D1488563

TARGETED KILLING

Looking beyond the events of the second intifada and 9/11, this book reveals how targeted killing is intimately embedded in both Israeli and US statecraft and in the problematic relationship between sovereign authority and lawful violence underpinning the modern state system. It details the legal and political issues raised in targeted killing as it has emerged in practice, including questions of domestic constitutional authority, the use of force in international law, the law of belligerent occupation, the law of targeting and human rights law. The distinctive nature of Israeli and US targeted killing is analysed in terms of the compulsion of legality characteristic of the liberal constitutional state, a compulsion that demands the ability to distinguish between legal 'targeted killing' and extra-legal 'political assassination'. The effect is a highly legalized framework for the extraterritorial killing of designated terrorists that may significantly affect the international law of force.

MARKUS GUNNEFLO is a postdoctoral researcher and lecturer in public international law at Lund University, Sweden, where he researches the theory and history of international law, particularly in the areas of the use of force, humanitarian law, human rights and migration.

TARGETED KILLING

A Legal and Political History

MARKUS GUNNEFLO

CAMBRIDGE
UNIVERSITY PRESS

University Printing House, Cambridge CB2 8BS, United Kingdom

Cambridge University Press is part of the University of Cambridge.

It furthers the University's mission by disseminating knowledge in the pursuit of
education, learning and research at the highest international levels of excellence.

www.cambridge.org
Information on this title: www.cambridge.org/9781107114852

© Markus Gunneflo 2016

First published 2016

A catalogue record for this publication is available from the British Library

Library of Congress Cataloguing in Publication data
Gunneflo, Markus, 1979– author.
Targeted killing : a legal and political history / Markus Gunneflo.
New York : Cambridge University Press, 2016.   Includes bibliographical references and index.
LCCN 2015048872   ISBN 9781107114852 (hardback)
LCSH: Targeted killing – Moral and ethical aspects.   Reprisals.   Intervention (International
law)   International criminal law.   Terrorism – Prevention – Government policy.
Terrorism – Prevention – Law and legislation.   Preemptive attack (Military science)
LCC KZ6362.G86   2016   DDC 341.6/3 – dc23
LC record available at http://lccn.loc.gov/2015048872

ISBN 978-1-107-11485-2 Hardback

'Only the State has the right to use force'
(and every use of its force stands in need of a particular law).

Walter Benjamin, 1920

CONTENTS

Acknowledgements   *page* ix

1   **Targeted Killing in the History of Israel, the United States and International Law**   1
History, Practice, International Law   2
Sovereignty, Protection, Liberal Legality   5
Chapter Overview   11

2   **The Emergence of Targeted Killing in the Israeli-Palestinian Common Entrapment of Enmity**   15
Public Committee Against Torture v. *The Government of Israel*   15
Walter Benjamin and the High Court of Justice   24
Trajectories of Israeli State Protection   32
Political Zionism as State Protection   34
Protection: The Difference a State Makes   38
'A Nation in Arms': The Israeli History of Wars of Existence and Assassinations   43
Occupation, Intifada, Targeted Killing   51
1967: Deepening the Common Entrapment of Enmity   52
The Legal Regime of the Occupation   55
Debating Legal Authority for Lethal Force in the First Intifada   60
Targeted Killing in the Second Intifada and Beyond   70

3   **The Emergence of Targeted Killing in an American Homeland which Is the Planet**   82
Al-Aulaqi v. *Obama*   83
Carl Schmitt and the US District Court for the District of Columbia   87
Carl Schmitt and the Law and Politics of Protection   89
Schmitt's Sovereign Protection   91
Protection: From Extra-legal to Apocryphal Sovereignty   94
Protection: From Westphalian to Post-Westphalian International Law   97

vii

NSDD 138 and George P. Shultz's Active Defense: Declaring War Against an Unspecified Terrorist Foe, to be Fought at an Unknown Place and Time with Weapons yet to be Chosen   109
   Measures to Neutralise Terrorist Leaders and Organisations   109
   From Passive to Active Defense against Terrorism   115
   Abraham D. Sofaer and the Legal Authority for Active Defense   127
   W. Hays Parks and the Lawful Killing of Terrorists under the Law of Armed Conflict   145
From Words to a Deed, Concept and Tool   154
   Attempts to Kill Osama bin Laden in Afghanistan   157
   Introducing the Targeted Killing Concept   161
   A New Tool for Targeted Killing: The Predator Drone   163
The American Targeted Killing Scheme after 9/11   166
   The Law of Targeted Killing after 9/11   167
   From Targeted Killing to Drone War   175
   9/11, a New Kind of Terrorism and a Planetary Homeland Security   177
   The Disease Metaphor in Targeted Killing: Death as a Means to Sustain Life   186

4   Targeted Killing and the Struggle over International Law's Sanctioning of Lethal Force   193
   Individualisation of Enmity?   194
   Deterritorialisation of Enmity?   206
   Enemy or Rights-bearer?   215
      Brief History of the Relation of Human Rights and Humanitarian Law   219
      The Doctrine of Lex Specialis   226
      Substituting a Hybridised for a Mutually Exclusive Relation   229

5   The Law of Targeted Killing   232

   Bibliography   240
   Table of Cases   266
   Index   268

ACKNOWLEDGEMENTS

First and foremost, thank you Bo for being an unfailing source of joy in the sometimes trying times of completing this book, and Annika for sharing this experience with me.

This book is a substantially revised version of a PhD thesis that was defended at Lund University in 2014. I would like to thank the supervisor of that work, Gregor Noll, for all the time spent reading and commenting on drafts, and for always maintaining a critical, yet constructive, mindset. More than anything else, I want to thank Gregor for stretching my imagination on what international legal scholarship might mean. His influence made this project possible and he continues to make international legal scholarship seem, to me, like a profession worth pursuing. Jens Bartelson's (my secondary supervisor) incisive comments and criticism were also a great help. Moreover, Jens provided confidence by always being clear about how the work could be improved and what it had already achieved.

At the public defence, I was enormously impressed by faculty opponent Anne Orford's ability to delicately unpick the nature and stakes of the project, while also being very attentive to detail. My notes taken during the defence provided both direction and a sense of purpose in revising the manuscript for publication as a book. My heartfelt thanks to Anne, as well as to the members of the grading committee – Susanne Krasmann, Ulf Linderfalk and Pål Wrange – for their contribution, questions and comments.

Numerous colleagues have read and commented, discussed or otherwise supported this work over the years. Thanks are due, in particular, to Matilda Arvidsson, Leila Brännström, Eduardo Gill-Pedro, Rens van Munster, Amin Parsa, Niklas Selberg and Daniel Steuer.

I am most grateful for the institutional and other support of the Faculty of Law at Lund University, and to the Ragnar Söderberg Foundation for financially supporting the postdoctoral position – the most important result of which is this book. Early in this project, I spent a few months as a visiting fellow at the Institute for International Law and the Humanities (IILAH) at Melbourne Law School. This visit would prove to have a lasting impact on the project. Several aspects of the study have been tested, at informal workshops in Lund and at the Faculty of Law at Helsinki University, between doctoral candidates with an interest in the heterodox strands of the legal discipline. At the end of the project, I was fortunate to participate in the Harvard Law School Institute for Global Law and Policy (IGLP) workshop in Doha and conference in Boston. This provided important input and energy at a time in which fatigue was becoming a serious factor. To all of these institutions – and to the people who make them what they are – thank you.

Gerhard Nordström kindly gave permission to use his 1965 etching, *The Attack*, for the cover. Although the medium is a different one, I would like to believe that the critical spirit of Gerhard's extensive 1960s and 70s production on war finds expression in this book.

Elizabeth Spicer, at Cambridge University Press, skilfully guided the manuscript through a publication process that had a very positive influence on the manuscript, not least through the comments by the anonymous referees. Thank you all.

Targeted Killing in the History of Israel, the United States and International Law

Current debates among critics of targeted killing suggest that the extraterritorial killing of designated terrorists has a tenuous relationship to law at best. This has led many to the conclusion that what is needed is to infuse more law and legal work into the practice; to ask the states engaging in targeted killing to articulate the legal framework in which they are conducted, perhaps even make decision-making in relation to such killings subject to judicial review. Numerous law scholars have also taken up the task of explaining the proper limits of such practices, whether the sources of those limits are found in constitutional law, international human rights law, the norms on the use of force or the law of armed conflict. This questionable relation to law has prompted yet other critics to conceptualise targeted killing in terms of sovereignty or exception, rather than law.

Contesting an assumption shared by these different responses, this book argues that targeted killing is steeped in law from the outset and that law, particularly international law, has both *shaped* and *been shaped* by this practice. In both Israel and the United States – the two states that have pioneered this practice – targeted killing did not emerge despite, or even necessarily in opposition to, law. In any case, it emerged through extensive legal work. Indeed, both the concept and the practice of targeted killing depend entirely on the ability to distinguish between *legal* 'targeted killing' and *extra-legal* 'political assassination'. This book offers a history of this ability. It allows us to see how targeted killing has emerged through a much longer and mutually productive relationship with law, particularly international law, than the contemporary debate and the prevailing focus on 9/11 and the second Intifada, suggests.[1]

---

[1] This association of targeted killing with 9/11 and the second intifada can be noticed inter alia in a dedicated encyclopaedia of international law: Georg Nolte, 'Targeted Killing' in Rudiger Wolfrum (ed.), *The Max Planck Encyclopedia of Public International Law* – online edition (Oxford University Press 2008) www.mpepil.com accessed 20 May 2015. Susanne Krasmann has argued for a mutually productive relationship between targeted killing

It must be stressed at this point that discriminate state killings by executive sanction are not at all new, and neither are Israel and the United States the only states practising it. What is new and distinctive about Israeli and American targeted killing is the framework in which these killings appear as legal, legitimate and necessary as a matter of both domestic and international law. By studying the development of a legal authority for targeted killing in the Israeli and the US contexts, we will learn about how this practice was emancipated from the sphere of secretive political assassinations and took the form of officially acknowledged targeted killing.

Targeted killing is intimately embedded in both Israeli and US statecraft and in the problematic relationship between sovereign authority and lawful violence underpinning the modern state system. This argument involves interweaving three central aspects for the emergence of targeted killing. The first aspect concerns fundamental questions of the law and politics of protection in the era of the liberal rule of law. Two incisive critics of the liberal rule of law, Walter Benjamin and Carl Schmitt, are the primary resources in this attempt to understand the centrality of state protection, but also the constant turn to law and to lawyers in the history of targeted killing. The second aspect concerns the particular histories of state protection, terrorism and assassination of Israel and the United States. This is because of the importance of understanding the historical trajectories and wider political developments of which targeted killing forms a part. The third aspect concerns iterative processes of the articulation of problems and threats; the provision of answers, definitions and interpretations; and the shaping and gaining in importance of practices over time. This final aspect is to account for the legal and political practices both constituting and constituted by targeted killing.

History, Practice, International Law

It will be clear from what has been said so far that this book represents both a turn to history and a turn to practice in the study of targeted killing. Robert W. Gordon argues that for lawyers the past is primarily a source of authority and legitimacy. 'History reassures us that what we do now flows continuously out of our past, out of precedents, traditions,

and international law (Susanne Krasmann, 'Targeted Killing and Its Law: On a Mutually Constitutive Relationship' 25 (2012) Leiden Journal of International Law 665).

fidelity to statutory and Constitutional texts and meanings'.[2] Indeed, frequent references to how today's drone strikes against terrorist suspects in Pakistan, Yemen or Somalia, for example, are no different from the deliberate US downing of the aircraft carrying Japanese Admiral Yamamoto in the Second World War play just such a role.[3] So too do references to the fact that attacks actually must be 'targeted' if they are to comply with the law of armed conflict and that targeted killing therefore represents a step forward as far as law of war compliance is concerned.[4] Indeed, such a reassuring progressivism may play an even more important role for the inherently repulsive act of intentional state death dealing.

This book does not turn to history as a source of authority or legitimacy but, instead, to make comprehensible shifting perceptions of the legality of the extraterritorial killing of designated terrorists. The importance of specifically studying legal practice in dealing with cases on the edge of the legal has recently been stressed by Fleur Johns.[5] Referring specifically to targeted killing, Johns suggests that somewhat less attention might be focused on explaining the proper limits of targeted killing,

> more attention might, instead, be directed towards those normative practices that already regulate critical decision-making surrounding targeted killing ... to ask how those existing norms have developed and what sort of knowledge practices, experiences and tendencies they appear to be fostering.[6]

The insistence of Fleur Johns that it matters that international lawyers disavow or downplay their role in constituting seemingly exogenous phenomena – in this case targeted killing – and the role of those phenomena, legally construed, in constituting international law leads us further to an important dimension of the way in which international law is treated in this study: *international law in history* and the *history of international law*.[7]

Suggested by Matthew Craven, *international law in history* and the *history of international law* are two different ways of conceiving the

---

[2] Robert W. Gordon, 'Foreword: The Arrival of Critical Historicism' 49 (1997) Stanford Law Review 1023.

[3] See, for example, US Attorney General Eric Holder, 'Attorney General Eric Holder Speaks at Northwestern University School of Law' (2012) www.justice.gov/opa/speech/attorney-general-eric-holder-speaks-northwestern-university-school-law accessed 10 May 2015.

[4] Michael N. Schmitt, 'Review of Nils Melzer's Targeted Killing in International Law' 103 (2009) American Journal of International Law 813.

[5] Fleur Johns, *Non-legality in International Law: Unruly Law* (Cambridge University Press 2013).

[6] *Ibid.* p. 9f.   [7] *Ibid.* p. 24.

relationship between international law and history.[8] Investigating the emergence of targeted killing in Israel and the United States in Chapters 2 and 3, I take up the perspective of *international law in history*. While stressing the importance of international law in social and political developments, this perspective may be used in describing how international law or international lawyers have been engaged, or involved themselves, in the creation of history in a wider sense, that is, outside the disciplinary history.[9] Moreover, the perspective of international law in history allows me to suspend a priori understandings of the oppositions between domestic and international law, law and politics, legal validity and political practice by, instead, proceeding bottom up – by studying interpretations, definitions, concepts and categories as produced by actors in the field.[10] This, in turn, provides a sense of historical motion and political struggle in the study of key aspects of targeted killing and the war on terrorism such as the 'constitutional structure' of the law of belligerent occupation, pre-emptive or preventive self-defence, 'unlawful combatants' and the concept of civilians taking a direct part in hostilities.

When we subsequently turn to investigate the effect on international law of the emergence and contemporary debate over targeted killing in Chapter 4, the perspective is shifted from *international law in history* to the *history of international law*. Craven sees in *history of international law* the seeking of trajectories or teleologies within the discipline of international law itself.[11] The particular concern here is the struggle over international law's sanctioning of lethal force in the debate on targeted killing.

Treating law in this empirical way is not a sign of *disinterest*, but of acute *interest* in its inherent normativity. Indeed, the understanding of international law as 'a bridge between the social past and the social future through the social present'[12] gives serious pause for thought when studying a

---

[8] Matthew Craven, in fact, considers three ways of conceiving this relationship – 'international law in history', 'history of international law' and 'history in international law' – but I shall only make use of the first two in this investigation. Matthew Craven, 'Introduction: International Law and Its Histories' in Matthew Craven, Malgosia Fitzmaurice and Maria Vogiatzi (eds.), *Time, History and International Law* (Leiden: Martinus Nijhoff Publishers 2007) 1–25 at 7.

[9] *Ibid.*; cf. Thomas Skouteris, 'Engaging History in International Law' in José María Beneyto (ed.), *New Approaches to International Law* (The Hague: T.M.C. Asser Press 2012) p. 104.

[10] Nikolas M. Rajkovic, Tanja Aalberts and Thomas Gammeltoft-Hansen, *The Power of Legality: Practices of International Law and Their Politics* (Cambridge University Press forthcoming 2016).

[11] Craven, 'Introduction: International Law and Its Histories' p. 6.

[12] Philip Allott, *The Health of Nations: Society and Law Beyond the State* (Cambridge University Press 2002) p. 317.

development that would appear to lock terrorism and counterterrorism in something that looks more and more like a self-fulfilling prophecy.[13] Moreover, it is precisely the normativity of law that makes it important to study the legal practices through which targeted killing emerged, in both a historical and political context. It is important to recognise the circumstances, knowledge practices and patterns of reasoning through which such an exceptional legal authority can emerge, but also to study the connections between the way in which international law is practiced in specific domestic jurisdictions and the development of international law as such.

Sovereignty, Protection, Liberal Legality

Kenneth Anderson has written about how the 'overpowering', 'strategic', and 'moral and humanitarian' logic of targeted killing will lead to the proliferation of this practice in both space and time:

> Just as crucial programs of Predator-centered targeted killings are under way now in Afghanistan and, accompanied by increasing international controversy, in Pakistan, such programs will be an essential element in U.S. counterterrorism operations in the future – against targets having little or nothing to do with today's iteration of the war on terror. Future administrations, even if they naturally prefer to couch the matter in softer terms, will likely follow the same path. Even if the whole notion seems to some disturbingly close to arbitrary killing, not open combat, it is often the most expedient – and, despite the civilian casualties that do occur, the most discriminatingly humanitarian manner to neutralize a terrorist without unduly jeopardizing either civilians or U.S. forces.[14]

The future of targeted killing and of drone warfare has captured the imagination of not just international lawyers but national security and human rights lawyers, political geographers and international relations specialists, as well as the broader public. At the same time, the focus on *protection* in targeted killing points us to the past; it points us way back

---

[13] The notion of a self-fulfilling prophecy in the context of terrorism and counterterrorism is taken from Joseba Zulaika, *Terrorism: The Self-fulfilling Prophecy* (The University of Chicago Press 2009). On 'blowback' caused by the American targeted killing campaign see Michael J. Boyle, 'The Costs and Consequences of Drone Warfare' 89 (2013) International Affairs 1; Leila Hudson, Colin S. Owens and David J. Callen, 'Drone Warfare in Yemen: Fostering Emirates Through Counterterrorism?' 14 (2012) Middle East Policy 142.

[14] Kenneth Anderson, 'Targeted Killing in U.S. Counterterrorism Strategy and Law' in Benjamin Wittes (ed.), *Legislating the War on Terror: An Agenda for Reform* (Washington DC: Brookings Institution Press 2009) 346–400 at 347.

in the thinking and practicing of sovereignty. In fact, it brings us all the way back to Hobbes' *Leviathan*, a book that inaugurates a tradition that makes protection the defining characteristic of sovereignty. As formulated by Anne Orford,

> Hobbes sought to argue that the creation of a political order depended upon the establishment of a common power with the capacity to protect its subjects. According to Hobbes, the lawful authority is recognisable as the one who achieves protection in the broad sense of bringing into being a condition in which the safety of the people can be achieved. This was the 'office', or in other words the responsibility of the sovereign.[15]

Roberto Esposito has stressed Hobbes' importance for protection-centric thinking on sovereignty. For Esposito, Hobbes' state of nature, in which all lived in continual fear and danger of violent death, is not simply the necessary counter-pole justifying political authority. For him it is a daunting image of human co-existence, or, as he prefers it, of men given over to one another in community. The 'immunisation' or protection of community in Hobbes' *Leviathan* proceeds through the institution of a commonwealth with a sovereign that is granted responsibility for protecting life.

Esposito likens the way in which conflict is neutralised in Hobbes with the practice of vaccinating the individual body. As is well known, this is a procedure in which a fragment of the pathogen from which the body needs to be protected is introduced into the body in order to block and contradict 'natural development'.[16] In Hobbes' schema this takes the form of the subjugation of the individual subject to a juridical order in which the subject is deprived of his or her right to self-defence through delegation to a sovereign that henceforth exercises it for the subject. Thus, 'the state of nature is not overcome once and for all by the civil, but it resurfaces again in the same figure of the sovereign, because it is the only one to have preserved natural right in a context in which all the others have given it up'.[17] From Esposito's account we also learn that state protection proceeds by presupposing the threat that makes it necessary, but also by

---

[15] Anne Orford, *International Authority and the Responsibility to Protect* (Cambridge University Press 2011) p. 57.

[16] Roberto Esposito, *Biós: Biopolitics and Philosophy* (Timothy Campbell tr, Minneapolis: University of Minnesota Press 2008) p. 46.

[17] Roberto Esposito, *Communitas: The Origin and Destiny of Community* (Timothy Campbell tr, Stanford University Press 2010) p. 30.

functioning through the use of what it opposes. State protection entails violence against violence in order to control violence.[18]

Jens Bartelson has stressed that due to its contingency and mutability this *double bind* between authority and force survived the transition from just war theology to secular statecraft and remains a powerful structuring principle for the legitimate exercise of force up until today.[19] This book gives careful attention to the double bind between authority and force emerging from the law of targeted killing, the consequences of which we can observe in the day-to-day reports of the killing of designated terrorists in Pakistan, Yemen, Somalia and Gaza, for example, in the name of protecting the population.

The extraterritorial dimension of targeted killing will be studied through the particular histories of state protection, terrorism and assassination of Israel and the United States in the chapters that follow. The international legal issues raised by this extraterritorial dimension are a key concern, particularly in the chapter on the United States. Two other aspects of central importance for the question of contemporary state protection should be mentioned at this point: changes in the subject of protection, from Hobbes through to today, and the consequences of the rise of the liberal rule of law.

Esposito notes how during the course of the modern state the body politic ceased to be the juridico-politico metaphor that it was in works such as Hobbes' *Leviathan* and that it would effectively 'eclipse itself simply because it is "realized" in the actual body of the people'.[20] This realisation had as its effect the inversion of the relation of domination between power and life through which 'life – its reproductive protection – became the ultimate criterion for legitimizing power'.[21] We should note here that Esposito both draws on the influential account of Michel Foucault and is cautiously at odds with it. In his works from the mid-1970s, Michel Foucault argued that at the beginning of the second half of the eighteenth century a rearticulation of sovereign power took place, a rearticulation that he refers to as a shift towards 'biopolitics', which he explains as a form of power that takes the security and welfare of populations as its

[18] Roberto Esposito, *Immunitas: The Protection and Negation of Life* (Zakiya Hanafi tr, Cambridge: Polity Press 2011) p. 29.

[19] Jens Bartelson, 'Double Binds: Sovereignty and the Just War Tradition' in Hent Kalmo and Quentin Skinner (eds.), *Sovereignty in Fragments: the Past, Present and Future of a Contested Concept* (Cambridge University Press 2010) 81–95.

[20] Esposito, *Immunitas: The Protection and Negation of Life* p. 15.   [21] *Ibid.*

object.[22] Esposito is entirely in agreement with Foucault on the significance of these developments. The only point at which Esposito parts with Foucault is that he finds that the contrasting distinction that Foucault sometimes makes between sovereignty and biopolitics underappreciates the protective character of sovereignty. If sovereignty is understood in the way suggested by Esposito, it becomes the first and most influential form that the biopolitical regime takes. As Esposito states: 'Sovereignty isn't before or after biopolitics, but cuts across the entire horizon, furnishing the most powerful response to the modern problem of the self-preservation of life'.[23]

Another significant aspect is the decline of absolutism and the ascent of the liberal rule of law. Hobbes' positing of protection as the supreme end of the state leads him to grant the sovereign the right to be the judge of the hindrances and disturbances of peace, as well as the means necessary for its recovery:

> And because the end of this institution, is the peace and defence of them all; and whosoever has right to the end, has right to the means; it belongeth of right, to whatsoever man, or assembly that hath the sovereignty, to be judge both of the means of peace and defence; and also of the hindrances, and disturbances of the same; and to do whatsoever he shall think necessary to be done, both beforehand, for the preserving of peace and security, by prevention of discord at home, and hostility from abroad; and, when peace and security are lost, for the recovery of the same.[24]

Such formulations led Carl Schmitt to categorise Hobbes, in his 1934 *On the Three Types of Juristic Thought*, as a 'classic case of decisionist thinking'. Schmitt writes about Hobbes:

> All *Recht*, all norms and statutes, all interpretations of laws, and all orders are for him essentially decisions of the sovereign, and the sovereign is not a legitimate monarch or established authority, but ... whoever establishes peace, security, and order is sovereign and has all authority.[25]

---

[22] See, in particular, Michel Foucault, '*Society Must be Defended': Lectures at the Collège de France 1975–76* (David Macey tr, New York: Picador 2003); Michel Foucault, *Security, Territory, Population: Lectures at the Collège de France, 1977–78* (Graham Burchell tr, New York: Palgrave Macmillan 2007); Michel Foucault, *The History of Sexuality: An Introduction* (Robert Hurley tr, New York: Pantheon 1978) but also a vast body of literature influenced by Foucault and usefully mapped in Thomas Lemke, *Biopolitics: An Advanced Introduction* (Eric Frederick Trump tr, New York University Press 2011).

[23] Esposito, *Bíos: Biopolitics and Philosophy* p. 57.

[24] Thomas Hobbes, *Leviathan* (Oxford University Press 1996) p. 118.

[25] Carl Schmitt, *On the Three Types of Juristic Thought* (Joseph W. Bendersky tr, London and Westport CT: Praeger Publishers 2004) p. 61.

Schmitt is often referred to as the Hobbes of the twentieth century and his work reveals the significant tensions created by a Hobbesian emphasis on protection in the era of the liberal rule of law. This is because liberal legality shuns this kind of sovereign decisionism, in which the sovereign is granted the right to be the judge of the hindrances and disturbances of peace as well as the means necessary for its recovery, insisting that all aspects of public authority are subject to law. Schmitt was very aware that liberalism's contribution to modern politics was the rule of law as a precondition for the exercise of public authority, but he continuously maintained the position that, despite all efforts, liberalism can only change the modalities – not the centrality and force – of the politics of protection. To cut a long story short, this is where legal practice enters the picture.

As has already been mentioned, this book turns to two iconic thinkers of this dynamic: Schmitt himself, but also one of Schmitt's contemporaries in Weimar Germany, the German-Jewish critic Walter Benjamin. Benjamin's description of the indistinct relationship between 'lawmaking' and 'law-preserving' violence and Schmitt's lesser-known concept of 'apocryphal' sovereignty both describe the tensions created by a protection-centric conception of the state in the era of the liberal rule of law. Both thinkers conceptualise the seeming paradox that even in situations of emergency it is 'highly unlikely that any liberal democratic state would claim an authority openly to act outside of the law'.[26] And still, 'they do seem to be able to procure, or at least to claim, a legal authority to exercise the power that past governments claimed under the rubric of prerogative'.[27] Benjamin will be the primary reference point in this regard in the chapter on Israel (Chapter 3), and Schmitt the same in the chapter on the United States (Chapter 4).

The reason for turning to Schmitt and Benjamin – in an investigation that admittedly takes us quite far away from Weimar Germany, as far as both space and time is concerned – is not to validate timeless, and a-contextual truths about sovereignty, law or state protection. This deserves to be mentioned because both Schmitt and Benjamin have been subject to de-historicised theory – 'a mode of inquiry that [plunder] the past for its insights but often [neglect] its historical character and efface the salient (though by no means insurmountable) differences between

---

[26] David Dyzenhaus, 'Emergency, Liberalism, and the State' 9 (2011) Perspectives on Politics 69 at 70.

[27] *Ibid.* p. 71.

past and present'.[28] In keeping with what was referred to earlier as a bottom up approach, the reason for turning to Schmitt and Benjamin is instead to analyse, clarify, make visible and thus to intensify the struggles that take place around power in the history of targeted killing.[29] This is possible because although there are important differences between the circumstances and situations that Schmitt and Benjamin faced and the circumstances and situations to which we will turn in this book, there are also similarities. The most obvious is that of responding to political crisis – times in which there is a sense that even the monopoly of violence of the state is at stake – *within* the framework provided by the liberal constitutional state. For the reason of these similarities, it is indeed possible to think of the philosophical and legal theoretical texts used in this study not as external theoretical resources imposed on the history of targeted killing but as part of the *relevant historical context*.[30] It is even possible to imagine that although the context, outlook and ambition of their work differ in significant ways, Schmitt, Benjamin and some of the protagonists of this history of targeted killing are positing essentially the same question: how is protection achieved in an era that accepts no outside to *legal* authority.

Against this background we are prepared to give a more nuanced answer to the question: why focus on Israel and the United States when plenty of other states kill people determined to be terrorists and a threat to the public? The fact that Israel and the United States have both been committed to engaging terrorism more or less openly by military means in application of the law of armed conflict is crucial. As Wouter Werner argues, this sets Israel and the United States apart from states that are denying any involvement in targeted killing, states that are not articulating a legal justification for them or are justifying lethal force as an exceptional measure of law enforcement.[31] What makes Israel and the United States

---

[28] Peter E. Gordon and John P. McCormick, 'Introduction: Weimar Thought: Continuity and Crisis' in Peter E. Gordon and John P. McCormick (eds.), *Weimar Thought: A Contested Legacy* (Princeton University Press 2013) 1–11 at 2.

[29] This is the way Anne Orford conceives of the place for political theory in the writings of Michel Foucault in 'In Praise of Description' 25 (2012) Leiden Journal of International Law 609 at 622. It is also reflective of her own use of the writings of Thomas Hobbes and Carl Schmitt in her study of the responsibility to protect concept (Orford, *International Authority and the Responsibility to Protect*).

[30] Anne Orford, 'On International Legal Method' 1 (2013) London Review of International Law 166 at 174.

[31] Wouter Werner, 'The Changing Face of Enmity: Carl Schmitt's International Theory and the Evolution of the Legal Concept of War' 2 (2010) International Theory 351 at 354f.

different is therefore, in part, precisely the legal work scrutinised in this book.

Another reason for our focus on Israel and the United States is the particular ways in which state protection is inscribed in their respective histories: in Israel through several important trajectories stretching as far back as the establishment of the state and its fraught relationship with the Palestinian population; in the United States by adapting conceptions of the global national security interests of the United States to the policy area of terrorism and the conception of terrorism as war since the early 1980s. Despite these differences, it is also true that there are points at which the developments of targeted killing in these two states intersect, whether it be for reason of shared geopolitical interests or extensive military, intelligence and legal cooperation.

Chapter Overview

Chapter 2 considers the emergence of targeted killing in Israel. The point of departure is a careful reading of the 2006 so-called targeted killing judgment of the Israel Supreme Court. In this judgment, the Court gave its permission for the Israel Defence Forces to continue to exercise targeted killing, provided that certain criteria were met. I focus on the Court's exercise of jurisdiction over these killings in the first place and the Court's decision on the applicable law, as well as the particular interpretation of that law. I claim that all of these aspects suggest that the Court, in an exercise of what Walter Benjamin calls 'law-preserving violence', makes itself actively involved in the continued 'lawmaking violence' of the Israeli state.

This analysis of the targeted killing judgment gives reason for taking a rather long historical perspective on targeted killing in Israel. This is a perspective that reads the development of targeted killing against the background of several trajectories of Israeli state protection, in particular how calls for protection have affected Jewish–Arab co-existence in Palestine from the founding of the state all the way to the contemporary war on terrorism. The legal perspective, particularly how both domestic and international law depends on the state for its distribution of the legitimate use of violence but also the problematic relationship between sovereign authority and lawful violence, is thoroughly integrated in this long historical perspective. As in the subsequent chapter on the United States, the perspective on international law is that of *international law in history*.

The chapter takes to task, in particular, the law of belligerent occupation – a legal regime imposed on the Palestinians, in 1967, through the
establishment of effective control over the lands they inhabited – for a
'constitutional structure' that institutionalises the indistinction of lawmaking and law-preserving violence in the resumption of a plenitude of
power and the rejection of the theory and practice of the separation of
powers. Palestinian perceptions of the illegitimacy of the occupation are
important for understanding the outbreak of the first Intifada, beginning
in the late 1980s, while the 'constitutional structure' of the legal regime
of the occupation is important for understanding the Israeli military
authority's response to it, in particular the debates over the authority of
undercover units to exercise lethal force in the pursuit of wanted individuals in the Intifada. It is equally important for understanding the shift
occurring in the context of the second Intifada, in the early 2000s, through
which targeted killing became the officially proclaimed legal means for
the occupying power to counter the Intifada and to kill designated Palestinian terrorists perceived to constitute a threat to Israeli soldiers, Israeli
settlers in the occupied territories and the Israeli population at large.

There are several aspects of international law that will be broached in
this chapter only to be taken up again in the subsequent chapter on the
emergence of targeted killing in the United States, when an authority not
dissimilar to the authority of the military commander on occupied territories would be constructed and adopted in a much more indeterminate
transnational space.

Chapter 3 details the emergence of targeted killing in the United States
and also takes a recent case of the adjudication of targeted killing as its
point of departure: the 2010 case of *al-Aulaqi* v. *Obama*. I argue that the
case reveals an exceptional legal authority and a direct relation between
the American executive and those subject to targeted killing. For precisely the reason of the exceptional nature of this authority, the Court
refused to exercise jurisdiction over the case. However, it is crucial to see
that this authority did not come about through sovereign decision but
rather through extensive policy and legal work stretching over several
decades. This chapter studies the emergence of targeted killing against the
background of the particular history of state protection, terrorism and
assassination, but also the discursive moves and knowledge practices that
have formed targeted killing in the United States.

In order to understand the development of a legal authority to carry
out targeted killing, this chapter turns to Carl Schmitt. The focus is on
Schmitt's thoughts concerning state protection in the context of the liberal

constitutional state. In order to take the implication of international law in targeted killing one step further, focus is also on Schmitt's thinking on the transition from a Westphalian to a post-Westphalian international law.

The analysis proceeds chronologically in three steps. The first step is Secretary of State George P. Shultz's push for an 'active defense' against terrorism during the Reagan years in the White House in the 1980s. Shultz articulated the necessity of engaging terrorism more actively and globally, specifically, of doing so with targeted military force. The rather unknown National Security Decision Directive 138 was adopted in 1984 and included directives to the CIA to find lawful measures through which the neutralisation of terrorist organisations and terrorist leaders could be achieved. Serious efforts of high-ranking lawyers within the administration to create the necessary domestic, as well as international, legal justifications to do so were also made in that time. This includes the question of the constitutional authority to target and kill designated terrorists, but also squaring such an active defense against terrorism with an international law distributing the right to wage legitimate force along the lines of territorial jurisdiction. I claim that this is a largely neglected formative era for present-day American targeted killing practices, both in terms of law and policy. In the second step I consider how an active defense against terrorism was, in the 1990s, transformed from words to a deed, concept and tool, in response to the allegedly new form of terrorism that al-Qaeda represented. This phase would reveal the military- and intelligence-related difficulties, as well as the strategic repercussions of engaging terrorism by military means. It would also reignite the controversy over legal authority and cause the frantic development of a particular military technology to be used for intelligence and for striking terrorists on foreign territory – the Predator drone. Moreover, this is the context in which the targeted killing concept was introduced in American counterterrorism. In the third step I consider the legal and political developments after 11 September 2001, developments that, as far as the legal framework for targeted killing is concerned, constitute a much less distinct break with the past than is usually perceived, but that would act as a catalyst for the dynamics that had caused a globalisation of US counterterrorism efforts decades earlier.

The question pursued in Chapter 4 is raised by the implication of international law and international lawyers in the history of targeted killing, but also by the recent rise of targeted killing on the agenda of international law. In this chapter the extension of the right to kill the enemy in application of the law of armed conflict to extraterritorial counterterrorism operations is considered from the perspective of *the history of interna-tional law.* Three questions arise in this context: first, the position of the subject of targeted killing as, at the same time, enemy, criminal and risk and the way in which this involves a shift away from international law's traditional concern with public forms of enmity to individual or private forms of enmity are studied. In this context the shift from exclusion to inclusion in international law of those subject to targeted killing is also considered. Second, the shift from enmity based on territorial jurisdic-tion to enmity as relation or, in other words, the deterritorialisation of enmity is analysed. Third and finally we turn to consider the fact that this individualised and deterritorialised enmity has emerged simultane-ously with an equally individualising and deterritorialising movement in international law – international human rights. The focus here is the encounter of the enemy and the rights-bearer in the subject of targeted killing. This encounter is considered through the history of the relation between human rights and humanitarian law, the doctrine of *lex specialis derogat legi generalis* and, finally, tendencies to substitute a hybridised for a mutually exclusive relation in the context of targeted killing.

The fifth and concluding chapter returns to reflect on the conception of law that has seen the emergence of targeted killing; a conception of law that heeds to the compulsion of legality and yet is able to produce a legal authority to engage in targeted killing.

As indicated already, while each chapter fulfils its own separate task, the chapters are written and arranged with a gradually progressing under-standing in mind. This is true in particular for the involvement and impli-cations for international law, moving from rather fundamental questions of the problematic relationship between sovereign authority and lawful violence in the chapter on Israel and only introducing some of the more particular problems and doctrines of international law raised in this prac-tice. The analysis of these problems and doctrines is taken significantly further in the chapter on the United States only to take centre stage in the fourth chapter when the perspective is shifted from *international law in history* to the *history of international law.*

The Emergence of Targeted Killing in the Israeli-Palestinian Common Entrapment of Enmity

Public Committee Against Torture v. *The Government of Israel*

The highest judicial authority of the state of Israel – The Israel Supreme Court, sitting as the High Court of Justice – has twice pronounced on what it refers to in English as 'targeted killing' and describes as 'a policy of preventative strikes' known to have caused the deaths of hundreds of designated Palestinian terrorists, but also numerous collateral deaths on the West Bank and Gaza.[1]

In 2002 the Court issued a decision on a petition by a member of the Knesset (the Israeli parliament), Mohammed Barakeh, to stop the killings. In a condensed decision, reproduced here in its entirety, the court effectively determined the targeted killing policy non-justiciable:

> We read and widely listened to the claims of the Applicant's representative. It seems to us that the announcement given on behalf of the Respondents [Prime Minister Ariel Sharon and Defence minister Benjamin Ben-Eliezer] supplied an exhaustive response to the Applicant's claims. The choice of means of warfare, used by the Respondents to preempt murderous terrorist attacks, is not the kind of issue the Court would see fit to intervene in. This is the case a fortiori when the appeal lacks a firm factual foundation and seeks a sweeping redress.[2]

An article published in the Israeli daily *Haaretz* quoted an exchange from the hearing between the attorney Nali Atiya and judge Mazza: the former

---

[1] Israel Supreme Court sitting as the High Court of Justice, *The Public Committee Against Torture et al.* v. *The Government of Israel et al.* (2006) HCJ 769/02. Available in English at the website of the Court: http://elyon1.court.gov.il/Files_ENG/02/690/007/a34/02007690 .a34.pdf accessed 10 May 2015. B'Tselem – The Israeli Information Center for Human Rights in the Occupied Territories, keeps statistics over Israeli targeted killings on the West Bank and Gaza: www.btselem.org/statistics accessed 10 May 2015.

[2] Israel Supreme Court sitting as the High Court of Justice, *Barakeh* v. *Prime Minister* (2002) HCJ 5872/01. Translated from Hebrew in Orna Ben-Naftali and Keren R. Michaeli, 'Justice-Ability: A Critique of the Alleged Non-Justiciability of Israel's Policy of Targeted Killings' 1 (2003) Journal of International Criminal Justice 368 at 369.

spoke of the distinction between fighters and civilians; Justice Mazza spoke about another possibility, 'There is a third thing that is called terror, and it is the enemy of all humanity. All countries view terror as a joint shared enemy'.[3] Justice Mazza is also quoted as having told attorney Atiya:

> Madam, go out to the streets of Jerusalem and you will see that this is a daily war. The request to prohibit targeted killing means that the court would become involved in administering the war. That would be akin to us telling the defense minister and the chief of staff to use only the infantry rather than tanks when entering Ramallah.[4]

In a critical review of the decision Orna Ben-Naftali and Keren Michaeli wrote:

> A court that declines to decide on the merits of the legality of state targeted killings, is not a court that merely made no decision. The decision not to decide is, too, a decision entailing far-reaching ramifications. Its substantive effect has contributed to the wholesale legitimization of the policy of targeted killings, in the eyes of the government, the legislature, the IDF [Israel Defence Forces] and the public. Its material effect has been the continuation of the practice of targeted killings . . . its institutional effect has been to don a judicial mantle of approval on the flexed muscles of the body politic, rendering the court a silent accomplice – rather than a normative counterweight – to the executive.[5]

As critical as Ben-Naftali and Michaeli are of the Court's decision not to consider the case on its merits, they add: 'It should, however, be noted that the same, or even worse, result would have emanated were the court to decide that the issue is justiciable, and then proceed to determine on the merits that all such actions fall within the reasonable margin of appreciation of the government'.[6]

The 2002 decision by Justices Mazza, Sheshin and Levi was reversed in late 2006 when the Court issued a judgment on a second petition to halt the killings, this time by one Israeli and one Palestinian NGO. The judgment was written and decided by the internationally renowned former President of the Israel Supreme Court, law professor, former Attorney General and Israel Prize laureate, Aharon Barak, with the concurring opinions of

---

[3] Moshe Gorali, 'Easier to Kill, Harder to Judge' *Haaretz* (31 January 2002) www.haaretz.com/print-edition/features/easier-to-kill-harder-to-judge-1.54240 accessed 10 May 2015.

[4] *Ibid.*

[5] Ben-Naftali and Michaeli, 'Justice-Ability: A Critique of the Alleged Non-Justiciability of Israel's Policy of Targeted Killings' p. 381.

[6] *Ibid.*

Eliezer Rivlin and Dorit Beinisch. In what follows I will pick up on three significant aspects of the case: the Court's exercise of jurisdiction over these killings in the first place, the Court's decision on the applicable law and the particular interpretation of that law.

In relation to the issue of the Court exercising jurisdiction over these killings in the first place, the following fact needs to be addressed: this judgment is issued by a national Court invoking an Israeli basic law as the source of its jurisdiction. At the same time, this national Court exercises jurisdiction, indeed, has the final power to decide, on the actions of military commanders in what was referred to in the 2002 decision as the 'choice of means of warfare'.

At this point it might be worth considering how this extraordinary situation came about. The jurisdiction exercised by the Israel Supreme Court over the occupied territories and its population is unique. While there are cases before and after in which the domestic courts of an occupant have tried the measures of its military forces under occupation ex post facto, before the Israel Supreme Court, no domestic court of an occupying power has been competent to prevent measures of the military from taking effect.[7] As much as this is a unique practice internationally, it is one with a long-standing history in the Israeli context. It was established when, in the early days of the occupation, Attorney General Meir Shamgar decided not to question the jurisdiction of the Court in relation to petitions from the occupied territories.[8]

Based on a comprehensive review of the jurisprudence of the Court in relation to the occupied territories, David Kretzmer argues that the judicial review of the Israel Supreme Court is a 'central feature of Israel's legal and political control over the occupied territories'.[9] Ronen Shamir

---

[7] Eyal Benvenisti, *The International Law of Occupation* (2nd edn, Oxford University Press 2012) p. 218.

[8] David Kretzmer, *The Occupation of Justice: The Supreme Court of Israel and the Occupied Territories* (New York: SUNY Press 2002) p. 19f.

[9] *Ibid.* p. 1. David Kretzmer mentions a few rationales for the Israeli military authorities' decision not to challenge the jurisdiction of the Court. Shamgar himself has held that the idea was to ensure some form of external control over the occupation authorities in order to maintain the rule of law. Kretzmer, however, also writes that it is 'fair to assume' that the implicit recognition of the state of Israel when the residents of the occupied territories petitioned the Israel Supreme Court also plays a part, as does the political legitimization of Israeli rule over the territories (*ibid.* p. 20). Subsequently, the Court argued that its jurisdiction was not dependent on the government authorities' tacit approval but was mandated by law. In the absence of any international legal obligation, the court reasoned that the military commander in the occupied territories is a state official who is part of

has argued that, in particular, the rare 'landmark cases' that have forced the occupation authorities to amend their policies have reinforced this legitimising role of the Court.[10] It should also be mentioned in this context that the decision of Aharon Barak to reverse the 2002 decision declaring targeted killing to be non-justiciable is consistent with his inclination to 'judicial activism' and the notion ascribed to him that 'everything is justiciable'.[11]

The targeted killing judgment provides interesting leads with regard to how this peculiar exercise of jurisdiction by the Supreme Court of the occupying state might play out when put to the test. In fact, Barak suggests as much when he writes, 'the State's fight against terrorism is the fight of the state against its enemies. It is also law's fight against those who rise up against it'.[12] But how exactly does law 'fight against those who rise up against it' in the context of a Supreme Court exercising jurisdiction over military commanders, indeed, having the power to decide on the choice of means of warfare in the context of a belligerent occupation? In the following I will focus on the Court's decision on the applicable law as well as the particular interpretation of that law.

The 2006 judgment was decided primarily on the basis of international law. Barak considers the status of international law within the Israeli legal system by declaring that international customary law is part of Israeli law 'by force of the State of Israel's existence as a sovereign and independent state'.[13]

In its 2004 advisory opinion on the consequences of the construction of a wall in the occupied Palestinian territories, the ICJ had side-lined much of the international law of force by determining that the right to self-defence does not apply in relation to occupied territories.[14] Further, the law applicable for the conduct of hostilities in armed conflict was held inapplicable because the military operations leading to the occupation

---

the IDF hierarchy and their actions are thus subject to the judicial review of the Court. Yoram Dinstein, *The International Law of Belligerent Occupation* (Cambridge University Press 2009) p. 25.

[10] Ronen Shamir, '"Landmark Cases" and the Reproduction of Legitimacy: The Case of Israel's High Court of Justice' 24 (1990) Law and Society Review 781.

[11] Amichai Cohen and Stuart A. Cohen, *Israel's National Security Law: Political Dynamics and Historical Development* (Abingdon: Routledge 2012) p. 133.

[12] *Public Committee Against Torture v. The Government of Israel* para. 62.

[13] *Ibid.* para. 16. Internal citations omitted.

[14] ICJ, *Legal Consequences of the Construction of a Wall in the Occupied Palestinian Territory* (Advisory Opinion) 2004 available at the website of the Court: www.icj-cij.org/docket/ files/131/1671.pdf accessed 10 May 2015 paras. 138–139.

ended a long time ago.[15] In keeping with the ICJ advisory opinion, the petitioners in the targeted killing case were of the view that the lawfulness of the targeted killing policy should be decided on the basis of the norms for law-enforcement in which there is no place for killing suspects without due process or without arrest or trial.[16] The pivotal norm here would, from an international law perspective, be the right to life recognised in human rights treaties that bind Israel as well as in customary international law. That goes for both those targeted and for any bystanders affected. To be sure, positive law provides circumstances under which life may be taken in an act of law enforcement. Far from an uncompromising proscription, the right to life certainly would have provided a more restrictive normative framework for the Israeli policy of targeted killings than that adopted by the Israel Supreme Court.

The Israel Supreme Court does not adopt the law suggested by the ICJ and the petitioners. The Court instead adopts the argumentation put forward by the government, declaring that 'the general, principled starting point' for the judgment is that since the beginning of the Intifada a 'continuous situation of armed conflict' has existed between the state of Israel and 'various terrorist organisations active in Judea, Samaria and the Gaza Strip'.[17] Barak corroborates this most significant determination by reference to previous case law of the Israel Supreme Court and further claims that it is 'in line with the definition of armed conflict in the international literature'.[18]

Barak describes the 'normative system' that applies to this armed conflict as 'complex'.[19] With reference to Antonio Cassese's textbook of international law, Barak determines that an armed struggle between an occupying state and 'terrorists' who come from the territory under belligerent occupation amounts to an *international armed conflict*.[20] Barak states that these laws include, but are not limited to, the law of belligerent

---

[15] *Ibid.* paras. 124–125.

[16] *Public Committee Against Torture* v. *The Government of Israel* para. 4.

[17] *Ibid.* para. 16. There has been some confusion in the English-speaking commentary on the case because of the fact that the first English language version published by the Court speaks of an armed conflict since the 'first Intifada', whereas the second version published in the series *Judgments of the Israel Supreme Court: Fighting Terrorism Within the Law*, published by the Israel Foreign Ministry, speaks of an armed conflict since 'the Intifada' see, for example, Marko Milanovic, 'Lessons for Human Rights and Humanitarian law in the War on Terror: Comparing Hamdan and the Israeli Targeted Killing Case' 89 (2007) International Review of the Red Cross 373 at 382f.

[18] *Public Committee Against Torture* v. *The Government of Israel* para. 16.

[19] *Ibid.* para. 18.   [20] *Ibid.*

occupation. There are also the norms for the conduct of hostilities applicable to 'any case of an armed conflict of international character – in other
words, one that crosses the border of the state – whether or not the place in
which the armed conflict occurs is subject to belligerent occupation'.[21] No
further reason is given for the very significant finding that the armed conflict between the state of Israel and 'various terrorist organisations' on the
West Bank and Gaza is an international armed conflict.

Referring to ICJ case law Barak acknowledges that, in addition to
international humanitarian law, human rights law also is applicable in
international armed conflicts.[22] Thus, potentially the right to life could
still be the appropriate norm in considering the legality of Israeli targeted killings. However, Barak states: 'humanitarian law is the lex specialis which applies in the case of an armed conflict. When there is a
gap (lacuna) in that law, it can be supplemented by human rights law'.[23]
With that laconic statement Barak effectively prioritise a legal paradigm
for targeted killing that crucially includes the right to target and kill the
enemy.

With regard to the killing or injuring of bystanders in a targeted killing
attack, this is also less of a problem in this legal framework due to the
so-called principle of proportionality.[24] According to this principle, it is
not unlawful to kill or injure bystanders as long as the civilian casualties
are not excessive in relation to the concrete and direct military advantage
anticipated from the attack, in this case, the killing of the designated terrorist. From the point of view of this norm, bystanders killed in a targeted
killing attack constitute collateral damage given that the proportionality
test has been satisfied.[25]

---

[21] *Ibid.*   [22] *Ibid.*   [23] *Ibid.*

[24] The treaty-based version of this norm is found in Article 51.5 of Additional Protocol 1 to
the Geneva Conventions of 12 August 1949.

[25] The loose contours of this test as it is conceived by Israeli military lawyers is illustrated
in a Haaretz article reporting on an exercise in which a team of IDF lawyers were asked
to address the following situation: 'Assume that there is a terrorist in Gaza and you know
that the terrorist is a Palestinian male bachelor between the ages of 18 and 45 and that
tomorrow he is for certain going to kill an Israeli male aged between 18 and 45, and there
is only one opportunity to kill him: by means of a missile, which will definitively succeed.
How many Palestinian bachelors aged 18–45 do you agree have to die, with certainty,
from the missile?' The Haaretz article continues: 'The team members jotted down their
response on a piece of paper; they ranged from zero to "as many as needed" (no end). The
average number of permitted collateral deaths was 3.14(pi). Maybe it is not surprising
that the outcome generated by the question was an irrational number'. Colonel Daniel
Reisner of the international law division of the Military Advocate General's office tells the
reporters that his response was two people. He continues 'if you formulate the question

Having already established the normative framework to be the rules governing the conduct of hostilities in the context of an international armed conflict, Barak turns to the question of how the individuals targeted under the targeted killing policy should be categorised.

A complication of Barak's determination of the applicable law is that the law applicable for the conduct of hostilities in the context of *international armed conflicts* grants all belligerents equal right to conduct hostilities. In order to avoid the prospect of being obliged to acknowledge a right for Palestinian militants to use violence against Israeli soldiers, even a right for them to kill civilians as collateral damage, and still maintain these rights for the state of Israel, there are essentially two different paths of interpretation available. Both work by way of exception to the principle of distinction determining combatants, but not civilians, to be eligible for attack.

The Israeli government had argued before the Court that those subject to targeted killing are 'unlawful combatants', unprotected by the law of armed conflict. The government's argument on this matter is summarised in the judgment in the following way:

> The status of terrorists actively participating in the armed conflict is not that of civilians. They are party to the armed conflict, and thus they can be attacked. They do not obey the law of war, and thus they do not benefit from the rights and protections granted to legal combatants, who obey the law of war. Respondent's position is, then, that according to each of the alternatives, 'the State is permitted to kill those who fight against it, in accordance with the fundamental principles of the law of war which apply in every armed conflict'.[26]

The Court rejects this line of reasoning. This is so because:

> It is difficult for us to see how a third category [unlawful combatant in addition to civilian and combatant] can be recognised in the framework

differently and ask whether I agree to sacrifice an Israeli man for three Palestinians, the answer might be different, but eight, for example, doesn't seem right to me. I learned a few things from that exercise: that young people tend toward higher numbers than older people, that people with families tend to give higher numbers than bachelors, that a correlation exists between political outlook and the number given . . . I don't know what the right answer is, but I know that the question has to be asked before an attack. If the commander asked the question and answered it based on a test of reasonableness; the task of the legal expert has been fully carried out'. Yotam Feldman and Uri Blau, 'Consent and Advise' Haaretz (29 January 2009) www.haaretz.com/consent-and-advise-1.269127 accessed 10 May 2015.

[26] *Public Committee Against Torture* v. *The Government of Israel* para. 11.

of the Hague and Geneva Conventions. It does not appear to us that we
were presented with data sufficient to allow us to say, at the present time,
that such a third category has been recognised in customary international
law.[27]

Barak instead proceed[s] to the hybrid category of '*civilians* who constitute *unlawful combatants*'.[28] The legal reasoning behind it can be found
in the alternative position of the government as far as the legal status of
those targeted is concerned.

Such civilians may, according to customary international law, be
attacked 'for such time as they take a direct part in hostilities'.[29] With
regard to the scope of this exception, Barak determines the 'accepted view'
to be that this includes acts that 'by nature and objective are intended to
cause damage to the army'.[30] However, Barak adds that it 'is not limited
merely to the issue of "hostilities" toward the army or the state. It applies
also to hostilities against the civilian population of the state'.[31]

Barak refers to 'the accepted definition' in saying that someone takes
part in hostilities when this person uses a weapon within the framework
of the armed conflict but also when collecting intelligence or preparing
for hostilities.[32] This means that there 'is no condition that the civilian
use his weapon, nor is their [sic] a condition that he bear arms (openly or
concealed). It is possible to take part in hostilities without using weapons
at all'.[33] Barak further determines the following cases to be instances of
direct participation in hostilities: a person who collects intelligence on
the army whether on issues regarding the hostilities or beyond those
issues; a person who transports unlawful combatants to or from the place
where the hostilities are taking place; a person who operates weapons
that unlawful combatants use or supervises their operation or provides
service to them;[34] a person serving voluntarily as a 'human shield'[35]; a
person who 'enlist[s]' another person to take a direct part in hostilities,
or, 'send[s]' others to do so; a person who 'decide[s]' upon, or, 'plan[s]'
'the act'.[36]

On the other hand, Barak writes, someone who 'sells food or
medicine to an unlawful combatant'; someone who 'aids the unlawful

---

[27] *Ibid.* para. 28.   [28] *Ibid.*, my emphasis.

[29] The treaty-based version of this norm is found in article 51.3 of Additional Protocol 1 to
the Geneva Conventions of 12 August 1949. The Position of the International Committee
of the Red Cross (ICRC) is that there is an equivalent in customary international law to
this norm, a position that Barak finds 'acceptable'. *Ibid.* para. 30.

[30] *Ibid.* para. 33.   [31] *Ibid.*   [32] *Ibid.*   [33] *Ibid.*

[34] *Ibid.* para. 35.   [35] *Ibid.* para. 36.   [36] *Ibid.* para. 37.

combatants by general strategic analysis, grants them logistical, general support including monetary aid'; someone who 'distributes propaganda supporting those unlawful combatants' takes an 'indirect part'.[37] This means that they may not be targeted but 'if such persons are injured, the State is likely not to be liable for it if it falls into the framework of collateral or incidental damage'.[38] With regard to the temporal element – 'for such time' – Barak concludes that 'a civilian who has joined a terrorist organization which has become his "home", and in the framework of his role in that organization he commits a chain of hostilities, with short periods of rest between them, loses his immunity from attack "for such time" as he is committing the chain of acts'.[39]

Before someone is considered as falling into the category in question, Barak determines that there needs to be 'information which has been most thoroughly verified . . . regarding the identity and activity of the civilian who is allegedly taking part in the hostilities'.[40] Also, a civilian taking a direct part in hostilities cannot be attacked if 'a less harmful means can be employed'.[41] This last criterion is derived not from international humanitarian law but from the principle of proportionality of Israeli domestic law.[42]

Interestingly, Judge Rivlin in his concurring opinion to the judgment compares the option of determining those subject to targeted killing as 'unlawful combatants' unprotected by the law and Barak's category of *civilians* who constitute *unlawful combatants* determining that 'there is no difference between the two paths in terms of the result, since the interpretation of the provisions of international law proposed by my colleague President Barak *adapts the rules to the new reality*'.[43] In fact, Barak explicitly writes that his interpretation of civilians taking a direct part in hostilities proceeds 'in the spirit' of 'dynamic interpretation'.[44]

From this summary I think it is clear that the judgment provides the government with a flexible category of persons who may lawfully be killed in this policy of preventive strikes against designated Palestinian terrorists. The judgment also provides the government with some lee-way with regard to the lawful killing of uninvolved bystanders in the form of 'collateral damage'. Hence, effectively, the judgment enables the

---

[37] *Ibid.* para. 35.
[38] *Ibid.* It remains somewhat unclear if Barak here means to introduce a presumption to the effect that harm done to persons taking an 'indirect part' constitutes lawful 'collateral damage' or if he, in this instance, merely refers to the 'ordinary' proportionality assessment.
[39] *Ibid.* para. 39.   [40] *Ibid.*   [41] *Ibid.* para. 40.   [42] *Ibid.*
[43] *Ibid.* concurring opinion by Judge Rivlin para. 2. My emphasis.   [44] *Ibid.* para. 28.

Israeli government to proceed with its policy of targeted killing within the bounds of law. Accordingly, just a few days after the judgment was delivered, the Israel Ministry of Foreign Affairs issued a press release. The first paragraph states: 'the Court's decision enables Israeli security forces to continue carrying out targeted killings on condition that the merits of every instance are individually examined'. It is specifically mentioned that the press release was written with the aid of the legal department of the Foreign Ministry in coordination with IDF legal staff.[45]

Walter Benjamin and the High Court of Justice

The targeted killing judgment has received a significant amount of attention since it was handed down in December 2006. Not least has it been scrutinised from the point of view of international law and has, from that particular point of view, received both praise and criticism.[46] We will come back to some of the substantive points of international law raised in

---

[45] Israel Ministry of Foreign Affairs, 'Israel Supreme Court Decision on Targeting Terrorist Operatives' (2006) http://www.mfa.gov.il/MFA/Government/Law/Legal+Issues+and+Rulings/Israel+Supreme+Court+decision+on+targeting+terrorist+operatives+20-Dec-2006.htm accessed 10 May 2015.

[46] Orna Ben-Naftali, 'A Judgment in the Shadow of International Criminal Law' 5 (2007) *Journal of International Criminal Justice* 322; Orna Ben-Naftali and Keren R. Michaeli, '*Public Committee Against Torture et al. v. The Government of Israel et al.*' 101 (2007) *American Journal of International Law* 459; Ariel L. Bendor, 'Justiciability of the Israeli Fight Against Terrorism' 39 (2007) The George Washington International Law Review 149; Antonio Cassese, 'On Some Merits of the Israeli Judgment on Targeted Killings' 5 (2007) Journal of International Criminal Justice 339; Amichai Cohen, 'Legal Operational Advice in the Israeli Defense Forces: The International Law Department and the Changing Nature of International Humanitarian Law' 26 (2011) Connecticut Journal of International Law 367; Kristen Eichensehr, 'On Target: The Israeli Supreme Court and the Expansion of Targeted Killings' 116 (2006) Yale Law Journal 1873; Helen Keller and Magdalena Forowicz, 'A Tightrope Walk Between Legality and Legitimacy: An Analysis of the Israeli Supreme Court's Judgment on Targeted Killing' 21 (2008) Leiden Journal of International Law 185; Even Khen and Hilly Moodrick, 'Can We Now Tell What "Direct Participation in Hostilities" Is?' 40 (2007) Israel Law Review 213; Mordechai Kremnitzer, 'Targeted Killing Policy: Insufficiently Limited' 44 (2007) Justice – The International Association of Jewish Lawyers and Jurists 38; Michelle Lesh, '*Public Committee Against Torture in Israel v. The Government of Israel*: The Israeli High Court of Justice Targeted Killing Decision' 8 (2007) Melbourne Journal of International Law 373; Nils Melzer, 'Targeted Killing or Less Harmful Means? Israel's High Court Judgment on Targeted Killing and the Restrictive Function of Military Necessity' 9 (2006) Yearbook of International Humanitarian Law 87; Milanovic, 'Lessons for Human Rights and Humanitarian law in the War on Terror: Comparing Hamdan and the Israeli Targeted Killing Case'; Roy S. Schondorf, 'The Targeted Killing Judgment' 5 (2007) Journal of International Criminal Justice 301; Mark E. Wojcik,

the judgment later in this book, but here I shall take up Walter Benjamin's perspective on positive law in reading the judgment and its declaring targeted killing legal, granted certain criteria are met.[47] First, however, let us see a brief introduction to Benjamin's essay *Critique of Violence*.

Benjamin lets the reader know in his 1921 text that, 'for the sake of simplicity', his discussion will relate to 'contemporary European conditions'.[48] Thus, at the same time as his critique has a transhistorical metaphysical strain there are clear traces of the particular political circumstances in which Benjamin led his life: the politically turbulent Weimar Germany. This explains the references to the recent war, constitutional turmoil, general strike, failed revolution, parliament and police.[49] Opting neither for a transhistorical reading nor for a reading restricted to Weimar Germany, the Israeli legal scholar Shai Lavi has suggested that Benjamin's text 'transcends its original historical and political context and can serve as a more general critique of force under *modern liberal conditions*'.[50]

At the outset it is important to keep two things in mind in reading Benjamin's essay, both of which can be illustrated by way of a consideration of the translation of *Kritik der Gewalt* into English as 'Critique of Violence'. As Beatrice Hanssen has argued, the German *Kritik* should not be understood here along the lines of simply an exercise of evaluative judgment or 'criticism' but instead in terms of the Greek *krinein* denoting to cut, rift, separate, discriminate, but also to decide. This meaning is particularly strong in the Kantian tradition of *Kritik*. At least initially in the essay, Benjamin follows this tradition, in an attempt to analyse what separates legitimate power from sheer force or violence. Further on in the essay, Benjamin points to the difficulties of upholding such a distinction and ultimately abandons it.[51] This ties in neatly with the German *Gewalt*

'Introductory Note to *Public Committee against Torture in Israel* v. *Government of Israel*' 46 (2007) International Legal Materials 373.

[47] The reading of the judgment provided here draws extensively on: Markus Gunneflo, 'The Targeted Killing Judgment of the Israeli Supreme Court and the Critique of Legal Violence' 23 (2012) Law and Critique 67.

[48] Walter Benjamin, 'Critique of Violence' in Peter Demetz (ed.), Edmund Jephcott (tr), *Reflections: Essays, Aphorisms, Autobiographical Writings* (New York: Schocken Books 1978) 277–300 at 280.

[49] Anthony Auerbach, 'Remarks on Walter Benjamin's Critique of Violence' (aauerbach.info) http://aauerbach.info/research/urban/benjamin_violence.html accessed 10 May 2015.

[50] Shai Lavi, 'The Use of Force Beyond the Liberal Imagination: Terror and Empire in Palestine, 1947' 7 (2006) Theoretical Inquiries in Law 199 at 203. My emphasis.

[51] Beatrice Hansen, *Critique of Violence: Between Poststructuralism and Critical Theory* (Abingdon: Routledge 2000) p. 3f.

and its translation into violence. For *Gewalt* signifies at the same time violence and legitimate power, something that is lost in the English translation to violence. More particularly, *Gewalt* signifies 'the dominance or the sovereignty of legal power, the authorizing or authorized authority; the force of law'.[52]

That the text is dedicated to a critique specifically of the violence or power of positive law is already made clear at the outset. Benjamin argues that natural and positive laws offer very different points of view on violence and he privileges the latter for the purpose of his critique. Benjamin reasons as follows: if violence were a means, a criterion for criticising it would seem immediately available in natural law: 'it imposes itself in the question whether violence, in a given case, is a means to a just or an unjust end'.[53] Positive law on the other hand sees 'violence as a product of history' and thus asks an entirely different question, namely whether violent means are employed for ends that have been historically sanctioned and thus are 'legal ends' or whether they are employed for unsanctioned 'natural ends'.[54] In other words, positive law demands of violence a 'proof of its historical origin, which under certain conditions is declared legal, sanctioned'.[55] Positive law's emphasis on the legality of means (as opposed to the justness of ends) does not entail a complete disregard for questions of justice. What it does mean is that positive law seeks to 'guarantee' the justness of the ends through the legal justification of the means.[56]

The bulk of Benjamin's text is dedicated to explaining how it can be that such 'fate-imposed violence' is determinative for law's justice.[57] The distinction between violence for 'natural ends' and sanctioned violence for 'legal ends' is but a preliminary step in this undertaking. It is preliminary because the focus of Benjamin's attention is really the 'sphere' in which such distinctions can be made, a sphere from which his 'historico-philosophical' view of law will emerge.[58] A first step in this undertaking is

---

[52] Jacques Derrida, 'Force of Law: The Mystical Foundation of Authority' in Gil Anidjar (ed.), *Acts of Religion: Jacques Derrida* (Abingdon: Routledge 2002) 230–300 at 264f.

[53] Benjamin, 'Critique of Violence' at 277.   [54] *Ibid.* p. 278.   [55] *Ibid.* p. 279f.

[56] *Ibid.* p. 278. Ultimately, that one could arrive at something like justice in this way is, according to Benjamin, unrealistic: 'For it is never reason that decides on the justification of means and the justness of ends, but fate-imposed violence on the former and God on the latter' (*Ibid.* p. 294). Considering this 'God's eye view on justice' James Martel highlights that it 'does not tell us anything at all; it merely suggests to us the limitations or nonabsoluteness of our own view' (James R. Martel, *Textual Conspiracies: Walter Benjamin, Idolatry, and Political Theory* (Ann Arbor: University of Michigan Press 2011) p. 48).

[57] Benjamin, 'Critique of Violence' p. 294.   [58] *Ibid.* p. 279.

to re-evaluate unsanctioned violence or violence for 'natural ends', focus-ing on its productive aspect. This aspect reveals how such violence is able 'to found and modify legal conditions', the 'fortuitous and isolated' func-tion of which Benjamin rebuts by considering military violence.[59] Military violence, Benjamin claims, is 'primordial and paradigmatic of all violence used for natural ends' and it has inherently a 'lawmaking character'.[60] This is the first modality of *Gewalt*, lawmaking [Ger. *rechtsetzend*] violence. Jacques Derrida describes moments of lawmaking violence as 'terrifying moments', exemplified by 'the sufferings, the crimes, the tortures that rarely fail to accompany [the founding of states]'.[61]

Apart from this military and physical form of violence, the founding of states is also associated with violence of another kind. Hence, what occurs in the very moment of the inauguration of law and polity can be described as the performative that provides the entirely necessary basis for violence for legal ends: the 'proof of historical origin'. This instance can be summarised in the claim that 'This will be law' or, more emphatically, 'This is now the law'.[62] The fact that this is done, as it were, by fiat, is underscored by Benjamin by declaring it a work of 'fate'; hence the notion 'fate-imposed violence' referred to earlier.[63] It is important to note that according to this account, the military violence as well as the performative that founds law does not amount merely to an historical embarrassment for the law but is always already at stake in all the different instances and practices of application or enforcement. Put otherwise, it is inherent in the rule of law.

These considerations lead us immediately to the second modality of legal violence: law-preserving [Ger. *rechtserhaltend*] violence. A number of state institutions may be singled out as significant in law-preserving violence. Benjamin speaks of 'the police' but Derrida points out that 'the police' in this instance does not only refer to policemen in uniform with batons; rather, 'by definition, the police are present or represented everywhere that there is force of law', that is to say, when law is enforced.[64]

---

[59] *Ibid.* p. 283.   [60] *Ibid.*

[61] Jacques Derrida, 'Force of Law: The Mystical Foundation of Authority' in Drucilla Cornell and others (eds.), *Deconstruction and the Possibility of Justice* (Abingdon: Routledge 1992) 3–67 at 35.

[62] Judith Butler, 'Critique, Coercion and Sacred Life in Benjamin's "Critique of Violence"' in Hent De Vries and Lawrence E. Sullivan (eds.), *Political Theologies: Public Religions in a Post-Secular World* (New York: Fordham University Press 2006) 201–219 at 202.

[63] Benjamin, 'Critique of Violence' p. 294.

[64] Derrida, 'Force of Law: The Mystical Foundation of Authority' p. 44.

In accordance with this understanding, Judith Butler, in a recent reading of Benjamin's text, characterises the enforcement of law by courts as a paradigmatic case of law-preserving violence, something that leads us back, finally, to the Israel Supreme Court targeted killing judgment.[65]

One motivation behind the distinction between lawmaking and law-preserving violence appears to be to show that law-preserving violence is fundamentally dependent on lawmaking violence. The logic here is simple: before law can be 'preserved' it needs to be 'made'. A rather basic fact about the targeted killing judgment was mentioned in the foregoing: a national Court invoking an Israeli Basic Law as the source of its jurisdiction issues this judgment. This clearly determines the judgment as a case of what Benjamin would call law-preserving violence. On the other hand, that there is a court and a Basic Law in the first place is due to the historical processes through which the Israeli state came into being, or, in other words how Israeli state law was 'made' in Palestine.

The same is made quite clear when Barak declares customary international law (the law that was determinative in the Court declaring targeted killing legal, granted certain criteria were met) to be part of Israeli law 'by force of the State of Israel's existence as a sovereign and independent state'. While this may be read as a straightforward explication of the English law's so-called 'doctrine of incorporation',[66] from Benjamin's perspective, it takes on the meaning of a reference to a rather more fundamental form of incorporation, the fact that the positive legality at work in the judgment is a product of history: the history through which Israel came into being as a sovereign and independent state. Above all, this reveals the continued normative significance of the factual institution of a territorialised political community.

There is yet another indicator of lawmaking violence in the Court's exercise of jurisdiction over the policy of targeted killing. Benjamin writes that 'where the highest violence, that over life and death, occurs in the legal system, the origins of law jut manifestly and fearsomely into existence'.[67] I take this to suggest that the distinction between the two modalities of legal violence is annulled in such fatal cases, when the origin of law – described by Benjamin as 'violence crowned by fate' – is exposed.[68] In

---

[65] Butler, 'Critique, Coercion and Sacred Life in Benjamin's "Critique of Violence"' p. 202.

[66] See David Kretzmer, 'Israel' in David Sloss (ed.), *The Role of Domestic Courts in Treaty Enforcement: A Comparative Study* (Cambridge University Press 2009) 273–325 at 278f.

[67] Benjamin, 'Critique of Violence' p. 286.

[68] *Ibid.* One can certainly see how this corresponds with Benjamin's conception of history from his *Theses on the Philosophy of History*, where he writes that 'the true picture of the

such instances law 'reaffirms itself' and in this very violence, according to Benjamin, 'something rotten in law is revealed'.[69] What is this origin of law that the court cloaks in law-preserving violence in this instance? It is the lawmaking violence of 1948, to which the Israeli Basic Law and the Court itself owe their existence. It is also the lawmaking violence of the 1967 war, in which what remained of British mandate Palestine and the territories inhabited by those targeted were placed under belligerent occupation. What was achieved through these historical developments was a source for the positive legality at work in the judgment or the conventions that guarantee the validity of the performative, thanks to which the Court gives itself the means to decide between legal and illegal violence.[70]

This leads me further to consider the Court's choice of the applicable law, for this choice is, as we have seen, key for the Court's being able to declare targeted killing legal, granted certain criteria are met. Although he pays tribute to the continuous application of human rights law in armed conflict by way of the maxim of *lex specialis derogat legi generalis,* Barak relied heavily on the norms applicable for the conduct of hostilities. And, as has already been noted, the starting point for the judgment was a determination that since the beginning of the Intifada, a continuous situation of armed conflict has existed between the state of Israel and various terrorist organisations active in Judea, Samaria and the Gaza Strip. While the Court in 2002 by determining targeted killing non-justiciable decided not to get actively involved in Israeli targeted killings (although the Court in the brief formulation that accompanied the decision unambiguously aligned itself with the Government), in 2006 the Israel Supreme Court made itself actively complicit in lawmaking violence. 'Complicit' might even be considered an understatement, since the Israel Supreme Court indeed has the ultimate power to decide whether such killings may be carried out or not. As Barak points out, 'the starting point which has guided the Court has been that the military commanders and officers who answer to the commander of army forces in the area [the West Bank and

---

past flits by. The past can be seized only as an image which flashes up at the instant when it can be recognized and is never seen again . . . To articulate the past historically does not mean to recognize it "the way it really was." It means to seize hold of a memory as it flashes up at a moment of danger' (Walter Benjamin, 'Theses on the Philosophy of History' in Hannah Arendt (ed.), Harry Zohn (tr), *Illuminations: Essays and Reflections* (New York: Schocken Books 1968) 253–264 at 255).

[69] Benjamin, 'Critique of Violence' p. 286.

[70] Derrida, 'Force of Law: The Mystical Foundation of Authority' p. 33.

Gaza] are public officials fulfilling roles pursuant to law'.[71] And, quoting another decision of the Court, 'the final and decisive decision as to the interpretation of a statute, as per its wording at any given time, is granted to the court'.[72]

Benjamin writes that there is inherent in all military violence a 'law-making character'; and the targeted killing judgment appears to be a case of *lawmaking violence* exercised by a state body institutionally prede-termined to exercise *law-preserving violence.*[73] Apparently the law's fight against those who rise up against it in this case includes a supreme judicial authority not just bestowing a mantle of approval on the flexed muscles of the body politic (to use the language of Ben-Naftali and Michaeli in their review of the 2002 decision of the Court) by declaring the policy non-justiciable, but a Court that has the final and decisive say on the choice of means of warfare and thus takes something akin to a commanding role over it.

This extraordinary exercise of jurisdiction leads us further to consider the Court's interpretation of the applicable law. For, as already noted, a problem with the Court's determination that the norms applicable in an international armed conflict applies in this case is that this law grants all participants equal right to exert violence against the other, something that is directly contrary to, to quote Benjamin, 'law's interest in a monopoly of violence'.[74] In fact, Benjamin addresses the fact that the state according to 'military law' is obliged to acknowledge the lawmaking violence of others when 'external powers force it to concede them the right to conduct warfare', something he (along with the right to strike) describes as an 'objective contradiction in the legal situation'.[75] Having placed himself in this situation by deciding that the case is to be decided on the basis of the norms governing the conduct of hostilities in *international armed conflict*, Barak needs to interpret away the contradiction noted by Benjamin. There are two ways of doing so and, as mentioned, both work by way of exception to the principle of distinction determining combatants, but not civilians, to be eligible for attack. As was also mentioned, Barak did not opt for the category of unlawful combatants but instead for his own category of '*civilians* who constitute *unlawful combatants*'. Again, we may note the re-emergence of something akin to lawmaking violence when Barak

---

[71] *Public Committee Against Torture* v. *The Government of Israel* para. 55.
[72] *Ibid.* para. 56.   [73] Benjamin, 'Critique of Violence' p. 283.
[74] *Ibid.* p. 281.   [75] *Ibid.* p. 283f.

not only decides that targeted killing falls under the international law governing the conduct of hostilities in the context of *international armed conflict* (when the defining characteristic of this type of conflict always has been its interstate, rather than its cross-border nature),[76] but also writes that his understanding of the hybrid category of *civilians* who constitute *unlawful combatants* proceeds 'in the spirit' of 'dynamic interpretation' – elsewhere referred to by Barak as 'judicial lawmaking'.[77]

In a book that came out in Hebrew in 2002 and in English in 2005, Barak develops a comprehensive theory of legal interpretation that he calls 'purposive interpretation'. One of the ways in which he describes this approach to legal interpretation is as a way for the interpreter to 'bridge the gap between law and the needs of society'. According to Barak, such change is a 'natural phenomenon'. For while 'law must be stable . . . it cannot stand still. Change is necessary, and interpretation is a legitimate and crucial tool to achieve it'.[78] Barak's decision concerning the applicability of the norms governing the conduct of hostilities in an international armed conflict in combination with the category of *civilians* who constitute *unlawful combatants* may be considered an example: this novel construction answers perfectly to the 'needs of society' to preserve the Israeli monopoly to exercise legitimate force in the conflict with the Palestinians while maintaining the right to continually exercise the 'active self-defence' measure of targeted killing.[79] Civilians who constitute unlawful combatants are legitimate targets for attack for such time as they take a direct part in hostilities, a norm which, as we have seen, may be stretched to apply

---

[76] Milanovic, 'Lessons for Human Rights and Humanitarian law in the War on Terror: Comparing Hamdan and the Israeli Targeted Killing Case' p. 384.

[77] *Public Committee Against Torture* v. *The Government of Israel* para. 28; Aharon Barak, 'The Role of the Supreme Court in a Democracy' 3 (1998) Israel Studies 6.

[78] Aharon Barak, *Purposive Interpretation in Law* (Sari Bashi tr, Princeton University Press 2005). For two very different assessments of Barak's practice of this legal theory in his judgments on questions of the occupation and the Israeli war against terror, see Owen Fiss, 'Law Is Everywhere' 117 (2007) The Yale Law Journal 256 and Nimer Sultany, 'The Legacy of Justice Aharon Barak: A Critical Review' Harvard International Law Journal Online www.harvardilj.org/wp-content/uploads/2011/05/HILJ-Online_48_Sultany.pdf accessed 15 May 2015. For the legacy of Barak from the perspective of Israeli national security law, see Cohen and Cohen, *Israel's National Security Law: Political Dynamics and Historical Development*, passim.

[79] This was the way in which Amos N. Guiora of the Military Advocate General's Corps of the IDF described the policy a couple of years before the judgment: Amos N. Guiora, 'Targeted Killing as Active Self-Defense' 36 (2004) Case Western Reserve Journal of International Law 319.

to a rather wide group. However, they do not themselves have the right to resort to violence, but may be tried, judged and punished for their participation in hostilities.[80] Furthermore, they do not enjoy the rights granted to combatants. Thus, for example, the laws of prisoners of war do not apply to them.[81]

In this respect the judgment ties in with Benjamin's reflections on the 'law of the Police' (and remember the wide interpretation of the Police institution given earlier). For Benjamin, the police provide an instance in which 'the separation of lawmaking and law-preserving violence is suspended'.[82] How and when does this suspension occur? Derrida writes that the police 'invent law, make themselves lawmaking, legislate each time law is indeterminate enough to give them the chance'[83] and Benjamin specifically says that this is done 'for security reasons' when the law cannot guarantee the ends that it 'desires at any price to attain'.[84]

For these reasons, I claim that the Court's exercise of jurisdiction over targeted killing in the first place, the Court's decision on the applicable law as well as the particular interpretation of that law all point in the direction of the fact that the Court, in an exercise of what Benjamin calls 'law-preserving violence', makes itself actively involved in the continued 'lawmaking violence' of the Israeli state.

Trajectories of Israeli State Protection

This reading of the targeted killing judgment suggests that cutting straight to the Intifada and the lethal targeting of designated Palestinian terrorists in application of the law of armed conflict is insufficient in accounting for the emergence of targeted killing in Israel. Instead, we will consider this practice against the background of a much longer Israeli history of state protection, terrorism and assassination. As we will see, the question of state protection was intimately related to the founding of the Israeli state and the call for state protection has affected Jewish–Arab co-existence in Palestine from the founding of the state all the way to the contemporary war on terrorism. Further, the history of the state of Israel provides important perspectives on how both domestic and international laws depend on the state for its distribution of the legitimate use of violence.

---

[80] *Public Committee Against Torture* v. *The Government of Israel* para. 25.
[81] *Ibid.*   [82] Benjamin, 'Critique of Violence' p. 286.
[83] Derrida, 'Force of Law: The Mystical Foundation of Authority' p. 43.
[84] Benjamin, 'Critique of Violence' p. 287.

Because Benjamin's *Critique of Violence* will continue to be a point of reference in this chapter it might be worth noting that Benjamin died in 1940 in Portbou, Spain, while attempting to escape the Nazi persecution of Jews on the European continent by embarking for America.[85] Little is known about his position on Zionist debates except that he was critical towards both the political Zionism that ultimately would succeed in establishing a Jewish state in Palestine and its main contestant, the assimilationism typical of the bourgeois Jewish environment in which he grew up.[86] In what appears to be an attempt to excuse his Marxist inclinations to his friend Gershom Scholem (who did not share them), Benjamin wrote from Berlin in 1931 that if he would be with Scholem in Palestine, his political outlooks quite possibly might have looked 'completely different'. This was so because, for Benjamin, Scholem's 'position on the Arab question' and his participation in 'Brit Shalom' (a group of intellectuals that fought for Arab–Jewish cooperation and a bi-national state) showed that there were other opportunities for 'unambiguously differentiating yourself from the bourgeoisie there than there are here'.[87] In his exchange of letters with Scholem, the issue of travelling to Palestine to see his friend or even move there permanently comes up repeatedly, however, he never made the trip.[88]

---

[85] Benjamin committed suicide after having realised that he would be put on a train back to France by the Spanish police following a decision that he did not have permission to leave for America. Noah Limone, 'Chronicling Walter Benjamin's Final Hours' *Haaretz* (9 July 2012) http://www.haaretz.com/chronicling-walter-benjamin-s-final-hours-1 .449897 accessed 10 May 2015.

[86] Benjamin's biographer Bernd Witte writes that 'Benjamin distanced himself from Zionism as a political and social movement; its "nationalism", he felt, was diametrically opposed to the mission of Judaism to become an international "radical cultural will". He also quotes Benjamin in correspondence with a friend declaring how it 'is idle to ask which is more important, Jewish work for Palestine or Jewish work for Europe. I am tied here. And it would be bad indeed for Europe if the cultural energies of the Jews were to be withdrawn from it'. On this basis Witte describes Benjamin as a 'cultural Zionist' (Bernd Witte, *Walter Benjamin: An Intellectual Biography* (James Rolleston tr, Detroit, MI: Wayne State University Press 1997) p. 26f).

[87] Walter Benjamin, *The Correspondence of Walter Benjamin 1910–1940* (Gershom Scholem and Theodor W. Adorno eds., Manfred R. Jacobson and Evelyn M. Jacobson trs, University of Chicago Press 1994) p. 378.

[88] Bernd Witte argues that it was Benjamin's commitment to cultural as opposed to political Zionism that persuaded him not to go (Witte, *Walter Benjamin: An Intellectual Biography* p. 27). In a recent article in which they map the reception of Benjamin in Israel, including in Israeli legal academia, Vivian Liska and Tamara Eisenberg have reasoned that although Benjamin never saw Palestine, his work certainly has (Vivian Liska and Tamara Eisenberg,

Political Zionism as State Protection

The idea of organised Jewish self-defence precedes the establishment of a Jewish state in Palestine. Jewish self-defence groups were formed in Eastern Europe in the beginning of the twentieth century against the backdrop of anti-Jewish pogroms. One such group, the All-Jewish Workers Union or *Bund*, defined nationalism in terms of Jewish rights within Russia at a time in which Zionist ideas were beginning to win support in Eastern Europe.[89] For young Zionists arriving in Palestine from Eastern Europe at the turn of the century, the protection of Jewish communities was a primary concern and *Shomer* and the *Hagana* was formed to protect Jewish presence in Ottoman-controlled pre-First World War Palestine.[90] These paramilitary groups would eventually form the backbone of the Israeli state army.

Much more generally, Jacqueline Rose has described a line that was central not just to Zionism but to the future of the Israeli nation – 'the line that runs from suffering to political power'.[91] This highlights that political Zionism was never simply a form of nationalism[92] or settler colonialism[93] but was, and still is, driven by the idea of state protection. This is the French political scientist Alain Dieckhoff:

> The state model, an organ of Reason whose task is to transcend all traditional forms of solidarity, has spread throughout the world, and still has an irresistible attraction for all peoples aspiring to full independence. This inevitably has a political dimension, involving the establishment of a state which alone can guarantee a nation the full enjoyment of its rights in a territorially defined space where it exercises its sovereignty and can ensure its security. Without the state a people remains fundamentally vulnerable.

'A Travel Guide to Palestine: Walter Benjamin in Israel' 2 (2009) Naharaim-Zeitschrift für deutsch-jüdische Literatur und Kulturgeschichte 301).

[89] Arie Perliger and Leonard Weinberg, 'Jewish Self-Defence and Terrorist Groups Prior to the Establishment of the State of Israel: Roots and Traditions' 4 (2003) Totalitarian Movements and Political Religions 91 at 94.

[90] *Ibid.* p. 95.

[91] Jacqueline Rose, *The Question of Zion* (Princeton University Press 2005) p. 113.

[92] The gloss of the preeminent theorist of nationalism Benedict Anderson in his influential *Imagined Communities* can serve as an example: 'The significance of the emergence of Zionism and the birth of Israel is that the former marks the reimagining of an ancient religious community as a nation, down there among the other nations – while the latter charts an alchemic change from wandering devotee to local patriot'. Benedict Anderson, *Imagined Communities: Reflections on the Origin and Spread of Nationalism* (Revised edn, London: Verso 2006) p. 149.

[93] See in particular Gabriel Piterberg, *The Returns of Zionism: Myths, Politics and Scholarship in Israel* (London: Verso 2008).

Subjected to the appetites of the powerful and caught up in strategies over which it has no control, it is constantly threatened with being scattered, suppressed or massacred. This basic fragility is the lot of all peoples without a state, but the Jews have experienced it in a paroxysmal fashion. Their original destitution could only be put right by the building of a nation state that would definitively end the basic statelessness of the Jews. Normalisation means a state.[94]

This road from suffering to political power, to use the expression of Jacqueline Rose, was not travelled without challenge by Jewish critics. Writing in the run-up to the establishment of the state Hannah Arendt finds the assumption that there is an escape from antisemitism in a promised land 'whose upbuilding', in chairman of the President of the Zionist Organisation and subsequently the First President of the state of Israel Chaim Weizmann's words, 'would be the answer to antisemitism', faulty.[95] This was proved, Arendt notes, when Rommel's army threatened Jews in Palestine with exactly the same fate as in European countries.[96] Moreover, this is a faulty assumption on the grounds that the idea that there is a place on earth where a people could live like an 'organic national body' is a dream. 'The real historical development of a nation' simply does not take place 'inside the closed walls of a biological entity'.[97]

What Arendt feared in the establishment of a state was not only the end of that which represented for her the idea of a 'Jewish homeland', the *yishuv* and the kibbutz movement.[98] Arendt also feared that the

[94] Alain Dieckhoff, *The Invention of a Nation: Zionist Thought and the Making of Modern Israel* (Jonathan Derrick tr, London: Hurst & Company 2003) p. viii.

[95] Hannah Arendt, 'The Jewish State: Fifty Years After, Where Have Herzl's Politics Led? [originally published 1945–46 in Commentary 1]' in Jerome Kohn and Ron H. Feldman (eds.), *The Jewish Writings: Hannah Arendt* (New York: Schocken Books 2007) 375–401 at 383.

[96] Hannah Arendt, 'Zionism Reconsidered [originally published October 1944 in the *Menorah Journal*]' in Jerome Kohn and Ron H. Feldman (eds.), *The Jewish Writings: Hannah Arendt* (New York: Schocken Books 2007) 343–374 at 360. Arendt refers to 'antisemitism' rather than the more commonly used 'anti-Semitism'. In a footnote to her essay *Antisemitism* Arendt describes how the term "semitic" first was a purely linguistic one and that it subsequently was turned into an anthropological and ethnic one (see Arendt, 'Antisemitism' p. 111f endnote 2). As noted by the editors of *The Jewish Writings*, since there never was an ideology or movement called "Semitism", anti-semitism and its cognates may be considered logical misnomers. Hannah Arendt, Jerome Kohn and Ron H. Feldman, *The Jewish Writings: Hannah Arendt* (New York: Schocken Books 2007) p. xxxiii.

[97] Arendt, 'The Jewish State: Fifty Years After, Where Have Herzl's Politics Led? [originally published 1945–46 in Commentary 1]' p. 382.

[98] For a consideration of the sharp distinction that Arendt makes between the notion of a 'Jewish homeland' and a 'Jewish state', see the introduction to *The Jewish Writings*: Ron

establishment of a Jewish state in Palestine made the dispossession of the Palestinians inevitable and that this reality could only be avoided through 'wilful blindness'.[99] Indeed, already in 1923, revisionist Zionist Ze'ev Jabotinsky described how Palestinian Arabs inevitably will be opposed to extensive Jewish settlement in Palestine and that this therefore must take place under the protection of an 'iron wall' of military force that refused to be in any way influenced by Arab interests or pressure:

> Zionist colonization, even the most restricted, must either be terminated or carried out in defiance of the will of the native population. This colonization can, therefore, continue and develop only under the protection of a force independent of the local population – an iron wall which the native population cannot break through. This is, in toto, our policy towards the Arabs. To formulate it any other way would only be hypocrisy.[100]

While Jabotinsky had the idea that Jewish steadfastness would provide ground for mutual concessions and that both peoples eventually would be able to live 'like good neighbors...in peace'[101], Arendt feared that the '"victorious" Jews would live surrounded by an entirely hostile Arab population, secluded inside ever-threatened borders, absorbed with physical self-defense to a degree that would submerge all other interests and

---

H. Feldman, 'Introduction: The Jew as Pariah: The Case of Hannah Arendt (1906–1975)' in Jerome Kohn and Ron H. Feldman (eds.), *The Jewish Writings: Hannah Arendt* (New York: Schocken Books 2007) xli–lxxvi.

[99] Arendt, 'Zionism Reconsidered [originally published October 1944 in the *Menorah Journal*]' p. 346.

[100] Ze'ev Jabotinsky, 'The Iron Wall (We and the Arabs)'(1923) First published in Russian in *Rassvyet* in 1923, published in English in *Jewish Herald* (South Africa) in 1937, published online by Marxistsde: www.marxists.de/middleast/ironwall/ironwall.htm accessed 10 May 2015. This is the kind of thinking that makes Dieckhoff consider Jabotinsky's stance on Jewish–Arab relations in the light of Carl Schmitt's friend–enemy distinction. In fact, Dieckhoff writes: 'Jabotinsky was the Carl Schmitt of Zionism: the irreducible reality of the political sphere consisted in the distinction between friend and enemy. Politics meant the assertion of the Same against the Other. It assumed identification of the enemy, who in one way or another challenged the existence of the people, and an all-out struggle against him to reduce his capacity to do harm'. Dieckhoff continues: 'It was considered not to be the job of ethics to guide political action, which had another objective: to ensure the survival, prosperity and security of the body politic, by means that possibly included what was morally contestable (war)' (Dieckhoff, *The Invention of a Nation: Zionist Thought and the Making of Modern Israel*. p. 216f). Historian Avi Shlaim reads the entire history of the Israeli state and its relationship to the Arab population through the lens of Jabotinsky's 'iron wall': Avi Shlaim, *The Iron Wall: Israel and the Arab World* (New York: W. W. Norton & Company 2001) 11–16.

[101] Jabotinsky, 'The Iron Wall (We and the Arabs)'.

activities'.[102] In other words she feared that the state Palestine Jewry would form not only would be one that would solve the 'Jewish question' by creating its very own 'Palestinian question', but one whose external as well as internal affairs would be entirely absorbed by the question of protection. Above all, Arendt realised in 1948 that a Jewish state in Palestine would have to be forged in violence and feared its effect on the 'idea of Arab-Jewish cooperation though never realized on any scale and today seemingly farther off than ever'.[103]

---

[102] Hannah Arendt, 'To Save the Jewish Homeland [originally published 1948 in *Commentary* 5]' in Kohn J and Feldman RH (eds.), *The Jewish Writings: Hannah Arendt* (New York: Schocken Books 2007) p. 396.

[103] Arendt, 'The Jewish State: Fifty Years After, Where Have Herzl's Politics Led? [originally published 1945–46 in *Commentary* 1]' p. 396. Although she would rarely refer to the processes through which the Israeli state was founded in her publications after 1948, I find it hard to believe that her intense engagement in Zionist debates throughout the 1940s did not have an impact on her later work in law and politics. There is a theme in her subsequent writings according to which it seems as if she wants to rid the political sphere of violence, but she would also, again and again, show that she is aware of law and politics' entanglement with it. Against this background the claim by Fraser and Hutchings that 'Arendtian politics remains haunted by the violence it supposedly excludes' seems apt (Elizabeth Frazer and Kimberly Hutchings, 'On Politics and Violence: Arendt Contra Fanon' 7 (2008) Contemporary Political Theory 90 at 94). Most pertinently in an attempt to retrieve a conception of law that is not imperative, Arendt referred to the Greek word for law: *nomos* (see Hannah Arendt, *The Human Condition* (University of Chicago Press 1958) and Hannah Arendt, 'The Great Tradition I. Law and Power' 74 (2007) Social Research: An International Quarterly 713). Arendt conceives of nomos in light of its etymological origin in the word *nemein* which means to distribute, to possess (what has been distributed), and to dwell: she was able to affirm this notion of law while at the same time maintaining that 'law . . . has something violent about it in terms of both its *origins* and its *nature*' (Arendt as quoted in Keith Breen, 'Law Beyond Command' in Marco Goldoni and Christopher McCorkindale (eds.), *Hannah Arendt and the Law* (Oxford: Hart Publishing 2012) 15–34 at 23). In this respect Carl Schmitt's challenge to Arendt's understanding of *nomos* is, very unfortunately, of great relevance. For Schmitt stressed how conceiving of *nomos* in terms of distribution and dwelling neutralises the political content of *nemein* (Hans Lindahl, 'Give and Take: Arendt and the Nomos of Political Community' 32 (2006) Philosophy and Social Criticism 881 at 893). This is so because it is not division but appropriation that comes first. 'Initially, there was no basic norm, but a basic appropriation. No man can give, divide, and distribute without taking' (Carl Schmitt, *The Nomos of the Earth in the International Law of the Jus Publicum Europaeum* (G. L. Ulmen tr, New York: Telos Press Publishing 2006) p. 345). This is the primordial act of 'land-appropriation' [Ger. *Landnahme*] or the 'radical title' by means of which 'a tribe, a retinue, or a people becomes . . . historically situated and turns a part of the earth's surface into the force-field of a particular order' (*ibid.* p. 70).

Protection: The Difference a State Makes

Dealing with the founding of the Israeli state, Honaida Ghanim has deployed a metaphor of the Palestinian poet Mahmoud Darwish: the descent into a 'common hole' or 'common entrapment' of enmity.[104] This metaphor is a good one because it captures the constitutive nature of the founding of the state not just for the respective group (the beginning of independence for one and the beginning of dispossession for the other), but for Jewish–Arab co-existence. In this metaphor, 1948 marks a shift from by no means always peaceful heterogeneous unity that characterised Jewish–Arab relations in Palestine under British and Turkish imperial rule to a community defined by the utmost degree of intensity of a union or separation, of an association and dissociation: the distinction between friend and enemy.[105] This is still a situation of co-existence, however, because Palestine would remain a place where Jews live together with Arabs also after 1948. This is not to suggest that Israelis and Palestinians are uniform groups, every member of which is, at all times, associated and dissociated. Judith Butler gives this cohabitation a more nuanced expression in a recent book:

> Even though neither 'Jews' nor 'Palestinians' are monolithic populations, they nevertheless are now in Israel/Palestine bound together in intractable ways through a regime of Israeli law and military violence that has produced a resistance movement that takes both violent and nonviolent forms.[106]

The legal and political arrangements of this co-existence would take different forms over the years. When the fighting stopped in 1949, Israel had claimed for itself not just the land that was reserved for the Jewish state in UN partition resolution 181 but 77 per cent of the territory of the former British mandate.[107] Roughly 800 000 Palestinians were displaced to the West Bank, Gaza and neighbouring Arab states,[108] remaining in

---

[104] Honaida Ghanim, 'The Urgency of a New Beginning in Palestine: An Imagined Scenario by Mahmoud Darwish and Hannah Arendt' 38 (2011) College Literature 75.

[105] Carl Schmitt, *The Concept of the Political – Expanded Edition* (George Schwab tr, University of Chicago Press 2007) p. 26.

[106] Judith Butler, *Parting Ways: Jewishness and the Critique of Zionism* (New York: Columbia University Press 2012) p. 30.

[107] Peter Malanczuk, 'Israel: Status, Territory and Occupied Territories', in Rudolf Bernhardt (ed.), *Encyclopedia of Public International Law II* (Elsevier 1995) 1468–1497 at 1483.

[108] In a recent article Roger O'Keefe considers the international lawfulness of the displacement of the Palestinians against the background of the unique circumstances of the end of a League of Nations Mandate in the United Nations era, without a geographically

the territory of the nascent state was a minority of Palestinians subject to a discriminatory military rule.[109]

Judith Butler notices, in the quote above, one critical characteristic of this common entrapment of enmity, one that is of immense importance for the question of state protection, the legal asymmetry of its 'partners'. This legal asymmetry explains how it can be that the violence of the one is unlawful terrorism by default, while the other may cast its violence as legally sanctioned counterterrorism. We can see this in the 2006 targeted killing judgment when Barak determined targeted killing lawful, granted certain criteria were met, relying on a customary international law which is part of Israeli law 'by force of the State of Israel's existence as a sovereign and independent state'.[110] I reasoned that this could be read as a direct reference to the fact that the positive legality at work in the judgment is a product of history: the history through which Israel came into being as a sovereign and independent state.

coextensive independent state succeeding it: 'It is difficult to resist the conclusion that, on the failure of the UN partition plan (which was not binding on the inhabitants of Palestine anyway) and the subsequent unilateral end of the British mandate (which, as it was, imposed no international legal obligations on either the Jewish or Arab communities), the Jewish population of the territory of the defunct Mandate was not prohibited by international law from seizing as much land as it could within its borders, in the same way that the Palestinian Arabs were at liberty to do. Neither the Jewish nor Arab community was constrained – nor, at the time, was a sub-state group considered even capable of being constrained – by any rule of international law. Nor, once the state of Israel could be said to have come into existence . . . did any relevant rule of international law apply to prevent it from claiming territory within the confines of the former Mandate. It is not that the territory was *terra nullius*: the presence of communities whose rights were explicitly recognized in the provisions of the Mandate and in Security Council resolutions of 1948 almost certainly prevented reversion of the territory covered by the Mandate to the international legal state of nature on the mandate's termination. The point, rather, is that any territory within the frontiers of the former Mandate that had not been incorporated into the state of Israel was not protected by the prohibition on the use of interstate force, whether under Art. 2(4) of the UN Charter (such territory not belonging to a Member of the United Nations) or, optimistically, under customary international law (such territory not belonging to a state). Nor does the now-recognized right of the Palestinian people to self-determination make any difference to the analysis, most fundamentally for the reason that this right did not exist in 1947–1949 as a rule of positive general international law' (Roger O'Keefe, 'Israel/Palestine Sixty Years On' in Thomas Giegerich and Alexander Proelß (eds.), *Krisenherde im Fokus des Völkerrechts – Trouble Spots in the Focus of International Law* (Berlin: Duncker & Humblot 2010) 13–55 at 18ff).

[109] See the database of Adalah: The Legal Center for Arab Minority Rights in Israel, 'Discriminatory Laws In Israel' www.adalah.org/en/law/index accessed 20 May 2015.

[110] *Public Committee Against Torture* v. *The Government of Israel* para. 16 (internal citations omitted).

A debate in the Security Council on 17 July 1948 is particularly illuminating in this regard. The meeting took place over a resolution from Syria that the Security Council should request an advisory legal opinion as to the status of Palestine arising from the termination of the mandate, a question that clearly would force the ICJ to determine the legal status of the newly proclaimed state.[111] At this point a handful of states had already recognised the state of Israel, including the *de facto* recognition of the United States the same day as the state was declared and the *de jure* recognition by the USSR three days later.

In his statement, the representative of Egypt, Mahmoud Bey Fawzi, broadened the debate to consider not just a request for an advisory opinion but the implications of a Jewish state in Palestine from a long-term perspective (and was interrupted by the Ukrainian President of the Council for doing so). He argued that, from this point onwards, Jewish–Arab relations would be characterised by an asymmetry that would have wide-ranging implications including on questions of Jewish immigration to Palestine, the right of Arabs to return to the land from which they were in the process of being expelled and questions relating to the use of force:

> On every occasion when we speak to them of our fairness, of our rights, of our justice; they will say, 'But we have a State.' Even when we point out that there are already immigration laws governing all Palestine, that those laws are not yet repealed, and that neither the Mediator, nor the Security Council, nor the so-called Jewish authorities in Palestine, are in law empowered in the present situation to legislate for Palestine or any part of it, the Zionists, will again say, 'But we have a State.' This is their only retort. They have extorted what they wanted and they are simply sitting tight with, so far, no means of redress for the Arabs.[112]

The assertion 'but we have a state' gives expression to the legal asymmetry that has characterised Israeli-Palestinian relations since 1948. From Benjamin's perspective, the expression 'but we have a state' reveals how 'proof of historical origin' is the necessary basis of violence for legal ends.

It is important to realise that this historical origin of law is something that escapes both domestic and international law. Starting with domestic law, two cases decided by the Israel Supreme Court just a few months after the state was declared may be noted. On 2 December 1948 in the case of *Ziv* v. *Gubernik and Others* the Court held that

---

[111] UNSC, Verbatim Record (27 July 1948) UN Doc S/PV/339.   [112] *Ibid.* p. 24f.

the object of the Declaration of Independence of May 15, 1948, was to determine the *fact* of the establishment of the State for the purpose of recognition by international law. It gave expression to the national ideal and the beliefs of the people, but was not a constitutional law in the light of which the validity of other laws could be examined.[113]

This understanding was clarified by the Court in *Ahmed Shauki el Kharbutli* v. *Minister of Defence,* passed on 3 January 1949, when the Court with reference to *Ziv* v. *Gubernik and Others,* expressed: 'It was not stated that the Declaration of Independence was merely a political act. On the contrary, it was stressed that the Declaration has the force of law for the purpose of establishing the *fact* of the legal creation of the state.'[114] As I read these cases the Israel Supreme Court asserts on the one hand the significance of the declaration of independence for the coming into being of law and on the other explains how the declaration itself relies not on law but on military and performative effectiveness.

The Court's statement in *Ziv* v. *Gubernik* that the purpose of the declaration of independence was to determine the fact of the establishment of the state for the purpose of international legal recognition leads us further to consider the acquisition of *international* legal subjectivity by the state of Israel.[115] Here, the mentioning of General Assembly resolution 181 and the 'natural right' of the Jewish people to 'their own sovereign state' in the declaration of independence may be noted. However, since both fail to provide a positive international law basis for the establishment of the Israeli state, we need to continue to the question of the founding from the point of view of the general international law of statehood, a question that leads us back to the 17 July 1948 deliberations of the Security Council.[116]

---

[113] Israel Supreme Court, '*Ziv* v. *Gubernik and Others* (2 December 1948)' 16 (1948) Annual Digest of Public International Law Cases 7 at 7.

[114] Israel Supreme Court, '*Ahmed Shauki el Kharbutli* v. *Minister of Defence* (3 January 1949)' 16 (1949) Annual Digest of Public International Law Cases 7 at 7.

[115] Roger O'Keefe states that 'the legal fact' of the Israeli state was achieved sometime between 14 May 1948 and the conclusion of the first of its general armistice agreements on 24 February 1949. O'Keefe, 'Israel/Palestine Sixty Years On' p. 17.

[116] Partition Resolution 181 fails to provide a positive law basis for the establishment of the Israeli state because formulated in a non-binding manner and, more fundamentally, because according to Articles 10 to 14 of the UN Charter, the General Assembly has the power to make recommendations only. Moreover, the creation of the Israeli state did not comply with Partition Resolution 181 inter alia in claiming substantially greater territory than accorded to it and in not complying with the prescribed conditions for protection of minorities (James Crawford, *The Creation of States in International Law* (2nd edn, Oxford University Press 2006) p. 233). The claim about the natural right of the Jewish people to their own sovereign state (which can be interpreted as an invocation of a nascent right of

At the outset it may be noted that the Israeli representative Abba Eban pointed to the irony of the fact that, should the Egyptian resolution be adopted, then the only state in history to have had its juridical status subject to judicial review would be, at the same time, the only one whose existence was proclaimed on suggestion of the UN General Assembly:

> There is one particular aspect of this question which would make it especially incongruous for the International Court of Justice to take the juridical status of Palestine under review. All States known to history have become States by their own unilateral assertion, without any injunction or permission from the organized international community. There is, however, one exception to the general rule. There is one State alone which came into existence at the behest and the summons of the international community: the State of Israel. If legitimate origin were relevant – which it is not – in determining statehood, there would be only one instance in which it could be established, for the General Assembly required and demanded the establishment of the State of Israel . . . Israel, in fact, possesses the only international birth certificate in a world of unproven virtue, and by a strange irony, it is precisely in this instance – the only instance in which the international community has pronounced itself – that the legitimacy of statehood is to be submitted to the International Court of Justice for investigation.[117]

With regard to the Israeli position on the Egyptian resolution, Abba Eban stated: 'it is not within the capacity of the International Court of Justice to determine the existence or the non-existence of the State of Israel, which is a question of fact and not of law, based on criteria of effectiveness and not of legitimacy'.[118]

The failure of the Syrian resolution to obtain the necessary affirmative votes can, of course, not be taken as proof of the extreme position on the pure fact of statehood in international law taken by Eban. However, the many declarations of recognition of the state of Israel during and shortly after the Israeli war of independence or *Nakba* (Arabic for catastrophe), some of which recognised Israel *de facto*, and others *de jure*, without a clear sense of the meaning of that distinction emerging, points to the fragile nature of the distinction between law and fact in the international

---

self-determination) fails on the grounds of the inter-temporal rule, requiring that events occurring at a particular period be judged by the valid law at that time. As Crawford claims, self-determination was not a rule of positive general international law at the time. Were it so, it could equally well be considered an obstacle to Israeli statehood because of the majority of Palestinians residing in the territory of the former British mandate. *Ibid.* p. 234.

[117] UNSC, Verbatim Record (27 July 1948) UN Doc S/PV/339 p. 30.   [118] *Ibid.* p. 32.

law of the creation of states. So does the inconclusive discussion of the legal or political nature of the recognition of states that was undertaken on the basis of the example set by Israel becoming a subject of international law.[119]

'A Nation in Arms': The Israeli History of Wars of Existence and Assassinations

International law scholar Anthony Carty has argued that there is a link between the 'independent force and energy' with which the state establishes itself and 'the dynamic or drive underlying state actions... to preserve itself' in general and in the case of Israel in particular.[120]

In this section we will consider the legal implications of this drive or dynamic of self-preservation in the context of the Israeli history of wars of existence and assassinations. One characteristic of the establishment

---

[119] Philip Marshall Brown, 'The Recognition of Israel' 42 (1948) American Journal of International Law 620; Herbert W. Briggs, 'Recognition of States: Some Reflections on Doctrine and Practice' 43 (1949) American Journal of International Law 113; Josef L. Kunz, 'Critical Remarks on Lauterpacht's "Recognition in International Law"' 44 (1950) American Journal of International Law 713. Following Peter Fitzpatrick's consideration of the question of statehood in international law I would argue that both the pure fact theory of statehood and the theory that the acquisition of statehood is regulated by international law overstress their cases. Fitzpatrick has argued: 'Now, common assurance to the contrary, facts do not speak for themselves. They come to be through various performative modes endowing them with operative existence. This could be an observational mode, for instance – a recognition of the existence of the facts through the way in which they are observed. And doubtless law, any system of living law, depends upon some such observation. It depends upon recognizing what, as it were, comes to it factually. But this ability, as Derrida has it, is of the law itself: the incipient relation to "nonlaw" is "in law". What is involved here becomes not just the "declaratory" observation of some factual evidence. What is involved is also a "constitutive" legal decision responding to a legal claim, with both decision and claim being based on legal criteria relating to whether an entity is to be endowed with the requisite legal personality to participate in an international legal system'. Peter Fitzpatrick, 'Latin Roots: The Force of International Law as Event' in Fleur Johns, Richard Joyce and Sundhya Pahuja (eds.), *Events: The Force of International Law* (New York: Routledge Cavendish 2010) 43–54 at 45. For a rigorous analyses of the constitutive and the declaratory theory of international legal statehood that support this view see Martti Koskenniemi, *From Apology to Utopia: The Structure of International Legal Argument* (2nd edn, Cambridge University Press 2005) pp. 272–282.

[120] Carty argues that this dynamic or drive 'is central to an analysis of international relations from a critical perspective, because it prepares one for the compulsive repetitive nature of the lust of states for security, a mark of all states and a fundamental characteristic of inter-state relations'. Anthony Carty, 'Israel's Legal Right to Exist and the Principle of the Self-determination of the Palestinian People?' 76 (2013) The Modern Law Review 158 at 158.

of the state of Israel was that the declaration of the state did not coincide with the 'peace ceremony' of which Benjamin writes, signifying that the victory establishes a new law, marking the threshold between lawmaking and law-preserving violence.[121] Instead, the Israeli state was declared in the midst of a war, a war that did not end with peace, but with an armistice with Israel's Arab neighbours and with a dispossessed Palestinian population. This implied that the military violence that founded the state was not discontinued. As a consequence of these dire circumstances, 'once victory was attained, Ben-Gurion emphatically ruled that there be no relaxation in the overall public mood of national security vigilance'.[122] Amichai Cohen and Stuart A. Cohen refer to Ben-Gurion as having 'from 1949 . . . repeatedly warned that the Arabs were preparing for "a second round" of fighting and hence insist[ing] that Israel had no choice but to remain a "nation in arms"'.[123]

This is a fact that corresponds with Honaida Ghanim's acute observation that Israel 'has never waged a single war since 1948 that was not presented by it as a war of "existence", so that regardless of the particular issues at any moment, what matters is that Israel as a state deems itself to be perpetually in a process of formation'.[124] As far as domestic law is concerned, it can be mentioned that the state of Israel has remained in an officially proclaimed state of emergency since 19 May 1948, four days after the declaration of independence, until today. This is explained in the 2013 fourth periodic report to the UN Human Rights Committee in the following way:

> The original declaration of a state of emergency was issued by the Provisional Council of State, in the midst of the war that began several months prior to the declaration of Israel's independence on May 14, 1948, with neighboring states and the local Arab population. Since then, the state of emergency has remained in force due to the ongoing state of war or violent conflict between Israel and its neighbors, and the constant attacks on the lives and property of its citizens.[125]

---

[121] Benjamin, 'Critique of Violence' p. 283.
[122] Cohen and Cohen, *Israel's National Security Law: Political Dynamics and Historical Development* p. 54.
[123] *Ibid.*
[124] Ghanim, 'The Urgency of a New Beginning in Palestine: An Imagined Scenario by Mahmoud Darwish and Hannah Arendt' p. 78f.
[125] Human Rights Committee, 'Consideration of reports submitted by States Parties under article 40 of the Covenant pursuant to the optional reporting procedure – (Fourth periodic reports of States parties due in 2013) Israel', (14 October 2013) Advance Unedited Version

These historical facts may be helpful in appreciating the continuation of military lawmaking violence, and the particular breed of such violence that targeted lethal force, often referred to as assassination, constitute.

In a book published in 1993 entitled *Political Assassinations By Jews: A Rhetorical Device For Justice*,[126] Nachman Ben-Yehuda of the Department of Sociology and Anthropology at the Hebrew University of Jerusalem undertakes 'an in-depth inquiry into the nature, scope, meaning and results of political assassinations within one complex cultural matrix... political assassinations by Jews in Palestine-Israel'.[127] Even though he also gives an historical background ranging as far back as the *Sicariis*, the book is first and foremost a case study of ninety-one cases of political assassinations dating from 1903 to the 1980s. This is accomplished by a study of both primary and secondary sources, including the archives of groups and by interviews with individuals involved in these historical developments. Indeed, most of the cases occurred in the British mandate period between 1939 and 1947 and were carried out by three Jewish groups who saw themselves as 'involved in an actual struggle with the British and the Arabs for the creation of a new and independent Jewish state':[128] the *Haganah*, which, unlike the other groups was the 'operational arm' of the Jewish Agency and was used and controlled by that political organisation;[129] and two outbreak revisionist Zionist paramilitary groups, *Lehi* (also referred to as the Stern Gang)[130] and *Etzel* (also referred to as *Irgun*).[131]

Ben-Yehuda argues that the tradition, ideology and practice of political assassinations carried out by pre-state Jewish self-defence groups were continued 'under a different guise' within the state structure after 1948.

> Before 1949, most cases were committed by the three main pre-state underground Jewish groups... After the State of Israel was formally established, the incidence of political assassination events declined very sharply and significantly. The reason for this is that before 1949 political assassinations were used to explain and justify acts that seemed like justice to the assassins in situations where they felt that they could not get a fair justice because the opportunities for such justice were blocked. After 1949, a new system of political and judicial justice came into being as the State of Israel was

published on the website of the Human Rights Committee: http://www.ccprcentre.org/country/israel/ accessed 10 May 2015 p. 52.
[126] Nachman Ben-Yehuda, *Political Assassinations by Jews: A Rhetorical Device for Justice* (New York: SUNY Press 1993).
[127] *Ibid.* p. 4f.   [128] *Ibid.* p. 379.   [129] *Ibid.* p. 88ff.
[130] *Ibid.* p. 91ff.   [131] *Ibid.* p. 94ff.

established, hence the need to resort to political assassinations declined sharply. Since 1948 instead of political assassinations we have cases of state sponsored assassinations: political executions.[132]

Political execution is, for Ben-Yehuda, a subcategory of *political assassination*, denoting 'an official organisation of a state, or a country, which makes a decision to assassinate a particular actor, for political reasons . . . and the decision is made not in a due, fair and open, process'.[133] Examining further the distinction Ben-Yehuda makes between 'political assassination' and 'political execution', it becomes clear that the distinction is not devised in order to make the case that political executions are entirely different from political assassinations. Instead, Ben-Yehuda appears to want to emphasise the organisational, ideological and personal continuities between pre-state political assassinations carried out by Jewish self-defence groups and the state-sponsored political assassinations or 'political executions' of the Israeli state. Accordingly, Ben-Yehuda writes:

> It must be remembered that the legacy of Etzel, Lehi and the Hagana was that political assassination events were, under certain circumstance [sic], possible and rightful. These three pre-state Jewish underground groups were definitely involved in several political assassination events. The Palmach, which was the operational military arm of the Jewish Agency and the Hagana and, to a very large extent, the precursor of the Israeli Army, was definitely involved in a few political assassinations/executions. Thus, Gilad [Gilad Zerubavel in the book *Palmach's Chapters*] tells of how, at an unknown date, the Palmach hit some specific and un-named Arab Actors, at unknown dates and places, for political reasons. These Arabs were considered dangerous enemies and held responsible for atrocities against Jews. Furthermore, the Hagana had *specific* units which could be used for this purpose: the Pum, the 'Mista'arvim' the Pelugot Meiuchadot in Tel Aviv, and other special units . . . The Lehi, obviously, had an *open* and public policy of political assassinations, and the Etzel was involved in such acts too. The legacy of political assassinations, therefore ideologically and organizationally was in existence. I remember talking to Isser Harel, Israel's former chief of the Mossad, and asking him about political executions. His response was 'we stopped that.' I never received a detailed answer to my question of what it was exactly that they stopped. Since many of the main figures in the Hagana, Etzel, and Lehi found themselves, after 1948, in key decision-making positions, in various political and command posts, we can certainly expect them to continue to carry the tradition, ideology and practice of political assassinations, *under a different guise,* into their new roles.[134]

---

[132] *Ibid.* pp. xxi–xxii.   [133] *Ibid.* p. 299.

[134] *Ibid.* p. 300f. My emphasis, internal citations omitted.

What does it mean when Ben-Yehuda writes that the tradition, ideology and practice of political assassination carried on 'under a different guise' through the main figures of the Jewish self-defence groups when they, after 1948, found themselves in various political and command posts of the Israeli state?[135]

I gather that this suggests on the one hand a factual continuity and on the other hand a normative discontinuity. For the 'different guise' of which Ben-Yehuda writes concerns the transformation of unsanctioned violence for 'natural' ends into sanctioned violence for 'legal' ends, or from lawmaking to law-preserving violence. Put otherwise, from the point of the founding of the state, the violence needed for protection is *potentially* legal. In this light, the 'different guise' may be said to concern the shift from the sphere of illegality to that of legality, when legality includes the *extra-legal,* or acts committed in excess of legal authority. The fact that Ben-Yehuda refers to such political assassinations as 'political *executions*' is revealing in this respect. This is so because 'execution' signifies not only a fatal action but also the fulfilment of a public office or the carrying into effect of law. This, in turn, directs our attention to another feature of Benjamin's distinction between lawmaking and law-preserving violence: the precarity of this distinction in the carrying into effect or enforcement of law or, in other words, how law-preserving violence is always at risk of lapsing back into lawmaking violence.

As noted, when considering the 'police', Benjamin writes about how measures will be taken – 'for security reasons' – when the state is no longer able to guarantee, through the application of general law, the legal ends that it 'desires at any price to attain'.[136] The distinction that is made in many jurisdictions between the application of general law and the measure tailored to deal with a specific situation, such as the distinction in French between *loi* and *acte,* and in German between *Gesetz* and *Maßnahme,* highlights this executive dimension of legality.

Ben-Yehuda notes that no country is overeager to reveal the possibly discrediting and 'dark' information that political executions constitute.[137]

---

[135] The matter does not become less obscure when Stahl considers the same processes, writing: 'As assassinations continued post-independence, this meant that the killings were quasi-institutionalized, as Israel was now a sovereign nation-state'. Adam Stahl, 'The Evolution of Israeli Targeted Operations: Consequences of the Thabet Thabet Operation' 33 (2010) Studies in Conflict and Terrorism 111 at 113.

[136] Benjamin, 'Critique of Violence' p. 287.

[137] Ben-Yehuda, *Political Assassinations by Jews: A Rhetorical Device for Justice* p. 300. In addition to the methodological considerations in the book itself, Ben-Yehuda has written an article laying out methodological problems and considerations for the study: Nachman

Even so he does find evidence for the involvement in political executions of the Israeli military intelligence and the Mossad (which has the
role of collecting information and performing operations outside Israel).
Ben-Yehuda's investigation did not yield any known cases of political
executions carried out by the Shabak (the Israel Security Agency) who
are responsible for internal security, including security on the occupied territories. However, he also notes that this is hardly surprising
because information about the Shabak is virtually non-existent in public
sources.[138]

Among the cases of political execution brought up by Ben-Yehuda
are the killing in July 1956 of Mustafa Hafez and Salah Mustafa, both
suspected of leading Fedayeen incursions and deadly attacks against Israeli
citizens.[139] These killings are directly linked to the unresolved Palestinian
refugee situation. Between 1948 and 1956 Palestinians who had taken
refuge from the war in Gaza and the West Bank started to make raids
into Israel. By 1956, 300 Israelis had died.[140] With the killing of Mustafa
Hafez and Salah Mustafa, political executions became part of the Israeli
response to such 'infiltration', alongside beefed up border security and
retaliatory strikes into Jordan and Egypt.[141]

Another case of political execution mentioned by Ben-Yehuda is the
killing of top Palestine Liberation Organization (PLO) aide Khalil el-Wazir
(a.k.a. 'Abu Jihad') in 1988 in his house in Tunis, Tunisia.[142] According to
a letter from the permanent representative of Tunisia to the President of
the Security Council, an Israeli commando team equipped with subma-
chine guns entered the residence of el-Wazir, killed a Tunisian employed
as a gardener as well as two guards, only to then assassinate el-Wazir in
the presence of his wife and daughter.[143] The Security Council adopted
a resolution noting with concern that the 'act of aggression' caused the
loss of human life, particularly the 'assassination' of el-Wazir.[144] The

Ben-Yehuda, 'Gathering Dark Secrets, Hidden and Dirty Information: Some Methodological Notes on Studying Political Assassinations' 13 (1990) Qualitative Sociology 345.
[138] Ben-Yehuda, *Political Assassinations by Jews: A Rhetorical Device for Justice* p. 301.
[139] *Ibid.* p. 303f.
[140] Avery Plaw, *Targeting Terrorists: A License to Kill?* (Burlington and Hampshire: Ashgate
   Publishing Company 2008) p. 38.
[141] *Ibid.* p. 39f. See also Benny Morris and Ian Black, *Israel's Secret Wars: A History of Israel's
   Intelligence Services* (New York: Grove Press 1991) p. 123ff.
[142] Ben-Yehuda, *Political Assassinations by Jews: A Rhetorical Device for Justice* p. 313f.
[143] UNSC, 'Letter dated 19 April 1988 from the permanent representative of Tunisia to the
   United Nations addressed the President of the Security Council' (1988) UN Doc S/19798.
[144] UNSC, Res 611 (25 April 1988) UN Doc S/RES/611.

resolution included the following very critical statement about the violation of Tunisian sovereignty:

> *Gravely concerned* by the act of aggression which constitutes a serious and renewed threat to peace, security and stability in the Mediterranean region... *condemns* vigorously the aggression, perpetrated on 16 April 1988 against the sovereignty and territorial integrity of Tunisia in flagrant violation of the Charter of the United Nations, international law and norms of conduct.[145]

The resolution's strong condemnation of both the 'assassination' of el-Wazir and of the violation of Tunisian sovereignty is a testament to the strong opposition to such extraterritorial use of lethal force in counter-terrorism operations at the time. The US ambassador to the UN Vernon A. Walters explained the abstention of the United States by on the one hand describing the Israeli action as 'an all too familiar pattern of escalating force and counter-force' and by deploring all 'acts of violence from whatever quarter they come'.[146] On the other hand ambassador Walters states that the United States

> strongly support the principle that a state subjected to continuing terrorist attacks may respond with appropriate use of force to defend against further attacks. This is an aspect of the inherent right of self-defense recognized in the United Nations Charter. We support this principle regardless of attacker and regardless of victim. It is the collective responsibility of sovereign states to see to that terrorism enjoys no sanctuary, no safe haven, and that those who practice it have no immunity from the responses their acts warrant. Moreover, it is the responsibility of each state to take appropriate steps to prevent persons or groups within its sovereign territory from perpetrating such acts.[147]

It should be mentioned in this context that the US government was split over how to deal with the emerging threat of international terrorism in general and the legality and legitimacy of assassination in counterterrorism in particular. In fact, the Israeli representative to the UN at the time, Benjamin Netanyahu, had convened a conference and edited a book volume in which the person in the US administration pushing hardest for deploying what he termed an 'active defense' against terrorism had

---

[145] *Ibid.*, emphasis in the original.
[146] US Mission to the UN Press Release No. 106(85), 4 October 1985, extract reprinted in 80 (1986) American Journal of International Law 165.
[147] *Ibid.*

participated: Secretary of State George P. Shultz. It is clear from the reasons given by ambassador Walters for the US abstention but also from
Shultz and other contributors to that book that even though the idea
of assassinating designated terrorists did not sit well with the Security
Council it did resonate elsewhere. Thus, in a chapter on 'the Legal Foundations for the War against Terrorism', we find a contribution by Burton
M. Leiser in which it is suggested that 'the most fitting term for a terrorist
is *hostis humani generis*, enemy of mankind' and, following from this, the
principle of 'hot pursuit' in counterterrorism operations should be internationally recognised. 'Any nation that is attacked in any way by terrorists
ought lawfully to be able to pursue these predators wherever they might
flee . . . these international outlaws can no longer be permitted to roam
free'.[148]

We will have good reason to return to both the domestic political
context of the United States and international legal aspects of the 'hot
pursuit' of terrorists 'wherever they might flee' in the coming chapter.
Going back specifically to the Israeli context, the killing of el-Wazir can be
interpreted as forming part of the end phases of the transnationalisation
of the struggle, the driving forces of which were the 1967 occupation of the
Palestinian territories and the emergence of new nationalist Palestinian
organisations. For, as Plaw has argued,

> The longer-term consequence of the Israeli victory [in the Six Day War]
> was to radicalize Palestinian groups, and to prompt them to invent and lead
> in the new terror. Now that the West Bank and Gaza strip were occupied by
> Israel, rather than annexed to Jordan and controlled by Egypt respectively,
> the Palestinian groups perceived an opportunity to reclaim these lands
> by focusing international pressure against Israel. The key was to capture
> international attention, and that was better done by spectacular actions in
> the capitals of the West than by sabotaging water conduits in the Judean
> desert.[149]

Part of this internationalised struggle was, alongside a number of spec-
tacular hijackings, the Black September hostage taking and subsequent
killing of eleven Israeli athletes during the 1972 Olympics in Munich,
West Germany. Just a few days later, Prime Minister Golda Meir conveyed
to the Knesset:

---

[148] Burton M. Leiser, 'Enemies of Mankind' in Benjamin Netanyahu (ed.), *Terrorism: How
the West can Win* (New York: Farrar, Straus and Giroux 1986) 155–156 at 156.
[149] Plaw, *Targeting Terrorists: A License to Kill?* p. 43.

> The actions and ways of the terrorists are continually evolving. It is our duty to prepare ourselves for this type of war, more than we have been to this day ... methodically, knowledgeably, decisively, and expansively; this is a dangerous and critical task ... We have no choice, but to strike terrorist organizations wherever we can reach them. That is our obligation to ourselves and to peace. We shall fulfil that obligation undauntedly.[150]

During the following decades this transnationalised struggle would take its toll, not only in Israeli and Palestinian lives but others as well. However, few of the assassinations known to have been conducted by the Israeli security agency have been admitted. Instead they have been linked to Israel by the work of investigative journalists and historians.[151] In fact, as late as 2012, Israeli military censors, in a rare decision, cleared the publication of an interview that was conducted more than a decade earlier with the Israeli commando who killed el-Wazir in 1988.[152] This means also that no attempts were made by the Israeli government to claim that the killings that took place in the period of the transnationalisation of the struggle were legal and legitimate. This turn from *extra-legal* secretive 'assassination' to *legal* targeted killing would instead occur in the distinctly localised struggle of the 1967 Israeli occupation of Palestinian lands and the Intifada or 'shaking off' of Israeli rule. Not only did the occupation exacerbate the problem of Jewish-Arab co-existence and thus deepen the common entrapment of enmity entered into in 1948, it also provided a legal regime, the 'constitutional structure' of which would enable this shift from secretive assassination to official and legal targeted killing.

Occupation, Intifada, Targeted Killing

In due course I will turn to consider the shift to targeted killing in the context of the occupation and the Palestinian Intifada. However, to understand this shift we must first get a better understanding of the particular

---

[150] Golda Meir cited in Aaron J. Klein, *Striking Back: The 1972 Munich Olympics Massacre and Israel's Deadly Response* (New York: Random House 2005) p. 100.

[151] See Simon Reeve, *One Day in September: The Full Story of the 1972 Munich Olympics Massacre and the Israeli Revenge Operation "Wrath of God"* (New York: Skyhorse Publishing Inc. 2000); Klein, *Striking Back: The 1972 Munich Olympics Massacre and Israel's Deadly Response*.

[152] 'Israel Acknowledges Killing Palestinian Deputy in 1988 Raid' *The Guardian* (1 November 2012) www.guardian.co.uk/world/2012/nov/01/israel-acknowledges-killing-palestinian-deputy accessed 10 May 2015.

circumstances of the occupation and the specific characteristics of the legal regime in which this shift occurs.

1967: Deepening the Common Entrapment of Enmity

The Six-Day War in 1967 was a swift Israeli victory over Egyptian, Syrian and Jordanian armed forces. The war was heralded as pre-emptive self-defence against Arab aggression and thus falls into the pattern of Israeli wars of existence considered earlier. It was also a war in the process of the formation of the Israeli state, because it resulted in the military occupation of the remaining parts of the territory of the British mandate, an occupation that has lasted long enough to be fairly counted as a 'constitutive element of the Israeli regime'.[153]

Honaida Ghanim describes the effect of these developments as a deepening of the common entrapment of enmity entered into in 1948. Moreover, she describes the subsequent policies of the Israeli occupation as having (perhaps unintentionally) intensified the entanglement of Israelis and Palestinians in it.[154] A few basic facts about the 1967 war and the occupation can be used to substantiate this dire assessment of Israeli-Palestinian relations post-1967.

First and foremost, the Israeli victory in the 1967 war and the subsequent occupation implied that the borders that had separated the Palestinians of the West Bank, the Gaza strip and the Palestinian minority within Israel proper, were removed. The structure of the regime that succeeded it implied a three-fold *naksah* (Arabic for setback) for the Palestinians: first, and as already mentioned, what was left of Palestine after 1948 was captured by Israel; second, there was another wave of refugees, estimated at around 210,000;[155] third, those who did not flee or were driven out found themselves under Israeli military rule.[156] Avi Raz describes how, 'by all accounts, the Palestinians were in a state of shock'.[157] Raz also describes a question broached earlier, how the change that 1967 brought about spurred Palestinian nationalism:

---

[153] Ariella Azoulay and Adi Ophir, *The One-state Condition: Occupation and Democracy in Israel/Palestine* (Tal Haran tr, Stanford University Press 2013) p. 203.

[154] Ghanim, 'The Urgency of a New Beginning in Palestine: An Imagined Scenario by Mahmoud Darwish and Hannah Arendt' p. 84.

[155] Avi Raz, *The Bride and the Dowry: Israel, Jordan, and the Palestinians in the Aftermath of the June 1967 War* (New Haven: Yale University Press 2012) p. 5.

[156] *Ibid.*   [157] *Ibid.* p. 25.

> Their sense of humiliation and despair notwithstanding, a large number of West Bank leaders realized in the wake of the defeat that a new situation had arisen, and with it new prospects: after seventeen years as Jordanian citizens, they could now become Palestinians again – and turn the Palestinian problem, a humanitarian issue since 1948, back into a national one.[158]

When both the 'Palestinian option' (the suggestion of leaders of the West Bank to form a Palestinian state) and the 'Jordanian option' (the attempts made by the king of Jordan to reach a peace) for Israeli withdrawal had been turned down, the option that was left for Israel was to remain in the territories as an occupying power.[159]

A number of reasons for the Israeli decision not to withdraw from the occupied territories have been presented, one of them being the geopolitical 'strategic depth' provided by the occupied territories in the defence of Israel proper.[160] What was likely more important was the strong reluctance to part with what was referred to not as the West Bank and Gaza but Judea and Samaria, evoking historical Jewish associations to the land, in combination with the 'demographic danger' that the more than one million Palestinians living on the desired territory in 1967 constituted.[161] In fact, Neve Gordon in his *Israel's Occupation* considers 'Israel's unwillingness to incorporate the occupied Palestinians and the distinction it made between the inhabitants and their land... the overarching logic informing the occupation'.[162] This points to how one of the most significant effects of the 1967 war was that it reignited the 'Palestinian question' in Israeli politics.[163] Apparently, the very being of Palestinians so threatened the body politic of the Jewish people that their inclusion in it was inconceivable. This was made abundantly clear by Abba Eban (no longer at this point Israeli ambassador at the UN but Israeli Foreign Minister) when, at a *Mapai* (Labour) party meeting, he asserted that there was a limit to the amount of arsenic the human body could absorb.[164]

---

[158] *Ibid.* p. 25f.
[159] The way in which these two options were handled are given careful consideration in: *ibid.* pp. 25–52.
[160] *Ibid.* p. 268.   [161] *Ibid.*
[162] Neve Gordon, *Israel's Occupation* (Berkeley: University of California Press 2008) p. 6.
[163] *Ibid.*
[164] Raz, *The Bride and the Dowry: Israel, Jordan, and the Palestinians in the Aftermath of the June 1967 War* p. 268.

Gordon's book considers the shifting and contradictory forms of control that have been deployed by the occupying power to govern the Palestinian population. He cites military reports published after the 1967 war, revealing that Israel's intention was to implement 'a policy of normalization' which would 'allow the population of the areas to carry on their life and activities just as they had been used to until the 5th of June 1967'.[165] Or, as put by the then Israeli Defence Minister Moshe Dayan, the goal was to make the 'occupation invisible'.[166] To achieve this, the civil institutions and the vast majority of local representatives and civil servants in public office were retained and a power-sharing agreement with Jordan was reached. A three-pronged policy of non-presence, non-interference and open bridges was devised, although Gordon stresses that in practice all three were frequently breached.[167]

The attempt to normalise the occupation did not mean that force was not used. In particular, during the first four years, Israel employed military force against the population in the West Bank and Gaza Strip, 'categorizing all forms of resistance as insurgency – including protests and political meetings, raising flags or other national symbols, publishing or distributing articles or pictures with political connotations, and even singing or listening to nationalist songs – and deployed security forces to suppress opposition'.[168] The security measures included: orders which restricted or supervised the movement of an individual; administrative detention orders; deportation orders; orders for the sealing or demolition of a house.[169] Interestingly, the power to impose such administrative sanctions could be found in the British mandate's Defence or Emergency Regulations of 1945, still in force in the area. As noted in a text that was published by the IDF as a legal defence of the measures taken in the context of the Intifada, these regulations had been aimed primarily against the Jewish community in Palestine and against its efforts at promoting Jewish immigration and securing British withdrawal and the establishment of a state. It is also noted that the regulations had, at the time, come under harsh criticism from representatives of the Jewish Community, as well as by the Federation of Jewish Lawyers.[170] For reasons of security they were now used to control the Palestinians residing in the occupied

---

[165] Gordon, *Israel's Occupation* p. 49.   [166] *Ibid.* p. 7.
[167] *Ibid.* p. 50.   [168] *Ibid.*
[169] David Yahav and others, *Israel, the "Intifada" and the Rule of Law* (Tel Aviv: Israel Ministry of Defense Publications 1993) p. 103.
[170] *Ibid.* p. 46.

territories. The opposition against the Israeli occupation was particularly fierce in Gaza.[171] After the armed resistance against the occupation was crushed, however, there was a shift of emphasis in the forms of control of the occupation. Gordon writes that the logic behind the new forms of control was to 'render the occupied inhabitants docile not so much by the deployment of military force as by raising their standard of living and transforming the population's lifestyle'.[172]

The Legal Regime of the Occupation

The legal regime of belligerent occupation constitutes a particular case of the double bind between authority and force, constituted, in the expression of Richard Baxter, 'solely by force'.[173] Because, while the occupation regime relies on the international legal title of the occupant, this title hinges on the factual question of exercising 'effective control' over a certain territory. Yoram Dinstein remarks that the occupying regime that is under the commander's responsibility is 'not derived from the will of the people' and is not designed to 'win the hearts and minds of the local inhabitants'. It has military or security objectives, 'its foundation is the "power of the bayonet"'.[174]

Israeli 'effective control' was established not by fighting against the Palestinians but by the ousting of the previous occupants of the West Bank and Gaza by military force. In 1971, Coordinator of the Government

---

[171] Ian Black and Benny Morris describe in *Israel's Secret Wars* how the job of pacifying Gaza was given to General Ariel Sharon and how 'Working closely with the Shin Bet, the army divided the Gaza Strip into squares, which were given codenames. An elite commando unit was ordered to comb the area, square by square, until no terrorists were left . . . Rumours circulated about the general roaming the area with a list of wanted men in his hand, crossing off the names as they were eliminated. Army units were indeed issued with regularly updated Shin Bet lists with the names – and when they were available, the photographs – of fugitive fedayee. Ordinary "Wanted" names were printed in black; "Wanted and Dangerous" in red'. (Morris and Black, *Israel's Secret Wars: A History of Israel's Intelligence Services* p. 261.)

[172] Gordon, *Israel's Occupation* p. 51f. Gordon suggests that behind this was not only sheer tactics to control the Palestinian population but the 'colonial fantasy' of bringing progress to the uncivilised Palestinians. In fact, Gordon claims that this was a contributing factor to the slow realisation of the occupying power that it was facing a large-scale Palestinian uprising in 1987. Israeli leaders were slow to react because they had convinced themselves that the indigenous Palestinians were grateful to the Israeli military government for improving their living conditions. *Ibid.* p. 148.

[173] Richard R. Baxter, 'The Duty of Obedience to the Belligerent Occupant' 27 (1950) British Yearbook of International Law 235 at 243.

[174] Dinstein, *The International Law of Belligerent Occupation* p. 35.

Authorities in the Administered territories Shlomo Gazit described how the situation of 'administering' the entire territory of the British mandate and more caught Israel off guard. However, he also described how this did not apply to the Military Advocate General's office, headed by Meir Shamgar.[175] Shamgar is an example of someone who has been at the frontline throughout law's violent constitution in Israel. Shamgar fought in the war of independence and later joined the Military Advocate General staff. Subsequently he became Military Advocate General of the Army, Attorney General and Justice and President of the Israel Supreme Court.

In the early 1960s, Shamgar, in his role as Military Advocate General, had developed courses, prepared a manual for the military advocate in military government, 'emergency kits' including legal textbooks and other materials such as precedents, proclamations and orders, as well as detailed legal and organisational instructions and guidelines for the IDF if it should find itself in the situation of a military occupation.[176] Shamgar describes the legal regime that was put in place in the occupied territories according to this 'previously planned scheme' in the following way:

> The Legal system operative in the Territories as a whole may be viewed in terms of a layer of proclamation law enacted by the Military Commanders of the area, called 'Security Enactments,' which has been superimposed on the local law existing before the entry of the Israel Defense Forces (I.D.F.).[177]

The early proclamations, Shamgar explains, followed the direction of Article 43 of the 1907 Hague Regulations concerning the Laws and Customs of War on Land annexed to the Hague Convention (IV), according to which:

> The authority of the legitimate power having in fact passed into the hands of the occupant, the latter shall take all the measures in his power to restore, and ensure, as far as possible, public order and safety, while respecting, unless absolutely prevented, the laws in force in the country.[178]

---

[175] Shlomo Gazit, 'Policy in the Administered Territories' 1 (1971) Israel Yearbook on Human Rights 278 at 278.

[176] Meir Shamgar, 'Legal Concepts and Problems of the Israeli Military Government: The Initial Stage' in Meir Shamgar (ed.), *Military Government in the Territories Administered by Israel 1967–1980: The Legal Aspects* (Hebrew University Jerusalem – Faculty of Law, The Harry Sacher Institute for Legislative Research and Comparative Law 1982) 13–59 at 25 footnote 27.

[177] Meir Shamgar, 'The Observance of International Law in the Administered Territories' 1 (1971) Israel Yearbook on Human Rights 262 at 267.

[178] Hague Regulations Respecting the Laws and Customs of War on Land, Annexed to Hague Convention (IV) (18 October 1907).

In order to see how this provision was made operational in the legal regime of the Israeli occupation, the first three military orders adopted during the very first day of the occupation are significant: that a new regime was in place was made clear to the Palestinians inhabiting the land through Proclamation no. 1, published on the first day of the occupation. Shamgar summarises the order in the following: 'Proclamation no. 1, published on the day of entry of the I.D.F. into the area, declared the assumption of Government and the responsibility for order and security by the I.D.F.'.[179]

Through Sections 2, 3a and 3b of proclamation no. 2 the military commander for the occupied territories declared:

> 2. The law which existed in the area on the 7th June 1967, shall remain in force in so far as there is nothing therein, repugnant to this proclamation, any other proclamation or order which will be enacted by me, and subject to such modifications as may result from the establishment of the rule of the I.D.F. in the area.

> 3. (a) All powers of government, legislation, appointment, and administration in relation to the area or its inhabitants shall henceforth vest in me alone and shall be exercised by me or by whomsoever shall be appointed by me in that behalf or act on my behalf.

> 3. (b) Without derogating from the generality of the foregoing it is hereby provided that any duty to consult, obtain consent and the like prescribed in any law as a condition – precedent for legislation, enactment or appointment, or as a condition for the entry into force of any legislation or appointment – is hereby repealed.[180]

Proclamation no. 3 in turn lays down the basic 'criminal security code of the area'; it 'deals with the trial of breaches of the Security Provisions Order, other security enactments, and criminal offenses against local law which, according to their facts are in the nature of security offenses'.[181] It also lays down the provisions for the Military court system, a system constituted by a military commander who also appoints the president and the judges.

Already from this brief introduction to how the international law of belligerent occupation was made operational in the legal regime of the Israeli occupation, we can see that it constitutes a resumption of a plenitude of power (or rather, the assertion of the occupation authorities to determine its own competence). It also rejects the theory and practice of

---

[179] Shamgar, 'The Observance of International Law in the Administered Territories' p. 267.
[180] Ibid.   [181] Ibid. p. 269.

the separation of powers because in this regime the legislative, executive and judicial powers are all in the hands of the military commander.[182] In fact, this is not only a feature of the legal regime of the Israeli occupation but a feature of the international law of belligerent occupation upon which this legal regime was built.

Although this legal regime was built on the model of the international law of belligerent occupation, the occupier preferred to consider itself as 'administering' rather than occupying the Palestinian territories. This reasoning found a clear expression with regard to the applicability of the Fourth Geneva Convention.[183] Meir Shamgar held that since both Jordan and Egypt had been occupying powers in the West Bank and Gaza respectively and that therefore these territories were, after 1948, sui generis, the Fourth Geneva Convention was not de jure applicable. This assessment pivots on the idea that the West Bank and Gaza do not fall within the scope of the phrase 'territory of a High Contracting party' which appears in the second paragraph of Article 2 of the Fourth Geneva Convention.[184] However, Shamgar at the same time pronounced that Israel nevertheless 'decided to act *de facto*, in accordance with the humanitarian provisions of the Convention'.[185]

By making this distinction between de jure and de facto application, Shamgar was able to make the point that neither of the displaced rulers, Egypt or Jordan, were displaced sovereigns but rather mere displaced occupants of the areas they had held between 1948 and 1967. Naturally this is of relevance for the question of historical Jewish association to Judea and Samaria.[186] Moreover, to admit that the Fourth Geneva Convention was de jure applicable could conceivably be interpreted as a renunciation, by Israel, of sovereign rights to the areas. 'After all, one does not "occupy" one's own territory, and one most certainly is not bound therein by the International Law of Belligerent occupation'.[187] Thus, the sui generis argument as regards the status of the territories and the de facto application

---

[182] Peter M. Stirk, *The Politics of Military Occupation* (Edinburgh University Press 2009) p. 111.

[183] Geneva Convention Relative to the Protection of Civilian Persons in Time of War (12 August 1949) 75 UNTS 287 (Fourth Geneva Convention).

[184] Shamgar's position on this question is referred to by Yoram Dinstein as 'patently sterile', Dinstein, *The International Law of Belligerent Occupation* p. 21.

[185] Shamgar, 'The Observance of International Law in the Administered Territories' p. 266.

[186] This point is made in Lisa Hajjar, *Courting Conflict: The Israeli Military Court System in the West Bank and Gaza* (University of California Press 2005) p. 53f.

[187] Yahav and others, *Israel, the "Intifada" and the Rule of Law* p. 21.

of the Fourth Geneva Convention avoided the Scylla and Charybdis of a formal claim for sovereignty and a renunciation of any potential future claims to sovereignty over Judea and Samaria.[188]

In what follows I will argue that what might be referred to as the 'constitutional structure' of the law of belligerent occupation in general and the Israeli occupation in particular are characterised by the institutionalised indistinction of what Benjamin terms lawmaking and law-preserving violence. As such, it is a particularly emblematic case of what he refers to as the law of the police because its characteristic function is the assertion of legal claims for *any* decree (lawmaking) and is simultaneously at the disposal of the ends thus established (law-preserving). Benjamin describes the phenomenology of this 'formless power' as a 'nowhere tangible, all-pervasive ghostly presence'.[189] In agreement with this understanding of the constitutional structure of belligerent occupation, Peter Stirk writes that the occupied population is 'subject to the holder of undifferentiated power' guided by the technical objective demands of the situation in which general laws are irrelevant or where laws can no longer be distinguished from administrative decrees.[190] This is a law entirely based on the executive dimension of legality discussed earlier, a law that has more of the character of *acte* than *loi, Maßnahme* than *Gesetz*.[191] As we will see, this is a question of significant importance for the emergence of targeted killing in the Israeli context.

---

[188] Cf. *Ibid.*   [189] Benjamin, 'Critique of Violence' p. 287.

[190] Peter M. Stirk, 'Carl Schmitt, the Law of Occupation, and the Iraq War' 11 (2004) *Constellations* 527 at 529.

[191] That being the case, the powers of the military commander resemble the commissarial dictatorship envisioned in the emergency powers sometimes laid down in liberal constitutions. In his *Legality and Legitimacy*, Carl Schmitt considers how the administrative state measure or *Maßnahme* displaces the parliamentary legislative state statute in the context of emergencies. Thus, for the extraordinary lawmaker of Article 48 of the Weimar constitution, 'the distinction between statute and statutory application, legislative and executive, is neither legally nor factually an obstacle. The extraordinary lawmaker combines both in his person ... in other words, he unites in himself lawmaking and legal execution and can enforce directly the norms he establishes, which the ordinary legislature of the parliamentary legislative state cannot do, so long as it respects the separation of powers with its distinction between law and legal application so essential for the legislative state'. (Carl Schmitt, *Legality and Legitimacy* (Jeffrey Seitzer tr, Durham: Duke University Press 2004) p. 71.) On Commissarial dictatorship see further: Carl Schmitt, *Dictatorship: From the Origin of the Modern Concept of Sovereignty to Proletarian Class Struggle* (Michael Hoelzl and Graham Ward trs, Cambridge and Malden: Polity 2014). For the link between commissarial dictatorship and the law of belligerent occupation see Nehal Bhuta, 'The Antinomies of Transformative Occupation' 16 (2005) European Journal of International Law 721.

Debating Legal Authority for Lethal Force in the First Intifada

Although the facts of the events remain disputed, the response of the occupying authorities to the first Palestinian Intifada and the debate over the legal authority to use lethal force in this context can be used to illuminate the constitutional structure of the occupation. This in turn is helpful for understanding the shift to *legal* targeted killing in application of the law of armed conflict that would occur in the second Intifada. However, before I come to this it is necessary to consider the circumstances of the outbreak of the Intifada.

The Palestinian lawyer and novelist Raja Shehadeh described in 1988 how the more or less open borders between Israel and the occupied territories had failed to promote a workable co-existence between the two nations because of the oppression and injustice of Israeli rule and how this spurred claims for self-determination.

> Among the Palestinians of the occupied territories, twenty years of Israeli occupation have only intensified the will to exercise self-determination in their land. There are no changes or improvements that can make the occupation tolerable. The expropriation of land, the establishment of settlements, the exploitation and strangulation of Palestinian society and institutions, and the corruption of the legal system lead one to the obvious conclusion that there can be no justice under occupation. This is perhaps stating the obvious. What has been less obvious – at least until the current uprising – is that twenty years of more or less open borders between Israel and the occupied territories have *not* increased the chances of co-existence and peace between the two nations. The Palestinians have experienced only oppression and injustice under Israeli rule. The continuation of this rule can only result in increasing bitterness and hatred.[192]

From the Israeli side, the occupation continually provided a passage between the Scylla and Charybdis of a formal claim for sovereignty and the demographic consequences this would entail and a renunciation of any future potential claim to sovereignty. Moreover, on the eve of the first Intifada there was the added dimension of Israel having seized more than 40 per cent of the land in the territories, building 125 settlements and numerous bypass roads, and allowing approximately 60,000 settlers to move to the West Bank and Gaza.[193] This implied that Israel had more to lose if it failed to maintain the status quo of the occupation. Moreover,

---

[192] Raja Shehadeh, 'Occupier's Law and the Uprising' 17 (1988) Journal of Palestine Studies 24 at 36f. Emphasis in the original.
[193] Gordon, *Israel's Occupation* p. 146.

with the settlements came the problem not only of maintaining law and order on occupied territory but also of protecting the parts of the Israeli population living on occupied land.[194]

When the Intifada finally erupted it was treated as a law and order problem. As it was expressed in the text that was published by the IDF as a legal defence for the measures taken in the Intifada:

> The IDF's goal in subduing the disturbances in the Territories has remained unchanged since the 'Intifada's' inception. This goal has been to restore law and order in the Areas, as it is required by International Law, with a minimal number of casualties on both sides in an effort to allow residents of the Areas, both Arabs and Jews to carry on normal lives.[195]

For the Palestinians partaking in the uprising, the preservation of law and order clearly had come to be perceived as serving the interests of an illegitimate rule.[196] If occupation is a situation in which protection is offered and obedience expected, clearly this link had now been severed.

In the IDF text, there is a mention of how, when the 'mass character' of the uprising receded, its continuation was secured by 'hard-core' activists from both the PLO and Hamas, and how

> the IDF reacted to this transformation by creating special anti-terrorist units who specialize in the handling of terror in accordance with International Law. These units work to capture terrorists on a piecemeal basis in order to cause minimal disturbances to the population at large.[197]

As early as 1988 there were press reports claiming that undercover units had been assigned to kill leaders of the Arab uprising, a claim that was dismissed by the then Israeli Defence Minister Yitzhak Rabin in *The New*

---

[194] On the other hand, in the case of *Ayoub* v. *Minister of Defense* the Israel Supreme Court, sitting as the High Court of Justice, argued that settlements contribute to the security on the occupied territories: 'there is no doubt that the presence of [Jewish] settlements in an administered territory significantly contributes to the security situation in that area and makes the work of the army easier. One does not have to be an expert on security to understand that subversive elements operate more easily in a space inhabited only by sympathetic or indifferent residents than in a space where there are also people who keep an eye on them and are willing to report suspicious movements'. As quoted in: Ronen Shamir, 'Occupation as Disorientation: The Impossibility of Borders' in Adi Ophir, Michal Givoni and Sari Hanafi (eds.), *The Power Of Inclusive Exclusion: Anatomy of Israeli Rule In The Occupied Palestinian Territories* (New York: Zone Books 2009) 587–596 at 590.

[195] Yahav and others, *Israel, the 'Intifada' and the Rule of Law* p. 38

[196] Shehadeh, 'Occupier's Law and the Uprising' p. 154.

[197] Yahav and others, *Israel, the 'Intifada' and the Rule of Law* p. 39.

York Times as 'total nonsense'.[198] The press credentials of three foreign correspondents who had reported on the claims were suspended and an investigation was initiated to see if the reporters had violated military censorship regulations.[199] However in June 1991 the IDF admitted the existence of undercover units, referred to as *mista'arvim*, the Hebrew word for masqueraders, within its ranks – in this context, IDF soldiers in Arab guise.[200] This was an explicit invocation of the name of special units within Haganah's Palmach or strike force devised to penetrate Arab territory to perform intelligence and operational activities in pre-state Palestine.[201] Stuart A. Cohen of the Begin-Sadat Center for Strategic Studies argued in 1993 that on a tactical level the units deployed in the Intifada differ from their pre-state predecessors because whereas the latter were employed mainly in a 'surveillance role', 'the emphasis of most contemporary mista'arvim is on "active" measures (the arrest or killing of suspects)'.[202] In relation to the 'active' nature of the work of the undercover units, Cohen writes: 'Instead of simply having to react – often indiscriminately – to the insurgency, the *mista'arvim* (it seems) are enabling the IDF to adopt the far wiser and more effective tactic of initiating pinpoint attacks on its principal instigators'.[203]

In 1992, Anita Vitullo of the Middle East Research and Information Project (MERIP) reported that three human rights organisations disputed military claims that soldiers only shot in self-defence and how investigations based on field investigations and eyewitness affidavits, 'concluded that real events differed markedly from accounts given to the press by the Israeli military spokesperson, and that an apparent policy of liquidating "wanted" Palestinians exists'.[204]

---

[198] 'Israel Bars 3 Reporters over "Undercover" Articles' *The New York Times* (25 October 1988) www.nytimes.com/1988/10/26/world/israel-bars-3-reporters-over-undercover-articles .html accessed 10 May 2015.

[199] *Ibid.*

[200] Stuart A. Cohen, '"Masqueraders" in the IDF: The Military Unit and the Public Debate, 1991–1992' 2 (1993) Low-Intensity Conflict and Law Enforcement 282 at 282.

[201] Ben-Yehuda, *Political Assassinations by Jews: A Rhetorical Device for Justice* p. 255f.

[202] Cohen, '"Masqueraders" in the IDF: The Military Unit and the Public Debate, 1991–1992' p. 297. However, it should be noted in this context that Ben-Yehuda points out that such units were not only involved directly in at least two cases of political assassination but also in a full-scale plan, named Operation Zarzir and launched in January 1948 in the war leading up to the proclamation of the Israeli state, to assassinate various Arab leaders. Ben-Yehuda, *Political Assassinations by Jews: A Rhetorical Device for Justice* p. 408.

[203] Cohen, '"Masqueraders" in the IDF: The Military Unit and the Public Debate, 1991–1992' p. 285.

[204] Anita Vitullo, 'Yitzhak Rabin and Israel's Death Squads' 22 (1992) *Middle East Report* 40 at 42. The three reports are: Na'ama Yashuvi, *Activity of the Undercover Units in*

Although clearly of great significance, our primary concern here is not to determine the extent to which killings by Israeli undercover units in fact took place or to investigate the exact circumstances of these killings. Rather, what is in focus is the discussion over the legal authority of the occupying authorities to exercise lethal force that arose following allegations that the occupying authorities had in effect taken up a policy of assassination. This in turn will help us better understand the emergence of an official Israeli policy of targeted killing in the second Intifada.

In the appendix to a report of the Middle East Watch there are letters from the organisation to officials of the occupying authorities accompanied by the responses. In a 1992 response to a request for details concerning incidents involving IDF special anti-terrorist units in the West Bank and Gaza, Deputy IDF Military Advocate General Colonel David Yahav takes as his point of departure that Israel, according to Article 43 of the 1907 Hague Regulations, is responsible for maintaining public order and safety in the areas.[205]

At the outset we may note that referring Middle East Watch to Article 43 of the 1907 Hague Regulations is a natural thing for Yahav to do. This is so because, as we saw earlier, the legal regime de facto put in place on the territories was based on the law of belligerent occupation and, as formulated by the law of belligerent occupation scholar Eyal Benvenisti, Article 43 of the 1907 Hague Regulations 'is a sort of mini-constitution for the occupation administration; its general guidelines permeate any prescriptive measure or other acts taken by the occupant'.[206]

---

the Occupied Territories (Jessica Bonn tr, Jerusalem: B'Tselem – The Israeli Information Center for Human Rights in the Occupied Territories 1992) www.btselem.org/Download/199205_Undercover_Units_Eng.doc accessed 10 May 2015; Zureik Elia, Vitulla Anita and Mohammad Abu Harthiyeh, Targeting to Kill: Israel's Undercover Units (Palestine Human Rights Information Center), published online at: www.thejerusalemfund.org/ht/a/GetDocumentAction/i/2942 accessed 10 May 2015; Middle East Watch, A License to Kill – Israeli Operations against 'Wanted' and Masked Palestinians (James Ron and others eds., New York, Washington, Los Angeles and London: Human Rights Watch 1993).

[205] Middle East Watch, A License to Kill – Israeli Operations against 'Wanted' and Masked Palestinians p. 228.

[206] Benvenisti, The International Law of Occupation p. 69. Considering the rationale behind this 'mini-constitution', Benvenisti observes that the obligation of ensuring public order and security was originally suggested by the delegates of countries that could see themselves as at some point being occupied by greater powers. The reason was a fear that occupants might choose not to get involved in matters concerning the civilian population in occupied territories. However, eventually this duty 'was transformed into a legal tool extensively invoked by the occupants in those areas in which they wished to intervene'. In this way, 'Article 43 proved an extremely convenient tool for the occupant: if it wished, it could intervene in practically all aspects of life; if it was in its interest to refrain from action, it could invoke the "limits" imposed on its powers' (Ibid., p. 78).

As far as forceful means to the end of ensuring public order and safety are concerned, the broad authority granted to the military commander of occupied territories is striking. This authority passed on from the law of the Hague to the law of Geneva in the fourth paragraph of Article 27 of the Fourth Geneva Convention, which states that 'the Parties to the conflict may take such measures of control and security in regard to protected persons as may be necessary as a result of the war'.[207] In the International Committee of the Red Cross (ICRC) commentary to this provision, Jean S. Pictet notes that the various security measures that states might take are not specified: 'the Article merely lays down a general provision ... A great deal is thus left to the discretion of the parties to the conflict as regard the choice of means'.[208] Consistently with this understanding Dinstein writes: 'the choice of means deemed necessary to contend with the problems of control and security is left to the occupying power'.[209]

In keeping with this understanding, the chapter on the maintenance of law and order in occupied territories in Dinstein's book considers 'individual resistance to occupation' (saboteurs, prisoners of war and Levée en masse), 'riot control' and 'hostilities in occupied territories' in separate subsections, in that order. Whereas the first two categories of the 'maintenance of law and order' on occupied territories are developed by means of analogy to police law enforcement in a domestic state context, the latter is considered as a matter of 'hostilities' governed by the law of armed conflict. What is important to note is that, in the constitutional structure of the legal regime of belligerent occupation, there are no clear distinctions between the kind of 'maintenance of law and order' that implies peace and that which implies war or armed conflict.[210] Apparently, even this is left to the occupying power to determine.

Revealingly, in a round of expert meetings on the law of belligerent occupation conducted by the ICRC involving representatives of States, international organisations, academics and NGOs, forceful means for the preservation of public order and safety on occupied territories are described under three main headings: the 'situation-based' or 'sliding

---

[207] Geneva Convention Relative to the Protection of Civilian Persons in Time of War (12 August 1949) 75 UNTS 287 (Fourth Geneva Convention).

[208] Jean S. Pictet, *The Geneva Conventions of 12 August 1949: Commentary, Geneva Convention Relative to the Protection of Civilian Persons in Time of War* (Jean S. Pictet ed., Ronald Griffin and CW Dumbleton trs, Geneva: International Committee of the Red Cross (ICRC) 1958).

[209] Dinstein, *The International Law of Belligerent Occupation* p. 93.

[210] *Ibid.* chapter 4.

scale' approach, the 'mixed model' approach and the 'jump theory'.[211] The summary of the discussions of these different approaches is as follows:

> the experts agreed that the use of force and the identification of the pertinent normative framework should ultimately be based on the prevailing facts; it should not be constrained by a dogmatic approach to applying the law. In fact, a majority of experts affirmed that the context should always determine which of the two models should be applied. They argued that each model could apply in the appropriate circumstances. In addition, the experts said, even if one model is preferred, the other would be held in reserve, as it were, to be applied when required.[212]

The report goes on to say that even though no consensus was reached, a majority was eventually formed around the proposition that a law enforcement model would be the default model, however, 'this presumption was nonetheless regarded as rebuttable in favour of the "conduct-of-hostilities" model if certain conditions were fulfilled'.[213]

All that has been said thus far points to the fact that when Military Advocate General Yahav, in his letter to Middle East Watch, explains that the 'traditional international law, which is the legal basis of IDF activities in hostile regions, allows for considerable discretion regarding the use of fire by the army in fulfilling its obseverings [sic] to maintain security and public order', he is merely affirming the broad authority granted to the military commander with regard to the use of force to maintain public order and security in occupied territories.[214]

With regard to the circumstances of the outbreak of the Intifada, Military Advocate General Yahav explains that there has been an escalation in the violence, from mass popular demonstrations to 'increasing terrorist activity with a heightened emphasis on the use of firearms'.[215] The specific need for undercover units in this environment is explained as being due to the fact that 'every time an IDF force openly enters an Arab village, the soldiers encounter opposition from local residents. This opposition provides the terrorists with ample warning and as a result enables them to evade arrest'.[216] Yahav also states that the rules of engagement apply to these units as to all IDF soldiers.[217]

---

[211] Tristan Ferraro, *Occupation and Other Forms of Administration of Foreign Territory: Expert Meeting* (Geneva: International Committee of the Red Cross (ICRC) 2012) pp. 113–116.
[212] *Ibid.* p. 115.   [213] *Ibid.* p. 116.
[214] Middle East Watch, *A License to Kill – Israeli Operations against 'Wanted' and Masked Palestinians* p. 220.
[215] *Ibid.* p. 216.   [216] *Ibid.* p. 218.   [217] *Ibid.* p. 219.

With regard to the content of these rules of engagement, Yahav writes that 'it was decided, as a principle of internal state policy', that the authority in the hands of the soldiers, and in general the orders concerning opening fire, will be based on the principles for law enforcement and apprehension of suspects found in Israeli criminal law.[218] Roughly at the same point in time, Yahav was cited in *The New York Times* as saying that 'our open-fire regulations follow the same legal principles that govern the police in Israel and in Western countries where there is no war'.[219]

Concurring that the legal framework governing the activities of the undercover units is, and should be, that of law enforcement, the Middle East Watch report notes that

> the use of undercover units is evidence in itself that the security forces are operating in the framework of law enforcement. If they were to claim that their conflict with armed activists amounted to an armed conflict, then their disguising of soldiers in civilian dress in order to commit hostile acts – by blurring the distinction between combatants and noncombatans – would constitute impermissible 'treachery' under the laws of war.[220]

Additionally, as noted in the B'Tselem report, the use of the term 'wanted persons' and the pattern of behaviour of the special units suggests that the undercover units find the legal basis for their activities in the exemption from criminal liability granted to a person who commits an act 'in executing the law' as opposed to the conduct of hostilities.[221]

Although the reports welcome the fact that the military authorities did not apply the norms for the conduct of hostilities, but rather the more restrictive standards of law enforcement, that is to say, that they treated 'wanted' activists as suspected offenders to be arrested and prosecuted, they are highly critical towards how such operations are carried out. Of great significance in this respect is that out of fear that the Palestinians would 'exploit' knowledge of the rules of engagement, they are kept secret and, furthermore, at the disposal for clarification or amendment by the military authorities without promulgation.[222]

[218] *Ibid.* p. 220.
[219] Joel Greenberg, 'Israelis Debate Army's Rights Record in Uprising' *The New York Times* (24 May 1993) http://www.nytimes.com/1993/05/24/world/israelis-debate-army-s-rights-record-in-uprising.html accessed 10 May 2015.
[220] Middle East Watch, *A License to Kill – Israeli Operations against 'Wanted' and Masked Palestinians* p. 39.
[221] Yashuvi, *Activity of the Undercover Units in the Occupied Territories* p. 20f.
[222] Middle East Watch, *A License to Kill – Israeli Operations against 'Wanted' and Masked Palestinians* p. 44.

Even so, two kinds of circumstances in which soldiers were permitted to fire live ammunition at suspects were made known to the public: when soldiers or others are placed in life-threatening danger and in order to prevent the escape of a dangerous suspect who has disobeyed orders.[223] Even though Israeli officials claimed that the 'legal principles' which guide these open-fire regulations were the same ones that guided the IDF before the Intifada, the IDF spokesperson in a reply to B'Tselem writes:

> The new and complex situations with which the soldiers are forced to cope on a daily basis, coupled with the fact that the *intifada* is changing its character and forcing soldiers to face new dangers demand a clarification of opening fire regulations . . . The changing face of the *intifada* demanded that the regulations define the *new* situations with which soldiers are forced to deal . . . [224]

No detailed account of these 'clarifications' of the open fire regulations and 'definitions' of the 'new situations' that the Intifada presented was given by Israeli officials.[225] In the reports there are mentions of a few such clarifications and definitions revealed in interviews with IDF personnel and in reports by the Israeli press. The Middle East Watch report goes as far as to claim that they constitute 'parallel rules of engagement for troops engaged in the pursuit of targeted Palestinians'.[226]

---

[223] *Ibid.* p. 45.

[224] Yashuvi, *Activity of the Undercover Units in the Occupied Territories* p. 85. Emphasis in the original.

[225] In a meeting of the Knesset Defense and Foreign Affairs Committee on 28 April 1992 the then Chief of Staff Lieutenant General Ehud Barak stated that 'there are no new instructions about opening fire, only adjustments, in order to respond appropriately to the reality in the field, and to enable IDF soldiers to capture *wanted* persons, while reducing the danger to their own lives'. The Chief of Staff added that all the updates in regulations are submitted to the legal administration for approval before being implemented. They are not promulgated however. *Ibid.* p. 11.

[226] Middle East Watch, *A License to Kill – Israeli Operations against 'Wanted' and Masked Palestinians* p. 167. This includes a new definition of 'life-endangering situation'. According to B'Tselem the adjusted orders state: 'fire is to be opened at armed persons [live or non-live weapon], without warning even if they can be apprehended by other means' (Yashuvi, *Activity of the Undercover Units in the Occupied Territories* p. 10). The same is true with regard to 'masked individuals' 'under suspicious circumstances' – that is, according to explanations given to the soldiers, if they are holding a stick, a chain, or any other object suspected of being a non-live weapon (*ibid.*). The Middle East Watch report reasons that this is made possible by the adoption of a logic which determines all 'wanted' activists as extremely dangerous, something which 'gives soldiers a pre-approved basis for shooting them in "self-defense"' (Middle East Watch, *A License to Kill – Israeli Operations against "Wanted" and Masked Palestinians* p. 147). The Middle East Watch report states that Military Advocate General Yahav had confirmed in interviews that there was a

Irrespective of the question of the exact circumstances and the extent to which wanted Palestinians in fact were killed by undercover units in the first Intifada, the legal discussion triggered by allegations that the occupation authorities had taken up a policy of assassinating individuals designated as terrorists is revealing with respect to the 'constitutional structure' of the legal regime of the occupation. This is a law where the military commander is free to interpret what the requirement of ensuring public order and safety in the occupied territories at any given moment entails, as well as what means to employ to achieve this end. As such it is a formless power entirely at the disposal of the objective demands of the situation. Yet, it is a power exercised for 'legal ends' or is, in other words, law-preserving. This latter point is something that we are reminded of over and over again in the text published by the IDF in legal defence of the measures taken in response to the Intifada, revealingly entitled: *Israel, the 'Intifada' and the Rule of Law.*[227]

It should be noted in this context that, during the first Intifada, the rules of engagement were still based on the more restrictive legal principles applicable for law enforcement, even though the restraints this implies apparently were diminished by undisclosed adjustments and definitions. This was so despite the fact that a number of the heads of the military establishment claimed that there was a war in the territories and that the IDF therefore functioned as on the battlefield.[228] In fact, Deputy Military Advocate General Yahav explained in a 1992 interview with Middle East Watch that international law views 'armed terrorists' as 'illegal combatants' who can be 'shot on the spot' and that the practice of treating these individuals as mere criminals instead had been taken 'as a principle of

shortened procedure but declined to reveal when and how it could be used. It mentions a document accompanying the rules of engagement entitled 'sheet on situations and responses' addressing various situations soldiers may face and enabling them at times to use a shortened procedure without, however, spelling out what this shortened procedure entails (*ibid.* p. 59). The B'Tselem report quotes an article published in the Hebrew newspaper *Hadashot*: 'The short procedure includes calling out in Arabic "Halt or I'll shoot", and shooting at the feet, in it, they skip the stage of shooting into the air. The very short procedure is applicable when there is a fear that calling a warning in Arabic will endanger the forces. In such a case, it is permissible to shoot at the legs also without warning' (Yashuvi, *Activity of the Undercover Units in the Occupied Territories* p. 13).

[227] Yahav and others, *Israel, the "Intifada" and the Rule of Law.* The Palestinian lawyer and novelist Raja Shehadeh published a review of the book in *Journal of Palestine Studies* with an equally revealing title: Raja Shehadeh, 'Apologia for Occupation: Israel, the "Intifada" and the Rule of Law' 23 (1994) *Journal of Palestine Studies* 104.

[228] Middle East Watch, *A License to Kill – Israeli Operations against "Wanted" and Masked Palestinians* p. 58.

internal state policy', not a requirement of international law.[229] Far from just a rash remark Yahav may here be understood as drawing conclusions for the use of lethal force from an international legal position of 'armed terrorists' that goes as far back in the Israeli context as the early days of the occupation.

In its 1969 *Military Prosecutor v. Omar Mahmud Kassem and Others*, the Ramallah Military Court held that armed Members of the *Popular Front for the Liberation of Palestine (PFLP)* who had entered the occupied territories from Jordan formed part of a 'type of underground activity' which 'is unknown in the international community'. This was so because they constituted an irregular force unaffiliated to a state. The Court asserted, 'we have found no direct reference in the relevant available literature to irregular forces being treated as illegal by the authorities to whom by the nature of things they should be subject'.[230] The court continued:

> If these authorities look upon a body such as the Popular Front for the Liberation of Palestine as an illegal organization, why must we have to regard it as a body to which international rules relating to lawful bodies are applicable?[231]

The Court nevertheless proceeded to look at the criteria for being a *lawful* combatant in the Hague regulations and the Geneva Conventions, only to conclude that the PFLP fighters could not fulfil them. The conclusion of the Military Court reads:

> International law is not designed to protect and grant rights to saboteurs and criminals. The defendants have no right except to stand trial in court and to be tried in accordance with the law and with the facts established by the evidence, in proceedings consonant with the requirements of ethics and International Law... We therefore reject the plea of the defendants as to their right to be treated as prisoners of war and hold that we are competent to hear the case in accordance with the charge-sheet.[232]

The *Kassem* case does not concern the use of lethal force but whether or not Kassem and the other PFLP militants captured could be considered prisoners of war in application of the law of armed conflict in view of the effect such status would have on their detention and criminal charges. The response was that the law of armed conflict offered no protection for

---

[229] *Ibid.* p. 25 footnote 31.
[230] '*Military Prosecutor v. Omar Mahmud Kassem and Others* (Israel, Military court sitting in Ramallah 13 April 1969)' 42 (1969) International Law Reporter 470 at 478.
[231] *Ibid.*   [232] *Ibid.* p. 483.

them: 'they are to be regarded as combatants not protected by the International Law dealing with prisoners of war, and the occupying power may
consider them as criminals for all purposes'.[233] In other words, they are
'unlawful combatants'[234] included in the law of armed conflict as combatants only to be excluded from almost all of its protection as *unlawful*
combatants.

   Accordingly, when Yahav, in the context of the first Intifada, glosses the
international legal position of 'armed terrorists' as 'illegal combatants'
who can be 'shot on the spot', this appears to me to be a case of drawing
conclusions concerning the use of lethal force from a law of armed conflict
status of such individuals that goes as far back, in the Israeli context, as
the *Kassem* case. As we are about to see, the 'internal state policy' decision
to treat them not as unlawful combatants but mere criminals would be
reassessed in the second Intifada.

Targeted Killing in the Second Intifada and Beyond

Honaida Ghanim has noted the changing modalities of Palestinian resistance after the deepening of the Israeli-Palestinian common entrapment
of enmity in 1967: the activities of the military resistance cells or *Fedayees*
formed in the 1960s intensified in the 1970s and 80s with the hijacking
of aeroplanes, bombs in Israeli compounds, attacks on Israelis in Europe
and guerrilla attacks on Israeli troops in Lebanon. This was the transnationalisation of the struggle referred to earlier. At the time of the first
Intifada, 'a new mythological character embodied in the "stone child"
or stone-throwing youth assumed the role of the *Fedayee* who had been
worn out by his conflict abroad'.[235] The hopes for a prospective solution
at the time of the signing of the Oslo Agreement turned into despair
when a Jewish rightist killed Yitzhak Rabin and a Jewish settler massacred
Palestinian worshippers in Hebron, resulting in Palestinian retaliation in
the form of suicide bombings in Israeli cities. This in turn caused intensified settlement activity and an Israeli disregard for signed agreements. By
the time of the second Intifada, Ghanim notes, 'in an extremely surreal
and tragic turn, the "suicide bomber" replaced the "stone child" who had
previously substituted for the *"fedayee"*'.[236]

---

[233] *Ibid.* p. 477.   [234] *Ibid.* p. 481.
[235] Ghanim, 'The Urgency of a New Beginning in Palestine: An Imagined Scenario by
      Mahmoud Darwish and Hannah Arendt' p. 88.
[236] *Ibid.* p. 89.

Daniel Reisner and the Turn to Targeted Killing in the Context of the Intifada

A couple of months into the second Intifada, the first officially proclaimed case of targeted killing occurred: the killing of Hussein Abayat in the West Bank village of Beit Sahour.[237] Abayat was killed in a helicopter attack while driving his car. Two women standing on the sidewalk were also killed and seven others were wounded. On 15 November 2000, Colonel Daniel Reisner, head of the international law department of IDF's Legal Division, held a press briefing in Jerusalem.[238] That it was the commanding officer of the international law branch who gave the briefing was no coincidence, but consistent with a shift in the way the occupying authorities perceived the nature of the conflict with the Palestinians. In a review of the work of the International Law Department, based on interviews with its officers, Amichai Cohen writes:

> Until 2000, the conflict was seen mainly as a law enforcement operation one of [sic] restoring public order to occupied territories. In September 2000 the IDF began to view the conflict as something similar to war, albeit in a civilian setting. IDF commanders had very little experience as to the IHL limits under this kind of conflict. In order to receive some legal instructions, the IDF commanders turned to the ILD [International Law Department] for advice.[239]

Analysing Reisner's statement at the press conference, one might note how Reisner initially assumes a mutually exclusive understanding of the relationship between peace and war. Reisner asserts that this is the choice 'classic international law' asks him to make, but also that 'life isn't as simple as that' and that, for this reason, there are 'lots of terms running around ... concerning the in-between'.[240] Reisner says that 'there is no basis for comparison between the Intifada of 1987–1992 and the current situation'.[241] This is not only due to the nature of the violent resistance

---

[237] Alina Korn, 'Israeli Press and the War against Terrorism: The Construction of the "liquidation policy"' 41 (2004) Crime, Law and Social Change 209 at 217.

[238] Daniel Reisner, 'Press Briefing by Colonel Daniel Reisner – Head of the International Law Branch of the IDF Legal Division 15 November 2000' (*Israel Ministry of Foreign Affairs*, 15 November 2000) http://mfa.gov.il/MFA/PressRoom/2000/Pages/Press%20Briefing%20by%20Colonel%20Daniel%20Reisner-%20Head%20of.aspx accessed 10 May 2015.

[239] Cohen, 'Legal Operational Advice in the Israeli Defense Forces: The International Law Department and the Changing Nature of International Humanitarian Law' p. 374.

[240] Reisner, 'Press Briefing by Colonel Daniel Reisner – Head of the International Law Branch of the IDF Legal Division 15 November 2000'.

[241] *Ibid.*

that Israeli authorities meet, but also with regard to the change following the handing over of the responsibility for maintaining order in certain areas to Palestinian authorities after the Oslo agreement. Supplanting the mutually exclusive understanding of the relationship between peace and war with that of a 'spectrum' between the two, Reisner asks himself 'where are we?'[242]

> While we are not at the end of the spectrum, which is war, because war is a conflict between two armies or two states, we are definitely in the area of armed conflict . . . whatever the term you wish to use that's fine with us, but please understand that for us, we have reached the decision . . . that the current situation has more of a semblance of war than of peace.[243]

Reisner continues, 'as a result, we are also applying the principles applicable to warfare to the current situation, and no longer the principles applied in a time of peace'.[244] Reisner refers to this as a 'general statement' that is 'implemented . . . into different fields', the most important of which is rules of engagement.[245] In a key section of the briefing, Reisner states:

> Up to the current events, the rules of engagement of the Israel Defense Forces in the West Bank and Gaza Strip were police rules of engagement. Use of live weapons only in self-defense, or after a warning shot to carry out an arrest, which is not relevant right now because we are not involved in arresting people at this point in time – that's historical from our perspective . . . When this new situation came about, and we came to the legal decision that we have crossed the line between the area of peace and the area of let's say active hostility, I came to the Israeli military and said, 'We can, at this juncture, look again at our rules of engagement, and they can move down that scale a bit more'.[246]

Reisner explains how the military was reluctant to agree to such changes because of the risk that further violence would play into the hands of the Palestinians, but also because of the risk of further escalating the violence. He then proceeds by saying 'and yet, we have made at least two, I won't call them amendments, but we made two modifications to adapt to the new circumstances'.[247] The first concerns the use of attack

---

[242] *Ibid.*   [243] *Ibid.*   [244] *Ibid.*   [245] *Ibid.*
[246] *Ibid.*   [247] *Ibid.*

helicopters to attack 'specific locations'. Reisner explains: 'Now, obviously that's not part of a peace-time operation. I mean, when you're in normal peace-time policing activities, you don't fire missiles from attack helicopters'.[248] Reisner here speaks of the changing of the rules of engagement '*in a specific instance* as a result of the new situation'.[249] The second modification concerns the fact that the circumstances in which live fire can be used in a 'life-threatening' situation have been given an extended meaning.[250]

In the foregoing I noted the broad authority that the law of belligerent occupation grants the military commander as far as forceful means for ensuring public order and safety on occupied territories are concerned. The casualness with which Reisner explains how modifications to the rules of engagement were made with regard to giving a wider interpretation of what constitutes a 'life-threatening situation' – more importantly, 'in a specific instance' in preparation for a deliberate attack against a 'specific location' using attack helicopters – is symptomatic of this broad authority and, more generally, of the constitutional structure of the legal regime of the occupation.

Inspired by Walter Benjamin's dictum that such a situation of simultaneous lawmaking and law-preserving bears witness to the 'greatest conceivable degeneration of violence',[251] Israeli legal scholar Roy Kreitner has asserted that targeted killing is 'one of the most degraded forms of violence used by modern states'.[252] However, in doing so, he misses that Israeli targeted killing has emerged in the context of a legal regime that institutionalises this indistinction and, as we have seen, gives great leeway to the occupying authorities to both decide and implement forceful means to the end of ensuring public order and safety. This is the 'spectral mixture' of lawmaking and law-preserving violence: violence for legal ends but with the simultaneous authority to decide these ends themselves within wide limits. Benjamin specifically mentions that a situation of simultaneous lawmaking and law-preserving 'is less devastating where they represent, in absolute monarchy, the power of a ruler in which legislative and executive supremacy are united', and, as we have seen, the constitutional structure of the international law

---

[248] *Ibid.* [249] *Ibid.*, my emphasis.
[250] *Ibid.* [251] Benjamin, 'Critique of Violence' p. 287.
[252] Roy Kreitner, 'Justification Between Positivism and Decisionism' 7 (2006) *Theoretical Inquiries in Law* 229 at 243 footnote 41.

of belligerent occupation has more in common with absolute monarchy than with the liberal constitutional state.[253]

In the questions and answers session of the press briefing, Reisner was prompted to expand on the implications of these 'modifications' in relation to whether IDF soldiers had been investigated for causing unwarranted fatalities. Reisner's response is that, no, there have been no instances yet in which IDF soldiers have been investigated. He adds: 'as I told you, we are not carrying out investigations because we are in active warfare'.[254] Reisner was also asked about the international lawfulness of the November 9 helicopter attack in which Hussein Abayat was killed, which in the days before the press conference had been widely reported in the Israeli press.[255] Very significantly, Reisner clarifies the question by restating it not as a question of international lawfulness, but as the much more specific question of lawfulness in the application of the law of armed conflict: 'As for your second question, international law of targeting, that's your specific question'. After this he says: 'First of all, you can only fire at a legitimate military target. We have reached a decision, and I think it's generally accepted, that that specific person was a legitimate military target'.[256] Reisner does not go into specifics about either the classification of the armed conflict in which the state of Israel and Palestinian groups are involved or the status of such legitimate military targets in this armed conflict. Reisner does expand on the 'rule of proportionality', stating, 'I don't know the exact details of why there were casualties in addition to that person, but in that respect international law does allow you to attack military targets, even if it may cause damage to civilians, but you're supposed to take all possible steps to minimize it'.[257]

At a panel on *Constraints on the Waging of War: Jus In Bello and the Challenge of Modern Conflicts* at the 2003 ASIL meeting, Reisner has the following to say about these questions:

---

[253] Benjamin, 'Critique of Violence' p. 287.

[254] Reisner, 'Press Briefing by Colonel Daniel Reisner – Head of the International Law Branch of the IDF Legal Division 15 November 2000'.

[255] In an article by Alina Korn, extensive consideration is given to the coverage in Israeli press of this first officially proclaimed killing of a designated Palestinian terrorist: Korn, 'Israeli Press and the War against Terrorism: The Construction of the "liquidation policy"'.

[256] Reisner, 'Press Briefing by Colonel Daniel Reisner – Head of the International Law Branch of the IDF Legal Division 15 November 2000'.

[257] *Ibid.*

To me, a war is a conflict between the armies of two or more states, but international law has evolved. It now uses the term 'armed conflict' to denote a much wider range of situations. Today, one must recognize the possibility of an armed conflict with nonstate actors, just as international law has come to recognize non-international armed conflict beyond the 'traditional' international armed conflict.[258]

Reisner goes on to caution against the automatic application of the law of armed conflict to all counterterrorist operations, only to then add that especially in relation to 'the most organized, military-capable terrorist organizations, the laws of warfare will . . . apply. Such terrorists are combatants. They should be treated as such'.[259] Of course, what Reisner means to say here is not that designated Palestinian terrorists have the rights and the privileges of combatants, but simply that they are legitimate targets. We know this from the position taken by the Israeli government in the proceedings before the Israel Supreme Court, proceedings in which the Palestinians subject to targeted killing are described as unlawful combatants. A *Haaretz* report from the 2002 case in which Reisner was involved sums up the government argument in the following way: 'the terrorists that are eliminated are fighters, and worse – illegal fighters who are not entitled to the protection of international law. As such, it is permitted to harm them in order to prevent "future hostile acts"'.[260]

At the ASIL meeting Reisner explains his dynamic approach to the application of the law of armed conflict illustrated by his ready acceptance that international law has evolved beyond the international armed conflict and non-international armed conflict binary, by turning to the findings of Justice Barak of the Israel Supreme Court in the 2002 *Ajuri* case. In this case Barak issues 'doubt whether the drafters of the provisions of . . . the Fourth Geneva Convention anticipated protected persons who collaborated with terrorists and "living bombs". This new reality requires a dynamic interpretive approach to the provisions of . . . the Fourth Geneva Convention, so that it can deal with the new reality'.[261] As we saw

---

[258] Daniel Reisner, 'Remarks by Daniel Reisner (Panel on Constraints on the Waging of War: *Jus In Bello* and the Challenge of Modern Conflicts)' 97 (2003) Proceedings of the Annual Meeting (American Society of International Law) 200 at 202.

[259] *Ibid.*

[260] The article goes on to note that '"Future" was explicitly written, and the state does not limit itself to immediate current prevention'. Gorali, 'Easier to Kill, Harder to Judge'.

[261] Reisner, 'Remarks by Daniel Reisner (Panel on Constraints on the Waging of War: *Jus In Bello* and the Challenge of Modern Conflicts)' p. 203 internal citations omitted, quoting Israel Supreme Court sitting as the High Court of Justice, *Ajuri* v. *IDF Commander* (2002) HCJ 7015/02.

earlier, this is the approach to legal interpretation that Barak refers to as purposive interpretation or judicial lawmaking and that he claims is a crucial and legitimate tool to bridge gaps between law and the needs of society. Associating himself with this theory of legal interpretation Reisner says: 'My proposal is not that we reinvent the wheel, but that we adapt it to conform to the new roads that international terrorism has forced us to travel'.[262]

Reisner's and the International Law Department's work took the form of a classified legal opinion laying down criteria for the exercise of targeted killing operations but also a continued involvement in the operations at both the planning and the operational stage.[263]

Publicly available accounts of the classified legal opinion gives the impression that the Israel Supreme Court in its 2006 judgment followed the criteria laid down in it to a great extent. Apparently, because of the problem of applying criteria such as when arrest is viable, the legal advisers were asked to take part in targeted killing operations at both the planning (vetting individuals for targeting, sanctioning, setting limits or, potentially, stopping their 'prosecution') and the live stage (time-sensitive targets).[264]

When Daniel Reisner was interviewed for a *Washington Post* article on his legal work on the targeted killing policy, he related this task to that of giving legal advice on Arab-Israeli peace talks: 'It was a feeling of – what on earth has happened . . . Instead of two states living amicably side by side, I have to write opinions on how and when we kill each other'.[265] This statement points us back to the legal asymmetry of Israeli-Palestinian community, because only one of the partners in this common entrapment is able to rely on the services of an international lawyer like Reisner to write opinions on how and when the enemy can be killed.

[262] *Ibid.* p. 203.
[263] Alain Craig, *International Legitimacy and the Politics of Security: The Strategic Deployment of Lawyers in the Israeli Military* (Plymouth: Lexington Books 2013) p. 145ff.
[264] Craig Jones, 'Frames of Law: Targeting Advice and Operational Law in the Israeli Military' 33 (2015) *Environment and Planning D: Society and Space* doi:10.1177/0263775815598103.
[265] Laura Blumenfeld, 'In Israel a Divisive Struggle Over Targeted Killing' *The Washington Post* (27 August 2006) www.washingtonpost.com/wp-dyn/content/article/2006/08/26/AR2006082600917_pf.html accessed 15 May 2015.

Targeted Killing as Active Self-Defense

A few years into the second Intifada, Amos N. Guiora of the Military Advocate General's Corps gave the following factual description of the situation at the inception of the Israeli policy of targeted killing:

> In light of the fact that Israel is under armed attack as evidenced by both the nature and quantity of the attacks, its response has been fundamentally different than its response to the Intifada. During the Intifada, thousands of Palestinians were administratively detained, while others were brought to trial or deported. The present conflict has been characterized by a more aggressive operational response, required in large part by the Palestinian terrorist groups' decisions to attack innocent civilians with suicide bombers.

Describing the nature of this more aggressive operational response, Guiora particularly stresses its 'active' nature, referring to 'targeted killing as active self-defense'. He defines it in the following way:

> Targeted killing reflects a deliberate decision to order the death of a Palestinian terrorist. It is important to emphasize that an individual will only be targeted if he presents a serious threat to public order and safety based on criminal evidence and/or reliable, corroborated intelligence information clearly implicating him. Intelligence information is corroborated when it is confirmed by at least two separate, unrelated sources.[266]

Guiora's description of the policy of targeted killing appears to me to follow a pattern laid down in the early days of the Intifada and by the 9 November 2000 killing of Hussein Abayat in particular. Accordingly, Alina Korn, in a review of Israeli newspaper reports of this killing, argues that this reporting created a pattern for subsequent reporting of, and debates over, targeted killing in Israel; a pattern that can be described as

---

[266] Guiora, 'Targeted Killing as Active Self-Defense' p. 325. David Tal, a historian specialising in Israeli national security, places the turn to targeted killing in a long trajectory that he describes as a 'preemptive attack doctrine' which, however, relaxes the temporal criteria of preemptive attacks. 'While the revenge aspect should not be ruled out, the major rationale for the attacks was the assumption that killing the leaders would disrupt the terror activities of the assassinated leaders' organizations; that is, it was a preemptive measure, but one lacking the dimension of immediacy associated with the doctrine of preemptive attack' (David Tal, 'Israel's Concept of Preemptive War' 57 (2006) Syracuse Law Review 601 at 616). As formulated by Adam Stahl, what targeted killing 'brought to the fore was the necessity and philosophy of preemption and prevention, not killing and revenge' (Stahl, 'The Evolution of Israeli Targeted Operations: Consequences of the Thabet Thabet Operation' p. 116).

'self defense and a war waged against terrorism'.[267] Moreover, she quotes a military correspondent writing in Israel's most popular newspaper *Yedioth Ahronot* describing the merits of the strike against Abayat the day after the killing: 'No more actions directed at mere targets, but rather an action against a marked target, with the aim of harming directly the terrorist initiators . . . a targeted, surgical, and smart hit . . . which harms only the terrorists and not the wide population'.[268] This focus on targeted killing as a targeted, active form of self-defence even found its way into the concept used for this practice; for although the common English translation is 'targeted killing', the Hebrew *sikul memukad* does not necessarily imply 'killing' – a literal translation would be 'focused foiling', 'focused thwarting'[269] or 'targeted prevention'.[270]

The introduction of this concept received significant pushback on legal grounds. Steven R. David of the Begin-Sadat Center for Strategic Studies at Bar-Ilan University argued that targeted killing should be seen in the context of a state legitimately seeking to protect its people from terrorist attacks and that the policy is not a 'black-and-white issue' in international law because taking place neither in war nor in peace and between belligerents, one of which is not a state.[271] In response, Yael Stein, head of research at the Israeli human rights organisation B'tselem, argued that 'targeted killing' is a term so far unknown in international law and that 'the use of clean language to describe this policy may conveniently allow the perpetrators to persist in its implementation and believe it is legal'.[272] Stein recognises that David and others use the concept of targeted killing because they believe that Israel is engaged in an armed conflict and that those targeted are killed in military operations and considered to be combatants.[273] In response, Stein argues that defining the circumstances as one of '"armed conflict" disregards the occupation of the territories

---

[267] Korn, 'Israeli Press and the War against Terrorism: The Construction of the "liquidation policy"' p. 217.

[268] *Ibid.* p. 218.

[269] Stahl, 'The Evolution of Israeli Targeted Operations: Consequences of the Thabet Thabet Operation' p. 112.

[270] Michael Handelzalts, 'Advice and Dissent' *Haaretz* (21 December 2001) http://www .haaretz.com/culture/books/advice-and-dissent-1.77879 accessed 10 May 2015.

[271] Steven R. David, 'If Not Combatants, Certainly Not Civilians: Reply to Yael Stein' 17 (2003) Ethics & International Affairs 138 at 138.

[272] Yael Stein, 'By Any Name Illegal and Immoral' 17 (2003) Ethics & International Affairs 127 at 128.

[273] See Steven R. David, 'Israel's Policy of Targeted Killing' 17 (2003) Ethics & International Affairs 111 and David, 'If Not Combatants, Certainly Not Civilians: Reply to Yael Stein'.

for the last thirty-five years, which imposes on Israel, as an occupying power, an extra duty to protect the civilian population living there'.[274] Stein thinks that because of this duty to protect the civilian population, policing, not military operations, is the appropriate modality of dealing with the Intifada. Moreover, even if the situation would be considered an 'armed conflict', because the law of war limits the actions of belligerents, it would not automatically follow that the policy is legal. Stein particularly zeroes in on the fact that armed Palestinians cannot be considered lawful targets because they are not combatants and the scope of the exception for civilians taking a direct part in hostilities is so narrow that most operations would fall outside its scope.[275] Also the way in which they are carried out raises questions, particularly the extensive use of Palestinian collaborators and informers, usually recruited through the use of illegal means such as threats, extortion or bribes. For these reasons, and because this is the concept used by Human Rights organisations such as Amnesty International and Human Rights Watch, Stein claims that the policy in place in the occupied territories should be defined as 'assassination'.[276]

Constant Surveillance and Strike Capabilities Over Palestinian Areas

I will end this chapter by noting something else about the killing of Hussain Abayat that would prove of great significance for the Israeli practice of targeted killing going forward: the fact that he was killed from the air. Eyal Weizman has argued that a permanent ground presence was shifted towards the air in the context of the second Intifada and that

> the ability of the Israeli Air Force to maintain a constant 'surveillance and strike' capability over Palestinian areas was one of the main reasons for the Sharon government's confidence, and popular support, in pursuing unilateral ground withdrawals and accordingly transforming the logic of the occupation.[277]

The most conspicuous sign of this transformation is of course the disengagement from Gaza in 2005, spurring a controversy over whether Gaza is still occupied as a matter of international law.[278] Be that as it may,

---

[274] Stein, 'By Any Name Illegal and Immoral' p. 128.

[275] *Ibid.* p. 130.   [276] *Ibid.* p. 128.

[277] Eyal Weizman, *Hollow Land: Israel's Architecture of Occupation* (London: Verso 2007) p. 238.

[278] See on this issue Iain Scobbie, 'An Intimate Disengagement: Israel's Withdrawal from Gaza, the Law of Occupation and of Self-determination' 11 (2007) Yearbook of Islamic

subsection 1 of Section 3 of the 2004 Disengagement Plan would prove important for airborne targeted killings in Gaza after the disengagement. Here it is stated that in addition to guarding and monitoring the external land and sea perimeters of the Gaza strip, Israel 'will continue to maintain exclusive authority in Gaza air space'. Furthermore, 'the state of Israel reserves its fundamental rights of self-defense, both preventive and reactive, including where necessary the use of force, in respect of threats emanating from the Gaza Strip'.[279] This shift from ground presence towards the air implied that it would become easier to meet the criteria disallowing targeted killing if there is a 'less harmful means' or a viable arrest opportunity; criteria inserted in the legal opinion of the IDF international law department as well as the 2006 Israel Supreme Court targeted killing judgment. This explains why publicly recognised targeted killing operations predominantly have taken place in Gaza and not the West Bank after the disengagement.[280]

The use of Unmanned Aerial Vehicles or drones by the IDF goes way back. They were used to mislead the Egyptian Air Force in the 1973 Yom Kippur war and used as decoys also in the 1982 war against Syria in the Bekaa Valley. The 1983 US marine barracks bombing in Lebanon were mentioned earlier. Reportedly, Israel sent a drone, live-feeding images of the arrival of US Marine Commandant General P.X. Kelley to the scene a few days after the bombings. The images were shown to a shocked Kelley just a few hours later in Tel Aviv.[281] In December 2001 it was reported that the Israeli defence establishment had started to develop missile-carrying

and Middle Eastern Law 107. See also the contributions by Aeyal Gross, Sari Bashi, Valentina Azarov and Matthew Saul to a symposium on the topic hosted by the Opinio Juris blog: Kevin Jon Heller, 'Symposium on the Functional Approach to the Law of Occupation' (*Opinio Juris*, 23 April 2012) http://opiniojuris.org/2012/04/23/symposium-on-the-functional-approach-to-the-law-of-occupation/ accessed 10 May 2015.

[279] Israel Prime Minister's Office, 'The Cabinet Resolution Regarding the Disengagement Plan' (6 June 2004), published online by the Israel Ministry of Foreign Affairs: http://www.mfa.gov.il/mfa/foreignpolicy/peace/mfadocuments/pages/revised%20dis engagement%20plan%206-june-2004.aspx accessed 10 May 2015.

[280] Uri Blau, 'License to Kill' *Haaretz* (27 November 2008) www.haaretz.com/license-to-kill-1.258378 accessed 13 May 2015. Uri Blau claims that the military authorities refer to 'arrest operations' also when authorisation to kill the target has been granted. See also B'Tselem – The Israeli Information Center for Human Rights in the Occupied Territories, 'Documents Published by Ha'aretz Raise Grave Suspicions that the Army Performs Illegal Assassinations' (2010) www.btselem.org/press_releases/20100408 accessed 13 May 2015.

[281] Grégoire Chamayou, A Theory of the Drone (Janet Lloyd tr, New York: The New Press 2015) p. 28.

drones[282] and, according to Eyal Weizman, by the time of the disengagement from Gaza the Air Force had started to shoot missiles from drones, rather than from the more visible attack helicopters and jets.[283]

---

[282] Amnon Barzilai, 'New Israeli Drone Would Destroy Missile Launch Pads' *Haaretz* (17 December 2001) www.haaretz.com/print-edition/news/new-israeli-drone-would-destroy-missile-launch-pads-1.77561 accessed 15 May 2015.

[283] Weizman, *Hollow Land: Israel's Architecture of Occupation* p. 242. It should be mentioned in this context that the lack of reporting on the use of drones for targeted killing operations in Israeli media is due to the fact that the Israeli military censor forbids it (Craig Jones, 'Where Drones Matter: Notes on Israeli Sikul Memukad' *War, Law & Space – Thoughts on Violence in the Historical Present*, 8 May 2013 https://warlawspace.wordpress.com/2013/05/08/where-drones-matter-notes-on-israeli-sikul-memukad/ accessed 15 May 2015); Anshel Pfeffer, 'Israel Should Stop Suppressing Debate about its Drone Policy' *Haaretz* (19 February 2013) www.haaretz.com/opinion/israel-should-stop-suppressing-debate-about-its-drone-policy.premium-1.504482 accessed 10 May 2015.

The Emergence of Targeted Killing in an American Homeland which Is the Planet

The previous chapter traced the emergence of targeted killing in Israel against the background of the Israeli history of state protection and the way in which both domestic and international law depend on the state for its distribution of the legitimate use of violence. The shift from *extra-legal* political assassinations to *legal* targeted killing occurred in the particular context of the occupation and the Intifada, governed by a legal regime with a constitutional structure that gives great leeway to the occupying authorities to both decide and implement forceful means to the end of ensuring public order and safety.

The emergence of targeted killing in the United States, traced in the present chapter, tells a different story. It tells the story of the advent of a displaced transnational terrorist threat in relation to which similarly displaced means for protection are devised, to the point at which targeted killing is deployed in an American homeland which is the planet.

As in the previous chapter, a recent case of the adjudication of targeted killing provides the point of departure: the 2010 case of *al-Aulaqi* v. *Obama*. I argue that the case reveals an exceptional legal authority and a direct relation between the American executive and those subject to targeted killing. For precisely the reason of the exceptionality of this authority, the Court refused to exercise jurisdiction over the case.

In order to understand the development of this authority I turn to Carl Schmitt. I focus in particular on Schmitt's thoughts concerning state protection, from an extra-legal sovereignty exercised according to the monarchical principle to the apocryphal sovereignty characteristic of the liberal constitutional state, as well as on the shift from Westphalian to post-Westphalian international law.

I then turn to the emergence of targeted killing in the American con-text, and examine it in three steps. The first is Secretary of State George P. Shultz's push for an 'active defense' against terrorism during the Reagan years in the White House in the 1980s. Shultz articulated the necessity of engaging terrorism more actively and, specifically, of doing so with targeted military force. The rather unknown National Security Decision Directive 138 was adopted in 1984 and included directives to the CIA to find lawful measures through which the neutralisation of terrorist organisations and terrorist leaders could be achieved. Serious efforts of high-ranking lawyers within the administration to create the necessary domestic as well as international legal justifications to do so were also made during this time. I claim that this is a largely neglected formative era for American targeted killing practices in terms of both law and policy. In the second step I consider how an 'active defense' against terrorism was, in the 1990s, transformed from words to a deed, concept and tool, in response to the allegedly new form of terrorism that al-Qaeda represented. This phase would reveal the military- and intelligence-related difficulties as well as the strategic repercussions of engaging terrorism by military means. It would also reignite the controversy over legal authority and cause a frantic development of a particular military technology to be used for intelligence *and* for striking terrorists on foreign territory – the Predator Unmanned Aerial Vehicle or drone. Moreover, this is the context in which the targeted killing concept was introduced in American counterterrorism. In the third step I consider legal and political developments after 11 September 2001, developments that, at least as far as the legal framework for targeted killing is concerned, constitute a much less distinct break with the past than is usually perceived.

Al-Aulaqi v. Obama

In 2010, Anwar al-Aulaqi, an American citizen of Yemeni descent, was put on a CIA and JSOC (Joint Special Operations Command) list of persons subject to targeted killing.[1] Seth Jones, a terror analyst at the RAND Corporation and a US government consultant, referred to al-Aulaqi in *ABC News* as 'the modern day terrorist' using 'a combination of involvement in operations . . . and an almost unparalleled use of social media – YouTube, broader internet sites, Facebook, Twitter – to get his propaganda messages out'.[2] In particular, the attention given to al-Aulaqi's email

---

[1] Scott Shane, 'U.S. Approves Targeted Killing of American Cleric' *The New York Times* (6 April 2010) http://www.nytimes.com/2010/04/07/world/middleeast/07yemen.html accessed 10 May 2015.

[2] Brian Ross and Lee Ferran, 'How Anwar Al-Awlaki Inspired Terror From Across the Globe' *ABC News* (30 September 2011) http://abcnews.go.com/Blotter/anwar-al-awlaki-inspired-terror/story?id=14643383 accessed 10 May 2015. Jeremy Scahill traces the post-9/11 evolution of US targeted killing practices against the backdrop of the case of

correspondence with US army psychiatrist Major Nidal Malik Hasan, prior to Hasan's shooting at Fort Hood on 5 November 2009, has given the impression that, even from halfway across the world, al-Aulaqi threatened the United States so much, in part through his online activities, as to merit being put to death.[3]

When his presence on the list became known, Anwar al-Aulaqi had left America for Yemen but his father Nasser al-Aulaqi, living in the United States, filed a complaint with the US District Court for the District of Columbia seeking declaratory and injunctive relief on his own behalf and as next friend of Anwar al-Aulaqi.

Nasser al-Aulaqi claimed an infringement of constitutional rights, in particular the Fourth amendment or the right to be free from unreasonable seizure and the Fifth Amendment or the right not to be deprived of life without due process.[4] What is more, he claimed that the US 'policy of targeted killings violates treaty and customary international law by authorizing, *outside* of armed conflict, the killing of individuals, including Plaintiff's son, without judicial process'.[5]

In a decision delivered on 7 December 2010, the court declined jurisdiction over the case for reasons of the plaintiff's lack of standing but, more importantly, because the political question doctrine alongside the doctrine of sovereign immunity prohibited the consideration of Nasser al-Aulaqi's claims even if he were considered to have standing to bring them.[6]

Anwar al-Aulaqi. The book also includes a biographical account of how 9/11 affected the life of Anwar al-Aulaqi and his family: Jeremy Scahill, *Dirty Wars: The World is a Battlefield* (New York: Nation Books 2013).

[3] Jeremy Scahill writes about how 'Awlaki later told a Yemeni journalist that Hasan had reached out to him and primarily asked him religious questions. Awlaki claimed he neither "ordered nor pressured" Hasan to carry out any attacks, a contention supported by the e-mails once they were made public. But Awlaki's reaction to the shooting made such details once they were made public. But Awlaki's reaction to the shooting made such details irrelevant in the eyes of the US public and government'. Scahill goes on by quoting blog posts of al-Aulaqi in which he states that Nidal Hasan 'did the right thing' and 'is a hero' and 'a man of conscience who could not bear living the contradiction of being a Muslim and serving in an army that is fighting against his own people' (Scahill, *Dirty Wars: The World is a Battlefield* p. 286).

[4] United States District Court for the District of Columbia, *al-Aulaqi* v. *Obama*, Complaint for Declaratory and Injunctive Relief (Violation of Constitutional Rights and International Law – Targeted Killing) 30 August 2010. Available online at: https://www.aclu.org/legal-document/al-aulaqi-v-obama-complaint accessed 10 May 2015 p. 9f.

[5] *Ibid.* p. 10. My emphasis.

[6] United States District Court for the District of Columbia, *al-Aulaqi* v. *Obama*, 727 F.Supp.2d. 1, 8 (D.D.C. 2010) Available online at: https://www.aclu.org/legal-document/al-aulaqi-v-obama-decision accessed 10 May 2015.

The political question doctrine is, according to Judge John Bates, 'essentially a function of the separation of powers' which excludes from judicial review conflicts revolving around 'policy choices' and 'value determinations' that are constitutionally committed for resolution by Congress or the executive branch.[7] The Court's examination of the specific areas in which US courts have invoked this doctrine reveals that 'national security, military matters and foreign relations are "quintessential sources of political questions"'.[8] Thus 'if the political questions doctrine means anything in the arena of national security and foreign relations, it means the courts cannot assess the merits of the President's decision to launch an attack on a foreign target'.[9] Judge Bates continues by saying that this is precisely what the plaintiff asked the Court to do in this case: to 'assess the merits of the President's (alleged) decision to launch an attack on a foreign target'.[10] The fact that the 'foreign target' in this case is a human being rather than enemy property does not make a difference in this assessment. Neither does the fact that the 'foreign target' in this case is a US citizen. The same reasons that counsel against judicial resolution in cases concerning 'foreign targets' generally applies with equal force here.[11] This is so because 'the questions posed in this case do require both expertise beyond the capacity of the Judiciary and the need for unquestioning adherence to a political decision by the Executive'.[12] Judge Bates asserts that whether the alleged 'terrorist activities' of an individual so threaten the national security of the United States as to warrant that 'military action be taken against that individual is a political judgment which belongs in the domain of political power not subject to judicial intrusion or inquiry'.[13]

As mentioned, Nasser al-Aulaqi also claimed a violation of international law. The Alien Tort Statute enables US district courts to exercise jurisdiction over any civil action when an act is committed in violation of international law.[14] More specifically, the claim was that outside of armed conflict, international law

> prohibits defendants from carrying out the targeted killing of US citizens, including Anwar Al-Aulaqi, except in circumstances in which they present a concrete, specific, and imminent threat to life or physical safety, and there are no means other than lethal force that could reasonably be employed to neutralize the threat.[15]

---

[7] *Ibid.* p. 65.   [8] *Ibid.* p. 67.   [9] *Ibid.* p. 70.   [10] *Ibid.*   [11] *Ibid.*

[12] *Ibid.* p. 76f. Internal citations omitted.

[13] *Ibid.* p. 79. Internal citations omitted.   [14] *Ibid.* p. 49.

[15] *al-Aulaqi* v. *Obama* – Complaint p. 9. Internal citations omitted.

In response to these claims of violation of international law, the defendants invoked the doctrine of sovereign immunity. This is a doctrine derived from the English law doctrine that 'the King can do no wrong'. As the expression suggests, it is a doctrine that protects the sovereign from claims of unlawful behaviour in carrying out the duties and privileges of sovereignty.[16] Judge Bates begins his assessment of this question by stating that because Nasser-al-Aulaqi brings his claims under the Alien Tort Statute against the President, the Secretary of Defence and the Director of the CIA in their official capacities, his suit is tantamount to a suit against the United States itself. The United States, as much as any other state, cannot be sued without its consent. The Alien Tort Statute is not a waiver of sovereign immunity, and any other expression of consent must be unequivocally expressed in statutory text, will not be implied, and all purported waivers will be strictly construed in favour of the sovereign.[17] Without taking a definitive stance on whether the Administrative Procedure Act should be interpreted as a waiver of sovereign immunity, Bates uses his 'equitable discretion not to grant the relief sought'.[18] Bates' explanation is that Nasser al-Aulaqi asks the Court to interject itself into a '"sensitive" foreign affairs matter, by issuing discretionary relief that would prohibit military and intelligence activities against an alleged enemy abroad'.[19]

Ultimately, Judge Bates decided not to exercise jurisdiction over the case, concluding, 'because these questions of justiciability require dismissal of this case at the outset, the serious issues regarding the merits of the alleged authorization of the targeted killing of a US citizen overseas must await another day or another (non-judicial) forum'.[20] After several failed attempts, Anwar al-Aulaqi was killed along with some of his companions in a US drone strike in northern Yemen on 30 September 2011,

---

[16] Erwin Chemerinsky, 'Against Sovereign Immunity' 53 (2000) Stanford Law Review 1201 at 1201f.

[17] *al-Aulaqi* v. *Obama* p. 59.

[18] This ground is not available for the President, who is not an 'agency' within the definition of the Administrative Procedure Act, but is 'arguably available' for the Secretary of Defence and the CIA director. *Ibid.* p. 61f.

[19] *Ibid.* p. 62. Internal citations omitted. In doing this he follows a previous case where government officials had 'approved a plan submitted by the CIA for covert activities to destabilize and overthrow the government of Nicaragua', a case in which immunity was granted.

[20] *Ibid.* p. 4.

less than a year after Judge Bates handed down his decision not to exercise jurisdiction over the case.[21]

Carl Schmitt and the US District Court for the District of Columbia

In his 1950 *Nomos of the Earth*, Carl Schmitt gives brief consideration to the international law of belligerent occupation. The objective in the law of belligerent occupation 'was to establish a direct relation between the occupying power's military commandant and the population of the occupied territory'.[22] He also writes about the development of a provisional legal community between the enemy and the inhabitants of the occupied area.[23] This direct relation is incompatible with the dualism of domestic and international law, being neither a purely intrastate nor a purely interstate law.[24] Contemplating this provisional legal community further, Schmitt appears startled by the fact that no one before him has considered the striking parallels between the authority of the military commander in the occupied area and the constitutional authority of the holder of executive power in the space that originates as a result of the declaration of a state of exception.[25] Further on he writes about the 'remarkable and essential relation between enemy occupation and state of siege or state of exception within a constitutional state'.[26] The previous chapter on the emergence of targeted killing in the history of the state of Israel confirms both Schmitt's point about the 'direct relation' between

---

[21] See Mark Mazetti and Eric Schmitt, 'Two-year Manhunt Led to Killing of Awlaki in Yemen' *The New York Times* (30 September 2011) http://www.nytimes.com/2011/10/01/world/middleeast/anwar-al-awlaki-is-killed-in-yemen.html accessed 10 May 2015. Shortly after Anwar al-Aulaqi was killed, Anwar's 16-year old son Abdulrahman was also killed in a US drone strike in Yemen: Peter Finn and Greg Miller, 'Anwar al-Awlaki's Family Speaks out Against his Son's Death in Airstrike' *The Washington Post* (17 October 2001) https://www.washingtonpost.com/world/national-security/anwar-al-awlakis-family-speaks-out-against-his-sons-deaths/2011/10/17/gIQA8kFssL_story.html accessed 10 May 2015; Nasser al-Awlaki, 'The Drone That Killed My Grandson' *The New York Times* (17 July 2013) www.nytimes.com/2013/07/18/opinion/the-drone-that-killed-my-grandson.html accessed 10 May 2015; Scahill, *Dirty Wars: The World is a Battlefield* pp. 507–511.

[22] Schmitt, *The Nomos of the Earth in the International Law of the Jus Publicum Europaeum* p. 206.

[23] Schmitt here refers to Edgar Loening: *ibid.*

[24] *Ibid.* [25] *Ibid.* [26] *Ibid.* p. 209.

occupier and occupied and its character as neither an intrastate nor inter-state law. Moreover, our consideration of the constitutional structure of this legal regime and the great leeway it affords the military commander with regard to forceful means of maintaining public order and security, validates Schmitt's remarks about the exceptional legal authority of the military commander.

Now, I would like to suggest that these remarks about the affinities between the authority of the military commander and the constitutional authority of the holder of executive power in the context of a state of exception within a constitutional state, could tell us something about the case of Anwar al-Aulaqi and about targeted killing in the US context more broadly.

For is it not the case that *al-Aulaqi v. Obama* reveals just such an excep-tional legal authority and direct relation between the American executive and the subject of targeted killing, in this case Anwar al-Aulaqi? A legal authority and relation that, furthermore, is neither a purely intrastate nor a purely interstate affair. After all, Nasser al-Aulaqi asked the Court to intervene in and thus disturb the direct relation that allowed the US President to order the death of his son and the Court refused to do so with reference to precisely the exceptionality of this legal authority and with more than a hint to royal prerogative. However, and this is important, the space in which this legal authority is asserted is not limited in the way that Schmitt's references to the holder of constitutional authority in the space that originates as a result of a state of exception within a consti-tutional state seem to presuppose. Rather, this legal authority is wielded in a much more indeterminate space. The assertion of this exceptional legal authority and the establishment of this direct relation between the American executive and those subject to targeted killing would appear to require some serious thinking in terms of its legal justification as a matter of both domestic and international law. Particularly in the present era of the liberal rule of law.

The rest of this chapter will be dedicated to tracing this legal thinking, largely in the work of lawyers within the American executive starting in the early 1980s. To be sure, this was a time long before an individual could threaten a state from halfway across the world by, inter alia, inciting vio-lence on the internet, but already in the 1980s we can see how international terrorism was beginning to be perceived not simply as a nuisance but as a threat to US national security and a sufficiently threatening problem of co-existence to demand protective counter-thrusts of a forceful nature. This resulted in a major reassessment of the constitutional authorities of the President in extraterritorial counterterrorism operations, a reinterpretation of an executive order banning 'assassination' and the seeking of ways to overcome the inconveniences of a Westphalian distribution of the right to wage legitimate force and the resulting problems encountered by the state in seeking extraterritorial access to its non-state enemy.

I claim that to come to grips with these developments we must first go to Germany in the interwar to early post-war period and the state law and international legal theory of Carl Schmitt. A thorough consideration of Schmitt's thought will prove helpful not only for this chapter's account of the emergence of targeted killing in the United States but also for our gradually progressing understanding of the impact of targeted killing on international law: it thus points us towards Chapter 4 when targeted killing will be examined from the perspective of the *history of international law*.

Carl Schmitt and the Law and Politics of Protection

Early in this book, Thomas Hobbes' 1651 *Leviathan* was introduced, because of its assertion of protection as the essential characteristic of sovereignty. The fact that *Leviathan* remains an iconic text for the study of sovereignty, together with Hobbes' assertion that it was 'occasioned by the disorders of the present time'[27] makes this truly a book both in and out of its time.[28] *Leviathan* was published in London just after the Thirty Years' War ended with the peace of Westphalia and the civil war in England with the execution of King Charles I and the installation of a republican regime headed by one of the revolutionary leaders. Hobbes' comment in this context that he wrote the book 'with no other design than to set before men's eyes the mutual relation between protection and obedience'[29] can be taken simultaneously as a remark about the timeless nature of sovereignty, an answer to the dire circumstances of the time, and a concession to the republican regime that had come into power, Hobbes previously having publicly shown allegiance to the overthrown monarch.[30]

---

[27] Hobbes, *Leviathan* p. 475.
[28] Glen Newey, *Routledge Philosophy Guidebook to Hobbes and Leviathan* (Abingdon: Routledge 2008) p. 17.
[29] Hobbes, *Leviathan* p. 475.
[30] Cf. Newey, *Routledge Philosophy Guidebook to Hobbes and Leviathan* p. 17f.

It has been asserted that one of the reasons for Schmitt's continued interest in Thomas Hobbes was the similarity in the political situations the two thinkers faced.[31] Schmitt published the better part of his state law theory in the politically turbulent Weimar Germany. Indeed, in this context he followed Hobbes' lead and asserted that 'the *protego ergo obligo* is the *cogito ergo sum* of the state'.[32]

Because Weimar Germany also provided the backdrop for Walter Benjamin's 1921 *Critique of Violence*, it might be worth mentioning that I find Benjamin's analysis of state power in his *Critique* to be *descriptively* compatible with Schmitt's statism. This would appear to be particularly true if we, as I shall do here, focus on Schmitt's 1928 *Constitutional Theory* and on the 'apocryphal' sovereignty that Schmitt claims is the result of the liberal constitutional state. Both texts tarry with the question of protection or security in the era of the liberal rule of law.

Even if their accounts are descriptively compatible, Schmitt's affirmation and Benjamin's rejection of this state of affairs sets them apart. For Schmitt, liberalism cannot get rid of the law and politics of protection only obfuscate it and this needs to be accepted because the state secures the 'existential survival of a particular way of life'.[33] Ultimately, for Benjamin, state protection implies the 'establishing [and conserving] of frontiers' by means of 'bloody power [Ger. Blutgewalt] over mere life [Ger. bloßes Leben] for its own sake'.[34]

Not only were Schmitt and Benjamin on opposite sides of Weimar politically speaking; the advancement of the 'political unity' that Schmitt analysed in his 1933 apologia for National Socialism – *State, Movement, People* – would have very different effects on their lives.[35] Benjamin's attempt to escape the rapidly expanding Third Reich's persecution of Jews ended with his death at the Spanish border. Schmitt on the other

---

[31] Orford, *International Authority and the Responsibility to Protect* p. 126f.

[32] Schmitt, *The Concept of the Political – Expanded Edition* p. 52.

[33] The formulation is Ellen Kennedy's: Ellen Kennedy, *Foreword* to *Constitutional Theory*, by Carl Schmitt, (Jeffrey Seitzer ed., Jeffrey Seitzer tr, Durham: Duke University Press 2008) xv–xvi at xvi.

[34] Benjamin, 'Critique of Violence' p. 297.

[35] Carl Schmitt, *State, Movement, People: The Triadic Structure of the Political Unity* (Simona Dragichi tr, Corvalls: Plutarch Press 2001). This text, employing as it does the themes and categories of Schmitt's state law theory in an apology for Nazi Germany, shows that even if racism is not inscribed in his general theory of the state, the emphasis he places on the friend-enemy distinction and its blatant anti-pluralism leaves it wide-open to be exploited by himself and others for racist purposes. See Jan Müller, 'Carl Schmitt: an Occasional Nationalist?' 23 (1997) History of European Ideas 19.

hand would eventually find himself detained as a prospective defendant in the Nuremberg military trials for his collaboration with the Nazi Party.[36] It must be stressed that accounting for Schmitt's reprehensible political choices in this context is certainly not an attempt to incriminate either targeted killing or its proponents. What makes Schmitt relevant in the context of targeted killing is his thinking about how law, of both domestic and international legal origin, is implicated in the law and politics of protection.

I will begin by reconstructing Schmitt's conception of sovereign protection. I proceed by considering Schmitt's thoughts on the transition from state protection exercised according to the monarchical principle through to the *Rechtsstaat* or liberal rule of law, or from extra-legal to 'apocryphal' sovereignty. I also consider Schmitt's thoughts on the shift from Westphalian to post-Westphalian international law, particularly as regards the question of self-defence and the rise of irregular warfare.

Schmitt's Sovereign Protection

Schmitt claims that political anthropology, 'the answer to the question whether man is a dangerous being or not, a risky or harmless creature', is 'decisive for the presupposition of every further political consideration'.[37] Furthermore, Schmitt sees a direct link between this line of inquiry and what Hobbes and his contemporaries called the state of nature.[38] Like Hobbes', Schmitt's political anthropology is distinctly negative. He holds that the human being is 'by no means an unproblematic but a dangerous and dynamic being'.[39] On this account it may be worth noting that Leo Strauss, reviewing Schmitt's *The Concept of the Political*, claims that Schmitt's thought is a restoration of the Hobbesian concept of the state of nature to 'a place of honor'.[40] However, Strauss adds something essential

---

[36] Schmitt's Nuremberg dossier was published in English translation by Joseph W. Bendersky in Volume 87 (Summer 1987) of the journal *Telos*. Additional material was subsequently found and published in the same journal: Joseph W. Bendersky, 'The "Fourth" (Second) Interrogation of Carl Schmitt at Nuremberg' 139 (2007) *Telos* 35.

[37] Schmitt, *The Concept of the Political – Expanded Edition* p. 40.

[38] *Ibid.* p. 58f.   [39] *Ibid.* p. 61.

[40] Leo Strauss, 'Notes on Carl Schmitt, The Concept of the Political' in George Schwab (ed.), *The Concept of the Political Expanded Edition* (University of Chicago Press 2008) 99–122 at 105. As is made clear by Simon Critchley, Schmitt's political anthropology, just as Hobbes' state of nature, may be understood as grounded in the fall of man. Simon Critchley, *The Faith of the Faithless: Experiments in Political Theology* (London and New York: Verso 2012) p. 107ff.

to his statement: for Hobbes, the state of nature is a state of war of individuals; for Schmitt, it is the 'state of war of groups (especially of nations)'.[41] Through this transformative restoration, Hobbes' individualistic 'war of all against all' is turned into the state of war of groups, or, in other words, into the *political* status of man. This political status of man is given the following formulation by Schmitt: 'the political does not reside in the battle itself . . . but in the mode of behaviour which is determined by this possibility by clearly evaluating the concrete situation and thereby being able to distinguish correctly the real friend and the real enemy'.[42]

Given man's inclination to friend and enemy groupings, there is, Schmitt argues, a need for an authority that transcends societal antagonisms, establishing a monopoly of the political, and thus making the friend and enemy distinction its 'central business':[43]

> In reality there exists no political society or association but only one political entity – one political community. The ever present possibility of a friend-and-enemy grouping suffices to forge a decisive entity which transcends the mere societal-associational groupings. The political entity is something specifically different, and vis-à-vis other associations, something decisive.[44]

This move from political anthropology to a theory of the state mirrors the dialectic that we saw in Chapter 1 in Roberto Esposito's reading of Hobbes: the state of nature as a daunting image of men given over to each other in community and its overcoming through the institution of a commonwealth with a sovereign that is granted responsibility for protecting life. Further, with Schmitt as with Hobbes, the entire operation presupposes the threat that makes the immunitary procedure necessary (the primacy of the friend-enemy distinction), but also functions through the use of what it opposes (making the friend-enemy distinction the central business of the state).[45]

As we have seen, Schmitt follows Hobbes' lead in claiming protection to be the essential feature of sovereignty. Accordingly, the first sentence of Schmitt's *Political Theology* reads: 'Sovereign is he who decides on the

[41] Strauss, 'Notes on Carl Schmitt, The Concept of the Political' p. 106.
[42] Schmitt, *The Concept of the Political – Expanded Edition* p. 37.
[43] Gabriella Slomp, *Carl Schmitt and the Politics of Hostility, Violence and Terror* (New York: Palgrave Macmillan 2009) p. 9.
[44] Schmitt, *The Concept of the Political – Expanded Edition* p. 45.
[45] Cf. Esposito, *Immunitas: The Protection and Negation of Life* p. 7f.

exception'.[46] And, as Étienne Balibar puts it: 'what the sovereign decides on is the necessity of public safety and order: where and when it is in danger, and what means are to be used to preserve it'.[47]

The most frequently cited formulation of the friend and enemy distinction from *The Concept of the Political* is helpful for understanding more precisely what it is that Schmitt is so keen on protecting:

> The specific political distinction to which political actions and motives can be reduced is that between friend and enemy . . . The distinction of friend and enemy denotes the utmost degree of intensity of a union or separation, of an association or dissociation.[48]

What is clearly discernible in this quote is the reciprocal nature of the friend-enemy distinction. Thus, as much as the distinction is constitutive for the enemy it is constitutive for the self. For Schmitt, this is a decidedly existential matter. This distinction concerns, in Ellen Kennedy's formulation, the establishment of a 'boundary that secures the existential survival of a particular way of life'.[49]

The complex relationship between sovereignty, law and the protection of a 'form of life' [Ger. *Lebensform*] finds different expressions in Schmitt's work. Because of its importance for our further considerations I want to pick up on the notion of 'constitution' [Ger. *Verfassung*], which is the fundamental concept underwriting Schmitt's *Constitutional Theory*.

---

[46] Carl Schmitt, *Political Theology: Four Chapters on the Concept of Sovereignty* (George Schwab tr, London and Cambridge, Massachusetts: MIT Press 1985) p. 5.

[47] Étienne Balibar, *We, The People of Europe? Reflections on Transnational Citizenship* (James Swenson tr, Princeton University Press 2004) p. 136.

[48] Schmitt, *The Concept of the Political – Expanded Edition* p. 26.

[49] Kennedy, *Foreword* to *Constitutional Theory*, by Carl Schmitt, xv–xvi at xvi. As has been argued by Andrew Norris, Schmitt appears to want to draw out the existential quality of political community by establishing a link between individual human life and the collective way of life (Andrew Norris, 'Carl Schmitt on Friends, Enemies and the Political' 112 (1998) *Telos* 68 at 73). David Pan has argued that the 'way of life' must somehow be prior to individual self-preservation. Pan has formulated this in the following way: 'Rather than simply defending one's bare existence against the enemy, the decision establishes the existence of a group of people who see themselves as part of a particular cultural form that must be defended against what the group judges to be alien and threatening to this form' (David Pan, 'Against Biopolitics: Walter Benjamin, Carl Schmitt, and Giorgio Agamben on Political Sovereignty and Symbolic Order' 82 (2009) *The German Quarterly* 42 at 57). Accordingly, Schmitt writes in *The Concept of the Political* that there is no other reason than 'an existential threat to one's own way of life' (collective) that can justify 'physical destruction of human life' (individual). Schmitt continues: 'If there really are enemies in the existential sense as meant here, then it is justified, but only politically, to repel and fight them physically' (Schmitt, *The Concept of the Political – Expanded Edition* p. 49).

Defining 'constitution', Schmitt departs from the general meaning of 'constitution', which is the arrangement or combination of different parts or elements that determines the nature and character of a specific whole. According to this meaning, Schmitt maintains, 'everything, each man and thing, every business and association, is somehow included in a "constitution"'.[50] If this meaning is limited to the constitution of the *state*, we arrive at 'the concrete, collective condition of political unity and social order of a particular state'.[51] In the same work Schmitt describes the constitution as a 'political being' (singular).[52]

Protection: From Extra-Legal to Apocryphal Sovereignty

Schmitt's thoughts about how sovereign protection is to be achieved appear to have developed significantly over time. Schmitt's 1922 *Political Theology* can be read as Schmitt committing to sovereign protection through Hobbesian decisionism. We noted already how this work begins with the proclamation 'Sovereign is he who decides on the exception', and how this can be interpreted as a decision on the necessity of public safety and order: where and when it is in danger, and what means are to be used to preserve it. When sovereignty is exercised in this extra-legal monarchical mode it reveals how the sovereign, in Schmitt's words, 'stands outside the normally valid juridical order and yet belongs to it, for he is competent to decide whether the constitution has to be suspended in toto'.[53] In contrast, in his 1928 *Constitutional Theory* Schmitt considers how sovereign protection will be achieved in liberal constitutional states of the *Rechtsstaat* or liberal rule of law type where extra-legal sovereign power has been substituted for a supposedly all-encompassing rule of law.

---

[50] Carl Schmitt, *Constitutional Theory* (Jeffrey Seltzer tr, Durham: Duke University Press 2008) p. 59.

[51] *Ibid.*

[52] *Ibid.* p. 125. The nouns that Schmitt uses in the friend and enemy distinction, but also elsewhere in his work in similar contexts, confirms this picture. Both 'union' [Ger. Verbindung] and 'association' [Ger. *Assoziation*] denote the action of joining separate elements so as to form a whole or a body, or the condition resulting from such action. In Schmitt's *On the Three Types of Juristic Thought* the fundamental concept and form of 'juristic thought' to which Schmitt commits himself is that of 'concrete order' (Schmitt, *On the Three Types of Juristic Thought*). Here we may note that, as with 'unity' and 'association', the adjective 'concrete', stemming from *concrescere*, implies to grow together, coalesce, or in other words to form a whole.

[53] Schmitt, *Political Theology: Four Chapters on the Concept of Sovereignty* p. 7.

To understand Schmitt's argument here the distinction between on the one hand the 'constitution' and on the other hand 'constitutional laws' is key. It may be worth noting also that elsewhere in the same work this distinction is rendered as the distinction between an absolute concept of the constitution and a relative concept of the constitution, or between a political concept of law and a formal or *Rechtsstaat* concept of law.[54] It should be noted also that Schmitt's preference is always for the former over the latter.

'Constitutional laws' are essentially the multitude of provisions projected in the document promulgated as the constitution of a state, including the catalogue of constitutional rights. However, according to Schmitt, this is really only a supplement to the *political* component of the constitution or the 'constitution' proper. At this point we should add something important about Schmitt's distinction between constitution and constitutional laws: the nature of 'the concrete, collective condition of political unity and social order of a particular state'[55] is a 'concrete political existence',[56] as distinct from the merely normative nature of constitutional laws. The way in which the concreteness of this constitution proves itself – how, if you like, the 'fact' of a particular way of life is made normatively significant – is a key aspect of Schmitt's constitutional theory.

Schmitt emphasises that, particularly in circumstances in which a political community, or 'constitution', is under threat, the constitutional law may impede the exercise of self-defence, prompting demands for changes or revisions.[57] These are circumstances in which the constitution in the concrete sense, all the time having remained alongside and above the constitutional law, comes into play. Schmitt further describes how, in these circumstances, 'some decision-making authority that is definitive in critical cases of conflicts of interest and power' will step in as the representative or guardian of the constitution.[58] In this figure we may of course notice the re-emergence of something of that exteriority of legality that is out in the open when sovereignty is exercised according to the extra-legal model.

It is quite clear in *Constitutional Theory* that the authority that the protection of the constitution presupposes is very broad.[59] Accordingly,

---

[54] Schmitt, *Constitutional Theory* passim.   [55] *Ibid.* p. 58.
[56] *Ibid.* p. 60.   [57] *Ibid.* p. 156.   [58] *Ibid.* p. 59.
[59] This is evident from Schmitt's criticism of the theory that this authority only concerns constitution-regarding constitutional changes and thus may not 'infringe' a single constitutional provision except those enumerated as subject to exception in Article 48 of

Schmitt asserts that the protection of the constitution may involve both constitution-regarding and constitution-disregarding changes. From this we understand that 'constitutional laws' are violable but also that the 'constitution' is 'inviolable'.[60] The reason why this is the case is clear: because a particular political community exists, it has a right to exist, and not because of the 'rightness or usefulness of norms'.[61] Here we can certainly see the normative significance of the facticity of political community in Schmitt's thought. Stressing this, Schmitt even manages to marry the famous vitalist dictum of Baruch Spinoza with Article 74a of the Weimar constitution:

> Considered juristically, what exists as *political* power has value because it exists. Consequently, its 'right to self-preservation' is the prerequisite of all further discussions; it attempts, above all, to maintain itself in its existence, 'in suo esse perseverare' (Spinoza); it protects 'its *existence,* its *integrity,* its *security,* and its *constitution,*' which are all existential values.[62]

Schmitt recognises that the figure of the guardian of the constitution, but also the idea of legitimate 'constitution-disregarding' amendments to the constitution when political community is threatened, raises an issue of the standing of the principle of *Princeps legibus solutus est,* that is, the status and location of extra-legal authority in the liberal constitutional state. The difficulty here is that liberal rule of law takes as its point of departure the ability to comprehend and limit the exercise of *all* state power without exception to law. This implies that the locus of sovereign authority often remains undecided in liberal constitutions. However, as much as extra-legal authority is inconceivable in the liberal constitutional state – working as it does under the assumption that 'constitutional laws' are sovereign – it is inevitable. Sovereignty will still be exercised even though it will take apocryphal forms.

> The fiction of the absolute normative quality then has no consequence other than that such a fundamental question like the one regarding sovereignty is left unclear. For the inevitable sovereign actions, a method for *apocryphal acts of sovereignty* develops.[63]

the Weimar constitution. Schmitt asserts that this is only tenable if the protection of the 'constitution' is confused with the protection of every 'constitutional law' and so if there is, consequently, a misconstrual of the 'essence' of the commissarial dictatorship laid down in provisions on emergency powers. *Ibid.* p. 80f.

[60] *Ibid.*   [61] *Ibid.* p. 76.

[62] Schmitt, *Constitutional Theory* p. 78. Emphasis in the original.

[63] *Ibid.* p. 155. Emphasis in the original.

In her foreword to the 2008 English language edition of Schmitt's *Constitutional Theory*, Ellen Kennedy reminds the reader that even though the text was written in 1928 only a few paragraphs were added to it subsequently, and that Schmitt in a new 1954 foreword remarked that a 'systematic work' such as *Constitutional Theory* need not keep itself up to date with all the constitutional texts that emerge over time 'as long as the type remains'.[64] Kennedy ends the foreword on a note of significance for the investigation in the present chapter: 'The American Constitution of 1789 is one example of this type. It is scarcely mentioned here, but in Schmitt's discussion of "apocryphal acts of sovereignty" the observant reader will find much to ponder in our current circumstances'.[65]

Protection: From Westphalian to Post-Westphalian International Law

During the Second World War Schmitt's thoughts turned from questions of sovereignty and constitutional law to international affairs. This turn to international law has been described not only in terms of an attempt to justify Nazi expansionism[66] but also as an interest in the question of the foundations of international law and the international legal order.[67] While there may be truth in both of these statements I think Schmitt's international legal thinking reveals a keen interest also in the role of international law for the protection of political community.[68] As we will see, not only his assessments of historical periods but also a number of substantive issues of international law hinges on precisely this issue.

When Schmitt was detained after the war, facing the prospect of prosecution in Nuremberg for participation in a 'conspiracy to wage aggressive war', he found himself entangled in the historical processes he was writing about.[69] In a 1941 letter to Ernst Jünger, Schmitt expresses that he thinks

---

[64] Kennedy, *Foreword* to *Constitutional Theory*, by Carl Schmitt, xv–xvi at xvi.

[65] *Ibid.*

[66] Lars Vinx, 'Carl Schmitt' in *Stanford Encyclopedia of Philosophy* (2010) http://plato .stanford.edu/entries/schmitt/ accessed 20 May 2015.

[67] William Rasch, 'Introduction: Carl Schmitt and the New World Order' 104 (2005) South Atlantic Quarterly 177.

[68] See Markus Gunneflo, 'Political Community in Carl Schmitt's International Legal Thinking' in Matilda Arvidsson, Leila Brännström and Panu Minkkinen (eds.), *The Contemporary Relevance of Carl Schmitt: Law, Politics, Theology* (Abingdon: Routledge 2015) 50–63.

[69] Michael G. Salter, 'Neo-fascist Legal Theory on Trial: An Interpretation of Carl Schmitt's Defence at Nuremberg from the Perspective of Franz Neumann's Critical Theory of Law' 5 (1999) Res Publica 161 at 164.

of Herman Melville's *Benito Cereno* as a 'situation-symbol'.[70] In the summer of 1946 Schmitt, in what was to be published in his *Ex captivitate salus – Erfahrungen der Zeit 1945/47*, writes: 'I am the last conscious representative of the *jus publicum Europaeum*, its last teacher and student in an existential sense and I have experienced it as Benito Cereno did the voyage of the pirate ship'.[71] Schmitt was ultimately released without charge in 1947, but these sentences can be read as Schmitt perceiving himself, somewhat self-absolvingly, as a situation-symbol for the disintegration of European international law.

Schmitt sees the First World War in which US President Wilson had intervened as a watershed in this regard. It began as a conventional war among states along the lines of European international law, and ended as a global civil war.[72] This transformation can be seen in the guilt placed with the German Kaiser after the war for the *jus ad bellum* 'crime of war' as distinct from *jus in bello* 'war crimes'. In the logic of European international law the first is an unthinkable crime because war was at the disposal of sovereign equals; because heads of state did not pursue war personally but by the state as *Justus hostis;* and, finally, because of the principle of *par in parem non habet jurisdictionem.*[73]

One aspect of Schmitt's regret about this shift concerns the consequences of substituting equality for hierarchy in inter-state relations. If European international law was fundamentally characterised by an equality that bound (European) states together and bracketed war between them, with the resurgence of hierarchical relations and war as the suppression of illiberal rebellion, the notion of *justus hostis* and a public concept of enmity was in retreat. This in turn implied 'the intensification of the means of destruction and the disorientation of theaters of war'.[74] Instead of the bracketed 'war-as-duel' characteristic of European international law, war was put back in pre-Westphalian 'just war'. More fundamentally perhaps, Schmitt's appreciation of Westphalian international law (and regret about its demise) is grounded in its sanctioning of

[70] Ellen Kennedy gives an account of this letter in Ellen Kennedy, *Constitutional Failure: Carl Schmitt in Weimar* (Durham: Duke University Press 2004) p. 196 footnote 50.

[71] *Ibid.* p. 20f.

[72] Carl Schmitt, *Theory of the Partisan: Intermediate Commentary on the Concept of the Political* (G. L. Ulmen tr, New York: Telos Press Publishing 2007) p. 95.

[73] Schmitt, *The Nomos of the Earth in the International Law of the Jus Publicum Europaeum* p. 262.

[74] *Ibid.* p. 321.

the boundary that secures the existential survival of a particular way of life.[75]

Schmitt's *Nomos of the Earth* is first and foremost a eulogy for the international legal order that was established through the peace of Westphalia.[76] The *Jus Publicum Europaeum* or European international law was a 'spatial order' arising when 'centralized, spatially self-contained, continental European State[s] that faced emperor and pope, as well as other similarly organized neighboring states', effectively upset the previous spatial order of the *Respublica Christiana* supported by empire and papacy.[77] The sovereign power exercised within the territorial boundaries of Westphalian states was absolute and, crucially, included matters of religion.[78] This 'substituted *raison d'état* for the interminable struggles of religious righteousness'.[79] While religious differences would remain important for European domestic politics, it declined rapidly as a cause for war.[80]

European international law was, as the name suggests, Eurocentric. It was the mutually binding law between *European* sovereigns and 'this European core determined the *nomos* of the rest of the earth'.[81] This determination of the *nomos* of the rest of the world proceeded along the lines of a clear distinction between the Old World of Europe and the New World with regard to territorial rights. As has been stressed by Jennifer Beard, in remaining silent about the territorial rights of the peoples of the 'New World' and their territories, the peace of Westphalia

---

[75] This would be a case in point with regard to Martti Koskenniemi's observation that arguments about international law arose naturally from Schmitt's political and legal theory (Martti Koskenniemi, *The Gentle Civilizer of Nations: The Rise and Fall of International Law 1870–1960* (Cambridge University Press 2001) p. 423). Relatedly, Koskenniemi has pointed out that Schmitt's writings on European international law are neither based on a 'concrete analysis' of European societies under the roughly 400 years of European predominance nor the 'reality' of European warfare in that time but on the 'logical corollaries of a theory of domestic absolutism' (Martti Koskenniemi, 'International Law as Political Theology: How to Read Nomos der Erde?' 11 (2004) Constellations 492 at 495).

[76] Rasch, 'Introduction: Carl Schmitt and the New World Order' p. 179.

[77] Schmitt, *The Nomos of the Earth in the International Law of the Jus Publicum Europaeum* p. 66.

[78] This is made clear by Schmitt in referring to the expression *cujus regio, ejus religio* or whose is the realm, his is the religion. *Ibid.* p. 128.

[79] William Hooker, *Carl Schmitt's International Thought: Order and Orientation* (Cambridge University Press 2009) p. 18.

[80] Charles Tilly, *Coercion, Capital, and European States, AD 990–1990* (Cambridge: Basil Blackwell 1990) p. 61.

[81] Schmitt, *The Nomos of the Earth in the International Law of the Jus Publicum Europaeum* p. 126.

enabled European legal theorists to carry forward the older claims of the
legitimate rule of the Holy Roman Empire and the Catholic Church into
new theories sanctioning pan-European land-appropriation, conquest
and colonialism.[82]

Accepting for the moment the violent claim of statehood as a European
privilege, I want to think through the significance of European international law as far as protection is concerned. For, as already expressed, the
prime feature of European international law for Schmitt lies in the way in
which it sanctions the boundary that secures the existential survival of a
particular way of life: the forestalling of internecine struggle by means of
the monopolisation of the political and the gaining of independence to
make the distinction between friend and enemy or to remain neutral in
foreign affairs.[83]

Schmitt describes the interstatal system formed by European states in
the following way:

> This logic of an interstate international law was grounded in a balanced
> spatial structure of self-contained states, each with defined territorial limits
> and fixed borders. The sovereignty of every individual state in relation to
> all the others only was apparent. In reality the *aequalitas* bound them
> together.[84]

From this we can see that the self constituted in European international
law was not only a protected but also a *moral* self.[85] While the former
may explain the reason for war in the first place – whether internal or
external, war is the most extreme measure a state can take in protection
of its particular way of life – the latter has a bearing on the way war
was conducted. At the height of the era of European international law,

---

[82] Jennifer Beard, 'The International Law in Force' in Fleur Johns, Richard Joyce and Sundhya
      Pahuja (eds.), *Events: The Force of International Law* (New York: Routledge Cavendish
      2010) 18–28 at 18.

[83] Hooker, *Carl Schmitt's International Thought: Order and Orientation* p. 19. Pål Wrange
      reads Schmitt's state law theory and his theory of international law (and the relationship
      between the two) from the perspective of the concept of neutrality. For the reasons laid out
      above, neutrality is a vice for political community internally and a virtue (or precondition)
      externally: Pål Wrange, *Impartial or Uninvolved? The Anatomy of 20th Century Doctrine
      on the Law of Neutrality* (Visby: eddy.se 2007) 457–498.

[84] Schmitt, *The Nomos of the Earth in the International Law of the Jus Publicum Europaeum*
      p. 167. The emphasis placed on the self-contained [Ger. in sich geschlossenen] nature of
      the European state is revealing in giving expression to identity as well as integrity.

[85] In fact, states were considered juridical 'persons' or *magni homines:* 'A decisive step toward
      this great, new institution called "state" and the new interstate international law was
      taken in that these new, contiguous, and contained power complexes were represented
      as *persons* . . . as *magni homines*. In human fantasy, they actually were sovereign persons,
      because they were the representative sovereigns of human persons' (*Ibid.* p. 143).

war became somewhat analogous to a duel, or, in other words, war was bracketed, it became a 'war in form'.[86]

When the warring parties recognise each other as states with the same character and the same rights it is possible to distinguish an enemy from a criminal. Accordingly, war is rationalised and humanised. It also makes way for being neutral in relation to belligerent states. Schmitt writes rather triumphantly about the bracketing of war by European international law: 'It was a true European achievement that every aspect of war was limited to conflicts between sovereign European states, and that war could be authorized and organized by states'.[87] The spatial order of European international law construed the contiguity and co-existence of these persons, the concrete reality of several sovereign territorial orders existing side-by-side in a particular space at a particular time.[88]

Returning to the Eurocentrism of European international law, it was of course the case that war was neither bracketed in wars against internal enemies nor beyond the 'amity lines' where Europe ended and the 'New World' began. 'Everything that occurred "beyond the line" remained outside the legal, moral and political values recognized on this side of the line'.[89] 'As a practical justification', Schmitt even suggests that the freedom of European states in the 'New World' was indispensable for the order of Central Europe.[90]

Characteristically, Schmitt claims that the proper way to understand this state of affairs is not as an ethical but as a legal problem. He writes that this restriction of law to the land has been

> characterized sociologically as 'landlocked morality.' In my view, it is simply a matter of the age-old maxim: 'all law is law only in a particular location.' . . . Then the idea of amity lines and of an area designated as free of law easily becomes understandable as an antithesis to law in the Old World, i.e., to an old law in a particular location.[91]

He also writes that this construction is 'obviously' 'analogous' to a 'state of exception'.[92]

This view of the legal relations of colonialism has been criticised for being overly simplistic and unable to capture the rule of law specific to colonialism.[93] More important for our purposes, however, are claims about continuities as far as legalised hegemony in international law is

---

[86] *Ibid.* p. 141. [87] *Ibid.* [88] *Ibid.* p. 146. [89] *Ibid.* p. 94.
[90] *Ibid.* p. 97. [91] *Ibid.* p. 98. [92] *Ibid.*
[93] For example, Johan Geertsema, 'Exceptions, Bare Life and Colonialism' in Victor V. Ramraj (ed.), *Emergencies and the Limits of Legality* (Cambridge University Press 2008) 337–359.

concerned, all the way from the demarcation between Christian/non-
Christian, subsequently European/non-European to the *unequal* distribution of *equal* rights between Great Powers and outlaw states in the
present era of formal sovereign equality.[94] This is particularly so in debates
in which the territorial integrity and political independence of outlaw
states is diminished, resulting in highly permissive environments in which
great powers may legally intervene,[95] what Stuart Elden calls 'contingent
sovereignty'.[96]

Although this particular aspect of European international law may still
be with us it is not difficult to see that other aspects of this international legal order has changed drastically since. Accordingly, it is difficult
to describe states today as unified, impermeable and self-contained, and
exceedingly difficult to describe war as a 'duel' between equals.[97] However,
Schmitt's writing on international law not only eulogises European international law but also provides a number of important perspectives for
thinking about the question of state protection in what might be termed
a post-Westphalian international legal order.

In what follows I will consider Schmitt's thoughts on a number of
significant developments pertaining to the question of protection in the
post-Westphalian era: the 'ban on war' of the 1928 Kellogg-Briand Pact,
subsequently Article 2(4) of the 1945 UN Charter; the unmooring of the
friend-enemy distinction from its Westphalian spatial compartmentalisation, accompanied by the emergence of new paradigmatic figures of
international law; the classical Monroe Doctrine and its universalisation
with American Wilsonianism as well as the rise of irregular or partisan
warfare of both a tellurian and dislocated nature.

In *The Concept of the Political* Schmitt stated that the 1928 Kellogg-
Briand Pact's ban on war could not and in fact did not prohibit 'a people
which exists in the sphere of the political in case of need . . . determin[ing]
by itself the friend-enemy distinction'.[98]

[94] Gerry Simpson, *Great Powers and Outlaw States: Unequal Sovereigns in the International
Legal Order* (Cambridge University Press 2004).

[95] *Ibid.* p. 325.

[96] Stuart Elden, *Terror and Territory: The Spatial Extent of Sovereignty* (Minneapolis: University of Minnesota Press 2009).

[97] Schmitt, *Political Theology: Four Chapters on the Concept of Sovereignty* p. 47. On the rise
of war as policing see Caroline Holmqvist, *Policing Wars: On Military Intervention in the
Twenty-First Century* (New York: Palgrave Macmillan 2014).

[98] Schmitt, *The Concept of the Political – Expanded Edition* p. 50. See also Schmitt, *Legality
and Legitimacy* p. 34f.

Such a declaration is subject, first of all, to specific reservations which are explicitly or implicitly self-understood as, for example, the reservation regarding the autonomous existence of the state and its self-defense, the reservation regarding existing treaties, the right of a continuing free and independent existence, and so on. Second, these reservations are, according to their logical structure, no mere exceptions to the norm, but altogether give the norm its concrete content. They are not peripheral but essential exceptions; they give the treaty its real content in dubious cases. Third, as long as a sovereign state exists, this state decides for itself, by virtue of its independence, whether or not such a reservation (self-defense, enemy aggression, violation of existing treaties including the Kellogg Pact and so on) is or is not given in the concrete case.[99]

After the Second World War, the ban on war was articulated in the United Nations Charter Article 2(4), which proscribed 'the threat or use of force against the territorial integrity or political independence of any state'.[100] Applying Schmitt's analysis of the Kellogg-Briand pact to the international legal order under the UN charter, one would however be forced to recognise the significance of the exception in Article 51 or the 'inherent right of self-defense'. In this way, Samuel Weber has argued that Schmitt's definition of sovereignty under the UN Charter can be translated as 'the nation state able to decide what constitutes a threat to its survival and thus a situation of self-defense'.[101] Obviously, such a conception of sovereignty will be in unceasing tension with the terms of Article 51, restricting the right to self-defence, inter alia, with regard to *who* or *what* can trigger a self-defence measure and *when* self-defence may be exercised.

This leads us to consider another tendency that caused a strain in the spatial order of European international law: the definition of spheres of interest of a particular state and the resulting 'space for exceeding the boundaries of the state proper' in the name of self-defence.[102] The prime example that Schmitt refers to with regard to such a claim for *Großraum* (literally 'great space' but 'sphere of influence' or 'geopolitical space' may be closer to the meaning)[103] is the American Monroe doctrine, articulated in an address by President Monroe in 1823. Schmitt claims that it contains

---

[99] Schmitt, *The Concept of the Political – Expanded Edition* p. 50f.

[100] Charter of the United Nations (entered into force 24 October 1945) 1 UNTS XVI.

[101] Samuel Weber, 'Rogue Democracy' 38 (2008) Diacritics 104 at 109.

[102] Schmitt, *The Nomos of the Earth in the International Law of the Jus Publicum Europaeum* p. 281.

[103] Stuart Elden, 'Reading Schmitt Geopolitically: Nomos Territory and Großraum' in Stephen Legg (ed.), *Spatiality, Sovereignty and Carl Schmitt: Geographies of the Nomos* (Abingdon: Routledge 2011) 91–105 at 93. Elden furthermore adds that 'the word

'three simple thoughts': 'independence of states in the Americas; non-colonization in this space; non-interference of extra-American powers in this space, coupled with non-interference of America in non-American space'.[104] Hence, as it was originally conceived, the Monroe doctrine was a specifically Western-hemispheric and purely defensive form of regionalism, defensive, that is, in relation to European nations, because from the right to exclude other powers from the Western hemisphere followed the right of the United States to intervene militarily within that territory.[105]

Schmitt embraces the original Monroe doctrine as a greater-space assertion of political community and at the beginning of World War II he argues for the appropriateness of its application in relation to the *German Reich* and 'the East European space', which he referred to as a *völkischer Großraum.*[106] The original idea of the Monroe Doctrine would be turned into something entirely different in the hands of Presidents Theodor Roosevelt and Woodrow Wilson. Schmitt writes that President Woodrow Wilson's announcement in 1917 of what subsequently would become known as Wilsonianism had the meaning of applying the Monroe Doctrine to the entire world. 'In this way he sought a justification for his massive interference in non-European areas completely foreign to him and in military conflicts between the European powers'.[107] This transformation of the Monroe Doctrine was made possible 'by the fact that Woodrow Wilson substituted for the original and true Monroe Principle the ideological idea of liberal democracy and its associated images,

---

amounts to a qualitative escalation and not an increase in the sense of mere expansion'.

[104] Carl Schmitt, 'Großraum Versus Universalism: The International Legal Struggle over the Monroe Doctrine' in Stephen Legg (ed.) Matthew Hannah (tr), *Spatiality, Sovereignty and Carl Schmitt: Geographies of the Nomos* (Abingdon: Routledge 2011) 46–54 at 46.

[105] Detlev F. Vagts, 'Hegemonic International Law' 95 (2001) American Journal of International Law 843 at 846.

[106] Carl Schmitt, 'The Großraum Order of International Law with a Ban on Intervention for Spatially Foreign Powers: A Contribution to the Concept of Reich in International law (1939–1941)' in Timothy Nunan (ed. & tr), *Writings on War* (Cambridge and Malden: Polity 2011) 75–124 at 99. This was corroborated by a self-incriminating reference to the declaration by Adolf Hitler in the German parliament on 20 February 1938 that there 'existed a German right of protection for German national groups of foreign state citizenship, all on the foundation of our National Socialist national idea'. The 'völkischness' of this *Großraum* is corroborated by Schmitt through an equally self-incriminating racist argument that gives expression to the 'political idea for the Central and East European space in which there live many nations and national groups that are, however, not – apart from the Jews – racially alien from one another' (*Ibid.* p. 99).

[107] Schmitt, 'Großraum Versus Universalism: The International Legal Struggle over the Monroe Doctrine' p. 47.

especially those of "free" world trade and [a] "free" world market'.[108] Schmitt's embrace of the original Monroe Doctrine and his contempt for its Wilsonian universalisation can be understood in terms of his commitment to the protection of political community *qua* particular way of life. While the original Monroe doctrine can be understood as a greater-space assertion of a particular way of life, Wilsonianism represents the detachment of protection from any concrete form of political existence and its application along the lines of abstract liberal values or the world economy. While Schmitt could embrace the former, the latter is, to him, reprehensible.

As we will see, a similar distinction between the protection of political community in a concrete sense is at work in Schmitt's embrace of the tellurian partisan, and his rejection of the displaced or globalised Partisan. Irrespective of Schmitt's normative assessment, we will also find in these considerations important insights about the legal asymmetry that international law maintains between the state and its non-state enemies.

While Schmitt's 1963 *Theory of the Partisan* certainly has been read as a rather limited in scope genealogy of irregular warfare, it can also be read as a re-articulation of the concept of the political in the face of the on-going disintegration of European international law. The key to opening the piece up to such a reading is to be found in the subtitle *Intermediate Commentary on the Concept of the Political*. The subtitle is explained in the foreword as being related to the simultaneous re-issue of Schmitt's *Concept of the Political*. Schmitt refers to the theory of the Partisan as 'independent' in relation to the concept of the political, but also stresses how it 'unavoidably flows into the problem of the distinction between friend and enemy' and thus into the question of the protection of political community.[109]

The Partisan is defined by the criteria of: (1) irregularity, (2) mobility and agility, (3) intense political commitment and (4) tellurian character or deep-rooted attachment to a particular land and space.[110] The figure of the Partisan at the same time challenges and restores the political. What the Partisan challenges is state monopolisation of the political, in that it claims the right to make its own decision on the enemy when the state can no longer maintain the relationship between protection and obedience. As stated by Slomp:

---

[108] *Ibid.* p. 48.
[109] Schmitt, *Theory of the Partisan: Intermediate Commentary on the Concept of the Political.*
[110] Slomp, *Carl Schmitt and the Politics of Hostility, Violence and Terror* p. 66.

when the state is no longer able to protect, then the partisan emerges: partisan insurgence and partisan groups are, for Schmitt, the symptoms of a 'weak' state: the stronger the political bond of an individual to a group or party, the weaker the state. By choosing their own enemy, partisan groups both challenge the legitimacy of the state and claim legitimacy for themselves.[111]

You could be forgiven for assuming that the Partisan's conviction concerning the justness of her cause would make Schmitt contemptuous towards her. 'After all, it was the absolute commitment to a just cause which he [Schmitt] railed against in *The Nomos*', because of its devastating effects on the bracketed, public wars of European international law.[112] However, here, the tellurian element enters and with it an important distinction between different forms of partisanship is introduced. The tellurian character of the Partisan assures his or her defensiveness and 'guard[s] it against the absolute claim of an abstract justice'.[113] While the tellurian Partisan certainly poses a challenge to any given state, as long as the defensiveness that the tellurian character guarantees is retained and Partisan warfare takes place in the demarcated domains of the Westphalian state system, it does not challenge the system as such.

The legal relationship between the state and the tellurian Partisan is the legal hierarchy of civil war. This was codified in Common Article 3 of the 1949 Geneva Conventions.[114] It is described in the following way in the commentary of Jean Pictet, who was the ICRC representative responsible for drafting and negotiating the Geneva Conventions:

> Contrary to what may have been thought, the Article in its reduced form does not in any way limit the right of a State to put down rebellion. Nor does it increase in the slightest the authority of the rebel party. It merely demands respect for certain rules, which were already recognized as essential in all civilized countries and enacted in the municipal law of the States in question, long before the Convention was signed.[115]

---

[111] *Ibid.*

[112] Jason Ralph, 'War as an Institution of International Hierarchy: Carl Schmitt's Theory of the Partisan and Contemporary US Practice' 39 (2010) Millennium: Journal of International Studies 279 at 289.

[113] Schmitt, *Theory of the Partisan: Intermediate Commentary on the Concept of the Political* p. 20.

[114] The first three articles of the four 1949 Geneva Conventions are identical and thus referred to as 'common article' 1, 2 and 3.

[115] Pictet, *The Geneva Conventions of 12 August 1949: Commentary, Geneva Convention Relative to the Protection of Civilian Persons in Time of War* p. 50.

As Jason Ralph comments: 'the intense political commitment of the partisan sets him apart from the common criminal but his actions are still unlawful'.[116]

Schmitt considers another form of Partisan – the one that has lost the defensiveness guaranteed by the tellurian character, or, in other words, the dislocated or global Partisan. This was a development driven by ideologies of world revolution as much as by technological developments. In relation to the former, Schmitt in the early 1960s clearly has Communist world revolution in mind, invoking the writings of, for example, Ernesto 'Che' Guevara. In relation to the latter, Schmitt refers to 'motorization' but also modern weaponry. The dislocation of the partisan makes her something of a non-state equivalent of American imperialism's tendency to suppress illiberal rebellion wherever it sees fit. What unites the two is that both wage a just war against an absolute enemy with little or no regard for the demarcated domains of the Westphalian state system. In his considerations of the distinctly tellurian Spanish civil war, Schmitt refers to Napoleon's famous words: 'in fighting the partisan anywhere, one must fight like a partisan; il faut opérer en partisan partout où il y a des partisans', evoking the vicious circle of terror and counter-terror of partisan warfare.[117] Could this expression be adapted in order to capture how the dislocated Partisan and the state that it challenges might become entangled in ever-widening circles of terror and counter-terror?

One feature in particular of the kind of warfare that takes place between the state and its irregular enemy is the state's ability to invoke its monopoly on legitimate force. As we saw when considering the legal hierarchy of civil war, the sovereign state is able to adopt the simple and clear position that the law is on its side.

In the previous chapter we noticed how this simple and clear position was taken by the Israeli state in the distinctly tellurian Israeli-Palestinian conflict. In the present chapter we will trace the establishment of a similar asymmetry between the United States and what might be considered a dislocated form of partisanship, from the state-sponsored international terrorism of the 1980s all the way to the present and the allegedly new

---

[116] Ralph, 'War as an Institution of International Hierarchy: Carl Schmitt's Theory of the Partisan and Contemporary US Practice' p. 289. Although this description clearly is accurate, the following should be added: until the rebel party succeeds in its rebellion and shoulders the monopoly it used to rebel against.

[117] Schmitt, *Theory of the Partisan: Intermediate Commentary on the Concept of the Political* p. 13.

kind of transnational terrorism that al-Qaeda represents.[118] Although the rise of this particular breed of transnational irregular warfare may be seen as a challenge to the Westphalian state system and thus as yet another indication of a post-Westphalian era, the notion of post-Westphalian international law does not imply an age where nation-state sovereignty is finished or irrelevant. Wendy Brown has maintained, specifically with regard to this notion, that:

> the prefix 'post' signifies a formation that is *temporally after but not over* that to which it is affixed. 'Post' indicates a very particular condition of afterness in which what is past is not left behind, but, on the contrary, relentlessly conditions, even dominates a present that nevertheless also breaks in some way with this past.[119]

I claim that one aspect that relentlessly conditions the war on terrorism in general and targeted killing in particular, not only in the Israeli but also in the US context, is the legal asymmetry that international law maintains between the state and its non-state enemy. This is so even though the lawfulness of the measures taken by the state is often called into question. For, as Schmitt maintains,

> even the legality that is challenged in the modern state is stronger than any other type of right. That is a manifestation of the decisionistic power of the state and its transformation of right into law . . . legality is the irresistible functional mode of every modern state army.[120]

Further, this is the legality that transforms 'the irregularity of the partisan into a deadly illegality'.[121] I shall bear Schmitt's remarks in mind, along with Ellen Kennedy's considerations of the importance of apocryphal sovereignty in the American constitutional context as I now turn to consider the emergence of targeted killing in the United States.

---

[118] See Gregor Noll, 'Force, Dislocation, Partisanship: An Essay on International Law in the State of the Exceptional' in Jarna Petman and Jan Klabbers (eds.), *Nordic Cosmopolitanism: Essays in International Law for Martti Koskenniemi* (Leiden: Martinus Nijhoff Publishers 2003) 207–219. See also Nehal Bhuta, 'States of Exception: Regulating Targeted Killing in a "Global Civil War"' in Philip Alston and Euan Macdonald (eds.), *Human Rights, Intervention, and the Use of Force* (Oxford University Press 2010) 243–274.

[119] Wendy Brown, *Walled States, Waning Sovereignty* (New York: Zone Books 2010) p. 21. Emphasis in the original.

[120] Schmitt, *Theory of the Partisan: Intermediate Commentary on the Concept of the Political* p. 84.

[121] *Ibid.* p. 83.

NSDD 138 and George P. Shultz's Active Defense: Declaring War Against an Unspecified Terrorist Foe, to be Fought at an Unknown Place and Time with Weapons yet to be Chosen

On 28 June 1985, President Ronald Reagan gave a speech from the front steps of Bloom High School in Chicago Heights, Illinois. Prior to the speech the President had met in the school library with families of the hostages in the on-going Trans World Airlines (TWA) 847 hijacking by members of Hezbollah and Islamic Jihad. This prompted President Reagan to begin the speech in the following way:

> I came to talk about tax fairness and simplification. But first, I want to say a few words about a subject that I know is on all our minds: the outrage of international terrorism. When terrorism strikes, civilization itself is under attack; no nation is immune. There's no safety in silence or neutrality. If we permit terrorism to succeed *anywhere*, it will spread like a cancer, eating away at civilized societies and sowing fear and chaos *everywhere*.[122]

About a year before the TWA 847 hijacking and these remarks by President Reagan, the long-time terrorism expert with the Rand Corporation Brian Michael Jenkins wrote that since 1972, with the creation of the Cabinet Committee to Combat Terrorism, 'the United States has "combatted" terrorism. Now we are to fight it – with military force'.[123] The reason for Jenkins' comment was the signing by Reagan of a new National Security Directive on 3 April 1984, together with the foreign policy address of Secretary of State George P. Shultz on the same date.[124] Jenkins writes that Shultz's address, along with the National Security Directive, 'constitute a declaration of war against an unspecified terrorist foe, to be fought at an unknown place and time with weapons yet to be chosen'.[125]

Measures to Neutralise Terrorist Leaders and Organisations

National Security Decision Directive 138 (hereinafter NSDD 138 or the NSDD) was considered very sensitive. The NSDD itself would remain

---

[122] Ronald Reagan, 'Remarks to Citizens in Chicago Heights, Illinois' (*White House*, 28 June 1985) https://www.reagan.utexas.edu/archives/speeches/1985/62885b.htm accessed 10 May 2015. My emphasis.

[123] Brian Michael Jenkins, 'Combatting Terrorism Becomes a War, P-6988' (1984) The Rand Corporation, published online: http://www.rand.org/content/dam/rand/pubs/papers/2005/P6988.pdf accessed 10 May 2015 p. 1.

[124] George P. Shultz, 'Power and Diplomacy in the 1980s [Address before the Trilateral Commission on 3 April 1984]' 84 (1984) Department of State Bulletin 12.

[125] Jenkins, 'Combatting Terrorism Becomes a War, P-6988' p. 1.

classified until the year 2010.[126] It is noted in a 1984 Memorandum requested by and prepared for Edwin Meese (counsellor to President Ronald Reagan, and a member of both the President's Cabinet and the National Security Council) by the National Security Advisor Robert C. McFarlane that the content of the NSDD was briefed selectively and – although this was clearly a key focus of the NSDD – the 'attention placed' on 'pre-emptive covert activities' was minimised throughout 'in order to preclude adverse reactions which could constrain our options'.[127]

What was known about the NSDD during all the years in which it was classified was the sparse information given in historical accounts of Reagan-era counterterrorism policy[128] and political memoirs.[129] In George P. Shultz's *Turmoil and Triumph – My Years as Secretary of State* it is mentioned that NSDD 138 contained 'a passage authorizing operations to "neutralize" terrorists'. This, notes Shultz, encountered 'fierce opposition' because it 'sounded as if it authorized assassination'.[130]

With regard to the content of the NSDD, the memo to Meese indicates its 'basic purpose' to be to 'shift policy focus from passive to active defense measures'.[131] Also in the NSDD itself the adjective 'active' is frequently used to describe the measures that it directs different government agencies to take.

NSDD 138 authorises a long-term programme that will be guided by a few principles, the more important of which are: that 'the practice of terrorism by *any* person or group in *any* cause [is] a threat to our national security' and is to be resisted 'by all legal means available'; that the United States should work with other democratic nations 'to eliminate the threat of terrorism to our way of life'; that 'whenever we have evidence that a state is mounting or intends to conduct an act of terrorism against us, we have

---

[126] National Security Council, 'Combatting Terrorism', National Security Decision Directive 138 (NSDD 138) Signed by President Ronald Reagan on 3 April 1984. Published online by the Federation of American Scientists: www.fas.org/irp/offdocs/nsdd/nsdd-138.pdf accessed 15 May 2015. Mattia Toaldo has considered NSDD 138 in his analysis of Reagan era counterterrorism: Mattia Toaldo, *The Origins of the US War on Terror: Lebanon, Libya and American Intervention in the Middle East* (Abingdon: Routledge 2012) pp. 102–107.

[127] Robert C. McFarlane, *Background Material on Terrorism* (The White House, Washington (15 August 1984), published online by Washington Decoded: www.washingtondecoded .com/files/nsdd.pdf accessed 10 May 2015).

[128] For example, David C. Wills, *The First War on Terrorism: Counter-terrorism Policy During the Reagan Administration* (Maryland: Rowman & Littlefield Publishers, Inc. 2003).

[129] In particular George P. Shultz, *Turmoil and Triumph: My Years as Secretary of State* (New York: Charles Scribner's Sons Macmillan Publishing Company 1993).

[130] *Ibid.* p. 645.   [131] McFarlane, *Background Material on Terrorism.*

a responsibility to take measures to protect our citizens, property, and interests'; that 'intelligence collection against groups and states involved in international terrorism must be improved in order to better prevent or counter attacks; warn our citizens, friends, and allies; and, thereby, reduce the risk to them'.[132]

Among the directives for different government agencies, those for the Secretary of Defence and the Director of the Central Intelligence Agency (CIA) stand out as particularly important. The directives to the Secretary of Defence include to 'continue improvements to US capabilities to conduct *military operations to counter terrorism* directed against US citizens, military forces, property and interests' and to 'develop a military strategy that is supportive of an *active, preventive program* to combat state-sponsored terrorism *before* the terrorists can initiate hostile acts'.[133]

The directives to the director of the CIA include to 'develop, in coordination with other friendly security services, capabilities for the *preemptive neutralization* of anti-American terrorist groups which plan, support, or conduct terrorist acts against US citizens, interests, and property overseas', and to 'provide a new Finding on combatting terrorism which includes, inter alia, lawful measures to: . . . Unilaterally and/or in concert with other countries *neutralize or counter* terrorist organizations and *terrorist leaders*'.[134]

These last directions to the director of the CIA are without doubt the parts of the directive that Shultz noted in his memoirs encountered fierce opposition because they sounded as if they authorised assassination. Considering that the OED notes the origin of use of the word 'neutralize' as a euphemism for killing to be the 'coordinated intelligence and operational effort designed to route [sic] out Vietcong by killing them, capturing them, or converting them to the government side' (citing a US Senate Committee on Foreign Relations Protocol), this link was perhaps not so far-fetched after all.

In this context it is important to note that the NSDD repeatedly emphasises that lawfulness is a condition for any activities undertaken in its implementation and twice asserts that this includes the provisions of Executive Order 12333 of 4 December 1981. The authors of the NSDD were of course aware that Executive Order 12333 includes a prohibition on assassination in Section 2.11:

---

[132] National Security Council, NSDD 138 p. 1f. My emphasis.
[133] *Ibid.* p. 3. My emphasis.   [134] *Ibid.* p. 4. My emphasis.

No person employed by or acting on behalf of the United States Government shall engage in, or conspire to engage in, assassination.[135]

Before pursuing this investigation of the content of NSDD 138 any further
we must have a brief look at the context in which it was passed.

The memo to Meese describes the background of the NSDD to be that
'the US remains an attractive terrorist target with 271 Americans losing
their lives to terrorists in 1983. This represents more American deaths
from terrorism than were recorded in the preceding 15 years'.[136] Noting
the high number of casualties among diplomatic and military officers
abroad, the memorandum comments that the United States is a 'prime
target' because of its 'extensive official and commercial presence overseas,
which is high in numbers of people and profile'.[137] Moreover, and more
generally, the memorandum succinctly notes, 'our policies are opposed to
the interests of many terrorist groups; and we often support governments
which terrorists are attempting to bring down'.[138] In the minutes of the
National Security Planning Group meeting held on 2 March 1984, a particular event is pointed to by National Security Advisor John Poindexter
as having triggered the NSDD: the two separate bombings of the United
States and French military forces in Beirut, Lebanon, on 23 October 1983,
in which 241 American servicemen had been killed.[139]

The fact that the NSDD sounds as if it authorises assassination was a
problem because, as mentioned, President Gerald Ford had already put a
prohibition on assassination in place in 1976, in response to the findings
of the Senate Select Committee on Intelligence Agencies (the so-called
Church Committee, after its chairman Frank Church) that the CIA had
engaged in assassination plots involving foreign leaders.[140] The ban was
reiterated by Jimmy Carter and subsequently also by Reagan himself.

---

[135] Exec. Order No. 12,333, 3 C.F.R. 200 (1981), reprinted in 50 U.S.C. § 401. Published
online by the Federation of American Scientists: http://fas.org/irp/offdocs/eo12333.htm
accessed 10 May 2015.

[136] McFarlane, *Background Material on Terrorism*.   [137] *Ibid.*   [138] *Ibid.*

[139] National Security Planning Group, 'Summary of National Security Planning Group
Meeting on Combatting Terrorism', 2 March 1984. Retrieved from The Reagan Files:
www.thereaganfiles.com/nspg-meetings.html On file with author. p. 1.

[140] The 1954 report of the Special Study Group on the Covert Activities of the Central
Intelligence Agency, the so-called Doolittle Committee, is often referred to as having
laid down the rationale for extensive American covert action activities of the Cold War
era including the assassination plots revealed by the Church Committee. The report,
which was commissioned by President Dwight D. Eisenhower, included reference to 'an
implacable enemy whose avowed objective is world domination by whatever means and
at whatever cost'. Against this background the report asserted: 'There are no rules in
such a game. Hitherto acceptable norms of human conduct do not apply. If the United
States is to survive, long-standing American concepts of "fair play" must be reconsidered.

Given that assassination is prohibited, one is left wondering what exactly the frequent references to a military strategy with an active, preventive programme of combatting terrorism and, more pointedly, the references to the neutralisation of terrorist groups and terrorist leaders in NSDD 138 mean.

Might the 1975 intermediary report of the Church Committee, in which the recommendation was made to ban assassination, be of any help in answering this question? The report notes that a statute is needed because assassination plots did happen and even though internal CIA orders banning assassination already had been issued in 1972 and 1973, the interim report asserts, 'it would be irresponsible not to do all that can be done to prevent their happening again'.[141] A law is needed, according to the committee, because 'laws express our nation's values; they deter those who might be tempted to ignore those values and stiffen the will of those who want to resist the temptation'.[142] With all the importance placed on a legal ban against assassination, the concluding part of the section, in which a statute is recommended, is remarkable. Here it is noted that 'during the Committee's hearings, some witnesses, while strongly condemning assassination, asked whether assassination should absolutely be ruled out in a time of truly unusual national emergency'.[143] The answer that the report gives is negative. The reasons given are important:

> In a grave emergency, the President has a limited power to act, not in violation of the law, but in accord with his own responsibilities under the Constitution to defend the Nation. As the Supreme Court has stated, the Constitution 'is not a suicide pact'.[144]

In support of this there is, besides the 1963 judgment *Kennedy v. Mendoza-Martinez* – from which the Committee got the expression that the constitution 'is not a suicide pact' – Abraham Lincoln. The example of Lincoln is instructive in this regard because 'during an unprecedented emergency'

We must develop effective espionage and counterespionage services and must learn to subvert, sabotage and destroy our enemies by more clever, more sophisticated and more effective methods than those used against us. It may become necessary that the American people be made acquainted with, understand and support this fundamentally repugnant philosophy'. J. H. Doolittle and others, 'Report on the Covert Activities of the Central Intelligence Agency' published online by Cryptome: http://cryptome.org/cia-doolittle .pdf accessed 10 May 2015 p. 2f.

[141] US Congress, Senate, Select Committee to Study Governmental Operations with Respect to Intelligence Activities, 94 Cong., 2d sess., 'Interim Report: Alleged Assassination Plots Involving Foreign Leaders', 1975 available online at www.aarclibrary.org/publib/contents/ church/contents_church_reports_ir.htm accessed 10 May 2015 p. 282f.

[142] *Ibid.* p. 283.   [143] *Ibid.* p. 284.   [144] *Ibid.*

he claimed 'unprecedented power based on the need to preserve the nation'.[145] The Committee report quotes Lincoln explaining his actions:

> My oath to preserve the Constitution to the best of my ability imposed upon me the duty of preserving by every indispensable means, that government – that nation – of which that Constitution was the organic law. Was it possible to lose the nation, and yet preserve the Constitution? By general law, life and limb must be protected: yet often a limb must be amputated to save a life: but a life is never wisely given to save a limb. I felt that measures, otherwise unconstitutional, might become lawful, by becoming indispensable to the preservation of the Constitution through the preservation of the nation.[146]

I claim that this investigation into the legislative history of the prohibition on assassination helps us understand the seeming contradiction of NSDD 138 that, although assassination is banned by executive order, the head of the CIA is directed to find *lawful* means to neutralise or counter terrorist organisations and terrorist leaders. It seems that although the NSDD 138 makes explicit reference to an executive order prohibiting assassination, this does not mean that assassinations are entirely out of the question. The evidence for this is reinforced by the fact that the recommendation of the Church Committee to ban assassination by legislation was not met; the ban instead took the form of an executive order. And, as Nathan Canestaro points out,

> part of the advantage of employing an executive order to prohibit assassination is its inherent flexibility. Although each order has the effect of law, they are not immutable, and allow the President a variety of ways to circumvent them. The President has the authority to overrule the order, make an exception to it, or ask Congress to legislate its removal. Additionally, the President may designate any of these changes as classified if he considers them 'intelligence activities . . . or intelligence sources and methods,' effectively preventing them from ever reaching public view.[147]

Arguably, NSDD 138 constituted precisely such a circumvention of the ban on assassination.

---

[145] *Ibid.*   [146] Abraham Lincoln as quoted in *ibid.*

[147] Nathan Canestaro, 'American Law and Policy on Assassinations of Foreign Leaders: The Practicality of Maintaining the Status Quo' 26 (2003) British Columbia International and Comparative Law Review 1 at 23. See also Jonathan Ulrich, 'The Gloves Were Never On: Defining the President's Authority to Order Targeted Killing in the War Against Terrorism' 45 (2005) Virginia Journal of International Law 1029.

From Passive to Active Defense against Terrorism

Secretary of State George P. Shultz was without doubt the architect of NSDD 138. Not only in the 4 April 1984 speech referred to earlier but also in a number of other public statements on terrorism delivered in a relatively short period of time, Shultz articulated the necessity of engaging terrorism more actively and, more specifically, of doing so with military force. These speeches provide a rich resource for understanding these developments.[148] Further, understanding them is an urgent matter, not least because of the unconventional nature of these events. They are unconventional first of all because war is declared against an '*unspecified terrorist foe*' – that is, without knowing when, where, how, or above all, against whom, the war is to be fought. But most importantly, they are unconventional for the simple fact that 'war' in this case refers neither to 'armed combat between organized political entities' nor to 'armed combat within an organized unit' – in other words, neither interstate international armed conflict nor intrastate non-international armed conflict – but rather to something else.[149] Decades later it would be conceded that the notion of a war on terror 'is not an inapt metaphor, but rather a recognition of the way war is changing'.[150]

David C. Wills writes that after the bombing of the marine barracks in October 1983, for Secretary of State George P. Shultz 'terrorism was no longer just a nuisance, but war'.[151] This conclusion may have been influenced by the Department of Defence Commission report on the

---

[148] Shultz, 'Power and Diplomacy in the 1980s [Address before the Trilateral Commission on 3 April 1984]'; George P. Shultz, 'Terrorism and the Modern World [Address before the Park Avenue Synagogue New York City on 25 October 1984]' 84 (1984) Department of State Bulletin 12; George P. Shultz, 'Terrorism: The Problem and the Challenge [Statement before the House Foreign Affairs Committee on 13 June 1984]' 84 (1984) Department of State Bulletin 29; George P. Shultz, 'Terrorism: The Challenge to the Democracies [Address before the Jonathan Institute's second Conference on International Terrorism on 24 June 1984]' 84 (1984) Department of State Bulletin 31; George P. Shultz, 'New Realities and New Ways of Thinking' 63 (1984) Foreign Affairs 705; George P. Shultz, 'Low-Intensity Warfare: The Challenge of Ambiguity [Address Before the Low-Intensity Warfare Conference, National Defense University, Washington, D.C., 15 January 1986]' 86 (1986) Department of State Bulletin 204.

[149] This is how Schmitt defines war in 1922 (Schmitt, *The Concept of the Political – Expanded Edition* p. 32). It is a conception that subsequently would be codified in the 1949 Geneva Conventions' *international armed conflict* and *non-international armed conflict* binary.

[150] Philip Bobbitt, *Terror and Consent: The Wars for the Twenty-First Century* (New York: Anchor Books 2009) p. 133.

[151] Wills, *The First War on Terrorism: Counter-terrorism Policy During the Reagan Administration* p. 2.

attacks of 20 December 1983 in which the Commission had stated that 'the most important message it can bring to the Secretary of Defense is that the 23 October 1983 attack on the Marine Battalion Landing Team Headquarters in Beirut was tantamount to an act of war using the medium of terrorism'.[152]

Shultz had already lost a trusted advisor in the April 1983 bombing of the US embassy in Beirut. Furthermore, as a former Marine, Shultz was deeply affected by the bombing of the Marines.[153] Wills describes Shultz's personal reaction as a turning point in his political career and writes that speculations that Shultz would resign after the Presidential election of 1984 did not come true because the attacks 'gave him a renewed sense of purpose and a fire in his gut to do something about terrorism'.[154] From this point, 'Shultz became the administration's most ardent and outspoken proponent of using military force to combat terrorism' something he would describe as a shift from passive to active defense against terrorism.[155]

Terrorism as an Emerging Global National Security Threat

Because of the link between Shultz's efforts at bringing about a shift towards a policy of active defense against terrorism, the passing of NSDD 138 and the bombing of the Marine barracks in Lebanon, the reasons for the US presence in Lebanon in the first place are worth considering. President Ronald Reagan describes this in the 27 October 1983 address on the bombings. On the question, 'why should our young men be dying in Lebanon? Why is Lebanon important to us?', Reagan states:

> Well, it's true, Lebanon is a small country, more than five-and-a-half thousand miles from our shores on the edge of what we call the Middle East, but every President who has occupied this office in the recent years has recognised that peace in the Middle East is of vital concern to our

---

[152] Department of Defense, 'Report of the Department of Defense Commission on Beirut International Airport Terrorist Act', 23 October 1983. Published online by the Federation of American Scientists: www.fas.org/irp/threat/beirut-1983.pdf accessed 10 May 2015.

[153] Wills, *The First War on Terrorism: Counter-terrorism Policy During the Reagan Administration*. p. 27f.

[154] *Ibid.* p. 28, quoting Neil C. Livingstone, *The Cult of Counterterrorism: The Weird World of Spooks, Counterterrorists, Adventurers and Professionals* (Lexington: Lexington Books 1990) p. 233.

[155] Wills, *The First War on Terrorism: Counter-terrorism Policy During the Reagan Administration* p. 28.

nation and, indeed, to our allies in Western Europe and Japan. We've been concerned because the Middle East is a powderkeg; four times in the last 30 years, the Arabs and Israelis have gone to war. And each time, the world has teetered near the edge of catastrophe. The area is key to the economic and political life of the West. Its strategic importance, its energy resources, the Suez Canal, and the well-being of the nearly 200 million people living there – all are vital to us and to world peace. If that key should fall into the hands of a power or powers hostile to the free world, there would be a direct threat to the United States and to our allies. We have another reason to be involved. Since 1948 our Nation has recognized and accepted a moral obligation to assure the continued existence of Israel as a nation. Israel shares our democratic values and is a formidable force an invader of the Middle East would have to reckon with . . . As to that narrower question – what exactly is the operational mission of the marines – the answer is, to secure a piece of Beirut, to keep order in their sector, and to prevent the area from becoming a battlefield. Our marines are not just sitting in an airport. Part of their task is to guard that airport. Because of their presence, the airport has remained operational. In addition, they patrol the surrounding area. This is their part – a limited, but essential part – in the larger effort that I've described.[156]

Patrick Porter describes a struggle along a spectrum between 'shapers' and 'restrainers' in the American strategic tradition. 'To some the republic can secure itself only by actively championing its values abroad and remaking the world in its image. Others are wary of entanglement abroad arguing that America is better off embodying rather than spreading its values'.[157] Wilsonian concepts such as the Middle East's importance for the economic and political life of the West, the cold war opposition between the 'free world' and the Soviet Union and the US allegiance with Israel frames Reagan's explanation for the American presence in Lebanon. This means that Reagan here places himself firmly in the tradition of 'shapers' – the idea of making America secure by globalising its security interests. At the same time, there were indications within government agencies of the dangers this entails. A memo drafted for CIA director William Casey on 30 November 1983 recognises that the local perception of US presence was very different. Quoting the memo, Mattia Toaldo writes that the United States was seen as an actor in the civil war:

---

[156] Ronald Reagan, 'Address to the Nation on Events in Lebanon and Grenada' (*White House*, 27 October 1983) www.reagan.utexas.edu/archives/speeches/1983/102783b.htm accessed 10 May 2015.

[157] Patrick Porter, *The Global Village Myth: Distance, War and the Limits of Power* (Washington DC: Georgetown University Press 2015) p. 63.

The Lebanese Shiite groups, the memo argued, considered the American contingent 'to be less peacekeepers than supporters of the Maronite Christian faction of the Lebanese fabric. This perception was strengthened when the United States demonstrated its willingness to use naval gunfire in support of the Lebanese army in its battles against Muslim elements in the Shuf Mountains in September'.[158]

Outside of government Francis A Boyle referred to the bombing of the Marine Barracks as the

needless deaths of... marines and diplomats in Lebanon... as a direct result of the Reagan administration's illegal military intervention into that country's civil war in order to prop-up a supposedly pro-Western regime that was imposed by the Israeli army.[159]

Shultz's speech, *Power and Diplomacy in the 1980s*, delivered the same day as NSDD 138 was passed, may be used to obtain a richer understanding of the international legal order in which Shultz's call for active defense against terrorism was made. The picture he paints is one that probably exceeded the complexity of the international legal order Carl Schmitt had analysed in the early post-war era. He describes the present 'moment' as one 'when the old international order had been destroyed by two world wars but no new stable system had developed to replace it'.[160] This is an order determined by processes of globalisation, the bi-polar superpower structure, decolonisation and the accompanying universalisation of the formal equality of states. This is also an order that used to be focused on Europe but where military strength is now with the Soviet Union and the United States, and economic power is dispersed. Further, Shultz describes the dismantling of the former colonial empires, leading to more than 160 independent nations on the 'world scene'; he describes much of the developing world, where most of the major international conflicts since 1945 have taken place, as 'torn by a continuing struggle between the forces of moderation and the forces of radicalism'.[161]

Under the rubric of 'the world we face', Shultz closes in on the emerging problem of 'international terrorism':

---

[158] Toaldo, *The Origins of the US War on Terror: Lebanon, Libya and American Intervention in the Middle East* p. 96.

[159] Francis A. Boyle, 'Preserving the Rule of Law in the War Against International Terrorism' 8 (1986) Whittier Law Review 735 at 736.

[160] Shultz, 'Power and Diplomacy in the 1980s [Address before the Trilateral Commission on 3 April 1984]' p. 12.

[161] *Ibid.*

> On a planet grown smaller because of global communications, grown more
> turbulent because of the diffusion of power – all the while overshadowed
> by nuclear weapons – the task of achieving stability, security, and progress
> is a profound challenge for mankind. In an age menaced by nuclear pro-
> liferation and state-sponsored terrorism, tendencies toward anarchy are
> bound to be a source of real dangers. It is absurd to think that America
> can walk away from these problems. This is a world of great potential
> instability and great potential danger. There is no safety in isolation . . . [162]

What Shultz grapples with here concerns the question of order, peace and
security that we recognise from thinkers such as Hobbes and Schmitt.
However, this question is placed in a very different context. This can be
seen in the way in which it is framed by claims about how the planet
has grown smaller because of global communications and how we are
living in a *world* of great potential instability and great potential danger –
without, and this is important, reducing this to the anarchic 'state of
nature' between states. This tells us that Shultz finds that these classic
ends of modern statehood – order, peace and security – are challenged
in the spatial dimension. Moreover, in stressing that 'there is no safety in
isolation', Shultz signals that he thinks state borders are inadequate for
deactivating communal exposure in this context. In what is probably his
most famous speech on the topic of counterterrorism, entitled *Terrorism
and the Modern World*, delivered at the Park Avenue Synagogue in New
York City on 25 October 1984, Shultz is clearer about how the problem of
international terrorism fits into the situation described so far. The agonic
relationship between terrorism and the modern world hinted at in the
title is also what gives the speech its thrust:

> We have already seen the horrible cost in innocent lives that terrorist vio-
> lence has incurred. But perhaps even more horrible is the damage that
> terrorism threatens to wreak on our modern civilization. For centuries
> mankind has strived to build a world in which the highest human aspira-
> tions can be fulfilled. We have pulled ourselves out of a state of barbarism
> and removed the affronts to human freedom and dignity that are inherent
> to that condition. We have sought to free ourselves from that primitive
> existence described by Hobbes where life is lived in 'continual fear and dan-
> ger of violent death . . . nasty brutish, and short.' We have sought to create,
> instead a world where universal respect for human rights and democratic
> values makes a better life possible . . . Terrorism is a step backward; it is a
> step toward anarchy and decay. In the broadest sense, terrorism represents
> a return to barbarism in the modern age. If the modern world cannot

[162] *Ibid.*

face up to challenge, then terrorism, and the lawlessness and inhumanity that come with it, will gradually undermine all that the modern world has achieved and make further progress impossible.[163]

Hans Blumenberg has described how an invocation such as this of Hobbes' state of nature, along with its opposite pole, the civil state, performs the following trick: 'The zero point of the disappearance of order and the point of departure of the construction of order are identical; the minimum of ontological predisposition is at the same time the maximum of constructive potentiality'.[164] According to Blumenberg, this expresses a 'modern relation to the world' through the 'self-assertion' by which man in a 'revolutionary reduction of historical positivity to elementary anarchism' creates for himself something like a state of nature, so as to 'get behind his own history and reach the zero point for the *creatio ex nihilo* of a rational social condition'.[165] This minimum of ontological predisposition and maximum of constructive potentiality will be used by Shultz to adapt expansive ideas of America's security interests into counterterrorism policy. For as we have seen earlier in this chapter, what Patrick Porter refers to as 'globalism' has a long history in the United States and was heightened from the middle of the twentieth century onwards when

> the interlocking of shocks, growing power, the dynamics of empire, inter-national demand, and a well-organized lobby for activism persuaded mak-ers of American strategy that they inhabited a dangerous, small world and that they could reshape it. This tradition teaches policymakers that Amer-ica is a singular and therefore vulnerable superpower, that it can only be safe in an open-door world of absolute security, and that territoriality and space are less of a guide to America's security interests than more amorphous values and psychological perception. Globalism became the dominant working theory of American statecraft.[166]

Taking this tradition into a new policy area and, indeed, self-assertively, Shultz streamlines the complex and diverse problem of terrorism and guards against an understanding of terrorism as a 'new manifestation of

---

[163] Shultz, 'Terrorism and the Modern World [Address before the Park Avenue Synagogue New York City on 25 October 1984]' p. 12f.
[164] Hans Blumenberg, *The Legitimacy of the Modern Age* (Robert M. Wallace tr, Cambridge, Massachusetts: MIT Press 1985) p. 220.
[165] *Ibid.* p. 220f.
[166] Porter, *The Global Village Myth: Distance, War and the Limits of Power* p. 94f.

traditional social conflict'.[167] He does so with the claim that although their stated objectives range from separatist causes to revenge for ethnic grievances to social and political revolution; the 'overarching goal of all terrorist[s]' is to create an 'atmosphere of fear'.[168] Accordingly, terrorists

> are depraved opponents of civilization itself, aided by the technology of modern weaponry. The terrorists want people to feel helpless and defenseless; they want people to lose faith in their government's capacity to protect them and thereby undermine the legitimacy of the government itself, or its policies, or both.[169]

In a statement before the House Foreign Affairs Committee on June 13 the same year, Shultz recognises that the problem of 'international terrorism' is not 'confined to any geographic area'. He also says that 'the extensive travel of terrorists outside their own countries and regions to commit acts of terror abroad' is 'a source of growing concern'.[170] Also, whereas inside the United States there are relatively few incidents, the problem, he says, is primarily in other areas of the world, in Europe, Latin America and the Middle East.[171] It appears to me, then, that the problem, as Shultz sees it, is the simultaneous displacement of the subjects and objects of protection and the international terrorism that put them at risk.

Shultz argues that, in a world of increasing intertwinement, as much as there is no safety in isolating oneself, so protection cannot be achieved on one's own, or, in other words, without international cooperation. At the National Security Planning Group Meeting on 2 March 1984, CIA Director William Casey ascribes to Shultz a belief in the importance of international cooperation: 'Just as George (Secretary Shultz) indicated, what we need is the kind of international cooperation that we had in the 18th in the international laws against piracy'.[172] However, as much as he sees the need for inter-state cooperation on terrorism Shultz will not put his wager on international institutions but rather on American leadership.

---

[167] Shultz, 'Terrorism and the Modern World [Address before the Park Avenue Synagogue New York City on 25 October 1984]' p. 13.

[168] *Ibid.*   [169] *Ibid.*

[170] Shultz, 'Terrorism: The Problem and the Challenge [Statement before the House Foreign Affairs Committee on 13 June 1984]' p. 29.

[171] *Ibid.*

[172] National Security Planning Group, 'Summary of National Security Planning Group Meeting on Combatting Terrorism', 2 March 1984. Retrieved from The Reagan Files: www.thereaganfiles.com/nspg-meetings.html On file with author p. 5.

Active Defense Against Terrorism

The problem that Shultz faces is how the protection of political community is to be achieved, given that state borders no longer deliver on their promise of being the protective boundary that deactivates communal exposure even for an offshore nation such as the United States. With a not-so naïve domestic analogy, Shultz in the 4 April 1984 speech raises the question of the need for a 'world's policeman', a role which he asserts the United States cannot fulfil.[173] However, he raises it again, although in a distinctly more solipsistic way, in the immediately following sentence with the description of the responsibilities that come with being 'the world's strongest free nation': 'our values, our principles, our hopes for a better world rests [sic] in great measure, inevitably, on our shoulders'.[174]

'In this environment' the principal goal of the United States is the 'duty to protect and strengthen peace', Shultz writes. This, however, does not mean merely assuming a 'reactive posture' or being the 'victims of events'; what is needed instead are proactive measures that 'shape them'.[175] In support of this stance Shultz invokes 'the great seal of the United States', showing, as it does, the American eagle clutching arrows in one claw and olive branches in the other. On some of the older versions of the seal, Shultz explains, the eagle looks toward the arrows, on others, toward the olive branches.

> It was President Truman who set it straight; he saw to it that the eagle always looked toward the olive branches – showing that America sought peace. But the eagle still holds onto those arrows. It is clear today that a world of peace and security will not come about without exertion or without facing up to some tough choices.[176]

This idea that protection is to be achieved by tough choices, ultimately the choice of military action might be interpreted as the idea that the state of nature is not overcome by the civil state but is brought into that state, resurfacing in the sovereign, who is the only one to have preserved his natural right when everyone else has given it up. Similarly, we saw how Schmitt turned the friend-enemy distinction from a (negative) political anthropology into the 'central business' of the state. This is the double bind of political authority and force: violence against violence in order to control violence. Now, with the emerging threat of international terrorism and the protective counter-thrust that Shultz sees in active defense, such

---

[173] Shultz, 'Power and Diplomacy in the 1980s [Address before the Trilateral Commission on 3 April 1984]' p. 12.

[174] *Ibid.*   [175] *Ibid.*   [176] *Ibid.* p. 13.

political authority is wielded in a much more indeterminate transnational space.

It should be mentioned that by no means does active defense substitute for other forms of passive defence against terrorism. Hence, Shultz explains that if terrorists strike at home it is a matter for police action and domestic law enforcement. In most cases overseas, acts of terrorism against US citizens and installations can be dealt with best by the host government and its forces.[177] Shultz also speaks of using the law to its maximum extent through cooperation in law enforcement, international agreements against hijacking and terrorism, extradition and prosecution of terrorists when captured.[178] While these domestic and international measures are important elements, the 'purely passive defense' that they entail is, according to Shultz, insufficient to cope with the problem.[179]

> From a practical standpoint, a purely passive defense does not provide enough of a deterrent to terrorism and the states that sponsor it. It is time to think long, hard, and seriously about more active means of defense – about defense through appropriate preventive or preemptive actions against terrorist groups before they strike.[180]

The 'heart of the challenge', according to Shultz, lies

> in those cases where international rules and traditional practices do not apply. Terrorists will strike from areas where no governmental authority exists, or they will base themselves behind what they expect will be the sanctuary of an international border. And they will design their attacks to take place in precisely those 'gray areas' where the full facts cannot be known, where the challenge will not bring with it an obvious or clear-cut choice of response.[181]

Antony Anghie has argued that preventive war against terrorism may become the vehicle for a new form of 'defensive imperialism'.[182] Indeed, in his memoirs, Shultz notes that the Address before the Park Avenue

---

[177] Shultz, 'Terrorism and the Modern World [Address before the Park Avenue Synagogue New York City on 25 October 1984]' p. 16.

[178] Shultz, 'Low-Intensity Warfare: The Challenge of Ambiguity [Address Before the Low-Intensity Warfare Conference, National Defense University, Washington, D.C., 15 January 1986]' p. 206.

[179] Shultz, 'Terrorism: The Challenge to the Democracies [Address before the Jonathan Institute's second Conference on International Terrorism on 24 June 1984]' p. 33.

[180] *Ibid.*

[181] Shultz, 'Terrorism and the Modern World [Address before the Park Avenue Synagogue New York City on 25 October 1984]' p. 16.

[182] Antony Anghie, *Imperialism, Sovereignty and the Making of International Law* (Cambridge University Press 2004) p. 294.

Synagogue in New York, from which this last quote was taken, caused controversy within the administration. The speech had apparently been circulated within the administration and there had been complaints that he was going too far and that he was setting government policy on his own. Just before it was to be delivered, Shultz had received a message from the office of Vice President George H. W. Bush that the speech 'conveyed a belligerent approach that we would not be able to carry through'.[183] After the speech was delivered journalists apparently asked Bush whether he agreed with Shultz's position and particularly the risk it might pose to civilians. Shultz quotes Bush's reply in his memoirs: 'I think you have got to pinpoint the source of the attack. We are not going to go out and bomb innocent civilians or something of that nature. I don't think we ever get to the point where you kill 100 innocent women and children just to kill one terrorist'.[184] Shultz comments on this reply: 'I agreed, of course, that any action would have to be pinpointed, but the critical proposition was to let terrorists know that action was possible'.[185]

Fear of Indecision and the Need for a Legally Empowered American Executive

A prominent theme in Shultz's public statements on terrorism during the 1980s is the fear that the 'gray areas'[186] or 'ambiguities' constituted by the kind of warfare that terrorists wage[187] risks being met with 'inaction'[188], 'self-paralysis'[189], 'impotence'[190], 'wallowing in self-flagellation or self-doubt'[191], 'confusion'[192] or 'indecisiveness'.[193] In one speech Shultz also

---

[183] Shultz, *Turmoil and Triumph: My Years as Secretary of State* p. 648.
[184] *Ibid.*   [185] *Ibid.* p. 648f.
[186] Shultz, 'Terrorism and the Modern World [Address before the Park Avenue Synagogue New York City on 25 October 1984]' p. 15.
[187] Shultz, 'Low-Intensity Warfare: The Challenge of Ambiguity [Address Before the Low-Intensity Warfare Conference, National Defense University, Washington, D.C., 15 January 1986]' p. 205.
[188] *Ibid.*
[189] Shultz, 'Power and Diplomacy in the 1980s [Address before the Trilateral Commission on 3 April 1984]' p. 15.
[190] Shultz, 'Low-Intensity Warfare: The Challenge of Ambiguity [Address Before the Low-Intensity Warfare Conference, National Defense University, Washington, D.C., 15 January 1986]' p. 205.
[191] Shultz, 'Power and Diplomacy in the 1980s [Address before the Trilateral Commission on 3 April 1984]' p. 16.
[192] Shultz, 'Terrorism and the Modern World [Address before the Park Avenue Synagogue New York City on 25 October 1984]' p. 14.
[193] *Ibid.* p. 17.

airs his fears that Americans' conception of war and peace as distinct phenomena will be an inhibiting factor. In view of this risk Shultz writes: 'We cannot allow ourselves to become the Hamlet of nations, worrying endlessly over whether and how to respond'.[194]

Shultz's cautioning invocation of Hamlet might be understood as a warning to the executive of which he was a part, in particular to Secretary of Defence Caspar Weinberger, with whom Shultz was engaged in a 'battle royal' over the question of an adequate response to the threat of international terrorism.[195] While Weinberger understood terrorism as a danger, he did not conceive of it as a danger in relationship to which the United States should engage its military in war, and certainly not in preventive attacks, as advocated by Shultz. Weinberger understood terrorism to be 'criminal activity – reprehensible criminal activity – but not warfare'.[196] In a speech held at the National Press Club on 28 November 1984 Weinberger would articulate a policy of restraint with regard to the use of US military force abroad, what subsequently would be termed the Weinberger doctrine.[197] In the eyes of Shultz, Weinberger's position is 'a counsel of inaction bordering on paralysis'.[198]

Michael G. Salter has claimed that Hamlet signifies sovereignty in crisis: it dramatises an emphatic disturbance in a presumed constitutional 'normal situation'. The politically potent myth of Hamlet, concerns the 'embodiment of the perils of decision-making, of resolving to make a fateful decision about the practical significance of this exception'.[199] Moreover, Salter writes that the play dramatises Hamlet's character of a non-sovereign sovereign or an indecisive decider:

> The mythic figure of Hamlet teaches us something potentially still relevant about the responsibilities of sovereign decision-making. This is particularly the case within contexts where the comfortably deluded option of remaining indecisive until presented with a perfect, risk-free alternative, one guaranteed to have only predictable and beneficial outcomes, is no option at all. Hamlet's condition of inner torment and prevarication, which occupies the bulk of the play, dramatizes the perennial political truth that

---

[194] *Ibid.* p. 16f.

[195] Shultz, *Turmoil and Triumph: My Years as Secretary of State* p. 650.

[196] Wills, *The First War on Terrorism: Counter-terrorism Policy During the Reagan Administration* p. 30.

[197] Caspar Weinberger, 'The Uses of Military Power' (*PBS*, 1984) www.pbs.org/wgbh/pages/frontline/shows/military/force/weinberger.html accessed 15 May 2015.

[198] Shultz, *Turmoil and Triumph: My Years as Secretary of State* p. 650.

[199] Michael G. Salter, *Law as Politics, Ideology and Strategic Myth* (Abingdon: Routledge 2012) p. 185.

sometimes the worst decisions are those in favour of an indecisive and
irresponsible deferral of decision.[200]

With his policy shift from passive to active defense against terrorism
Shultz shows the kind of personal resolve that at the end of the play would
make Hamlet step up and meet the demands of the situation. At the
same time, and this is very important, Shultz is clearly concerned with a
lack of legal authority to sustain this policy shift, in particular the legal
authority to engage terrorism by military means. This shows how, in the
liberal constitutional state, the question of sovereign authority is not just
a question of decisiveness or of being an effective ruler, as dramatised
in Hamlet, but rather one of law and legal justification. Accordingly,
Shultz reflects upon the unfortunate coincidence of the 'disorderly and
dangerous new world' of which the threat of terrorism forms a part, and
what he refers to as 'a kind of cultural revolution at home', which over
the previous fifteen years had seen a 'web of restrictions on executive
action embedded permanently in [US] laws', particularly concerning war
powers.[201] What Shultz has in mind is in particular the way in which
Congress had seized the initiative on the question of War Powers with the
passing of the 1973 War Powers Resolution.[202] Shultz asserts that the

> micromanagement by a committee of 535 independent-minded individ-
> uals is a grossly inefficient and ineffective way to run any important enter-
> prise. The fact is that depriving the President of flexibility weakens our
> country. Yet a host of restrictions on the President's ability to act are
> now built into our laws and our procedures. Surely there is a better way
> for the President and the Congress to exercise their prerogatives without
> hobbling this country in the face of assaults on the free-world interests
> abroad.[203]

In this way, Shultz links his active defense against terrorism to a need for
the legal empowerment of the American executive to make the sovereign
decision on the terrorist enemy and to deal with him accordingly. Interestingly, in his 1925 book *The Crisis of Parliamentary Democracy*, Carl

---

[200] *Ibid.*
[201] Shultz, 'Terrorism and the Modern World [Address before the Park Avenue Synagogue
New York City on 25 October 1984]' p. 15.
[202] 'War Powers Resolution', P.L. 93–148 [HJ Res. 542], 87 Stat. 555, passed over President's veto 7 November 1973. Published online by the Yale Law School Lillian Goldman
Law Library's Avalon Project at http://avalon.law.yale.edu/20th_century/warpower.asp
accessed 20 May 2015.
[203] Shultz, 'Power and Diplomacy in the 1980s [Address before the Trilateral Commission
on 3 April 1984]' p. 15.

Schmitt refers to the American constitutional context, particularly the views expressed by Alexander Hamilton in the Federalist paper no. 70, as 'the least doctrinaire explanation' of the principle that executive power must be unlimited and 'in the hand of a single man because its energy and activity depend upon that'. He continues: 'Different opinions are useful and necessary in the legislative; but not in the executive, where especially in times of war and disturbance, action must be energetic; to this belongs a unity of decision'.[204] While Shultz, Hamilton and Schmitt prefer if the power to make war is accumulated within the executive, the liberal nature of the US constitution assures a competition of the different branches in acting in the name of 'we the people' by the deployment of military force.[205] Accordingly, the undetermined locus of sovereign authority creates a politics between the different branches and a need for the legal justification of each and every claim to it. Accepting this state of affairs Shultz would give high-ranking lawyers within the American executive the task of creating the legal authority for his active defense against terrorism.

Abraham D. Sofaer, the government lawyer to which we will turn next, is an important actor in the struggle over the legal authority for active defense against terrorism. The way he engages this question reminds us of Schmitt's insistence that as much as extra-legal authority is inconceivable in the liberal constitutional state, sovereignty will still be exercised, even though it will take apocryphal forms.

Abraham D. Sofaer and the Legal Authority for Active Defense

Abraham D. Sofaer was sworn in as Legal Adviser at the Department of State on 10 June 1985. Four days later (June 14) Trans World Airlines (TWA) Flight 847 was hijacked. Then came the hijacking of the *Achille Lauro* cruise ship. These events meant that Sofaer was confronted with the question of both constitutional and international legal aspects of counterterrorism from the very start of his time at the Department of State. Sofaer worked with Shultz on the two hijackings and Shultz wrote in his memoirs that after these experiences he told Sofaer to pursue the issue of counterterrorism 'forcefully'. Shultz continues: 'And he did. By

---

[204] Carl Schmitt, *The Crisis of Parliamentary Democracy* (Ellen Kennedy tr, London and Cambridge, Massachusetts: MIT Press 2000) p. 45.

[205] See Paul W. Kahn, *Political Theology: Four New Chapters on the Concept of Sovereignty* (New York: Columbia University Press 2011) p. 15.

the time we were through, we had had a significant impact on the legal issues that confronted us as we confronted terrorism'.[206]

The Legal Adviser, or 'L' as the office is referred to in the US government, is assigned the task of 'advising the Secretary of State on all legal issues, domestic and international, and with advising all branches of the US government on how to formulate and implement the foreign policies of the United States in accordance with international law'.[207] Stephen M. Schwebel, former Legal Adviser as well as former Judge and President of the ICJ, has referred to the Legal Adviser as the head of 'the most important office in the world for the practice of public international law'.[208]

Significantly, the professional background upon which Sofaer would draw in taking up this task was that of a constitutional lawyer specialising on war powers. At a luncheon session of The American Law Institute on 19 May 1988, Rod Perkins introduced Sofaer by reference to how a book Sofaer had published in 1976, entitled *War, Foreign Affairs and Constitutional Power*, had contributed to his appointment as Legal Adviser:

> In June of 1985 Judge Sofaer was called from the bench by a combination of Kenneth Dam, then the Deputy Secretary of State, and Secretary of State Shultz, who I understand had read Judge Sofaer's distinguished book and kept it on the shelf behind him. So the moral of this story is not one of publish or perish, but of publish and be appointed to high places.[209]

War, Foreign Affairs and Constitutional Power was written on a contract with the American Bar Association, which in 1971 had contracted Sofaer to conduct a study of 'the respective powers under the Constitution of the President and of Congress to enter into and conduct war'.[210] The reason for the American Bar Association commissioning this study was the war in Vietnam, which had set off what the famous scholar of American history Arthur Schlesinger Jr. in the introduction to the book describes

---

[206] Shultz, *Turmoil and Triumph: My Years as Secretary of State* p. 676.

[207] Harold Hongju Koh, 'Foreword: America's Conscience on International Law' in Michael P. Scharf and Paul R. Williams (eds.), *Shaping Foreign Policy in Times of Crisis: The Role of International Law and the State Department Legal Adviser* (Cambridge University Press 2010) xi–xvii at xi.

[208] Schwebel in endorsements for: Michael P. Scharf and Paul R. Williams, *Shaping Foreign Policy in Times of Crisis: The Role of International Law and the State Department Legal Adviser* (Cambridge University Press 2010).

[209] Abraham D. Sofaer, 'Luncheon Address (10 May 1988)' (1988) ALI Meeting Speeches 23 at 26.

[210] Abraham D. Sofaer, *War, Foreign Affairs and Constitutional Power: The Origins* (Cambridge, Massachusetts: Ballinger Publishing Company 1976) p. xiii.

as 'an impassioned constitutional debate in the United States...where the decision to go to war lay under the Constitution; what right the executive had to commit armed forces to hostilities without congressional authorization; what control of the war-making power remained to Congress'.[211] As noted by Schlesinger Jr., in these debates historical argument was ever-present but the knowledge of historical facts sketchy and imprecise.[212] For this reason Sofaer apparently decided that an historical investigation into the way powers relating to war and emergencies had been exercised by the various branches of the American government was needed, an investigation that furthermore would take the British constitutional tradition, the ratification process and the debates among the framers of the constitution into account. The bulk of the text reads as an elaborate account of how a range of military undertakings in the period from 1789 to 1829 found support in constitutional interpretation. One of the findings of Sofaer's study is that despite assertions of various leaders that one branch of government must not intrude on the area of power assigned to another branch, precedents that establish areas of exclusive responsibility in relation to war and emergency powers cannot be found:

> The legislative and executive branches functioned as separate entities, but with powers over the same matters. Each was jealous of its authority, and at times sought to increase its power. But, as Hamilton, Madison and others intended, neither branch prevailed consistently enough to subordinate the other.[213]

This is precisely the situation of undetermined location of sovereign extra-legal authority that Schmitt finds to be a distinctive feature of the liberal constitutional state leaving, in the words of Mariah Zeisberg, 'resources – textual, ideological, and institutional – through which actors occupy various roles, or offices, and in turn use those offices to advance their aims in politics'.[214] In doing so, 'the Constitution creates a politics every bit as much as it creates a legal order'.[215]

Just as Shultz respected Sofaer's work, so Sofaer held Shultz generally, and his call for an active defense against terrorism particularly, in high regard, even before he took up the office of the Legal Adviser. In a recent publication, Sofaer reflects on his path to becoming Legal Adviser: 'I had

---

[211] *Ibid.* p. xvii.   [212] *Ibid.* p. xviii.   [213] *Ibid.* p. xiv.

[214] Mariah Zeisberg, *War Powers: The Politics of Constitutional Authority* (Princeton University Press 2013) p. 8f.

[215] *Ibid.*

read speeches by Secretary Shultz on the need to deal more firmly with terrorism, and I greatly admired his stance on that and other issues. In particular, I agreed with his call for an "active defense" that involved using force to pre-empt attacks'.[216]

If Sofaer's work in constitutional history uncovered overlapping powers and a struggle between the different branches, in his position as Legal Adviser he would attempt to increase the powers of the executive in order to promote unity of decision in the context of Shultz's policy of active defense. This would be done against the backdrop of Shultz's assertions about the 'web of restrictions' on executive action embedded permanently in US law that he claimed had arisen since the 1970s.

During his time as Legal Adviser at the Department of State, Sofaer would identify a number of ways in which law (domestic as well as international) impeded active defense. I claim that the overarching task that Sofaer sets for himself mirrors Carl Schmitt's description of how, when a political community is endangered, law will appear as an undue hindrance, or even a threat to this community's right to self-preservation. However, because of the liberal constitutional state's insistence on an all-encompassing rule of law, the assertion of this right to self-preservation will not take extra-legal but apocryphal forms instead.

We noticed earlier in this chapter that a key to Schmitt's understanding of the exercise of sovereignty in the context of the liberal constitutional state is the distinction between the 'constitution' and 'constitutional laws', the latter denoting the multitude of provisions projected in the document promulgated as the constitution of a state, and the former the concrete political existence of a particular political community or way of life.

I claim Sofaer's legal thinking is characterised by a similar dynamic. This is particularly clear in a speech that Sofaer gave to the staff, faculty and graduate students of the Judge Advocate General (JAG) School of the Army on 4 May 1989, subsequently published in the Military Law Review under the title *Terrorism, The Law, and the National Defense*. In this speech Sofaer stresses the importance of law:

> The law has played – and must continue to play – an important role in marking the limits and conditions on measures used to protect our national security against state-sponsored terror. Many proposed military actions were considered and rejected during recent years on legal grounds. That must and will continue to occur. But the law must not be allowed

---

[216] Sofaer in Scharf and Williams, *Shaping Foreign Policy in Times of Crisis: The Role of International Law and the State Department Legal Adviser* p. 24.

improperly to interfere with legitimate national security measures. In important respects, it is doing so today.[217]

From this follows the undertaking of reviewing areas in which 'unwarranted limitations are being imposed on counter-terrorist actions under both international law and US domestic law' and, furthermore, of 'explain[ing] some of the dangers such limitations may pose'.[218] In this as well as in other statements, Sofaer asserts that this is not a struggle 'against the rule of law, but for a rule of law that reflects our values and methods'. It is a 'battle' to see that the rule of law 'serves the interests of freedom and the civilized world'.[219]

Addressing the JAG lawyers he takes the view that there is a 'special responsibility' on 'lawyers' 'to identify, and to revise or reject unjustifiable legal restrictions on our nation's capacity to protect its security'.[220] This is so because

> State-sponsored terrorism poses a threat to our national security, to which the United States must respond effectively. To succeed in this effort, our nation's policy planners and military strategists are entitled to as much flexibility as possible in combatting an enemy that accepts no limits based on law, but only those imposed by an effective defense.[221]

Guarding Against a 'Web of Restrictions on Executive Action' and Constructing the Presidential Authority to Designate the Terrorist Enemy

In his speech at the JAG school of the Army but also elsewhere, Sofaer highlights how the 1973 War Powers Resolution 'when applied rigidly or unintelligently' creates 'serious obstacles to carrying out lawful and useful military operations against state-sponsored terrorists'.[222]

The War Powers Resolution was a result of the constitutional debates that followed from the war in Vietnam. With tensions in the country running high after the war, Congress recognised that 'as a result of the powers that came to the president by accretion in particular' it had lost powers that it considered belonged to it, including that of war making.[223] Consequently, the War Powers Resolution was the US Congress' attempt at

---

[217] Abraham D. Sofaer, 'Terrorism, the Law and the National Defense' 126 (1989) *Military Law Review* 89 at 90.

[218] *Ibid.*   [219] *Ibid.* p. 122.   [220] *Ibid.* p. 91.   [221] *Ibid.*   [222] *Ibid.* p. 113.

[223] George Schwab, 'The Decision: Is the American Sovereign at Bay?' 16 (1978) Revue Européenne des Sciences Sociales 67 at 75.

regulating the overlapping powers and the struggle between the branches
over sovereign authority and taking back some of the powers it had lost.

The critical questions of sovereignty raised by the resolution are highlighted in a 1978 text entitled *The Decision: Is the American Sovereign At
Bay?* by the American Schmitt scholar George Schwab.[224] Two years after
having published the English translation of *The Concept of the Political*,
Schwab considers the constitutional debates following the defeat in Vietnam in general and the War Powers Resolution in particular and in this
context asks whether

> the resolve to act in the national interest that had in the past characterized
> the people of this huge, rich, and still militarily powerful country has
> not only dissipated considerably but [whether] the country also lacked an
> authority sufficiently effective to turn the switch that electrifies the state
> to act at crucial moments. In other words, the questions posed actually
> revolve around the complex issue of sovereignty.[225]

Addressing the very same Resolution in the context of active defense
against terrorism, Sofaer took the stand on 29 April 1986 in a hearing
before the Subcommittee on Arms Control, International Security and
Science to the House of Representatives Committee on Foreign Affairs.[226]
At the hearing, particular attention was given to the recent US naval
manoeuvres in the Gulf of Sidra as well as the attacks against 'terrorist-
related targets'[227] in Libya just weeks before; operations in which Sofaer
had given legal advice and that we will have reason to return to in what
follows.

Chairman Dante B. Fascell, who had been a co-sponsor of the War
Powers Resolution, opened the hearing with the following statement:

> Clearly, the President's actions against Libya have the strong support of
> the Congress and the American people. However, when we respond with
> military force to state-sponsored terrorism directed against the United
> States, should it not be consistent with our own laws and constitutional
> procedures?[228]

Fascell further emphasised how the matter of the President's authority
to engage the American military in a war against terrorism does not

---

[224] *Ibid.*   [225] *Ibid.* p. 67.

[226] US Congress, 'War Powers, Libya and State-sponsored Terrorism', Hearings before the
Subcommittee on Arms Control, International Security, and Science of the Committee
on Foreign Affairs, House of Representatives, Ninety-ninth Congress, second session, 29
April, 1 and 15 May 1986.

[227] W. Hays Parks, 'Crossing the Line' 4 (1986) US Naval Institute Proceedings 22 at 41.

[228] US Congress, 'War Powers, Libya and State-sponsored Terrorism' p. 1.

only raise questions under the War Powers Resolution but also profound questions concerning the constitutional prerogatives of the President:

> It would appear at the present moment, that what we are confronted with is not only the question of complying with the statutory requirements of the War Powers Resolution, which requires consultation with and report to the Congress, but also the question of whether or not there has not been a broad abrogation and interpretation of the constitutional prerogatives of the Chief Executive. In other words, can the President, as Commander in Chief, take the country to war wherever an act of state-sponsored terrorism has taken place, and do it all under the rubric of saying this is self-defense and every nation has the right to defend itself.[229]

In his statement before the Committee, Sofaer attempts to point out the numerous ways in which the 1973 War Powers Resolution inhibits an effective defence: he points to the fact that Section 2(c) fails to include instances in which the armed forces are used to protect or to rescue Americans from attack, including terrorist attacks, which is the most likely circumstance in which the President would need the authority to use the armed forces in combatting terrorism. The listing also fails to include the use of force to defend against attacks by state-sponsored terrorists on military personnel and equipment of the United States or on other states that the President might decide to assist in defending.[230] A further problem is that the resolution requires the President to consult with Congress 'in every possible instance' before introducing US armed forces 'into hostilities or into situations where imminent involvement in hostilities is clearly indicated by the circumstances'.[231] While this 'in principle' is an 'essential form of cooperation between the President and Congress', the President is responsible 'not only for defending the United States, but also for doing so successfully'.[232] Sofaer asserts that the President must be answerable to Congress for using armed force, 'but not in a manner that jeopardizes his ability to achieve the purposes for which such forces are placed at his disposal'.[233] For this reason, a consultation that would create an unreasonably great risk to life or to the success of a military mission should *not* be considered 'possible'.[234] The resolution furthermore restricts the length of time the President may use the armed forces in a military operation without Congress' approval to sixty days. While a

---

[229] *Ibid.* p. 2.   [230] Sofaer, 'Terrorism, the Law and the National Defense' p. 113.
[231] US Congress, 'War Powers, Libya and State-sponsored Terrorism' p. 5. See also Sofaer, 'Terrorism, the Law and the National Defense'.
[232] Sofaer, 'Terrorism, the Law and the National Defense' p. 114.
[233] *Ibid.*   [234] *Ibid.*

sixty-day limit poses no problem for most counter-terrorist operations, such operations may sometimes have to be sustained beyond sixty days, and in such circumstances a law that places an 'arbitrary time limit could undermine the nation's ability to conduct such operations successfully', according to Sofaer.[235]

Sofaer's conclusion from his review of the setbacks of the War Powers Resolution is neither that it should be amended, taking note of these omissions, nor that it should be repealed by Congress to relieve the President from these dangerous restrictions. Instead, he states,

> It seems fair to say, in conclusion, that it is not clear how the War Powers Resolution, which was originally designed to provide an appropriate role for the Congress with respect to U.S. involvement in hostilities with other states, should apply to the use of U.S. forces in other kinds of situations. Some such situations – the deployment of anti-terrorist units – would seem to fall completely outside the scope of the resolution.[236]

Michael J. Glennon wrote a critical editorial comment in the *American Journal of International Law* apropos of Sofaer's testimony arguing that the legal adviser 'ignores the most fundamental canons of statutory construction – those that require that every word be given effect, that presume Congress not to have enacted a nullity, that prefer an interpretation that saves to one that destroys'.[237] However, Sofaer did not change his mind and in his 1989 speech at the JAG school of the Army, the inapplicability of the War Powers Resolution to counterterrorism operations is explained further. Again pointing to the setbacks of the resolution in relation to counterterrorism operations, Sofaer states: 'In addition to these general difficulties, the Resolution should be regarded as *inapplicable* to ordinary counter-terrorist activities'.[238] This is so because 'counter-terrorist units should not generally be treated as armed forces for this purpose', as counterterrorism activity is 'more analogous to law enforcement activity by police in the domestic context than it is to the "hostilities" between states contemplated by the War Powers resolution'.[239] Furthermore, 'no need exists...for a War Powers Resolution that casts doubt upon the President's traditional and constitutionally-based authority to defend

[235] *Ibid.* p. 115.
[236] US Congress, 'War Powers, Libya and State-sponsored Terrorism' p. 11.
[237] Michael J. Glennon, 'Mr. Sofaer's War Powers "Partnership"' 80 (1986) American Journal of International Law 584 at 585.
[238] Sofaer, 'Terrorism, the Law and the National Defense' p. 115. My emphasis.
[239] *Ibid.*

Americans and American interests from attack without prior legislative approval'.[240]

The fact of the US constitution's undetermined locus of the sovereign authority to make war ensures that there will be no agreement as to whether the right of the President to engage the US military in 'ordinary counter-terrorist activities' is a prerogative that accords with, or one that conflicts with, the constitutional text. Sofaer's take on this matter in the 1986 Congress hearing is that it is 'inherent in the President's authority under the constitution, including his authority as Commander in Chief'. In the question and answer session of the hearing, Senator Berman makes clear that he is not content with the lack of concreteness in Sofaer's references to the President's authority under the constitution. With reference to the introductory statement by Chairman Dante B. Fascell about the consistency of counterterrorism force with US laws and procedures, as well as the specific authorisation of the use of force against terrorist-related targets in Libya, Berman asks:

> Your answer to the question that apparently has been raised over and over again, and perhaps by the chairman, is not clear to me. You say that it is clear that the limited actions undertaken by President Reagan in response to attacks on U.S. citizens fall well within the President's authority under the Constitution, and that authority is?[241]

In response, Sofaer, in addition to the Commander in Chief clause, refers to the 'power over foreign affairs' and 'the power to ensure that the laws of the United States are implemented'.[242]

It is tempting to follow Schmitt and read this exchange between Chairman Fascell, Senator Berman and Legal Adviser Sofaer as one over the 'constitution' in the concrete or existential sense and the normative 'constitutional law', between an absolute concept of the constitution and a relative concept of the constitution, or between a political concept of law and a formal or *Rechtsstaat* concept of law. When Berman requires that the authority of the President to make the decision on the terrorist enemy and deal with him accordingly be supported by 'constitutional law' and Michael J. Glennon complains about Sofaer ignoring the most basic tenets of statutory fidelity and construction, Sofaer's response is to point to the 'constitutionally-based' authority of the President. This is a case in point with regard to the notion of apocryphal sovereignty.

---

[240] *Ibid.* p. 123.
[241] US Congress, 'War Powers, Libya and State-sponsored Terrorism' p. 45. [242] *Ibid.*

As important as these Schmittian insights are to understand the stakes and the dynamics of this exchange it is important to resist Schmitt's tendency to naturalise its outcome and to privilege the 'unity of decision' provided by the executive. In fact, what is played out in Congress can be understood as a testament to the opposite: what Paul W. Kahn refers to as 'the competition over the sovereign voice in American political life', and, I would add, the place of law in that voice.[243] For, as this exchange vividly illustrates, this is not a competition that pits law against sovereignty but one between different politics of law.

On the front lines of that struggle is a specialist in war powers with the role of advising the Secretary of State on all legal issues, domestic and international, and all branches of the US government on how to formulate and implement the foreign policies of the United States in accordance with international law.

In the question and response session that followed his statement before the subcommittee, Sofaer is asked to comment on a pending bill, the 'Anti-Terrorism Act of 1986', which exempts counterterrorism action from the requirements of the War Powers Act and in Section 4(b) grants the President the sweeping authority 'to undertake actions to protect US persons against terrorists and terrorism activity through the use of all such anti-terrorism and counter-terrorism measures as he deems necessary'.[244] Sofaer's response to a question about his views on the bill is revealing:

> We certainly appreciate the intent of those bills and the support that they reflect for the President's policies. We do not think that the passage of those bills is necessary for us to continue doing those essential things in the national interest that are being done so we have no official policy of supporting those bills.[245]

Guarding Against the Protection Afforded by National Borders and Gaining Extraterritorial Access to the Terrorist Enemy

It is important to note that while discussions in Congress focused primarily on the question of constitutional authority, Sofaer's considerations about dangerous and unwarranted limitations on counterterrorism

---

[243] Kahn, *Political Theology: Four New Chapters on the Concept of Sovereignty* p. 15.

[244] US Congress, 'War Powers, Libya and State-sponsored Terrorism' Appendix 6 pp. 218–222. It may be noted that 'persons' refers to both juridical and natural persons in the proposed bill.

[245] *Ibid.* p. 35.

included extensive analysis also of international law. A lesson that Sofaer had learned from dealing with the hijackings of TWA flight 847 and the *Achille Lauro* cruise ship concerns the difficulties of squaring an American active defense against terrorism with an international law premised on the territorial compartmentalisation of the world characteristic of the Westphalian distribution of the right to wage legitimate force. Gregor Noll has formulated this inconvenience in the following way: 'dividing the world into states with power, territory and population, and assigning responsibility for non-state actors within that state network can deny an attacked state direct access to its non-state enemy outside its territory'.[246]

Shultz deemed law enforcement and the passive defence that it entails insufficient for countering international terrorism, suggesting a turn from passive to active defense. At a 1986 Symposium on *Terrorism and the Law*, professor of law and former employee at the Office of the Legal Adviser Christopher L. Blakesley warned against the '"infernal dialectic" of violence' that such a policy path entails:

> It is error of the highest order to accept the ideologues' argument that because some nations or rebel groups participate in oppression and terror-violence, it is inevitable and therefore necessary to combat it with like conduct. Self defense under the rule of law does not include the use of innocent civilians as tools.[247]

Blakesley's prescription of self-defense under the rule of law departs from the fact that international law condemns terrorism and provides ground for all states to assert jurisdiction over its perpetrations and perpetrators.[248] In an article published in 1986 in *Foreign Affairs*, Sofaer effectively debunks such efforts at 'bringing terrorists to justice': how extradition requests are often refused because the offence is characterised as 'political' and therefore exempted from extradition[249]; how the traditional law of piracy was amended with the 1958 Geneva Convention on the High Seas and the 1982 UN Convention on the Law of the Sea, in both cases excluding acts committed for a political purpose from the universal jurisdiction of sovereign states[250]; how 'radical groups' succeeded in

---

[246] Noll, 'Force, Dislocation, Partisanship: An Essay on International Law in the State of the Exceptional' p. 213.

[247] Christopher L. Blakesley, 'Jurisdiction as Legal Protection Against Terrorism' 19 (1987) Connecticut Law Review 895 at 942.

[248] *Ibid.*

[249] Abraham D. Sofaer, 'Terrorism and the Law' 64 (1986) Foreign Affairs 901 at 906.

[250] *Ibid.* p. 911f.

acquiring legal legitimacy in the Geneva Diplomatic Conference on the
Reaffirmation of International Humanitarian Law Applicable in Armed
Conflict, which met between 1974 and 1977, leading to the extension
of the privileges and protection of the law of armed conflict to groups
fighting against colonial domination, alien occupation or racist regimes
(Additional Protocol I)[251]; how the UN Convention Against the Taking
of Hostages precludes extradition to destinations where the suspect is
likely to be unfairly treated, and how it does not apply to the extent that
the 1949 Geneva Conventions and the 1977 additional protocols impose
substantively identical obligations.[252]

However, as much as a Westphalian distribution of the right to exercise legitimate force poses a problem for passive defence measures, it
also severely restricts active defense measures, particularly when they are
understood to require 'absolute deference to the principle of territorial
integrity'.[253]

It should be kept in mind that Shultz's and Sofaer's efforts at devising a
legal authority to engage in active defense coincide with what Christian J.
Tams has referred to as the 'heyday' of a '"restrictive analysis" of the norms
on the use of force: an approach seeking to limit the availability of military
force to the largest possible extent'.[254] Tams writes that a restrictive analysis
represented the mainstream approach to the *jus ad bellum* at this time and
was arguably more dominant than it had been before or would be after.
This restrictive analysis was expressed in influential writings of the time
such as the treatment of Articles 2(4), 39–43, and 51 of the UN Charter
in the first editions of the charter commentaries by Cot and Pellet and
Simma; in the majority of the contributions to Antonio Cassese's 1986 *The
Current Legal Regulations of the Use of Force* and in the 1985 proceedings
of the German Society of International law.[255] Of course, the examples
Tams mentions primarily originate in Europe, but the resolution of the
UN General Assembly calling the 1986 American airstrikes in Libya 'acts
of aggression' reveals that the restrictive approach was not just a European

---

[251] *Ibid.* p. 912ff. This makes for a ready defence in courts when a terrorist criminal may refer
to him- or herself as a combatant engaging in legitimate hostilities, something Sofaer
noted had already occurred in American courts. This was also what the PFLP fighters
attempted in the 1969 case of *Military Prosecutor* v. *Omar Mahmud Kassem and Others*
analysed in Chapter 2.

[252] *Ibid.* p. 915f.   [253] Sofaer, 'Terrorism, the Law and the National Defense' p. 93.

[254] Christian J. Tams, 'The Use of Force Against Terrorists' 20 (2009) European Journal of
International Law 359 at 363.

[255] *Ibid.*

phenomenon.[256] The equally critical resolution of the Security Council calling the 1988 Israeli killing of Khalil el-Wazir in Tunis an 'assassination' as well as an 'act of aggression', as we saw in the previous chapter, also shows that the restrictive approach was not only the dominant general approach to the *jus ad bellum* but, crucially, 'it informed the international community's approach to anti-terrorist force'.[257]

As noted earlier, part of the shift from Westphalian to post-Westphalian international law is the ban on war of the 1928 Kellogg-Briand Pact, subsequently Article 2(4) of the 1945 UN Charter, leaving the inherent right to self-defence in Article 51 of the UN Charter (and its equivalent in customary international law) as the only exception as far as unilateral resort to force is concerned. The tensions created between a conception of sovereignty focusing on protection and this norm restricting the right to self-defence, inter alia, with regard to *who* or *what* can trigger a self-defence measure, and *when* a measure of self-defence may be undertaken, was also noted. This tension is of course even greater when the prevailing view is a restrictive one.

This was a point in time in which the United States was facing the risk of having a restrictive framework for the use of force imposed on it not just as regards counterterrorism measures but also with regard to its military and paramilitary activities in and against Nicaragua.[258] At the 1986 annual meeting of the American Society of International Law (ASIL) Sofaer explained the United States' withdrawal of its acceptance of the Court's compulsory jurisdiction, a decision that was taken on his advice.[259]

> For the United States to recognize that the ICJ has authority to define and adjudicate with respect to our right of self-defense, therefore, is effectively to surrender to that body the power to pass on our efforts to guarantee the safety and security of this nation and of its allies ... interests of a

---

[256] UNGA, 'Declaration of the Assembly of Heads of State and Government of the Organization of African Unity on the aerial and naval military attack against the Socialist People's Libyan Arab Jamahiriya by the present United States Administration in April 1986' (20 November 1986) UN Doc A/RES/41/38.

[257] Tams, 'The Use of Force Against Terrorists' p. 363.

[258] See ICJ, *Case Concerning Military and Paramilitary Activities in and Against Nicaragua* (Jurisdiction and Admissibility) 1984 available at the website of the Court: www.icj-cij .org/docket/files/70/6485.pdf accessed 10 May 2015.

[259] Abraham D. Sofaer, 'The Reagan and Bush Administrations (1985–1990)' in Michael P. Scharf and Paul R. Williams (eds.), *Shaping Foreign Policy in Times of Crisis: The Role of International Law and the State Department Legal Adviser* (Cambridge University Press 2010) 65–86 at 65.

fundamentally political nature, going to our nation's security. Such matters cannot be left for resolution by judicial means, let alone by a court such as the ICJ; rather, they are the ultimate responsibilities assigned by our Constitution to the President and Congress.[260]

Commenting on Sofaer's statement at the meeting Oscar Schachter argued that the US withdrawal could be read as a rejection of the binding character of the principles on force in international law. Schachter understood Sofaer's arguments for American withdrawal as a rather thinly veiled argument for the idea that 'the inherent right of a state to self-defense is a matter for determination by that state alone'.[261]

Now, I claim that the view expressed by Sofaer with regard to interests of a fundamentally political nature going to US national security informs his understanding of the right to self-defence in counterterrorism force. For, granted that the international law of self-defence is accommodated to domestic law and its indeterminate concepts are subject to interpretation of the authority assigned in the American constitution, Sofaer's claim in his 1989 address at the JAG school of the Army that 'the principle of territorial integrity is a major – and proper – legal constraint to taking actions against terrorists or States that support terrorism' makes sense.[262] It makes sense despite the fact that the states in which designated terrorists live, work and train 'are almost invariably unable or unwilling to extradite them' and despite the fact that 'the only possible remedies against such terrorists often would require infringement of the territorial integrity of the State in which they are located'.[263] It makes sense because Sofaer claims: 'territorial integrity is not entitled to absolute deference in international law, and our national defense requires that we claim the right to act within the territory of other States in appropriate circumstances'.[264]

Among the measures Sofaer, in his 1989 JAG school address, considers within the purview of this right are 'attacks on terrorists and terrorist camps'.[265] Here, Sofaer asserts that the United States claims the right to 'strike terrorists within the territory of another State where the terrorists are using that territory as a location from which to launch terrorist attacks and where the State involved has failed to respond effectively to demand that the attacks be stopped'.[266]

[260] Abraham D. Sofaer, 'The United States and the World Court' 80 (1986) Proceedings of the Annual Meeting (American Society of International Law) 204 at 209f.

[261] Oscar Schachter, 'The United States and the World Court' 80 (1986) Proceedings of the Annual Meeting (American Society of International Law) 204 at 211.

[262] Sofaer, 'Terrorism, the Law and the National Defense' p. 106.

[263] *Ibid.*   [264] *Ibid.*   [265] *Ibid.* p. 108.   [266] *Ibid.*

In order to accommodate this right to attack terrorists and terrorist camps on foreign territory with the principle of territorial integrity, Sofaer asserts, 'the United States rejects the notion that the UN Charter supersedes customary international law on the right of self defense'.[267] However, in order to retain the positive nature of the norm of self-defence and at the same time make it responsive to the goal of the United States of being able to defend itself and its allies, a 'principled but practical approach' is adopted in constructing it.[268] This deference to customary international law but also the dynamic approach that Sofaer takes in establishing its content, is the means by which he eases the tension between an active defense against terrorism and the restrictive terms of Article 51 of the UN Charter. With regard to the content of this customary right of self-defence, Sofaer explains, 'we have always construed the phrase "armed attack" in a reasonable manner, consistent with a customary practice that enables any State effectively to protect itself and its citizens from every illegal use of force aimed at the State'.[269]

Furthermore, and stressing that the right to self-defence applies in relation to states and non-state enemies alike, Sofaer writes, 'the United States has long assumed that the inherent right of self defense potentially applies against any illegal use of force, and that it extends to any group or State that can properly be regarded as responsible for such activities'.[270] Finally, Sofaer links this protean inherent right to self-defence to Shultz's active defense:

> A sound construction of article 51 would allow any State, once a terrorist 'attack occurs' or is about to occur, to use force against those responsible for the attack in order to prevent the attack or to deter further attacks unless reasonable ground exists to believe that no further attack will be undertaken. In 1984 Secretary Shultz described this policy as an 'active defense'.[271]

This is not enough, however, because while in conventional war adequate proof of responsibility for an attack rarely presents a problem, in self-defence against terrorism this question is often less clear.[272] Sofaer realises the need for a two-pronged approach on this matter: first, adequate proof of the responsibility of the non-state actor and, second, proof of the

---

[267] *Ibid.* p. 94.
[268] Abraham D. Sofaer, 'International Law and the Use of Force' 82 (1988) Proceedings of the Annual Meeting (American Society of International Law) 420 at 422.
[269] Sofaer, 'Terrorism, the Law and the National Defense' p. 94.
[270] *Ibid.* p. 93.   [271] *Ibid.* p. 95.   [272] *Ibid.* p. 98.

involvement of the state whose borders protect him from American self-defence measures.

With regard to the former, Shultz had already stressed at a 1984 National Security Planning Group meeting that his active defense raised a 'moral issue . . . in that evidence will never be conclusive enough to "win a Supreme Court case." . . . At some point, we have to wrestle with the issue of how "sure" we have to be before we hit back'.[273] Along the same lines, Sofaer considers how in domestic law, aiding and abetting, conspiracy and racketeering charges are widespread and that, 'in protecting our national security the test should be no more exacting'.[274]

In relation to the latter question of state responsibility, Sofaer acknowledges that 'controversy and uncertainty exist as to the extent to which States that protect or support terrorist groups can legally be held responsible for such groups'.[275] Sofaer here contrasts the view of the United States with the 'present widespread acceptance of the premise that States can do virtually anything short of ordering a terrorist act or participating in its execution and still avoid being treated as responsible'.[276]

Interestingly, this was a view that was brought to bear on the United States in the 1986 judgment on the merits in the Nicaragua case.[277] The United States provided the Contras with significant support, including financing for food and clothing, military training, arms and tactical assistance. The court concluded, nonetheless, that the United States did not have 'effective control' over the Contras and therefore did not hold the United States accountable for their actions.[278] Sofaer asserts that 'the United States at no time during the Nicaragua litigation advanced as a defense for its support for the contras the claim that it had no responsibility for their actions' and that this part of the judgment in fact provides support 'for states that assist terrorist groups'.[279] The US position on this question is explained in relation to, inter alia, the 1987 rendition and subsequent prosecution and conviction on conspiracy, aircraft piracy and

---

[273] National Security Planning Group, 'Summary of National Security Planning Group Meeting on Combatting Terrorism', 2 March 1984. Retrieved from The Reagan Files: www.thereaganfiles.com/nspg-meetings.html On file with author. p. 3.

[274] Sofaer, 'Terrorism, the Law and the National Defense' p. 100.

[275] *Ibid.* p. 104.   [276] *Ibid.* p. 100.

[277] ICJ, *Case Concerning Military and Paramilitary Activities in and Against Nicaragua* (Merits) 1986 available at the website of the Court: www.icj-cij.org/docket/files/70/6503.pdf accessed 10 May 2015.

[278] *Ibid.* paras. 115–116.

[279] Sofaer, 'Terrorism, the Law and the National Defense' p. 101.

hostage-taking charges of Fawaz Yunis. Sofaer summarises the judgment by Judge Barrington Parker:

> Nations cannot be permitted to seize terrorists anywhere in the world in an unregulated manner. Governments must act in accordance with international law and domestic statutes. But he said that where a State, such as Lebanon, is 'incapable or unwilling . . . [to] enforce its obligations under the [Montreal] Convention,' or when a government 'harbors international terrorists or is unable to enforce international law, it is left to the world community to respond and prosecute the alleged terrorists.'[280]

Sofaer concludes these considerations of a proposed shift from direct attribution of state responsibility for terrorist crimes to more indirect responsibility in the form of harbouring or being unable or unwilling to extradite by stating, 'the ultimate remedy for [a] State's knowingly harboring or assisting terrorists who attack another State or its citizens is self defense'.[281]

Guarding Against Improper Use of the Statutory Ban on Assassination

Following on from the previous section we may note that Sofaer claims a right to attack 'terrorists and terrorist camps' on foreign territory in self-defence. In this context he raises the question of the legal implications of such use of force, sometimes taking 'the form of an attack aimed at one or more *individuals*'.[282] Sofaer recognises that such conduct invariably leads to allegations of 'assassination', which is prohibited by Executive Order 12333. However, Sofaer continues:

> The standard by which the propriety of such attacks should be judged is the same applied to more general attacks. Attacks aimed at specific individuals potentially involve claims of 'assassination,' which is prohibited by an Executive Order . . . When such attacks are lawful under international law, and therefore are not an 'assassination,' they are often less damaging to innocent persons than bombings and other less discriminate actions. Yet we seem to disfavor such conduct. The U.S. is obliged in principle, by international law and by sound ethics, to utilize the most discriminating measures reasonably possible in exercising self defense.[283]

---

[280] *Ibid.*

[281] *Ibid.* The distinction between direct and indirect responsibility is taken from Vincent-Joël Proulx, *Transnational Terrorism and State Accountability: A New Theory of Prevention* (Oxford: Hart Publishing 2012).

[282] Sofaer, 'Terrorism, the Law and the National Defense' p. 109. My emphasis.

[283] *Ibid.*

Engaging this distinction between unlawful 'assassinations' and the lawful targeting of individual terrorists under international law, Sofaer affirms that the United States 'should not and need not authorize its military personnel or its special forces, any more than its police, to engage in murder for the alleged purpose of advancing our national security'.[284] A ban on assassination is 'legally, militarily and morally sound'. What cannot be permitted, however, is 'the *improper* use of the assassination prohibition to limit or to prevent the legitimate resort to lethal force in defending our nationals and friends'.[285]

We saw earlier how Sofaer argued that no need exists for a War Powers Resolution that casts doubt upon the President's traditional and constitutionally-based authority to defend Americans and American interests from attack without prior legislative approval. Sofaer applies a similar logic in arguing 'no need exists to construe the assassination prohibition in a manner that inhibits the *lawful* exercise of lethal force'.[286]

Sofaer thinks that both the lexical meaning of the term 'assassination' and the historical background of the prohibition supports limiting the use of the term to '*illegal*, politically motivated killing'.[287] Virtually all available definitions of the term 'assassination' include references to 'murder', a 'most serious form of criminal homicide'. They also include the element of killing with a political purpose.[288] Accordingly, Sofaer reasons, the lexical definition would exclude *lawful* killing for political purposes. This corresponds to the historical background of the prohibition, which suggests that it was devised against the backdrop of plots by CIA officials to assassinate foreign leaders '*without express authorization from the President*'. 'No effort was made to justify any of them as an act of self defense or on any other legally sufficient basis'.[289] According to Sofaer, all of the above points to the conclusion that there is no support for 'applying the Executive Order to *lawful* killings undertaken in self defense against terrorists who attack Americans or against their sponsors'.[290]

At this point, Sofaer turns to the law of war, which 'also supports limiting the assassination prohibition to illegal killing'. This is so because 'the most fundamental protection that the law of war extend[s] to combatants is the right to use lethal force against any person who is a legitimate military target'. Furthermore, the law of war accepts the 'harsh' consequence of 'collateral death of noncombatants pursuant to lawful attacks'.[291]

---

[284] *Ibid.* p. 117.   [285] *Ibid.*, my emphasis.   [286] *Ibid.* p. 123. My emphasis.
[287] *Ibid.* p. 118. My emphasis.   [288] *Ibid.* p. 117.
[289] *Ibid.* p. 119. My emphasis.   [290] *Ibid.*, my emphasis.   [291] *Ibid.*

On the matter of the prohibition on assassination Sofaer draws extensively on the 'excellent analysis' of the ban written by W. Hays Parks, entitled *Memorandum of Law: Executive Order 12333 and Assassination*.[292] Parks wrote this memo in his capacity as Chief of the International Law Branch of the International Affairs Division of the Judge Advocate General of the Army. Since Parks' memo was coordinated with the Department of Defence, the CIA, the Office of Legal Counsel of the Department of Justice, the National Security Council Legal Adviser and the Legal Adviser of the Department of State, Sofaer apparently had the opportunity to oversee its drafting or even contribute to it.

As mentioned earlier, Sofaer had given the President legal advice on the operation against terrorist-related targets in Libya in 1986. However, the airstrike planning also involved law of war aspects. The task of dealing with these had been given to W. Hays Parks. This means that Parks had had reason to think through the law of armed conflict implications of engaging terrorism militarily before he wrote his memo on the ban on assassination.

W. Hays Parks and the Lawful Killing of Terrorists under the Law of Armed Conflict

In a career of US government service that spans from the late 1960s to the present, or from the war in Vietnam to the war in Afghanistan, W. Hays Parks has fulfilled a number of significant legal roles within the American military: legal adviser in military operations; US representative in law of war negotiations in New York, Geneva, The Hague and Vienna; contributor to US law of war manuals.[293] He is also a well-regarded teacher

---

[292] *Ibid.* p. 116 footnote 55.

[293] In order to stay close to W. Hays Parks' conception of this area of international law, I will use the term 'law of war' in this section. In a book review published in 1994, Parks explained the fact that he sticks to this term rather than the more commonly used law of armed conflict or International Humanitarian Law (IHL). On the notion of the 'law of armed conflict' his primary concern seems to be that such a language becomes too technical inasmuch as 'war' is still the widely used term for the practice in question even after the point at which war as state policy was prohibited. This goes for general public use as well as in international law treaties and by governments. With regard to the notion of 'humanitarian law of armed conflict' or 'international humanitarian law', in addition to being unduly long and complicated, Parks' concern here is that it simply does not reflect the reality of war as he has experienced it. He explains this in a note of some importance for this investigation: 'The law of war authorizes a combatant to take the life of an enemy combatant; speaking from this reviewer's personal experience of combat service in Vietnam, there is nothing humanitarian about such an act'. (W. Hays Parks, 'Book Review (Review of the Books *Terrorism in War – The Law of War Crimes*

of the law of war and has published extensively on a range of law of war topics.[294]

Throughout his career Parks has emphasised how the law of war does not merely impose constraints but also affords significant privileges to its state subjects.[295] Parks' writing on counterterrorism stretches from the 1980s to the present, and here he also stresses how the law of war affords significant privileges to states. In the memo referred to earlier – the 1989 *Memorandum of Law: Executive Order 12333 and Assassination* – Parks would bring a very significant such privilege to bear on counterterrorism operations: the right to kill the enemy. The memo was written in the context of rewriting the 1956 Army Field Manual 27–10 *The Law of War*, with the aim of ensuring consistency with Executive Order 12333.[296]

Before analysing the content of the memo it might be useful to consider Parks' approach to the question of terrorism and the law of war more generally. Being a law of war lawyer with a keen interest in the history of the field, Parks has asserted that a concept that pre-dates the modern law of armed conflict by many centuries, millennia even, is essential in the context of applying the law of war to the transnational terrorism threat: the principle of 'right authority'.[297]

As Just War theorist James Turner Johnson has explained, while going back all the way to the Roman legal concept of *auctoritas principis*, the concept of right authority found its way into Just War theory by way of

---

by Dobbs Ferry and *Non-Combatant Immunity as a Norm of International Humanitarian Law* by Judith G. Gardam)' 28 (1994) George Washington Journal of International Law and Economics 207 at 207 footnote 1).

[294] In 1987 Parks published an article in the Army Lawyer entitled 'Teaching the Law of War' (W. Hays Parks, 'Teaching the Law of War'(1987) The Army Lawyer 4). In honour of twenty years since its publication the IDF Law Review published 'The W. Hays Parks Symposium on Teaching the Law of War' in which, among others, Parks returned to this topic. W. Hays Parks, 'Teaching the Law of War: A Reprise' 3 (2007) IDF Law Review 9.

[295] This is exemplified by Parks' complaints about overly restrictive rules of engagement in for example, the Rolling Thunder air campaign in Vietnam between 1965 and 1968 (W. Hays Parks, 'Rolling Thunder and the Law of War' 33 (1982) Air University Review 112); in the 1986 airstrikes against terrorist-related targets in Libya (Parks, 'Crossing the Line'); and in the rules of engagement that apply for circumstances of self-defence to all U.S. forces in peacetime (Joint Chief of Staff's Standing Rules of engagement) (W. Hays Parks, 'Deadly Force is Authorized' 127 (2001) US Naval Institute Proceedings 32).

[296] W. Hays Parks, 'Memorandum of Law: Executive Order 12333 and Assassination' (1989) The Army Lawyer 4.

[297] W. Hays Parks, 'Combatants' 85 (2009) International Law Studies Series – US Naval War College 247; W. Hays Parks, 'Jus in Bello in the Struggle Against Terror' in John Norton Moore and Robert F. Turner (eds.), *Legal Issues in the Struggle Against Terror* (Durham, North Carolina: Carolina Academic Press 2010) 359–401.

the need to 'discourage the spread of lawlessness in medieval society by proscribing the use of force for private purposes'.[298] Against this backdrop, the concept came to mean that only those civil authorities that had no formal superior were allowed to authorise the use of force. This was in agreement with 'prevailing medieval political theory, in which right politics aimed at establishing three goods: order, justice and peace':[299]

> Order was conceived as first among these, for without order there would be chaos; without order, just relationships among the members of the political community could not be ensured; and without both order and justice there could be no true peace, for peace meant far more than an absence of violence. This final goal of a good politics envisioned a community in which justice and orderly relations would prevail among men. The use of force for private ends was therefore seen as an attack on the society as a whole.[300]

Johnson further notes that translated into the modern state system the concept of right authority is sovereignty.[301]

A comparison of James Turner Johnson's description of the reasons for the upholding of right authority in mediaeval society given in the foregoing and Parks' 'practical, political and humanitarian' reasons for governments retaining the 'exclusive authority to wage war' throughout the history of the law of war illustrates how war requires right authority, but this authority is legitimised with reference to the violence and disorder that would obtain in its absence.[302]

Parks mentions three reasons in particular for this exclusive authority:

> First is the responsibility of a government to protect its citizens. Second, a desire for stability in international relations necessitates a prohibition of unilateral acts by a civilian or civilians that may lead to war between nations. Third, the prohibition on civilians engaging in combatant acts serves to implement and enforce the law of war principle of *discrimination*.[303]

---

[298] James Turner Johnson, 'Just War Tradition and Low-Intensity Conflict' in Alberto R. Coll, James S. Ord and Stephen A. Rose (eds.), *Legal and Moral Constraints on Low-Intensity Conflict*, vol 67 (Newport, Rhode Island: U.S. Naval War College 1995) 147–169 at 158. Giorgio Agamben deals extensively with *auctoritas principis* in his analysis of the state of exception in Rome: Giorgio Agamben, *State of Exception* (Kevin Attel tr, University of Chicago Press 2005) p. 80ff.

[299] Johnson, 'Just War Tradition and Low-Intensity Conflict' p. 158.   [300] *Ibid.*

[301] *Ibid.*   [302] Bartelson, 'Double Binds: Sovereignty and the Just War Tradition' p. 88.

[303] Parks, 'Jus in Bello in the Struggle Against Terror' p. 361f.

The combatant's privilege represents the *jus in bello* instantiation of the *jus ad bellum* principle of right authority. Parks explains the link between right authority (or sovereignty) and this privilege in the following way:

> The law of war recognizes the combatant's privilege – to lawfully target enemy combatants and civilians while the latter are taking a direct part in hostilities and, conversely, to be targeted by lawful enemy combatants. The law of war denies the combatant's privilege and entitlement to prisoner of war status to private citizens (other than members of a *levee en masse*) who resort to armed violence without government authority. It preserves and protects the centuries-old monopoly of governments to resort to violence in order to provide the greater good to, and protection for, the peaceful civilian population.[304]

What Parks expresses here is that the history of the law of war is also the history of the double bind between authority and force. The Combatant's privilege retains the ability of states to exercise violence against violence in order to control violence.

The concept of right authority or sovereignty, along with its *jus in bello* corollary in the combatant's privilege, are crucial to keep in mind as we now return to Parks' 1989 memorandum on the executive order banning assassination and the lawful killing of terrorists under the law of war.

At the outset Parks notes that while the assassination prohibition certainly is in force, the concept on which it rests – 'assassination' – is not *defined*. From a great many sources Parks distils the meaning of assassination that we saw Sofaer take up in the foregoing: that '*assassination* involves murder of a targeted *individual* for political purposes',[305] but also that assassination includes an element of covertness or surprise.

What Parks refers to as 'assassination in peacetime' provides the point of departure for the analysis. In keeping with the conception of the protection offered by the borders of the sovereign states, and relying on Article 2(4) of the UN Charter for international legal support, Parks notes: 'In peacetime, the citizens of a nation – whether private individuals or public figures – are entitled to immunity from intentional acts of violence by citizens, agents, or military forces of another nation'.[306] Parks continues:

---

[304] Parks, 'Teaching the Law of War: A Reprise' p. 10f.
[305] Parks, 'Memorandum of Law: Executive Order 12333 and Assassination' p. 4. My emphasis.
[306] *Ibid.*

> Peacetime assassination, then, would seem to encompass the murder of a
> private individual or public figure for political purposes . . . Assassination
> is unlawful killing, and would be prohibited by international law even if
> there was no executive order proscribing it.[307]

Under the category 'assassination in wartime', Parks considers the only
exception to this general prohibition in the form of 'lawful acts carried out
by military forces in time of war that do not constitute assassination'.[308]
Very significantly, this exception is further divided into not two but three
levels of military operations: conventional military operations (international armed conflict), counterinsurgency operations (non-international
armed conflict) and peacetime counterterrorist operations.

Referring to all three levels, Parks points to how political assassination
in this context 'takes on a different meaning'. This is so because war,
turning to Clausewitz, is the 'continuation of political activity by other
means'[309] and furthermore, turning to Grotius and Oppenheim, a political activity that involves 'the legalized killing (as opposed to murder)
of the enemy'.[310] Additionally, Parks notes, the death of non-combatants
ancillary to the lawful attack of a combatant or military objective 'is
neither assassination nor otherwise unlawful. Civilians and other non-
combatants who are within or in close proximity to a military objective
assume a certain risk through their presence in or in proximity to such
targets'.[311]

Parks begins his exploration of the three levels of conflict with that
which has always been the primary emphasis of the law of war: international or interstate armed conflicts:

> In conventional war enemy combatants normally wear uniforms, and
> those that are identifiable as belonging in the enemy group are legitimate
> targets at all times, regardless of their duties or activities at the time of
> their attack. Article 23(b) of the fourth Hague Convention of 1907 imposes
> certain constraints in prohibiting assassination, proscription or outlawry
> of an enemy, or putting a price upon an enemy's head, as well as offering
> a reward for an enemy 'dead or alive'. It does not prohibit operations that
> depend on an element of surprise, however.[312]

---

[307] *Ibid.*   [308] *Ibid.* p. 5.

[309] For Schmitt it was more than that: in a footnote in *The Concept of the Political* Schmitt
interprets Clausewitz's expression as meaning that war in fact is the '*ultima ratio* of
the friend-enemy grouping', or, in other words, is inseparable from the idea of political
community. Schmitt, *The Concept of the Political – Expanded Edition* p. 34 footnote 14.

[310] Parks, 'Memorandum of Law: Executive Order 12333 and Assassination' p. 4f.

[311] *Ibid.* p. 5.   [312] *Ibid.*

The practice of states relying on organised partisan forces in the Second World War triggered the 1949 Geneva Conventions' inclusion of this class of fighters in the group of combatants, granted all the criteria set out in Article 4 of the third Geneva Convention are met.[313] Civilians who participate in hostilities but do not fulfil these criteria are, Parks notes, considered unprivileged belligerents. There is no agreement as to the degree of participation necessary to make an individual civilian a combatant and thus subject to attack.[314] Parks continues, 'historically, however, the decision as to the level at which civilians may be regarded as combatants or "quasi-combatants" and thereby subject to attack generally has been a policy rather than a legal matter'.[315]

If one of the characteristics of conventional war is the requirement of soldiers to wear uniforms, counterinsurgency or non-international armed conflicts are characterised by civilians undertaking military activities dressed as civilians 'in order to conceal their presence or movement from the enemy'.[316] The wearing of civilian clothes does not make a guerrilla immune from lawful attack and consequently does not make a lawful attack on a guerrilla an act of assassination. However, Parks writes:

> As with the attack of civilians who have combatant responsibilities in conventional war, the difficulty lies in determining where the line should be drawn between guerrillas/combatants and the civilian population in order to provide maximum protection from attack to innocent civilians. The law provides no precise answer to this problem . . . if a member of a guerrilla organization falls above the line established by competent authority for combatants, a military operation to capture or kill an individual designated as a combatant would not be assassination.[317]

Furthermore, 'a civilian who undertakes military activities assumes a risk of attack, and efforts by military forces to capture or kill that individual would not constitute assassination'.[318]

The third form of 'assassination in wartime', Parks' 'peacetime counterterrorism operations', is particularly interesting. Parks writes that the United States recognises three forms of self-defence: against an actual use of force or hostile act; pre-emptive self-defence against an imminent use of force; and self-defence against a 'continuing threat'.[319] Most importantly, he adds:

---

[313] Geneva Convention Relative to the Treatment of Prisoners of War (12 August 1949) 75 UNTS 135 (Third Geneva Convention).
[314] Parks, 'Memorandum of Law: Executive Order 12333 and Assassination' p. 6.
[315] *Ibid.*   [316] *Ibid.* p. 7.   [317] *Ibid.*   [318] *Ibid.*   [319] *Ibid.*

A national decision to employ military force in self defense against a legitimate terrorist threat would not be unlike the employment of force in response to a threat by conventional forces; only the nature of the threat has changed, rather than the international legal right of self defense. The terrorist organizations envisaged as appropriate to necessitate or warrant an armed response by U.S. military forces are well-financed, highly organized paramilitary structures engaged in the illegal use of force.[320]

Parks particularly singles out self-defence against a 'continuing threat' as 'appropriate to the attack of terrorist leaders who through their actions pose a continuing threat to US citizens or the national security of the United States'.[321]

One crucial aspect of Parks' 'peacetime counterterrorist operations' is that the law of war status of those targeted for assassination is considered only by way of analogy to the 'unprivileged belligerents' of conventional armed conflict or 'guerrilla infrastructure' in the context of counterinsurgency, which in both contexts is already a 'policy' matter rather than a legal one. Accordingly, Parks writes:

> *In a conventional armed conflict*, such individuals would be regarded as unprivileged belligerents, subject to attack, but not entitled to prisoner of war protection or exemption from prosecution for their crimes. Employment of military force against terrorists does not bestow prisoner of war protection upon members of the terrorist organization.[322]

Employing an analogy with counterinsurgency, Parks writes: '*As with an attack on a guerrilla infrastructure*, the level to which attacks could be carried out against individuals within a terrorist infrastructure would be a policy rather than a legal decision'.[323]

I can see two reasons for this turn to law of war application *by analogy* in the context of 'peacetime counterterrorism operations': The first concerns its apparent confusion of peace and war. It appears to be the case that although peacetime counterterrorism operations are considered in the context of the *jus ad bellum* right to self-defence, they are not necessarily part of *jus in bello* armed conflict. Apparently, the law of armed conflict may still apply in such cases, but only the most rudimentary customary principles such as the principle of distinction and the principle of proportionality. The second reason is that terrorists are, in Carl Schmitt's words

---

[320] *Ibid.* p. 7f. [321] *Ibid.* p. 7 footnote 8.
[322] *Ibid.* p. 8 footnote 9. My emphasis. [323] *Ibid.* p. 7 footnote 8. My emphasis.

in *Theory of the Partisan*, 'outside the law', are 'particularly gruesome criminal[s]'.[324]

In order to get a better understanding of this last point in particular it might be useful to consider US practice with regard to the law of war status of designated terrorists at the time. As already mentioned, Parks provided legal advice focusing on law of war aspects in the 1986 US attacks against 'terrorist-related targets' in Libya. In a 1986 article entitled *Crossing the Line* and published in the November 1986 issue of the *Proceedings* of the US Naval institute, Parks reflects on this military operation.[325] By way of introduction he writes that the prospect of a military response to terrorism originating from Qadhafi's Libya brings into play, in addition to considerations of self-defence, 'another area of international law – the law of war'.[326]

Interestingly, although considered an act of self-defence by the United States, neither Libya nor the United States seems to have regarded the circumstances of the airstrikes as amounting to an armed conflict.[327] Yet as mentioned, the law of war was 'brought into play'.[328] Parks acknowledges that this includes certain responsibilities such as the obligation to 'minimize collateral civilian casualties', but at the same time 'it is neither a suicide pact nor a one-way street. It also establishes certain rights that serve as important planning factors for any combat operation'.[329] First among the rights listed by Parks is an instantiation of the combatant's privilege: 'a legitimate target may be attacked at any time, wherever it is located'.[330]

When Parks brings this first right to bear on the targeting of terrorism-related targets in conjunction with the obligation to minimise collateral civilian casualties, it reads like this:

> *Although terrorists are not protected by the law of war,* the tendency of terrorist organizations to use the civilian population as a shield from attack places a nation such as the United States under a law of war obligation to

---

[324] Schmitt, *Theory of the Partisan: Intermediate Commentary on the Concept of the Political* p. 10. See also G. L. Ulmen, *Translator's Introduction* to *Theory of the Partisan – Intermediate Commentary on the Concept of the Political,* by Carl Schmitt (New York: Telos Press Publishing 2007) p. xixf.

[325] Parks, 'Crossing the Line'.   [326] *Ibid.* p. 46.

[327] Jennifer K. Elsea, *Memorandum: Legal Issues Related to the Lethal Targeting of U.S. Citizens Suspected of Terrorist Activities* (CRS Report for Congress 2012), published online by the Federation of American Scientists: www.fas.org/sgp/crs/natsec/target.pdf accessed 10 May 2015 p. 7.

[328] Parks, 'Crossing the Line' p. 46.   [329] *Ibid.* p. 47.

[330] *Ibid.,* see also W. Hays Parks, 'Lessons From the 1986 Libya Airstrike' 36 (2002) New England Law Review 755.

take reasonable efforts to minimize collateral injury to innocent civilians in responding to terrorism.[331]

Now, this would appear to entail that terrorists are, as far as targeting is concerned, included in the law of war solely as legitimate targets.

This brings us back to Parks' 1989 memo on the executive order banning assassination, because if terrorists are unprotected by the law of war, yet legitimate targets, as both the memo and US practice at the time shows, there is no duty to capture rather than kill and whereas in some circumstances it might be preferable to use ground forces to capture a known terrorist, in other circumstances

> if the President has determined that the individual(s) in question pose such a threat to U.S. citizens or the national security interests of the United States as to require the use of military force, it would be legally permissible to employ (e.g.) an airstrike against that individual or group rather than attempt his, her, or their capture, and would not violate the prohibition on assassination.[332]

The conclusion of Parks' investigation is noteworthy for its extension of a right to use military force against individuals or groups that pose a threat to US citizens or national security not just in time of war but also in time of peace, as well as for its emphatic claim that this does not constitute assassination:

> Clandestine, low visibility or overt use of military force against legitimate targets in time of war, or against *similar targets* in time of peace where such individuals or groups pose an immediate threat to United States citizens or the national security of the United States, as determined by competent authority, does not constitute assassination or conspiracy to engage in assassination, and would not be prohibited by the proscription in EO 12333 or by international law.[333]

After having been signed by the Army's Judge Advocate General, Parks' memo was provided to the House and Senate Intelligence Oversight Committees and was published in the State Department's volume of significant international law documents: the *Cumulative Digest of United States in International law 1981–1988*.[334]

---

[331] Parks, 'Crossing the Line' p. 46. My emphasis.
[332] Parks, 'Memorandum of Law: Executive Order 12333 and Assassination' p. 7 footnote 6.
[333] *Ibid.*, my emphasis.
[334] W. Hays Parks, 'The Laws of War, Methods and Means of Combat, Assassination and the Law of War' in Marian Nash (ed.), *Cumulative Digest of United States in International Law 1981–1988*, vol. 3 (Office of the Legal Adviser, Department of State 1993) 3411–3421.

Concluding these considerations of the lawful killing of terrorists in application of the law of war, I want to turn to the question of how they fit into the broader picture of the law and policy of active defense considered so far in this chapter. This seems particularly important since I see in these developments the refashioning of the binaries of peace and war and internal and external affairs that is at the core of the international legal regulation of the exercise of legitimate force.

This refashioning takes place when Shultz notes that in order to succeed in his plea for a shift from passive to active defense against terrorism, the idea of war and peace as distinct phenomena would have to be overcome. It can further be noticed when Sofaer, in the context of constructing the constitutional authority for the executive to designate the terrorist enemy and deal with him accordingly, circumvents the War Powers Resolution with reference to the claim that extraterritorial counterterrorism operations are more analogous to law enforcement activity by police in the domestic context than they are to the hostilities between states contemplated by this law. It can also be observed in Sofaer's overcoming of the inconvenience of a Westphalian distribution of the right to exercise legitimate force and his construction of a theory of self-defence that accommodates pre-emptive attacks on terrorists and terrorist camps. Finally it is noticeable in W. Hays Parks' consideration of '*peacetime* counterterrorism operations' within the context of '*wartime* assassination' and the theory and practice of *jus ad bellum* self-defence measures without necessarily being linked to *jus in bello* armed conflict, in the context of the lawful killing of terrorists in application of the law of war. Against this background it may be worth asking whether an attack on a designated terrorist or terrorist camp in another state's territory, in the absence of an armed conflict with that state, is an attack against an internal or an external enemy.

From Words to a Deed, Concept and Tool

Even though Shultz successfully made active defense official government policy with the passing of NSDD 138 and also facilitated the development of the necessary domestic as well as international legal justification for it, active defense would by and large fail to be put into practice during his time at the Department of State.

To be sure, the American response to the *Achille Lauro* hijacking in 1985 and attacks against terrorist-related targets in Libya in 1986 following the La Belle Disco bombing in Berlin showed that the Reagan government was willing to use military force in response to acts of terrorism. In the case of

Libya, Reagan had even referred to the actions taken by the United States as 'pre-emptive action against terrorist installations', which, in and of itself, could be interpreted as a victory for Shultz's active defense.[335] However, the perception among participants in these developments was that, as far as Shultz's push for the proactive use of military force was concerned, he had failed. David C. Wills quotes Noel Koch (Principal Deputy Assistant Secretary of Defence for International Security Affairs in the Reagan administration) who maintains that Shultz's active defense represented a 'quantum leap in countering terrorism' but that it nevertheless 'was simply ignored. No part of it was ever implemented'.[336] Wills writes that the reason for this was that 'the bureaucracy never wholly embraced the proactive approach'.[337]

This failure notwithstanding, it would be a mistake to think that current American targeted killing practices are not indebted to Shultz's active defense in terms of both law and policy. This is something that the continued investigation in this chapter will show, but it is also something that Shultz, Sofaer and Parks themselves would point out once the tide had shifted in favour of active defense against terrorism in general and the extraterritorial killing of designated terrorists in particular.[338]

Although clearly not the most significant in terms of impact, a letter to the editor of *The Washington Post* by W. Hays Parks in reaction to the *Post*'s coverage of the killing of Osama bin Laden on 2 May 2011 may serve as an example. In his letter, Parks commends the *Post*'s reportage as well written but objects to 'the story refer[ing] to the deadly attacks as an "assassination"', adding: 'It was not'. Parks validates this by pointing to his 1989 memorandum and by enumerating the various parts of the US

---

[335] Ronald Reagan, 'Speech to the Nation on Air Strikes Against Libya' (*White House*, 14 April 1986) http://millercenter.org/president/reagan/speeches/speech-5864 accessed 10 May 2015. Shultz comments on the Libya attack in his memoirs: Shultz, *Turmoil and Triumph: My Years as Secretary of State* p. 687f.

[336] Wills, *The First War on Terrorism: Counter-terrorism Policy During the Reagan Administration* pp. 84 and 87.

[337] *Ibid.*

[338] See for example, George P. Shultz, 'A More Accountable World?' 13 (2002) Mediterranean Quarterly 1; Abraham D. Sofaer, 'Terrorism as War' 96 (2002) Proceedings of the Annual Meeting (American Society of International Law) 254; Abraham D. Sofaer and Paul R. Williams, 'Doing Justice during Wartime' 111 (2002) Policy Review 3; Abraham D. Sofaer, 'On the Necessity of Pre-emption' 14 (2003) European Journal of International Law 209; Abraham D. Sofaer, The Best Defense? Legitimacy & Preventive Force (Stanford, California: Hoover Institution Press 2010); Parks, 'Combatants'; Parks, 'Jus in Bello in the Struggle Against Terror'; Abraham D. Sofaer, 'Playing Games with Terrorists' 36 (2002) New England Law Review.

government that he coordinated it with and the fact that it was signed and submitted to the House and Senate Intelligence Oversight Committees and published in the Cumulative Digest of significant international law documents. On the question of substance he makes the following succinct remark:

> Assassination is murder committed for political purposes. The killing of enemy military personnel in time of armed conflict is not assassination. Nor is it assassination to attack the leadership of armed non-state actors such as Osama bin Laden who have been and remain engaged in planning and executing armed attacks against a sovereign state. Because bin Laden was a lawful target, the attack was neither murder nor assassination.[339]

I have already considered some of the reasons why Shultz's active defense failed to be put into practice. Among other things there were concerns about the 'standard of proof' for making a decision on the question of whom to direct the consequential military force against. Secretary of Defence Weinberger clearly thought that Shultz, with his understanding that the kind of evidence that can stand up in an American court of law would not be required, had gone too far in lowering this standard. Weinberger held that Shultz's approach was analogous to firing a gun in a crowded theatre in the slim hope of hitting the guilty party.[340] Questions were also raised with regard to the extent to which collateral damage could be accepted in directing military force against terrorists. Here the point made by George H. W. Bush comes to mind that it is necessary to

---

[339] W. Hays Parks, 'Washington Post Opinions: Reaction to Post Coverage of bin Laden's death' *The Washington Post* (6 May 2011) www.washingtonpost.com/opinions/reaction-to-post-coverage-of-bin-ladens-death/2011/05/02/AFMTojCG_story.html accessed 10 May 2015. Some years before Abraham D. Sofaer had made a similar point in the press stressing that 'it is essential not to allow loaded rhetoric to obscure the propriety of lawfully using deadly force in self-defense. When people call a targeted killing an "assassination," they are attempting to preclude debate on the merits of the action. Assassination is widely defined as murder, and is for that reason prohibited in the United States by executive order. U.S. officials may not kill people merely because their policies are seen as detrimental to our interests, and properly so. But killings in self-defense are no more "assassinations" in international affairs than they are murders when undertaken by our police forces against domestic killers. Targeted killings in self-defense have been authoritatively determined by the federal government to fall outside the assassination prohibition'. Abraham D. Sofaer, 'Responses to Terrorism: Targeted Killing is a Necessary Option' *SFGatecom* (26 March 2004) www.sfgate.com/opinion/openforum/article/Responses-to-Terrorism-Targeted-killing-is-a-2775845.php accessed 15 May 2015.

[340] Wills, *The First War on Terrorism: Counter-terrorism Policy During the Reagan Administration* p. 30.

pinpoint the source of the attack and that one should never get to the point where one kills hundred innocent women and children just to kill one terrorist. Also relevant here is Shultz's response, in his biography, that any action would have to be pinpointed, but the critical proposition is to let terrorists know that action is possible.

In what follows I will consider the transition of active defense against terrorism from words to a deed, concept and tool. As mistaken as it would be not to see how the contemporary American targeted killing scheme is indebted to the developments in the 1980s considered so far, a lack of attention to developments in the years between Shultz's time at the Department of State and 9/11 would be equally mistaken. In the late 1990s, under the presidency of Bill Clinton, steps toward a more proactive counterterrorism practice were taken. This shift would reveal the military- and intelligence-related difficulties involved in a proactive counterterrorism practice, cause a debate on the strategic repercussions of engaging terrorism by military means, reignite the controversy over legal authority and cause the frantic development of a particular military technology to be used for intelligence *and* for striking terrorists on foreign territory: the Predator unmanned aerial vehicle. Moreover, this is the context in which Sofaer's and Parks' efforts at interpreting Executive Order 12333 in a way that did not limit or prevent the legal and legitimate use of discriminate lethal force in countering terrorism would be linked to the concept of 'targeted killing'. That this would occur against the backdrop of the allegedly new kind of terrorism that al-Qaeda represents gives us reason to consider whether the failure of implementation of active defense in the 1980s was related to the fact that war was declared against, as Jenkins put it in 1984, 'an unspecified terrorist foe, to be fought at an unknown place and time with weapons yet to be chosen'. For each of these elements would materialise during the course of the 1990s.

Attempts to Kill Osama bin Laden in Afghanistan

Characterising terrorism as 'a potential threat to national security as well as a criminal act' and noting that 'all appropriate means to combat it' will be applied, the 1995 partly unclassified Presidential Decision Directive 39 *US Policy on Counterterrorism* is still somewhat reactively oriented:

> It is the policy of the United States to deter, defeat and respond vigorously to all terrorist attacks on our territory or against our citizens, or facilities, whether they occur domestically, in international waters or airspace or on

foreign territory . . . In doing so, the U.S. shall pursue vigorously efforts
to deter and pre-empt, apprehend and prosecute, or assist other governments to prosecute, individuals who perpetrate or plan to perpetrate such
attacks.[341]

Even so, starting in 1997, American authorities were beginning to go after
the leader of an organisation known as al-Qaeda, Osama bin Laden, in a
way that broke new ground in terms of the proactive use of military force.

The first attempt at capturing Osama bin Laden in Afghanistan was
in 1997. The responsible authority was the CIA but it would not be CIA
operatives who captured bin Laden but one of the agency's contacts in
Afghanistan, a group associated with tribes among Afghanistan's ethnic
Pashtun community. Apparently, the Justice Department was moving
towards indicting bin Laden, making possible a criminal trial in a New
York court.[342] The capture operation was never realised because decision-
makers considered the risk to the 'tribal assets', as well as other civilians,
too high. Furthermore, they were worried that 'the purpose and nature
of the operation would be subject to unavoidable misinterpretations –
and probably recriminations – in the event that bin Laden despite our
best intentions and efforts, did not survive', that is it could be seen as an
assassination.[343] After cancellation of this covert action, inquiries were
made into possibilities for military action and there was a proposal from
the Pentagon to strike eight terrorist camps in Afghanistan with cruise
missiles.[344]

Soon after the almost simultaneous 1998 bombings of the US embassies
in Nairobi, Kenya and Dar es Salaam, Tanzania, and after responsibility
was 'firmly fixed' on bin Laden and his associates, there was information
about 'terrorist leaders' gathering at a camp near Khowst, Afghanistan. A
consensus on attacking the gathering was reached. 'The strike's purpose
was to kill Bin Ladin and his chief lieutenants'.[345] A pharmaceutical plant
in Sudan, al-Shifa, was also attacked. Twenty to thirty people in the
camps were killed but the attack 'probably missed Bin Ladin by a few
hours'.[346] Since the missiles would have to fly over Pakistan, the Pakistani

---

[341] National Security Council, 'U.S. Policy on Counterterrorism', Presidential Decision Directive 39, signed by President Bill Clinton on 21 June 1995. Published online by the Federation of American Scientists: www.fas.org/irp/offdocs/pdd/pdd-39.pdf accessed 10 May
2015.

[342] National Commission on Terrorist Attacks upon the United States, *The 9/11 Commission
Report: Final Report of the National Commission on Terrorist Attacks upon the United States*
(1st edn, New York: W.W. Norton & Company 2004) p. 111.

[343] *Ibid.* p. 114.   [344] *Ibid.* p. 116.   [345] *Ibid.*   [346] *Ibid.* p. 117.

government had to be informed in order to prevent them from thinking that the missiles came from India, and speculations went in the direction that 'one or another Pakistani official might have sent a warning to the Taliban or Bin Ladin'.[347] In a letter to the Security Council President it was stated that the United States had exercised its inherent right to self-defence in accordance with Article 51 of the Charter, responding to armed attacks against US embassies and nationals.[348]

The military strikes in Afghanistan and Sudan were considered a dangerous mistake in some quarters. An editorial in *The Economist* feared that they 'created 10,000 new fanatics where there would have been none'.[349] Among the disadvantages of the strike, according to a 1999 Sandia National Laboratories (a contractor for US Department of Energy) report, were that

> by mirror imaging aspects of al Qaeda's own attacks (they bombed targets in independent third-world countries without concern for the sensitivities of the nations involved and we bombed targets in independent third-world countries with a similar disregard for the nations involved), we may have only muddied moral distinctions and given away the moral high-ground.[350]

Others made a different assessment. Richard Clarke (Counterterrorism coordinator and later Special Advisor for the National Security Council for the better part of the 1990s and early 2000s) hoped that they 'would mark the beginning of a sustained campaign against Bin Ladin'.[351]

In addition to approving the bombing, Clinton had asked for 'an overall plan to deal with al Qaeda'.[352] The team around Richard Clarke proceeded to write a 'Politico-military plan' or a Pol-Mil. Clarke writes,

---

[347] *Ibid.*

[348] UNSC, 'Letter from the Permanent Representative of the United States of America to the United Nations addressed to the President of the Security Council' (20 August 1998) UN Doc S/1998/780. The reactions of states are summarised in UNSC, 'International Political Relations' (1998) United Nations Yearbook 1219.

[349] Editorial, 'Punished and be Damned' *The Economist* (27 August 1998) www.economist.com/node/162475 accessed 10 May 2015.

[350] Sandia National Laboratories, 'Osama Bin Laden: A Case Study' (1999), published online by George Washington University: www2.gwu.edu/~nsarchiv/NSAEBB/NSAEBB253/sandia.pdf accessed 10 May 2015 p. 23.

[351] National Commission on Terrorist Attacks upon the United States, *The 9/11 Commission Report: Final Report of the National Commission on Terrorist Attacks upon the United States* p. 119.

[352] Richard A. Clarke, *Against All Enemies: Inside America's War on Terror* (New York: Free Press 2004) p. 185.

'to express the intent of the Pol-Mil plan for al Qaeda, I borrowed a phrase from Cato the Elder, Roman Senator and famous orator who in 201 B.C.E. had encouraged war by ending every speech with the line "Carthage must be destroyed", or as Cato would have said it, "Carthago delenda est"'. The Politico-Military plan for al-Qaeda was named 'Top Secret Delenda'.[353] Clarke acknowledged that 'destroying al Qaeda would require a multifaceted, detailed plan'. Some of the tasks he set out for the intelligence agencies were to 'identify and break up al Qaeda's cells, find its money, train and arm its enemies, and eliminate its leaders'.[354] While there was agreement that there should be less focus publicly on Osama bin Laden and more focus on the al-Qaeda network, one of the first steps on the path towards the destruction of al-Qaeda 'was to eliminate its leader'.[355] Apparently, 'the military component of Clarke's plan was its most fully articulated element. He envisioned an ongoing campaign of strikes against Bin Ladin's bases in Afghanistan or elsewhere, whenever target information was ripe'.[356]

For this purpose the Defence Department was asked to keep submarines with cruise missiles off the Pakistani coast. This brought the timeframe from the time the order was given to impact somewhere in Afghanistan down to about six hours.[357] With this plan the task for the CIA was, as described in a *Washington Post* article, 'to place him [bin Laden] inside the explosive radius of a warhead at a precise time at least six hours in the future'.[358]

Although on at least three occasions preparations for such acts were made (and on all occasions were approved by President Clinton), no further cruise missile attacks would be launched against bin Laden. As expressed by an 'intelligence official' cited in *The Washington Post*, 'cruise missiles are excellent weapons for shooting at fixed targets, but they're not so good at targets that have a mind of their own'.[359] Other options were also put on the table only later to be shelved, such as the deployment of attack aircrafts and ground troops.[360]

[353] *Ibid.* p. 196f.   [354] *Ibid.* p. 197f.   [355] *Ibid.* p. 198.

[356] National Commission on Terrorist Attacks upon the United States, *The 9/11 Commission Report: Final Report of the National Commission on Terrorist Attacks upon the United States* p. 120.

[357] Barton Gellman, 'Broad Effort Launched After '98 Attacks' *The Washington Post* (19 December 2001) www.washingtonpost.com/wp-dyn/content/article/2010/03/11/AR2010031102582.html accessed 10 May 2015.

[358] *Ibid.*   [359] *Ibid.*

[360] National Commission on Terrorist Attacks upon the United States, *The 9/11 Commission Report: Final Report of the National Commission on Terrorist Attacks upon the United States* p. 134ff.

Introducing the Targeted Killing Concept

The cruise missile attacks in Afghanistan and Sudan and other indications of the US government's intentions to kill bin Laden reinvigorated the debate about the legal authority of such action. An article in the *Los Angeles Times* dated September 1998 written by Paul Richter reports on influential Democrats having joined Republicans in 'asking whether the broad and vaguely worded Executive Order [12333] should be revised, perhaps to allow targeted attacks on terrorist leaders or greater latitude for opposition groups allied with the United States to strike at a common enemy'.[361] One of the influential Democrats mentioned in the article is Joseph R. Biden, who would later become the Vice President of the United States, but at the time was the ranking minority member of the Senate Foreign Relations Committee. Biden had apparently written to Attorney General Janet Reno seeking a clarification of what the order permitted.[362] Apparently, there would be no reason for Biden to take legislative steps to revise the executive order banning assassination because a little more than a month later the *Los Angeles Times* published another article by Paul Richter opening with the Clinton administration's contention 'that it has a legal right to use deadly force against terrorist leaders such as Islamic extremist Osama bin Laden, despite a 23-year-old presidential ban on assassinations'.[363] Further on in the article it is explained that this 'prerogative arises from a fundamental right of national self-defense'.[364] In relation to 'the link between the right of self-defense and the use of lethal force against individuals', the information provided by the Los Angeles Times reporter clearly relies on the memo written by W. Hays Parks (although his name is nowhere mentioned).[365] An excerpt from the concluding section of Parks' memo is even quoted: '"The clandestine, low visibility, or overt use of force against legitimate targets in time of war, or against similar targets in time of peace where such individuals or groups pose an immediate threat . . . does not constitute assassination," the memo states'.[366]

Apparently sources within the administration provided the reporter with conflicting views about how Parks' memo was perceived in the

---

[361] Paul Richter, 'Congress Ponders Whether the U.S. Should Ease Ban on Assassinations' *Los Angeles Times* (18 September 1998) http://articles.latimes.com/1998/sep/18/news/mn-24038 accessed 10 May 2015.

[362] *Ibid.*

[363] Paul Richter, 'White House Justifies Option of Lethal Force' *Los Angeles Times* (29 October 1998) http://articles.latimes.com/1998/oct/29/news/mn-37327 accessed 10 May 2015.

[364] *Ibid.*   [365] *Ibid.*   [366] *Ibid.*

American executive at the time. Some sources apparently played down its significance, noting that it was drafted nine years ago 'and may not fully reflect current administration thinking', while other officials expressed that 'the administration concurs with its basic view on the right of self-defense', specifically noting that the memo would be included in a 'new reference manual spelling out the law of war for the military services'.[367]

These debates about the legal authority for killing Osama bin Laden in Afghanistan provide the context for the introduction of the targeted killing concept in US counterterrorism discourse. The first article, as far as I can tell, in which the targeted killing concept is used in this context was published in the year 2000. In this article, Mark Vincent Vlasic considers the legality of state-sponsored assassination, concluding, 'those who think the United States is legally prohibited from engaging in what is commonly known as assassination are wrong'.[368] This is not what is most significant about the article however; what is, is that Vlasic, referring to both Sofaer and Parks, *names* the *lawful* counterpart to unlawful assassination 'targeted killing'. Vlasic writes:

> The failure of EO 12333 to define the term assassination has permitted U.S. officials to interpret its prohibition in a very restrictive manner. The current legal guidance seems to allow the United States to conduct the *targeted killing* of individuals during a period of armed conflict or when such individuals pose a threat to U.S. national security.[369]

Vlasic later explains the rationale of his own and others' use of the targeted killing concept in the following way: 'unlike assassination which carries the connotation of illegality, the legality of a particular targeted killing must be determined by looking at the applicable legal framework'.[370] Even though neither of them coined the concept of 'targeted killing', and Parks has even expressed that the term is unfortunate,[371] I want to stress the

---

[367] *Ibid.* That would be the Joint Services Law of War Manual that was proposed in 1995 and in the development of which Parks had a key role. See: W. Hays Parks, 'Update on the DOD Law of War Manual' American Bar Association 22nd Annual Review of the Field of National Security Law, Ritz Carlton Hotel, Washington DC, 30 November 2012, published online by the Lawfare blog: https://lawfare.s3-us-west-2.amazonaws.com/staging/s3fs-public/uploads/2012/12/Parks.Manual.pdf accessed 15 May 2015.

[368] Mark Vincent Vlasic, 'Cloak and Dagger Diplomacy: The U.S. and Assassination' 95 (2000) Georgetown Journal of International Affairs 95 at 95.

[369] *Ibid.* p. 98. My emphasis.

[370] Mark Vincent Vlasic, 'Assassination & Targeted Killing: A Historical and Post-bin Laden Legal Analysis' 43 (2012) Georgetown Journal of International Law 259 at 268.

[371] W. Hays Parks, 'Perspective and the Importance of History' 14 (2012) Yearbook of International Humanitarian Law 361 at 378.

importance of Shultz's, Sofaer's and Parks' contributions, in the 1980s, for the introduction of the terminology of targeted killing in the American counterterrorism context. One might understand the relationship between these efforts and the emergence of the targeted killing concept in terms of the fact that the creation of a legal basis for the extraterritorial pre-emptive killing of designated terrorists is also the creation of a potentiality for *naming* such killings. As we have seen, a new concept is particularly important when competing concepts such as 'assassination' and 'extrajudicial killing' have a discrediting normative connotation. Naturally, this does not give us an answer to the question: why, specifically, the term 'targeted killing'? As 'targeting' is a term of art in the law of armed conflict, one suspects that the part played by the law of war in legalising these killings might have something to do with the matter.[372] Might it be a case of the poor English translation of the Hebrew *Sikul Memukad* and the communication between Israeli and American counterterrorism law and policy? Might it be related to the wider shift in governance that Valverde and Mopas refer to as 'targeted governance' and that is 'linked to the idea of efficient, apolitical, knowledge-driven "evidence-based" policy', which they claim is exemplified by the use of smart drugs, smart bombs, targeted social programmes and targeted policing?[373]

A New Tool for Targeted Killing: The Predator Drone

Even though questions of legal authority were apparently still on the table and despite the fact that Clinton, along with his National Security Advisor Sandy Berger, expressed concern that unsuccessful attacks could 'enhance his [bin Laden's] stature and win him new recruits'[374], the main

---

[372] It should be mentioned that the term appears once in an article by Michael N. Schmitt from 1992. In this context it appears to be a consequence precisely of the particular understanding of the notion of 'targeting' in military doctrine and in the law of armed conflict. Schmitt writes in the first footnote of the piece: 'In military parlance, a "target" is a specific object of attack, and "targeting" involves directing operations toward the attack of a target. This article uses these terms in the context of assassination' (Michael N. Schmitt, 'State-Sponsored Assassination in International and Domestic Law' 17 (1992) Yale Journal of International Law 609 at 610).

[373] Mariana Valverde and Michael Mopas, 'Insecurity and the Dream of Targeted Governance' in Wendy W. Larner and William Walters (eds.), *Global Governmentality* (Abingdon: Routledge 2004) 233–250 at 245.

[374] National Commission on Terrorist Attacks upon the United States, *The 9/11 Commission Report: Final Report of the National Commission on Terrorist Attacks upon the United States* p. 120.

reason why we did not see more attempts to kill him appears to have been practical: the problem of knowing when and where to strike and actually possessing the ability to do so. A technological solution to this problem was eagerly sought in the late 1990s and early 2000s. The task has been described as 'getting reliable American eyes on Bin Laden in a way that would reduce the lag time between sighting and striking'.[375] One idea was to place a long-range telescope high up on a mountain but in range of one of bin Laden's training camps. This idea was abandoned as too risky. Another was to deploy one of the Defense Department's Predator unmanned aerial vehicles, or drones, over Afghanistan. After the first test-flight Richard Clarke clearly saw the potential of this technology and apparently suggested that even if bin Laden were not found, Predator missions might identify additional worthwhile targets, such as other al-Qaeda leaders or stocks of chemical or biological weapons.[376] High-ranking national security officials considered the fact that emergency meetings might have to be convened if the Predator was able to determine bin Laden's location. Experiments with arming the Predator with small rockets had been conducted. The deadline that was set for working capability was 2004. Clarke recalls that he asked the developers to speed up their efforts and to have it ready already by late spring 2001.[377]

At the end of Bill Clinton's presidency and in the early parts of George W. Bush's first term in office, the armed Predator was at the centre of attention of the US government's counterterrorism efforts. Accordingly, 'the main debate in the summer 2001 concentrated on the one new mechanism for a lethal attack on Bin Ladin – an armed version of the Predator drone'.[378] Secretary of Defense Donald Rumsfeld has said that he did not recall any particular counterterrorism issue that got his attention before 9/11 other than the development of the Predator. This included modifying the so-called 'Hellfire' missile to be mounted on the Predator because 'it had been built to hit tanks, not people'.[379] Efforts of arming the Predator drone was initially not linked to counterterrorism efforts.[380] However, the fact that a replica of the four-room villa in which bin Laden

---

[375] *Ibid.* p. 189.   [376] *Ibid.* p. 190.

[377] Clarke, *Against All Enemies: Inside America's War on Terror* p. 221.

[378] National Commission on Terrorist Attacks upon the United States, *The 9/11 Commission Report: Final Report of the National Commission on Terrorist Attacks upon the United States* p. 210.

[379] *Ibid.* p. 211.

[380] Richard Whittle, *Predator: The Secret Origins of the Drone Revolution* (New York: Henry Holt and Company 2014) p. 194.

lived outside Kandahar was built in the Nevada desert in June 2001 and used as a target for Predator-launched purpose-made Hellfire missiles, attest to the merging of the efforts of arming the predator and killing bin Laden.

In the 2002 *Washington Post* article which first made this public, an unnamed participant in the experiment is reported to have referred to this technology as '"the holy grail" of a three-year quest by the US government – a tool that could kill bin Laden within minutes of finding him'.[381]

At the same time, the legal debate on the authority to use this 'tool' was continuing. Since the CIA at the time was the leading government authority on counterterrorism when it came to intelligence and covert operations, it would also have the responsibility for operating the Predator. The Director of Central Intelligence of the CIA, George Tenet, raised a range of questions: 'What is the chain of command? Who takes the shot? Are America's leaders comfortable with the CIA doing this, going outside of normal military command and control?'.[382] Tenet held that neither he nor his colleagues at the CIA had the authority to do it. Apparently, the Deputies Committee of the National Security Council had a different opinion:

> They concluded that it was legal for the CIA to kill Bin Ladin or one of his deputies with the Predator. Such strikes would be acts of Self-defense that would not violate the ban on assassinations in Executive Order 12333. The big issues – who would pay for what, who would authorize strikes, and who would pull the trigger – were left for the principals to settle. The Defense Department representatives did not take positions on these issues.[383]

These issues were considered in the wider context of a new National Security Presidential Directive that was discussed in draft form by senior administration officials on 4 September 2001. This was the first major substantive National Security Presidential Directive issued by the Bush administration.[384] In 2004 the White House released a brief summary of

---

[381] Barton Gellman, 'A Strategy's Cautious Evolution' *The Washington Post* (20 January 2002) www.washingtonpost.com/wp-dyn/content/article/2006/06/09/AR2006060900885.html accessed 10 May 2015.

[382] National Commission on Terrorist Attacks upon the United States, *The 9/11 Commission Report: Final Report of the National Commission on Terrorist Attacks upon the United States* p. 211.

[383] *Ibid.* p. 212.

[384] National Security Council, 'Combatting Terrorism', National Security Presidential Directive 9 signed by President George W. Bush on 21 October 2001. Published online by the

the otherwise classified document entitled *Defeating the Terrorist Threat to the United States*.

National Security Presidential Directive 9 (NSPD 9) called on the Secretary of Defense to plan for military options 'against Taliban targets in Afghanistan, including leadership, command-control, air and air defense, ground forces, and logistics'. NSPD 9 also called for plans 'against al-Qaeda and associated terrorist facilities in Afghanistan, including leadership, command-control-communications, training, and logistics facilities'.[385] Secretary of Defense Donald Rumsfeld described the strategy of NSPD 9 in the following way:

> The objectives of the new strategy were: To eliminate the al-Qaeda network; to use all elements of national power to do so – diplomatic, military, economic, intelligence, information and law enforcement; To eliminate sanctuaries for al-Qaeda and related terrorist networks and if diplomatic efforts to do so failed, to consider additional measures.[386]

On September 10 George Tenet was instructed to prepare new draft legal authorities for this programme. He was specifically told that they should include 'a separate section "authorizing a broad range of other covert activities, including authority to capture or to use lethal force" against al Qaeda command-and-control elements'.[387]

The American Targeted Killing Scheme after 9/11

I dedicate this first section of my consideration of the American targeted killing scheme after 9/11 to the legal instruments adopted and legal positions taken in the aftermaths of the attacks on New York City and Washington on 11 September 2001, which killed close to 3,000 people. I will relate these instruments adopted and legal positions taken to the legal authorities for Shultz's active defense in the 1980s stressing both continuities and discontinuities.

As far as law is concerned, 9/11 constitutes a much less distinct break with the past than is usually believed. In the coming sections I turn to

---

Federation of American Scientists: www.fas.org/irp/offdocs/nspd/nspd-9.htm accessed 10 May 2015.

[385] *Ibid.*   [386] *Ibid.*

[387] National Commission on Terrorist Attacks upon the United States, *The 9/11 Commission Report: Final Report of the National Commission on Terrorist Attacks upon the United States* p. 214.

consider further reasons for the proliferation of targeted killing after 9/11 in the technological ability to carry them out and then in a radicalisation of the dynamics of globalism that had caused George P. Shultz to develop active defense against terrorism in the 1980s.

The Law of Targeted Killing after 9/11

An appropriate starting point for an assessment of the legal instruments adopted and legal positions taken in response to 9/11 is the Authorization for Use of Military Force (AUMF) bill. In the days immediately after 11 September, the President consulted with Congressional leaders on appropriate steps to deal with the situation confronting America after the attacks on New York and Washington, DC. According to a report of the Congressional Research Service (CRS), 'these discussions produced the concept of a joint resolution of the Congress authorizing the President to take military steps to deal with the parties responsible for the attacks on the United States'.[388]

Congress passed the AUMF bill on 14 September 2001 and President George W. Bush signed it into law on 18 September. The bill authorised the President

> to use all necessary and appropriate force against those nations, organiza-
> tions, or persons he determines planned, authorized, committed, or aided
> the terrorist attacks that occurred on September 11, 2001, or harboured
> such organizations or persons, in order to prevent any future acts of inter-
> national terrorism against the United States by such nations, organizations
> or persons.[389]

In past authorisations for use of US military force, Congress had permit-
ted action against unnamed nations in specific regions of the world or against named individual nations. Never before had Congress authorised use of military force against *organisations* or *persons*.[390] As the preceding analysis shows, it was certainly not the first time that an American President considered himself to hold such authority. The question is whether

---

[388] Richard F. Grimmet, *Authorization For Use of Military Force in Response to the 9/11 Attacks (P.L. 107–40): Legislative History* (CRS Report for Congress 2001), published online by the Federation of American Scientists: www.fas.org/sgp/crs/natsec/RS22357.pdf accessed 10 May 2015 p. 2.

[389] 'Authorization for Use of Military Force', Pub. L. No. 107–40, 115 Stat. 224 (2001).

[390] Grimmet, *Authorization For Use of Military Force in Response to the 9/11 Attacks (P.L. 107–40): Legislative History* (CRS Report for Congress 2001) p. 4.

the AUMF represents a shift in either the locus or scope of the authority of the President to designate the terrorist enemy and deal with him accordingly.

With regard to the *locus* of this authority it should be noted that although the passing of the bill in the first place is clearly significant, the sweeping authority granted in the AUMF to determine who 'planned, authorized, committed, or aided the terrorist attacks' makes it difficult to describe the AUMF as a shift of authority from the President to Congress. Furthermore, no requirements for the President to consult with Congress are included in the bill. The question of the impact of the AUMF on the *scope* of the authority to use force in the context of counterterrorism operations generally, and targeted killing specifically, is more complicated. One particular aspect of the AUMF stands out in this regard: the AUMF suggests that the authority of the President is limited to organisations and persons involved in the 9/11 attacks. That being the case, and contrary to what one might think, the AUMF actually threatens to *limit* the authority of the executive to designate the terrorist enemy and deal with him accordingly that Shultz had considered an entirely necessary protective counter-thrust to the international terrorism of the 1980s and that Sofaer, when pressed on its constitutional basis, had grounded on the Commander in Chief clause, the President's power over foreign affairs and the power to ensure that the laws of the United States are implemented.

Against this background, the draft joint resolution that the White House gave to the leaders of Congress on September 12 is of significant interest because it had a slightly different wording. The difference between the draft and the adopted bill is that whereas the authorisation in the adopted bill requires a link to 9/11 for the use of force, the draft bill authorises military force to deter and pre-empt future acts of terrorism and aggression even if *unrelated* to 9/11.[391] The Congressional Research Service report referred to earlier describes how the language of the draft bill

---

[391] Whereas the adopted bill ends 'or harboured *such organizations or persons*, in order to prevent any future acts of international terrorism against the United States by *such nations, organizations or persons* [my emphasis]' the draft proposal read, 'and to deter and pre-empt any future acts of terrorism or aggression against the United States'. (*Ibid.* p. 5f). See also Gregory D. Johnsen, '60 Words and a War Without End: The Untold Story of the Most Dangerous Sentence in U.S. History' (*BuzzFeed BuzzReads*, 16 January 2014) www.buzzfeed.com/gregorydjohnsen/60-words-and-a-war-without-end-the-untold-story-of-the-most accessed 14 May 2015.

seemingly authorized the President, without durational limitation, and
at his sole discretion, to take military action against any nation, terrorist
group or individuals in the world without having to seek further authority from the Congress. It would have granted the President open-ended
authority to act against all terrorism and terrorists or potential aggressors
against the United States anywhere, not just the authority to act against the
terrorists involved in the September 11, 2001 attacks, and those nations,
organizations and persons who had aided or harboured the terrorists.[392]

Apparently this was an authority that Congress was not ready to grant the
President. However, this does not mean that the President did not reserve
it for himself all the same. One of the 'whereas clauses' of the adopted
bill, as well as the statement of the President when signing the bill, is of
relevance in this respect. Whereas the draft proposal of the White House
contained four 'whereas clauses' the final bill included five. The added
clause reads: 'whereas the President has authority under the Constitution
to take action to deter and prevent acts of international terrorism against
the United States . . . '[393] and then proceeds to the substantive authorisation. According to David Abramowitz (at the time the Democratic Chief
Counsel on the Committee on International Relations of the US House
of Representatives and thus an insider to the negotiations), the clause was
proposed by the White House 'in part to address the failure to achieve the
broader authority to use force in response to future acts of terrorism or
aggression'.[394]

President George W. Bush's statement on the occasion of signing the
AUMF bill adds to the impression that the added 'whereas clause' was
meant to assert that the AUMF bill indeed did not limit the President's
authority to authorise force against designated terrorists, whether related
or unrelated to 9/11. President Bush declared:

> Senate Joint Resolution 23 recognizes the seriousness of the terrorist threat
> to our Nation and the authority of the President under the Constitution
> to take action to deter and prevent acts of terrorism against the United
> States. In signing this resolution, I maintain the longstanding position of
> the executive branch regarding the President's constitutional authority to

---

[392] Grimmet, *Authorization For Use of Military Force in Response to the 9/11 Attacks (P.L.
107–40): Legislative History* (CRS Report for Congress 2001).

[393] *Ibid.* p. 4.

[394] David Abramowitz, 'The President, the Congress, and Use of Force: Legal and Political
Considerations in Authorizing Use of Force Against International Terrorism' 43 (2002)
Harvard International Law Journal 71 at 77f.

use force, including the Armed Forces of the United States and regarding
the constitutionality of the War Powers Resolution.[395]

In addition to the fifth 'whereas clause' and the President's reference to
the longstanding position of the executive branch regarding the constitutional authority to use force in these circumstances, a September 25
memorandum written by John Yoo of the Department of Justice Office
of Legal Counsel supports the idea that whatever was achieved by the
adoption of the AUMF, it did not alter the broad scope of the President's
authority to address terrorism by military means.

In this memo, entitled *The President's Constitutional Authority to Conduct Military Operations Against Terrorists and Nations Supporting them,*
Yoo makes it unquestionably clear that he thinks the President has the
authority to take military action in response to the terrorist attacks of
11 September 2001.[396] However, Yoo does not base this authority on the
authority granted to the President in the AUMF bill but on the 'constitutional power' of the President under his authority as Commander in
Chief. Because this power is only 'acknowledged' in the AUMF bill and in
the War Powers Resolution neither statute

> can place any limits on the President's determinations as to any terror-
> ist threat, the amount of military force to be used in response, or the
> method, timing, and nature of the response. These decisions, under our
> Constitution, are for the President alone to make.[397]

Furthermore, this means that 'the President may deploy military force
pre-emptively against terrorist organizations or the States that harbour
or support them, whether or not they can be linked to the specific terrorist
incidents of September 11'.[398]

Because of the fact that the AUMF authorises all necessary and
appropriate force against, inter alia, *organisations* and *persons,* the question of whether the draft proposal to the AUMF would overturn the
ban on assassination was apparently already raised on the evening of

---

[395] 'President Signs Authorization for Use of Military Force bill' (*White House,* 18
September 2001) http://georgewbush-whitehouse.archives.gov/news/releases/2001/09/
20010918-10.html accessed 10 May 2015.

[396] John C. Yoo, 'The President's Constitutional Authority to Conduct Military Operations
Against Terrorists and Nations Supporting Them, U.S. Department of Justice, Office of
the Legal Counsel (September 25, 2001)' in Karen J. Greenberg and Joshua L. Dratel
(eds.), *The Torture Papers: The Road to Abu Ghraib* (Cambridge University Press 2005)
3–24 at 3.

[397] *Ibid.* p. 24.   [398] *Ibid.* p. 3.

September 12.[399] Addressing these concerns, David Abramowitz takes the position that, in fact, the ban would not be overturned by the AUMF and neither is the AUMF necessary in the first place for the exercise of targeted killing. Referencing Parks' 1989 memorandum, Abramowitz explains:

> It has long been the view of the executive branch that targeting the enemy's command and control structures, including those of insurgent groups, is permissible under the law of war and does not constitute 'assassination'. Thus regardless of whether S.J. Res. 23 had been enacted or not, the executive branch would take the view that the President could carry out targeted attacks on those responsible for the attacks of September 11, 2001, without violating this ban.[400]

Since 2001, differing understandings regarding the constitutional authority to carry out targeted killing have also been presented within the American executive branch. When the former Legal Adviser of the Department of State Harold Koh touched upon the topic in a speech at the 2010 Annual Meeting of the American Society of International Law (ASIL), he did not refer to any domestic legal authority other than the AUMF.[401] By contrast, Stephen Preston (at the time CIA General Counsel), in a speech from April 2012, pointed to the President's authority as Commander in Chief in discussing a hypothetical case of the covert use of lethal force abroad, only to then point out that 'a specific congressional authorization might also provide an independent basis for the use of force under U.S. law'.[402] In a Department of Justice white paper released in 2013 and based on a classified Office of Legal Counsel memo apparently drafted in the context of the killing of Anwar al-Aulaqi, a number of domestic as well as international legal grounds for the authority to exercise

---

[399] 'What War Powers Does the President Have?' *Slate* (13 September 2001) www.slate.com/articles/news_and_politics/explainer/2001/09/what_war_powers_does_the_president_have.html accessed 10 May 2015.

[400] Abramowitz, 'The President, the Congress, and Use of Force: Legal and Political Considerations in Authorizing Use of Force Against International Terrorism' p. 78. Abramowitz clearly knew about the positions taken in the American executive in the 1980s because he is thanked for his 'able assistance' in the published version of Abraham D. Sofaer's 1989 speech at the JAG school of the Army considered in the foregoing: Sofaer, 'Terrorism, the Law and the National Defense' p. 89.

[401] Harold Hongju Koh, 'The Obama Administration and International Law' (*Department of State*, 25 March 2010) www.state.gov/s/l/releases/remarks/139119.htm accessed 15 May 2015.

[402] Stephen W. Preston, 'CIA and the Rule of Law' (*Lawfare*, 10 April 2012) www.lawfareblog.com/2012/04/remarks-of-cia-general-counsel-stephen-preston-at-harvard-law-school/ accessed 10 May 2015.

lethal force were pointed to: the President's 'constitutional responsibility to protect the country', the inherent right of the United States to national self-defence under international law and Congress's authorisation of the use of all necessary and appropriate military force against al-Qaeda under international law.[403]

While lawyers within the American executive may have different views on the importance or otherwise of the AUMF for the legal authority of the President to carry out targeted killing, they are certainly in agreement on the matter of the compatibility of targeted killing with the prohibition on assassination. Hence Koh, in the same ASIL speech referred to earlier, follows closely the conclusions of W. Hays Parks in his 1989 memorandum, only adding to it a technological twist: 'the use of lawful weapons systems – consistent with the applicable law of war – for precision targeting of specific high-level belligerent leaders when acting in self-defense or during an armed conflict is not unlawful, and hence does not constitute "assassination"'.[404]

Koh's references to 'precision targeting' in *self-defence* or during an *armed conflict* leads us further to consider developments in international law after 9/11. First, we may pick up on the fact that on September 12 the United Nations Security Council had already provided recognition, albeit without further specification, of the inherent right to self-defence in the context of the 9/11 attacks.[405] As we have seen, such a right to self-defence in relation to violent acts by non-state actors was a right strenuously fought for by Shultz and Sofaer in the 1980s against the narrow interpretation of the *jus ad bellum* prevailing at the time, an interpretation that precluded a right to self-defence against non-state actors if the 'armed attack' for which they were responsible could not be attributed to a state according to the international law of state responsibility. Security Council resolution 1373[406] indicated that times had changed and, apparently, so had the opinion of international law scholars.[407]

---

[403] Department of Justice, 'White Paper: Lawfulness of a Lethal Operation Directed Against a U.S. Citizen who is a Senior Operational Leader of Al-Qa'ida or an Associated Force', published online at: www.law.upenn.edu/live/files/1903-doj-white-paper accessed 10 May 2015.

[404] Koh, 'The Obama Administration and International Law'.

[405] UNSC, Res 1368 (12 September 2001) UN Doc S/RES/1368.

[406] UNSC, Res 1373 (28 September 2001) UN Doc S/RES/1373.

[407] Ulf Linderfalk has considered this shift in international legal scholarship. The apparent avoidance of significant legal arguments that would restrain states' right to self-defence in this context makes Linderfalk question the integrity of international law as a scholarly discipline. Ulf Linderfalk, 'The Post-9/11 Discourse Revisited: The Self-image of the

Legal opinion in the American executive branch was more on the side of continuity. In the 2010 address at the ASIL referred to earlier, Koh stresses that American targeted killings comply with the *jus ad Bellum* inherent right to self-defence but he also emphasises that 'whether a particular individual will be targeted in a particular location will depend upon considerations specific to each case, including those related to the imminence of the threat, the sovereignty of the other states involved, and the willingness and ability of those states to suppress the threat the target poses'.[408] This would appear to be in keeping with Sofaer's efforts at guarding against absolute deference to the principle of territorial integrity and with his belief in the 'sound construction of article 51' which allows self-defence 'once a terrorist "attack occurs" or is about to occur, to use force against those responsible for the attack in order to prevent the attack or to deter further attacks',[409] in particular if coupled to his proposed shift from direct attribution of state responsibility for terrorist crimes to more indirect responsibility in the form of harbouring designated terrorists or being unable or unwilling to extradite them.

If post-9/11 developments with regard to the *jus ad Bellum* revealed signs of the international community conforming to long-held American positions, in the *Jus in Bello* the American position showed signs of renewal. The Executive Order of 13 November 2001 on the *Detention, Treatment, and Trial of certain Non-Citizens in the War Against Terrorism* found that

> International terrorists, including members of al Qaida, have carried out attacks on United States diplomatic and military personnel and facilities abroad and on citizens and property within the United States on a scale that has created a *state of armed conflict* that requires the use of the United States Armed Forces.[410]

The determination that there existed, at least after 9/11, an 'armed conflict' between the United States and international terrorists, including members of al-Qaeda, is a significant step as compared with the application

---

International Legal Scientific Discipline' 2 (2010) Goettingen Journal of International Law 893.

[408] Koh, 'The Obama Administration and International Law'.

[409] Sofaer, 'Terrorism, the Law and the National Defense' p. 95.

[410] 'Detention, Treatment, and Trial of Certain Non-Citizens in the War Against Terrorism – Military Order of November 13, 2001, Federal Register: 16 November 2001 (volume 66, Number 2) Presidential Documents Page 57831–57836' in Karen J. Greenberg and Joshua L. Dratel (eds.), *The Torture Papers: The Road to Abu Ghraib* (Cambridge University Press) 25–28 at 25.

of the law of armed conflict in previous counterterrorism operations. Referring back to Parks' three levels of military operations in which killing is lawful and therefore does not constitute assassination, targeted killing appears to have travelled from 'peacetime counterterrorism operations' to either conventional military operations (international armed conflict) or counterinsurgency (non-international armed conflict), or both.

What remained constant, however, was the exclusion of designated terrorists from the protection of the law of armed conflict and their simultaneous inclusion in the law of armed conflict as legitimate targets. This was made quite clear in a subsequent memorandum from 9 January 2002, written by two executive branch lawyers, John Yoo and Robert J. Delabunty, in which it was determined that the law of war does not protect members of the al-Qaeda organization 'which as a non-state actor cannot be a party to the international agreements governing war'.[411] This was about to change, however, with the 2006 Supreme Court judgment in *Hamdan* v. *Rumsfeld* in which it was declared that Common Article 3 of the Geneva Conventions did apply in the American war against terrorism, resulting in the concept of a *transnational non-international armed conflict*.[412] While the difference between being excluded from and being included in the law of armed conflict would appear to be great, it depends of course on the specific characteristics of the normative framework in question. Thus, as suggested by Jason Ralph, the judgment in *Hamdan* amounts to something of a pyrrhic victory for the critics of the exclusion of the terrorist adversary from law's protection. This is so because what *Hamdan* effectively does is to transnationalise the legal hierarchies of civil war.[413] Thus, the adversary in the American war against terrorism is transformed from being considered a particularly gruesome criminal and an unjust enemy outside the law to being considered a particularly gruesome criminal and an unjust enemy inside the law: in a transnational as much as an internal non-international armed conflict, only the state

---

[411] John C. Yoo and Robert J. Delabunty, 'Memorandum for William J. Haynes II General Counsel, Department of Defense – Re: Application of Treaties and Laws to al Qaeda and Taliban Detainees (January 9, 2002)' in Karen J. Greenberg and Joshua L. Dratel (eds.), *The Torture Papers: The Road to Abu Ghraib* (Cambridge University Press 2005) 38–79 at 38.

[412] US Supreme Court, *Hamdan* v. *Rumsfeld*, 126 S. Ct. 2749 (2006) available at the website of the Court: http://www.supremecourt.gov/opinions/05pdf/05-184.pdf accessed 10 May 2015.

[413] Ralph, 'War as an Institution of International Hierarchy: Carl Schmitt's Theory of the Partisan and Contemporary US Practice' p. 294.

party has 'right authority' or sovereignty. In terms of detaining and charging the terrorist enemy with a crime, *Hamdan* caused Congress to alter the clause 'murder by an unprivileged belligerent' to 'murder in violation of the law of war' in the 2006 Military Commissions Act.[414] In terms of killing the terrorist enemy, *Hamdan* does not necessarily imply additional constraint because, as Legal Adviser Harold Koh stated at the ASIL, 'individuals who are part of . . . an armed group are belligerents, and therefore lawful targets'.[415]

From Targeted Killing to Drone War

If it is the case that the legal authority to designate the terrorist enemy and deal with him accordingly had already developed in the 1980s, this would appear to suggest that while legal authority is a necessary condition for the exercise of exceptional state violence such as targeted killing, it is not a sufficient one.[416] I noted earlier in this chapter that the fact that Shultz's active defense failed to be put into practice during his time at the Department of State might have been related to the fact that he had declared war against 'an unspecified terrorist foe, to be fought at an unknown place and time with weapons yet to be chosen'; but I also showed how each of these elements materialised during the course of the 1990s and would become even more clear after 11 September 2001.

The armed Predator drone offered a technological solution to the problems that the Clinton administration faced when they were attempting to kill Osama bin Laden in the late 1990s by means of cruise missiles. Already by the end of October 2001 it was reported in *Aviation Week & Space Technology* that two US units were flying small numbers of Hellfire-missile-armed Predators over Afghanistan and that the CIA had started operations against the Taliban using the Predator.[417] These developments were described as key elements of a 'fast-reaction strike system designed to hit targets within 5 min. of their being detected'.[418] Apparently, no longer would the CIA have to play the difficult game of placing someone singled out for targeted killing inside the explosive radius of a warhead at a precise time at least six hours in the future because of intelligence lag

---

[414] *Ibid.*   [415] Koh, 'The Obama Administration and International Law'.

[416] I take this point from Samuel Weber, 'Bare Life and Life in General' 46 (2012) Grey Room 7 at 8.

[417] David A. Fulghum, 'More UAVs Shift to Afghan Duty' 155 (2001) Aviation Week and Space Technology 44.

[418] *Ibid.*

time and the time it takes for a slow-flying cruise missile to travel vast distances. Already at the time of the first test-flights of the Predator UAV over Afghanistan in 2000 White House chief counterterrorism official Richard Clarke had said that even if bin Laden was not found, Predator missions might identify additional worthwhile targets, such as other al-Qaeda leaders. This use of the drone technology, to search for and engage previously unknown threats, is reminiscent of the recent significant widening of the scope of the American targeted killing scheme to include not just what are referred to as 'personality strikes', but also so-called 'signature strikes'. In 2010, the *Los Angeles Times* reported that in 2008 the CIA received secret permission to attack not only individual, designated 'high-value' terrorists about whom the different authorities keep lists, but suspected militants whose names are not known, 'as part of a dramatic expansion of its campaign of drone strikes in Pakistan's border region'.[419] The expanded authority was approved by George W. Bush and continued under President Obama, and permits the agency to rely on 'what officials describe as "pattern of life" analysis, using evidence collected by surveillance cameras on the unmanned aircraft and from other sources about individuals and locations'.[420] These are 'signature strikes', where 'signature' does not denote that they are approved *by* signature, but rather connotes the sense of a 'pattern of life' with a distinguishing mark or signature sufficiently threatening to merit being put to death.[421]

---

[419] David S. Cloud, 'CIA Drones Have Broader List of Targets' *Los Angeles Times* (5 May 2010) http://articles.latimes.com/2010/may/05/world/la-fg-drone-targets-20100506 accessed 10 May 2015; Scahill, *Dirty Wars: The World is a Battlefield* pp. 248–253. See also Kevin Jon Heller, '"One Hell of a Killing Machine": Signature Strikes and International Law' 11 (2013) Journal of International Criminal Justice 89.

[420] Cloud, 'CIA Drones Have Broader List of Targets'.

[421] A particularly wicked species of such signature strikes are so called 'double taps', where individuals who have come to help victims of a first strike are killed in a second strike, or where strikes are conducted against mourners or funerals of victims of previous drone strikes. Presumably the idea is that those who come to the rescue of or mourn victims of a first strike also lead a 'pattern of life' sufficiently threatening to America and Americans to merit their being put to death. Glenn Greenwald, 'US Drone Strikes Target Rescuers in Pakistan – and the West Stays Silent' *The Guardian* (12 August 2012) www.theguardian.com/commentisfree/2012/aug/20/us-drones-strikes-target-rescuers-pakistan accessed 10 May 2015; Chris Woods and Christina Lamb, 'CIA Tactics in Pakistan Include Targeting Rescuers and Funerals' *The Bureau of Investigative Journalism* (4 February 2012) www.thebureauinvestigates.com/2012/02/04/obama-terror-drones-cia-tactics-in-pakistan-include-targeting-rescuers-and-funerals/ accessed 10 May 2015.

As important as technological capabilities are, we have yet to give more focused attention to developments in the aftermath of 9/11 and the heightened sense of vulnerability following from the terrorist attacks on that date. I claim that in addition to legal authority and technological capabilities, it is here that we can find the reason for the rapidly expanding American targeted killing scheme, through which thousands of designated terrorists whose names are known, individuals determined as threats through 'pattern of life analysis', but also uninvolved bystanders have been killed particularly in Yemen, Afghanistan, Iraq, Pakistan and Somalia since 9/11.[422]

9/11, a New Kind of Terrorism and a Planetary Homeland Security

The text that I will depart from in investigating these developments is the report of the *National Commission on Terrorist Attacks Upon the United States*, better known as the 9/11 Report.[423] A bipartisan Commission created by legislation in late 2002 produced a report that not only was lauded by Congressional leaders from both parties but also rose to the top of several bestseller lists quickly after its publication.[424] In addition to being lauded and widely read the Report is a good choice because it is as close as one can get to an official account of 9/11 and because the Commission had access to classified material and performed interviews with key officials. Moreover, the Committee took on its task by looking backwards in order to look forwards something which made it consider the rise of an allegedly new kind of terrorism threat directed towards

---

[422] See the statistics provided by the New America Foundation (http://securitydata .newamerica.net/), the Bureau of Investigative Journalism (www.thebureauinvestigates .com/category/projects/drones/drones-graphs/) and The Long War Journal (www.long warjournal.org/yemen-strikes.php and www.longwarjournal.org/pakistan-strikes/). All accessed 15 May 2015.

[423] National Commission on Terrorist Attacks upon the United States, *The 9/11 Commission Report: Final Report of the National Commission on Terrorist Attacks upon the United States*.

[424] Ben Yagoda, 'The Genius of The 9/11 Commission Report: How a Government Committee Made a Piece of Literature' *Slate Magazine* http://www.slate.com/articles/arts/books/ 2004/11/the_911_commission_report.html accessed 10 May 2015. Determining the report to be 'one of the most unlikely literary successes in American history', Craig Warren argues that the report demanded that readers train their interpretive powers 'on the accessible language of the commissioners, but also on the wounds behind that language. In American literary history, few bestsellers have required so much of the reader, or illustrated so clearly the public's hunger for literature as a means of shaping national identity'. Craig A. Warren, '"It Reads Like a Novel": The 9/11 Commission Report and the American Reading Public' 41 (2007) Journal of American Studies 533 at 534.

America and Americans as well as the counterterrorism policies set to deal with it.[425] Accordingly, what the report effectively does is reconsider American counterterrorism policy, stretching as far back as the 1980s, in order to determine the course it should take in the future, or, as expressed in the report, into the 'generational challenge' of 'how to protect our nation in this new era'.[426]

In the preface to the report we already get a glimpse of the enemy in relation to whom these efforts of protection would be devised. Here, the chair and the vice chair of the Committee (Thomas H. Kean and Lee H. Hamilton) write that during the course of the Committee's work they

> learned about an enemy who is sophisticated, patient, disciplined and lethal. The enemy rallies broad support in the Arab and Muslim world by demanding redress of political grievances, but its hostility toward us and our values is limitless. Its purpose is to rid the world of religious and political pluralism, the plebiscite, and equal rights for women. It makes no distinction between military and civilian targets. *Collateral damage* is not in its lexicon.[427]

The enemy that is referred to in this quote represents not merely a 'new terrorist organization' but a 'new kind of terrorism': al-Qaeda.[428] The report includes a fairly standard history of al-Qaeda and Osama bin Laden: how al-Qaeda was formed out of the national resistance movement that withstood invading Soviet forces in Afghanistan; how, after a successful war, a potential general 'headquarters for future jihad' was kept, of which bin Laden became the leader[429]; how 'the groundwork for a true global terrorist network was . . . laid' through the building of offices for financial and other support for activities in the Balkans, Africa, Europe and southeast Asia in the early 1990s[430]; how Osama bin Laden issued a 'self-styled' fatwa calling on Muslims to drive out the US military from Saudi Arabia in 1996 and in 1998 issued another one in the name of a 'World Islamic Front' for the killing of Americans and their allies in any country in which it was possible to do it.[431]

What the report's history of al-Qaeda does not dig deeper into is something that Richard Clarke (one of the few heroes of the 9/11 Report for his early belligerent approach to countering al-Qaeda) mentions in

---

[425] National Commission on Terrorist Attacks upon the United States, *The 9/11 Commission Report: Final Report of the National Commission on Terrorist Attacks upon the United States* p. xvi.

[426] *Ibid.* p. 361.   [427] *Ibid.* p. xvi.   [428] *Ibid.* p. 71.

[429] *Ibid.* p. 56.   [430] *Ibid.* p. 58.   [431] *Ibid.* p. 47f.

his book *Against All Enemies: Inside America's War on Terror*, namely two changes that occurred in 1979, the Iranian Revolution and the Soviet Invasion of Afghanistan, both of which according to Clarke 'rekindled the radical movement in Islam and ... drew America further into the realm of Islam'.[432]

Clarke writes that the 1974 Arab Oil Boycott of the United States 'had made clear to Washington the importance of Persian Gulf resources'.[433] Now, with the invasion and subsequent occupation of Afghanistan the Soviet Red Army had moved south in the direction of the Persian Gulf. The situation worsened with the overthrow of the Shah in Iran, who not only had provided a reliable source of oil but also had been an ally to the United States on the Soviet Union's southern flank. What drew America further into the 'realm of Islam' was the ensuing 'fevered campaign to develop the military capability to project force into the region and to create bases into which those forces could be sent'.[434] For roughly the same reasons Reagan would later bring the United States closer, militarily, to Israel. As is well known by now, both the establishment of American military bases in the Gulf region and America's political and military support for Israel are critical concerns for those engaging in the allegedly new kind of terrorism that al-Qaeda represents.[435]

While Clarke considers the measures taken in the Persian Gulf 'defensive', he describes the measures in Afghanistan as '[going] on the offensive, in a way that drew the United States further into the region'.[436] In Afghanistan the United States gave weapons to and trained the mujahideen through its staging base in Pakistan to fight and eventually defeat the Soviet Union. Although he clearly disagrees with this assessment, Clarke notes, 'there are many who believe that these were mistaken Cold War policies that laid the seeds of al-Qaeda'.[437]

I stressed earlier that when military force was used as a counterterrorism measure during Shultz's time at the Department of State it was primarily in retaliation for past terrorist attacks. Although retaliation was certainly something that Shultz supported, the more radical turn that he had pushed for was to use military force against terrorism proactively. The 9/11 Report's assessment of use of force with the aim of deterrence

---

[432] Clarke, *Against All Enemies: Inside America's War on Terror* p. 36.
[433] *Ibid.*   [434] *Ibid.* p. 38.
[435] This is acknowledged in the 9/11 Report: National Commission on Terrorist Attacks upon the United States, *The 9/11 Commission Report: Final Report of the National Commission on Terrorist Attacks upon the United States* p. 362.
[436] Clarke, *Against All Enemies: Inside America's War on Terror* p. 47.   [437] *Ibid.* p. 51.

is of great interest because effectively it appears to say that such application of military force is only effective for the 'old' forms of specifically state-sponsored terrorism. The report invokes the airstrikes against Libya as an example, saying that, at the time, the response was seen as a success. Hence, the experience of the 1980s had suggested that the proper role for the military in counterterrorism would be a traditional military role; it would act against state sponsors of terrorism. However, the report succinctly remarks that the 1988 bombing of Pan Am 103 over Lockerbie in Scotland 'showed that the operation did not curb Qadhafi's interest in terrorism'.[438] The next case in which retaliation with the aim of deterrence would be put to the test was in 1993 in response to Iraqi involvement in a plot to assassinate George H. W. Bush during his visit to Kuwait for the purpose of being honoured for his 'rescue' of that country in the Gulf War of 1991. Kuwaiti authorities had foiled the plot, arrested several individuals and had 'implicated the Iraqi intelligence service'.[439] The list of targets to be struck was reduced from the original twelve suggested by the Pentagon to one, something which the report explains resulted from debate in the White House and in the CIA about possible collateral damage. Ultimately twenty-three Tomahawk missiles would be fired at the Iraqi intelligence headquarters in Baghdad. The 9/11 Report understood the military response to the plot to assassinate the President to draw on the lesson from the airstrikes against Libya that 'terrorism could be stopped by the use of US air power that inflicted pain on the authors or sponsors of terrorist acts', that is, retaliation with the aim of deterrence. Unsurprisingly, the international legal defence of the strike was that it was an act of self-defence in application of Article 51 of the United Nations Charter. In the case of Iraq, the report notes, 'no further intelligence came in about terrorist acts planned by Iraq'.[440]

The report ends its evaluation of these early cases of the use of American military force in countering Libyan and Iraqi state-sponsored terrorism in the following way:

> The 1986 attack in Libya and the 1993 attack on Iraq symbolized for the military establishment effective use of military power for counterterrorism – limited retaliation with air power, aimed at deterrence. *What*

---

[438] National Commission on Terrorist Attacks upon the United States, *The 9/11 Commission Report: Final Report of the National Commission on Terrorist Attacks upon the United States* p. 97f.

[439] *Ibid.* p. 98.

[440] *Ibid.* Being an outspoken critic of the 2003 Iraq war, Richard Clarke adds: 'Until we invaded Iraq in 2003'. Clarke, *Against All Enemies: Inside America's War on Terror* p. 84.

> *remained was the hard question of how deterrence could be effective when*
> *the adversary was a loose transnational network.*[441]

Thus, while the 9/11 Report is open to the possibility that deterrence may have 'worked' with the 'old' state-sponsored terrorism, the Committee clearly is sceptical about its efficacy in responding to the 'new kind of terrorism' that al-Qaeda represents. This conclusion is related to differences in organising principle, that is, the new kind of terrorism has looser affiliations to a state that can be deterred: 'because large states were more powerful, they also had more to lose. They could be deterred'.[442] As we will soon see, this disenchantment with deterrence in American counterterrorism policy, contrary to what one might think, may actually have supported the use of *more* force, rather than less.

The report presents the 1993 World Trade Center bombing as the step 'from the old terrorism to the new',[443] where the novelty of the latter is characterised in terms of it being a kind of terrorism 'whose rage and malice had no limit'.[444]

Within days of the bombing, the FBI made an arrest and within two weeks they had four of those responsible in custody. As a result of the investigations and arrests a number of individuals were convicted for crimes related to the bombing and other plots that were revealed during the course of the investigations.[445] The way in which the report evaluates the state's response to the attacks is helpful for understanding the disenchantment with the process of seeking criminal liability for terrorist crimes. The report credits the FBI and the Justice Department with 'excellent work investigating the bombing' only to add: 'An unfortunate consequence of this superb investigative and prosecutorial effort was that it created an impression that the law enforcement system was well-equipped to cope with terrorism'.[446] The reason why law enforcement cannot cope with terrorism is that

> the law enforcement process is concerned with proving guilt of persons apprehended and charged. Investigators and prosecutors could not present all the evidence of possible involvement of individuals other than those

---

[441] National Commission on Terrorist Attacks upon the United States, *The 9/11 Commission Report: Final Report of the National Commission on Terrorist Attacks upon the United States* p. 98. My emphasis.

[442] *Ibid.* p. 362.   [443] *Ibid.* p. 71. My emphasis.

[444] The 'rage and malice' of which is corroborated by the fact that the person who had planted the bomb in the garage beneath the two towers later said that he had hoped to kill 250,000 people. *Ibid.* p. 72.

[445] *Ibid.*   [446] *Ibid.*

charged, although they continued to pursue such investigations, planning or hoping for later prosecutions.[447]

The success of the legal system, according to the 9/11 Report, 'had the side effect of obscuring the need to examine the character and extent of the new threat facing the United States', ultimately leading to a 'widespread underestimation of the threat'.[448] Apparently this underestimation was due to a failure to address the true *nature* of the threat. This is revealed in the following quote:

> An unfortunate consequence of this superb investigative and prosecutorial effort was that it created an impression that the law enforcement system was well-equipped to cope with terrorism. Neither President Clinton, his principal advisers, the Congress, nor the news media felt prompted until later, to press the question of whether the procedures that put the Blind Sheikh and Ramzi Yousef behind bars would *really protect Americans against the new virus of which these individuals were just the first symptoms.*[449]

'The existing mechanisms for handling terrorist acts' had, according to the 9/11 report, been 'trial and punishment for acts committed by individuals; sanction, reprisal, deterrence, or war for acts by hostile governments'.[450] The 9/11 Committee effectively consigns the application of military force in response to acts of terrorism with the aim of deterrence to the time of the 'old' form of state-sponsored terrorism, and rules out criminal prosecution as a somewhat misguided, symptomatic treatment with respect to the new kind of terrorism that al-Qaeda represents. These already existing solutions are insufficient to deal with al-Qaeda because 'the actions of al Qaeda fit neither category. Its crimes were on a scale approaching acts of war, but they were committed by a loose, far-flung, nebulous conspiracy with no territories or citizens or assets that could be readily threatened, overwhelmed, or destroyed'.[451] The combined effect of this critical assessment of past counterterrorism efforts is that the room for manoeuvre in terms of counterterrorism policy becomes ever more restricted, in particular when seen in the light of the Committee's framing of the enemy as an enemy with virtually limitless and non-negotiable goals.[452]

---

[447] *Ibid.* p. 73.   [448] *Ibid.* p. 72.   [449] *Ibid.*, my emphasis.
[450] *Ibid.* p. 348.   [451] *Ibid.*
[452] The report's preoccupation with the limitless and non-negotiable goals of this new form of terrorism is, according to terrorism scholar Martha Crenshaw, a standard contention of accounts of a new kind of terrorism. As an example Crenshaw quotes a speech of George W. Bush delivered in 2006: 'we're not facing a set of grievances that can be soothed and

In fact, in a passage that gives a description of the origins and goals of al-Qaeda, it is said that there is no common ground to address them. The origin and goals of this new kind of terrorism are said to derive from a long tradition of extreme intolerance motivated by religion, 'fed by grievances stressed by Bin Laden and widely felt throughout the Muslim world – against the US military presence in the Middle East, policies perceived as anti-Arab and anti-Muslim, and support of Israel'.[453] For Islamist terrorists, America must be 'converted or destroyed'. What is very important to see is how this analysis of the limitless and non-negotiable nature of the threat is turned into the need for an equally limitless and non-negotiable modality of defence. This can be seen when the Report continues from where it left off in stating that this 'is not a position with which Americans can bargain or negotiate. With it there is no common ground – not even respect for life – on which to begin a dialogue. It can only be destroyed or utterly isolated'.[454]

When the 9/11 Report prescribes destruction and utter isolation as the modalities in which al-Qaeda will have to be confronted, we are of course reminded yet again of the formula that equals state protection with using violence against violence in order to control violence.[455] In the section of the report in which these formulations appear, it is clear that what is to be destroyed or utterly isolated is a 'position', not necessarily the human beings embracing it.[456] However, the operative parts of the report, the Committee's 'global strategy', includes 'the struggle of ideas' as

---

addressed. We're facing a radical ideology with inalterable objectives: to enslave whole nations and intimidate the world . . . no concession, bribe, or act of appeasement would change or limit their plans for murder' (Martha Crenshaw, 'The Debate over "New" vs. "Old" Terrorism' 4 (2009) Values and Violence 117 at 123).

[453] National Commission on Terrorist Attacks upon the United States, *The 9/11 Commission Report: Final Report of the National Commission on Terrorist Attacks upon the United States* p. 362.

[454] *Ibid.*

[455] This matter has recently received an interesting twist in critical counterterrorism studies. Ersun N. Kurtulus has argued that what he terms the 'new counterterrorism' in being 'ideological-religious in its rhetorical outlook, networked in its organization structures, increasingly lethal in its operational tactics, and more and more brutal in its methods . . . display[s] similarities with the "new terrorism" – the foe that they are meant to fight – at discursive, organizational, tactical, and methodological levels' (Ersun N. Kurtulus, 'The New Counterterrorism: Contemporary Counterterrorism Trends in the United States and Israel' 35 (2012) Studies in Conflict and Terrorism 37 at 37).

[456] National Commission on Terrorist Attacks upon the United States, *The 9/11 Commission Report: Final Report of the National Commission on Terrorist Attacks upon the United States* p. 361ff.

well as the aims of 'attack[ing] terrorists and their organizations', where this is described in terms of 'identify[ing], disrupt[ing], captur[ing], or kill[ing] individual terrorists'. From this we understand that the Committee's strategy involves ideational as well as corporal destruction and utter isolation.[457]

It is of course the case that corporal destruction and utter isolation was already part of American counterterrorism policy at the time the report was published. The exemplary case of the latter was established in 2002, the detention camp at Guantanamo Bay, Cuba. As we have seen in this chapter, the idea of corporal destruction as a mode of counterterrorism has been long coming, but would not be practised until the late 1990s with the effort to kill bin Laden. It would be deployed more aggressively between 9/11 and the publication of the 9/11 Report, and would be taken to an entirely new level thereafter, at least as far as targeted killing outside the 'hot battlefields' of Afghanistan and Iraq is concerned.

This leads us to the question of how the 9/11 Report makes the global space in which this threat unfolds into America's defensive frontier (which is another way of saying that there is no frontier). This can be observed in an insight in the report that relates the emergence of this new form of terrorism to the unipolar world of the post-cold war period.

> The United States emerged in the post-Cold War world as the globe's pre-eminent military power. But the vacuum created by the sudden demise of the Soviet Union created fresh sources of instability and new challenges for the United States. America stood out as an object for admiration, envy and blame. This created a kind of cultural asymmetry. To us, Afghanistan seemed very far away. To members of al-Qaeda, America seemed very close. *In a sense, they were more globalized than we were.*[458]

These reflections about how al-Qaeda, through a kind of paradox of unipolarity, became more globalised than the United States are later formulated as a foresight with tremendous implications for American counterterrorism:

> In this sense, 9/11 has taught us that terrorism against American interests 'over there' should be regarded just as we regard terrorism against America 'over here'. In this same sense, *the American homeland is the planet.*[459]

I claim that this should be understood as a radicalisation of the dynamics of globalism initiated by Shultz in the sphere of counterterrorism and that triggered his call for a policy shift from passive to active defense.

---

[457] *Ibid.*   [458] *Ibid.* p. 340. My emphasis.   [459] *Ibid.* p. 362. My emphasis.

Shultz already saw at that point how the problem of international terrorism was not confined to any geographic area and how the extensive travel of terrorists outside their own countries and regions to commit acts of terror abroad was a source of growing concern (although I noted that the 1983 bombings of the Marine Barracks in Lebanon seemed to be less a case of the displacement of the terrorism threat as the displacement of the subjects and objects of American protection into the vertigo of a civil war). Now, this tendency seems to me to be radicalised with the 9/11 attacks, which were directed not against American troops or embassies stationed abroad, but were apparently planned in Afghanistan and put into effect on American territory. As far as counterterrorism is concerned we may note the targeted killing of 'the modern day terrorist' Anwar al-Aulaqi in Yemen who, in addition to involvement in operations, allegedly constituted a threat due to his use of social media, 'YouTube, broader internet sites, Facebook, Twitter – to get his propaganda messages out'.[460] Additionally, in 2009, President Barack Obama referred to the border regions of Afghanistan and Pakistan as 'the most dangerous place in the world' for the American people, a place where few Americans have ever set foot.[461] That same place saw a steep rise in targeted killing in the years that followed.[462] Not only does state protection in this case involve a certain symmetry in the *modality* of threat and response but also between the *space* of threat and response, to the point at which targeted killing is deployed in an American homeland which is the planet.

Perhaps the one who pushed the ideology of 'globalism' furthest in his testimony for the Commission was the Swedish terrorism expert Magnus Ranstorp:

> The world is truly a global village today and it has been made even more real than ever with September 11th. Among the first lessons is that the global community cannot allow conflict in one part of the world to fester – principally because, sooner or later, it has the propensity to reach around the globe and produce violence in any corner of the global village . . . above all, September 11th showed that when globalization meets extremist violence anything is possible for the future with threats of

---

[460] Ross and Ferran, 'How Anwar Al-Awlaki Inspired Terror From Across the Globe'.

[461] Barack Obama, 'Remarks by the President on a New Strategy for Afghanistan and Pakistan' (*White House*, 2009) www.whitehouse.gov/the_press_office/Remarks-by-the-President-on-a-New-Strategy-for-Afghanistan-and-Pakistan/ accessed 10 May 2015.

[462] See statistics from the Bureau of Investigative Journalism www.thebureauinvestigates.com/category/projects/drones/drones-graphs/ accessed 15 May 2015.

violence that can occur anywhere and anytime within our homelands
with incalculable and unimaginable consequences.[463]

The Disease Metaphor in Targeted Killing: Death as a Means to Sustain Life

In order to explain the aggressive shift in American counterterrorism,
perhaps the Commission's invocation, noted earlier, of a 'new virus' is
worth taking seriously as a metaphor for the problem of co-existence that
al-Qaeda represents for an American political body made vulnerable by
the forces of globalisation. Remember that this metaphor was invoked at
the point in the Report in which military deterrence had been declared
ineffective and criminal prosecution a somewhat misguided, symptomatic
treatment.

To be sure, this was neither the first time variations on the theme
of disease were used as a metaphor for terrorism, nor would it be the
last.[464] We need only remind ourselves about Reagan's remarks from

---

[463] Magnus Ranstorp, 'Statement of Magnus Ranstorp to the National Commission on
Terrorist Attacks Upon the United States March 31, 2003' (*National Commission on
Terrorist Attacks Upon the United States*) http://govinfo.library.unt.edu/911/hearings/
hearing1/witness_ranstorp.htm accessed 14 May 2015.

[464] This has been picked up in critical accounts in both law and politics (see, e.g. Ileana
M. Porras, 'On Terrorism: Reflections on Violence and the Outlaw' 1 (1994) Utah Law
Review 119 and Ronnie Lippens, 'Viral Contagion and Anti-terrorism: Notes on Medical
Emergency, Legality and Diplomacy' 17 (2004) International Journal for the Semiotics
of Law 125) and in medicine (Ann Mongoven, 'The War on Disease and the War on Terror – A Dangerous Metaphorical Nexus?' 15 (2006) Cambridge Quarterly of Healthcare
Ethics 403). Explicitly epidemiological approaches to counterterrorism have even been
suggested. In a report published by the Aspen Strategy Group, Paul B. Stares and Mona
Yacoubian have proposed to counter the problem of 'Islamist militancy' by viewing it
'as one would a global health threat or epidemic' drawing on 'the scientific principles
and practice of epidemiology as well as the insights from a growing body of research on
social contagion phenomena such as fashions, fads, rumors, civil disobedience, and revolutionary ideas' (Paul B. Stares and Mona Yacoubian, 'Unconventional Approaches to an
Unconventional Threat: A Counter-Epidemic Strategy' in Kurt M. Campbell and Willow
Darsie (eds.), *Mapping the Jihadist Threat – The War on Terrorism Since 9/11* (Washington
DC: Aspen Strategy Group 2006) 85–95 www.aclu.org/files/fbimappingfoia/20111110/
ACLURM000944.pdf accessed 10 May 2015 p. 87). The extensive use of the disease
metaphor in the aftermath of 9/11 by American leaders including by George W. Bush,
Richard N. Haass, Susan Rice and Paul Wolfowitz inspired Douglas R. Stickle to write a
thesis about it at the School of Advanced Airpower Studies. In addition to mapping these
statements, the thesis provides the immunological background against which they can
be understood and concludes that the metaphors can be understood not as short cuts to
solutions but as 'tools for education and exploration. They illustrate important facets of
the nature of our current adversary and the nature of the war. As such, disease imagery can

the beginning of this chapter about how no nation is 'immune' against terrorism and that it will spread like a cancer if decisive action is not taken. Furthermore, Shultz once asserted that 'the magnitude of the threat posed by terrorism is so great that we cannot afford to confront it with half-hearted and poorly organized measures. Terrorism is a contagious disease that will inevitably spread if it goes untreated'.[465] And what could be more natural, really? If our conception of political community is such that it lends itself to be analogised with an organism or body the protection of which is the essential feature of sovereignty, then it is indeed neither alien to compare a threat to this body to an illness or disease nor to use the language and images of medicine in devising appropriate responses to it.

In *Illness as Metaphor* Susan Sontag considers the evolution of the metaphor of illness in, inter alia, political philosophy.[466] She finds that the metaphor has changed with paradigmatic shifts in what we know about the causes of disease and how to treat them. Early analogies between political disorder and illness from Plato to Hobbes find their basis in the medical idea of balance.[467] In this model, illness is a sign of imbalance and treatment is aimed at restoring the right balance. An example of this is Machiavelli, whose invocations of illness never involve fatal illness, but maladies where the prognosis is largely optimistic.[468] The disease can be cured, particularly if detected at an early stage, with the proper foresight. As such it is less about the health condition of society and more about statecraft (conceived of as a therapeutic art).[469] Similarly in Hobbes, the analogy between disease and civil disorder 'is proposed to encourage rulers to pursue a more rational policy'. In support of this, Sontag quotes a section of the Leviathan where Hobbes writes:

> Yet, if men had the use of reason they pretend to, their Commonwealths might be secured, at least from perishing by internal diseases . . . Therefore when they come to be dissolved, not by external violence, but intestine disorder, the fault is not in men, as they are the Matter; but as they are the Makers, and orderers of them.[470]

---

frame the core "war" issues in a comprehensive and easily understandable way: immunity as protection; public health as prevention; medical treatment as intervention'. Douglas R. Stickle, 'Malignants in the Body Politic – Redefining War Through Metaphor' (School of Advanced Airpower Studies for Completion of Graduation Requirements 2002).

[465] Shultz, 'Terrorism and the Modern World [Address before the Park Avenue Synagogue New York City on 25 October 1984]' p. 14.

[466] Susan Sontag, *Illness as Metaphor* (New York: Farrar, Straus and Giroux 1978).

[467] *Ibid.* p. 76f.   [468] *Ibid.* p. 77.   [469] *Ibid.* p. 77f.

[470] *Ibid.* p. 78. Quoting Hobbes, *Leviathan* p. 212.

Sontag's conclusion is that the examples of Machiavelli and Hobbes suggest that rulers have the responsibility and the ability to use proper foresight and pursue a rational policy to control disorder: 'the importance of cutting off serious disease early, while it is relatively easy to control'.[471] Sontag does not say that elements of calls to foresight and to pursue a rational policy disappear in contemporary uses of the illness metaphor in politics. What she does say is that the metaphor has changed with development in medical knowledge. And, in modern medicine, health is not a question of balance or imbalance but a question of perilous co-existence and the overcoming of this predicament through an effective bodily defence.[472] Sontag suggests that, adapting to this significant medical shift, the illness metaphor in law and politics has become an incitement to violence.[473]

When the disease metaphor is meant in this inflammatory manner, Sontag notes that there are only two types of diseases used: the painful but curable, and the possibly fatal.[474] Particularly the possibly fatal 'gives the metaphor a much more pointed character. It enormously ups the ante'.[475] Recently having recovered from cancer at the time when *Illness as Metaphor* was published in 1977, Sontag notes that the particular disease that she had suffered from is something of a master illness of political polemics. She notes too that the intentions of those invoking it often have been implicitly genocidal. Among other historical examples Sontag notes how 'the Jewish problem' in Nazi propaganda from the 1930s was represented using this metaphor and how the propaganda pointed out that, in treating a cancer, one must cut out much of the healthy tissue around it. She also points to how, in Arab polemics, Israel is represented as the cancer of the Middle East. Lastly she points to how an officer with the Christian Lebanese rightist forces in August 1976 called the camp of Tal Zataar 'a cancer in the Lebanese body' in preparation for the massacre in which thousands of Palestinian refugees were killed.[476] What all these examples have in common is that they function so as to compel a political community into considering their continued existence to be dependent on the death of the other with whom they co-exist.

---

[471] Sontag, *Illness as Metaphor* p. 78f.
[472] The question of the shifting of language and images between law and politics and medicine is given the most serious consideration in Ed Cohen, *A Body Worth Defending: Immunity, Biopolitics and the Apotheosis of the Modern Body* (Durham and London: Duke University Press 2009).
[473] Sontag, *Illness as Metaphor* p. 84.   [474] *Ibid.* p. 72.   [475] *Ibid.* p. 83.
[476] *Ibid.* p. 83f.

It is not by coincidence that the most extensive use of this metaphor in the context of targeted killing is ascribable to John Brennan, close advisor to President Barack Obama since November 2008, a leader for the president-elect's review of the US Intelligence Community, and, eventually, homeland security advisor and deputy national security advisor for counterterrorism, with the rank of assistant to the President since Obama entered office, and presently the Director of the CIA. In these different roles Brennan has been instrumental in the Obama presidency's heavy reliance on countering terrorism by means of targeted killing particularly by means of drone strikes.

In his book *Kill or Capture*, Daniel Klaidman reports on a meeting between Brennan and Obama before Obama was elected. Klaidman writes about how Obama and Brennan agreed on the need for a more 'surgical strategy', one that focused on demonstrable threats to the United States, rather than a 'mow them all down approach'. Klaidman writes:

> It was like attacking a spreading cancer, Brennan told the president-elect: 'You need to target the metastasizing disease without destroying the surrounding tissue.' How to implement that strategy brought the discussion around what Admiral McConnell had briefed the president-elect on days before and what would become the new administration's weapon of choice: weaponized pilotless aircraft, or drones.[477]

In this quote we can see how Brennan's use of the cancer metaphor combines the call to foresight that Sontag associates with statecraft conceived as a therapeutic art with the fatalism of modern uses of the illness metaphor. Several years later Brennan returns to the same metaphor in a speech on *The Efficacy and Ethics of U.S. Counterterrorism Strategy*. He does so in a line of argument stressing their ethicality, where ethics is very significantly and emblematically reduced to 'the basic principles of the law of war'.[478]

Brennan says that targeted strikes conform to the principle of necessity, because al-Qaeda or its associated forces are legitimate military targets; they conform to the principle of distinction because 'never before has there been a weapon that allows us to distinguish more effectively between an al-Qaida terrorist and innocent civilians'.[479] They conform, further, to the

---

[477] Daniel Klaidman, *Kill or Capture* (New York: Houghton Mifflin Harcourt 2012) p. 23.
[478] John Brennan, 'The Efficacy and Ethics of U.S. Counterterrorism Strategy' (*White House*, 30 April 2012) www.wilsoncenter.org/event/the-efficacy-and-ethics-us-counter terrorism-strategy accessed 14 May 2015.
[479] *Ibid.*

principle of proportionality because 'by targeting an individual terrorist or small numbers of terrorists with ordnance that can be adapted to avoid harming others in the immediate vicinity, it is hard to imagine a tool that can better minimize the risk to civilians than remotely piloted aircraft'; for the same reason targeted strikes conform to the principle of humanity which requires that weapons are used that will not inflict 'unnecessary suffering'. For all these reasons, Brennan asserts, 'these targeted strikes against al-Qaida terrorists are indeed ethical and just', before arriving at the conclusion:[480]

> Compared against other options, a pilot operating this aircraft remotely, with the benefit of technology and with the safety of distance, might actually have a clearer picture of the target and its surroundings, including the presence of innocent civilians. It's this surgical precision, the ability, with laser-like focus, to eliminate the cancerous tumor called an al-Qaida terrorist while limiting damage to the tissue around it, that makes this counterterrorism tool so essential.[481]

First it may be noted that Brennan, in declaring the target to be 'the cancerous tumor *called* an al-Qaida terrorist', stresses the metaphor by substituting the subject which is to be compared, and the object of the comparison.[482] Apparently, a cancerous tumour is what he or she *is*, an al-Qaeda terrorist is simply what he or she is *called*. Moreover, the role that Brennan assigns to targeted killing by drones strikes – to, 'with laser-like focus', eliminate this cancer while limiting damage to the tissue around it – gives us reason to return to Sontag's consideration of shifts in medical knowledge and the use of the disease metaphor in law and politics. For Brennan does not invoke the cancer metaphor in pleading for a 'broad-spectrum' treatment like the ones exemplified by Sontag and referred to in the foregoing. Instead, Brennan uses it to suggest a specifically targeted form of killing, which, incidentally, is precisely what preoccupies contemporary medical research as well.[483] Accordingly, it would appear to be the case that developments in medicine have extended the repertoire of the cancer metaphor to include not just broad-spectrum but also targeted forms of state death dealing. Moreover, Brennan's image renews the cancer metaphor in another sense too: the body that is the subject of this quasi-medical intervention is a disincorporated political

---

[480] Brennan, 'The Efficacy and Ethics of U.S. Counterterrorism Strategy'.   [481] *Ibid.*

[482] Referred to as the 'tenor' and the 'vehicle', respectively, in metaphor theory.

[483] Markus Gunneflo, *The Life and Times of Targeted Killing* (Lund: Faculty of Law 2014) pp. 15–18.

body, a body whose borders are not the central locus of protection they once were and that is seen to require various forms of foreign internal defence systems, including targeted killing, to sustain itself.

Foreign internal defence is a term that the US military has used in counterinsurgency doctrine in the specific sense of 'the application of all instruments of national power [to] support *host nation* efforts to build capability and capacity to free and protect *its* society from subversion, lawlessness, and insurgency',[484] or, in the words of a leading thinker and practitioner of counterinsurgency doctrine, US General Stanley McChrystal, in the sense of creating 'in the nation-state the equivalent of [a] rebuilding of *their* immune system so that *they* have the ability to deal with the problem'.[485] McChrystal has famously led the way from an 'enemy-centric' to a 'population-centric' form of counterinsurgency. As his commands in both Iraq and Afghanistan have shown, this, however, includes extensive targeted killing operations using drones as well as 'kill or capture' night raids.[486]

Just as the United States has deployed drones and conducted targeted killing operations outside the wars in Afghanistan and Iraq, the notion of foreign internal defence can be adapted to resonate with the lesson drawn by the 9/11 Commission about regarding terrorism against American interests 'over there' just as they regard terrorism against America 'over here', that is, with the lesson that America should visualise its homeland as

---

[484] Joint Chiefs of Staff, 'Foreign Internal Defense', Joint Publication 3–22 (12 July 2010) available at: www.dtic.mil/doctrine/new_pubs/jp3_22.pdf accessed 14 May 2015 p. i. My emphasis. Thanks to Amin Parsa for alerting me to this.

[485] This deployment of medical thinking in counterinsurgency is not just a random metaphor for McChrystal but was uttered in the context of the presentation of a two-year project on 'Lessons on Counterinsurgency from the Human Body' pursued with Kristina Talbert-Slagle, an immunologist from the Yale Global Health Research Institute. The project was presented at the *Brookings Institution* on 19 December 2013 and broadcasted at the *Lawfare* blog (Benjamin Wittes, 'Lawfare Podcast Episode #57: General Stanley McChrystal and Kristina Talbert-Slagle on Lessons on Counterinsurgency from the Human Body' (*Lawfare* 9 January 2014) http://www.lawfareblog.com/2014/01/lawfare-podcast-episode-57-general-stanley-mcchystal-and-kristina-talbert-slagle-on-lessons-on-counterinsurgency-from-the-human-body/#.Us_VcPZZVC4 accessed 10 May 2015). For a critical consideration of medical thinking in Counterinsurgency see Colleen Bell, 'War and the Allegory of Medical Intervention: Why Metaphors Matter' 6 (2012) International Political Sociology 325.

[486] Against the background of both Iraq and Afghanistan Steve Niva refers to the 'doctrinal synergy between population-centric counterinsurgency and high-tempo kill-or-capture operations undertaken by JSOC [Joint Special Operations Command]'. Steve Niva, 'Disappearing Violence: JSOC and the Pentagon's New Cartography of Networked Warfare' 44 (2013) Security Dialogue 185 at 194f.

the entire planet. In this meaning, targeted killing becomes the American political body's *own* means of foreign internal defence.

The fatal implications of thinking about global co-existence in terms of diseases and immunitary responses is the same in these different conceptions of foreign internal defence: it suggests that the existence of political community is entirely dependent on the death of certain human beings with whom it co-exists or, in other words, that death is a precondition for sustaining life.

4

Targeted Killing and the Struggle over International Law's Sanctioning of Lethal Force

So far I have been focusing on the emergence of targeted killing in Israel and the United States. In the Israeli context I showed how, far from being just a means for the Israeli state to deal with the situation of insecurity of the second Intifada, targeted killing can be understood against the background of a long and vexing history of Israeli state protection and the common entrapment of enmity entered into with the Palestinians in 1948. The legal asymmetry between the partners in this entrapment, the 'constitutional structure' of the legal regime of the occupation and the extraordinary targeted killing judgment of the Israel Supreme Court sitting as the High Court of Justice, has enabled the emergence and functioning of this particularly 'active' form of counterterrorism. More than simply an emergency measure devised in response to the situation of insecurity following 9/11, targeted killing in the US context has emerged by adapting conceptions of the global national security interests of the United States to the policy area of counterterrorism starting with George P. Shultz's active defense in the 1980s.

The history of targeted killing in both contexts is also the history of the ability to distinguish between *extra-legal* 'political assassination' and *legal* 'targeted killing'. This ability turns on the extension of the right to kill the enemy in application of the law of armed conflict to extraterritorial counterterrorism operations. Because of this implication of international law in the emergence of targeted killing, the debate over this practice takes the form of a struggle over international law's sanctioning of lethal force. This struggle will be examined in this chapter from the perspective of the *history of international law*. As was already mentioned in the first chapter, the conception of the history of international law relied on here is one that seeks trajectories within the discipline of international law, in this case trajectories in international law's sanctioning of lethal force.[1]

---

[1] Cf. Craven, 'Introduction: International Law and Its Histories' p. 6f.

First I will investigate the position of the subject of targeted killing as at the same time enemy, criminal and risk, and the way in which this involves a shift in international law from its traditional concern with public forms of enmity to individual or private forms of enmity. In this context I will also consider the shift from exclusion to inclusion in international law of those subject to targeted killing. Second, I will investigate how targeted killing involves a shift from enmity based on territorial jurisdiction to enmity as relation, or, in other words the deterritorialisation of enmity. Third and finally I will turn to consider the fact that this individualised and deterritorialised enmity has emerged simultaneously with an equally individualising and deterritorialising movement in international law – human rights. In focus here is the encounter of the enemy and the rights-bearer in the subject of targeted killing and the conflicting demands that this would appear to entail as far as lethal force is concerned.

Individualisation of Enmity?

The application of the law of armed conflict in counterterrorism operations implies the emergence of a particular form of enmity. Wouter Werner has described the international legal position of this non-state enemy in a way that is consistent with our findings in the preceding chapters: 'the enemy under attack in policies of targeted killing is not the *justus hostis* of classical international law. Instead, he is individualised, denied the right to participate in hostilities and regarded as an enemy, criminal, and risk at the same time'.[2] What remains to be done here is to bring into sharper focus the place, if any, for such an individualised or private form of enmity in international law, based as it is on a public form of enmity in which combatants are killed not as individuals but because they are enrolled by a state that authorises their violence.[3]

---

[2] Werner, 'The Changing Face of Enmity: Carl Schmitt's International Theory and the Evolution of the Legal Concept of War' p. 374.

[3] The formulation is taken from Derek Gregory, 'Drone Geographies' 183 (2014) Radical Philosophy 7 at 12 but the law of war principle that it explicates is that of military necessity. The clearest expression of this principle as regards the killing of combatants is found in the 11 December 1868 St. Petersburg Declaration Renouncing the Use, In Time of War, of Explosive Projectiles Under 400 Grammes Weight. In this Declaration it is stated that 'the only legitimate object which States should endeavour to accomplish during war is to weaken the military forces of the enemy; That for this purpose it is sufficient to disable the greatest possible number of men . . . '

Early in the foregoing chapter I considered Carl Schmitt's analysis of the shift from Westphalian to post-Westphalian international law. In that context I noted that one of the reasons for Schmitt's praise of European international law was for its assertion of a fundamental equality between the belligerents, articulated in this notion of *justus hostis*. Schmitt deplored the disintegration of this order; particularly he deplored how increasing universalist tendencies, the imperial inclinations of the United States and the ban on war made way for a new kind of just war, or, in other words, he deplored the substitution of the *injustus hostis* for the *justus hostis*.[4] Another tendency in the shift from Westphalian to post-Westphalian international law was the rise of irregular or partisan warfare. I highlighted one feature in particular of such irregular warfare: the state's monopoly on legitimate force. In relation to a non-state enemy the sovereign state is able to adopt the simple and clear position that the law is on its side. Thus, in interstate as much as in irregular warfare the notion of *injustus hostis* is on the rise.

Ward Thomas has considered the effect of these changes on the perception of the legality and legitimacy of assassination in international law.[5] Although as I am concerned with the history of targeted killing my primary interest lies with war between a state and a non-state enemy, I will deal with his account of changing perceptions of the assassination of state enemies first. The reason is that it highlights a structural bias in international law offering state leaders greater protection from targeted death than non-state enemy leaders.

Thomas stresses that the negative perception of the assassination of foreign leaders is of relatively recent origin. He refers to Alberico Gentili, who in 1612 recounted numerous cases that make it clear that the murder of enemy leaders was 'an exceedingly common method of pursuing foreign policy among the ancients'.[6] In the sixteenth century the prevalence of assassination in Europe was accompanied by international

---

[4] For a consideration of the conflation of *jus ad bellum* and *jus in bello* that is the consequence of the resurrection of the concept of *injustus hostis* in contemporary regulation of interstate force see: Robert D. Sloane, 'The Cost of Conflation: Preserving the Dualism of Jus ad Bellum and Jus in Bello in the Contemporary Law of War' 34 (2009) The Yale Journal of International Law 47.

[5] Ward Thomas, 'Norms and Security: The Case of International Assassination' 25 (2000) *International Security* 105; Ward Thomas, *The Ethics of Destruction: Norms and Force in International Relations* (Ithaca and London: Cornell University Press 2001); Ward Thomas, 'The New Age of Assassination' 25 (2005) SAIS Review 27.

[6] Thomas, 'Norms and Security: The Case of International Assassination' p. 108.

lawyers such as Thomas More hailing assassination 'both as a useful tool of statecraft and as a means of sparing ordinary citizens the hardships of wars for which their leaders were responsible'.[7] Thomas in this context notes that although the taking of a life presented obvious moral problems, these did not give rise to 'a full-fledged international norm – a collective understanding that assassination in the conduct of foreign policy was improper – until considerably later'.[8] This would only occur after the rise of sovereign statehood in the seventeenth century and the idea that state leaders were agents of state interests pursuing war not for personal motives but in the pursuit of policy by other means. It was also linked to the rise of mass armies through which war was conducted on a very large, rather than a personal, scale.[9] In this very different context, in 1758 Emmerich de Vattel penned one of the more striking denunciations of assassination:

> I give, then, the name of assassination to treacherous murder . . . and such an attempt, I say, is infamous and execrable, both in him who executes it and in him who commands it . . . The sovereign who makes use of such execrable means should be regarded as an enemy of the human race, and all Nations are called upon, in the interests of the common safety of mankind, to join forces and unite to punish him.[10]

Apparently, while the use of assassination had previously been considered prudent statecraft, it was now condemned, prosecuted even, in interests of the common safety of mankind. Thomas also refers to Thomas Jefferson, who in a 1789 letter to James Madison expressed that civilisation had left assassination behind it: 'Assassination, poison, perjury . . . all of these were legitimate principles in the dark ages which intervened between ancient and modern civilizations, but exploded and held in just horror in the eighteenth century'.[11] Ninetieth century codifications of the law of war affirmed these negative perceptions of assassination. In doing so, they also solidified the dual character of the concept of assassination in use by the early writers: the targeting of selected *individuals* (the private individual or person as opposed to the public soldier or enemy) and the use of *treachery*.[12]

---

[7] *Ibid.* p. 110.   [8] *Ibid.* p. 108.   [9] *Ibid.* p. 118.
[10] Vattel as quoted in *ibid.* p. 112.   [11] *Ibid.*
[12] Michael N. Schmitt writes that 'all codification efforts attempted to define assassination as the targeting of specific individuals. For example, General Order 100 uses the phrases 'an individual . . . a citizen. . . . a subject . . . an outlaw. The Brussels Declaration speaks of "individuals", whereas the *Oxford Manual* forbids a treacherous attempt on the life of

It is of course true that these prohibitions do not forbid the wartime killing of the top echelons of the enemy's chain of command. From the point of view of international law, as long as the targeted individual is in the chain of command and the means used are not 'treacherous' such killings are lawful. As an authoritative source for the fact that the killing of leaders nevertheless is perceived negatively and is practised by states only with great circumspection Thomas cites a passage of W. Hays Parks' 1989 memorandum, given extensive consideration in the preceding chapter on the emergence of targeted killing in the United States. In the section cited by Thomas, Parks writes: 'while a civilian head of state who serves as commander-in-chief of the armed forces may be a lawful target . . . as a matter of comity such attacks generally have been limited'.[13] In particular, Thomas notes that the word 'comity' denotes courtesy or civility but also implies a sense of reciprocity in the observance of such courtesies.[14] This latter point Thomas explains by the association of assassination with disorder and systemic chaos.[15]

Arguing that the negative perception of the assassination of state enemies is changing, Thomas cites as recent examples, inter alia, the 1986 air strike on Tripoli, on which Abraham D. Sofaer and W. Hays Parks gave legal advice as well as attempts to kill Saddam Hussein in the first Gulf War. Thomas claims that in both cases targets were chosen with the hope that the raids would result in the death of the opposing leader, yet US officials denied this with indignation.[16]

"an enemy". The Hague Regulations likewise employ the term "individuals",' while Protocol I condemns the resort to perfidy against "an adversary". This textual evidence demonstrates the requirement of individual targeting' (Schmitt, 'State-Sponsored Assassination in International and Domestic Law' p. 632).

[13] Parks, 'Memorandum of Law: Executive Order 12333 and Assassination' p. 6 footnote 4.

[14] Thomas, *The Ethics of Destruction: Norms and Force in International Relations* p. 74 footnote 101.

[15] Thomas, 'Norms and Security: The Case of International Assassination' p. 116.

[16] *Ibid.* p. 115. In a 2002 article Parks provides the following brief comment on the matter: 'Media speculation about the raid raised the legal issue as to whether Ghadafi's death would violate Executive Order 12333, which prohibits assassination (it would not have)' (Parks, 'Lessons From the 1986 Libya Airstrike' p. 764). In a 2010 article Parks writes that 'a residence of Qadhafi was located within the heavily-fortified Tarabulus (Aziziyah) Barracks in Tripoli, a principal command and control center for Qadhafi's worldwide terrorist network, but neither Qadhafi (whose whereabouts were unknown) nor his residence were targeted'. W. Hays Parks, 'Part IX of the ICRC Direct Participation in Hostilities Study: No Mandate, No Expertise, and Legally Incorrect' 42 (2010) New York Journal of International Law and Policy 769 at 789 footnote 65.

Although each of these alleged attempts to assassinate state leaders of course had their specific reasons, it is also the case that the negative perception of inter-state assassinations does not appear to fit into the international legal order quite as neatly as it once did. In particular, the idea that leaders can and should be held accountable for transgressions committed in the name of the state is a significant blow to the ideational foundation on which the assassination ban is based.[17] Put differently, the relaxation of the stigma against assassination of state leaders is associated with the shift from *justus hostis* to *injustus hostis*. Thomas puts the matter in rather more drastic terms:

> The norm against assassinating foreign leaders gained purchase when the surrounding international context most favoured it. The Westphalian model's weakening has created a crisis of coherence for the norm, especially . . . the growing acceptance that leaders should be held to answer for their actions, whether in the dock or in the crosshairs.[18]

Ward Thomas issues a warning against the recent relaxation of the norm prohibiting assassination of state leaders. He takes the perspective of state sovereignty in doing so. For although Westphalian sovereignty may be waning, Thomas argues that the reasons for the negative perception of assassination at the height of the Westphalian era still apply, first and foremost among which is the destabilising effect that such assassinations have on international relations.[19]

Thomas does not consider the assassination of state leaders in the context of the UN Charter collective security system. In the lead-up to the 2003 Iraq war, Ann-Marie Slaughter (international law professor and former President of the American Society of International Law, whose career also includes a stint at the US Department of State) brought the authority of the Security Council to bear on the question of the assassination of state leaders. In a *Foreign Policy* article Slaughter argued for the inclusion of 'mercy killings' among the UN Security Council's forceful means for the maintenance of international peace and security, more particularly, that the UN Security Council, if all else fails, can and should 'issue death warrants against dangerous dictators' in the name of the common interest, something which includes national as well as human security:

> In this context, targeting dictators is not murder or assassination. Once the shift has been made to 'war,' army against army, killing becomes legitimate.

---

[17] Thomas, 'Norms and Security: The Case of International Assassination' p. 129.
[18] Thomas, 'The New Age of Assassination' p. 31.   [19] *Ibid.*

But once war breaks out, even direct targeting of the political leadership is bound to involve many civilian deaths. Surely, in these kinds of situations, it would be far better to target an individual political leader from the beginning of a crisis, not with the force of arms but the force of law. Identify him as a criminal and seek his arrest by any means possible. If all else fails, authorize the use of force, but against an individual, not a nation . . . the United Nations, and specifically the Security Council, is charged with acting in the common interest. That common interest includes not only national security but also human security. The Security Council can thus identify a leader as a threat not only to the world's nations but also to his own people. And if the Security Council does so – with the votes of at least nine diverse nations with no veto by any one of the five major powers – it can issue an international warrant, even a death warrant. This course would be far more moral than careening toward war. And it would be a course far more consistent with the mission of the United Nations itself: 'to reaffirm faith in fundamental human rights, in the dignity and worth of the human person, in the equal rights of men and women and nations large and small'.[20]

Indeed, even though no Security Council 'death warrant' was issued for Saddam Hussein, literally the first shots (or cruise missiles to be more precise) of the 2003 Iraq war were aimed at what was described as a 'target of opportunity': Saddam Hussein in an isolated private residence in southern Baghdad.[21]

More recently, when external interventions in civil wars are debated, the option of assassinating the leader who manifestly has failed in his responsibility to protect the population is often raised. Thus, immediately after news spread that Bashar al-Assad had used chemical weapons in the Syrian civil war, Foreign Affairs Columnist of the *Wall Street Journal* Bret Stephens wrote an op-ed, entitled 'Target Assad', declaring that

should President Obama decide to order a military strike against Syria, his main order of business must be to kill Bashar Assad. Also, Bashar's brother and principal henchmen, Maher. Also, everyone else in the Assad family with a claim on political power. Also, all of the political symbols of the Assad family's power, including all of their official or unofficial residences. The use of chemical weapons against one's own citizens plumbs depths of barbarity matched in recent history only by Saddam Hussein. A civilized

---

[20] Anne-Marie Slaughter, 'Mercy Killings' 136 (2003) Foreign Policy 72 at 72f.
[21] Barton Gellman and Dana Priest, 'CIA Had Fix on Hussein: Intelligence Revealed "Target of Opportunity"' *The Washington Post* (20 March 2003) AD1 http://www.washingtonpost .com/wp-dyn/articles/A58177-2003Mar20.html accessed 10 May 2015.

world cannot tolerate it. It must demonstrate that the penalty for it will be
acutely personal and inescapably fatal.[22]

Stephens' piece ends by linking his plea to target Bashar al-Assad to the
rise of the targeted killing of non-state actors:

> Yes, a Tomahawk aimed at Assad could miss, just as the missiles aimed at
> Saddam did. But there's also a chance it could hit and hasten the end of
> the civil war. And there's both a moral and a deterrent value in putting
> Bashar and Maher on the same list that once contained the names of Bin
> Laden and Anwar Al-Aulaqi.[23]

This leads us further to consider changing perceptions of assassination
specifically with regard to non-state enemies. However, a word of caution
concerning what it means to be speaking about the individualisation or
privatisation of enmity in this context is in order. For Gabriella Blum has
argued that the decline of war's public character need not necessarily lead
to its individualisation. The risk of individualising collectivism is that it
ends up collectivising individualism, manifesting itself in the development of 'groupings of individuals according to non-traditional features:
instead of territory or citizenship, groups would be identified according
to ethnicity, religion or ideology'. Already we see this move, argues Blum,
in 'speaking about "global Al Qaeda" or "radical Islam"'.[24]

Addressing the rise of irregular warfare and shifting perceptions of
the assassination of non-state enemies, Thomas sticks to the perspective
of state sovereignty. Interestingly, this yields an entirely different result
in terms of the propriety of relaxing the stigma against assassination.
Thomas writes:

> The most obvious and direct source of pressure on the norm [prohibiting
> assassination] has been the post-World War II rise of 'non-traditional'
> (the term is necessarily relative) modes of political violence, including
> guerrilla warfare and terrorism. These methods, which reject many existing

---

[22] Bret Stephens, 'Target Assad' *The Wall Street Journal* (27 August 2013) http://online.wsj
.com/news/articles/SB10001424127887323407104579036740023927518 accessed 10 May
2015.

[23] *Ibid.* 'Building on the tradition that is associated with Thomas More and others' Eamon
Aloyo constructs a Just War argument for what he appropriately terms 'just assassina-
tions'. The example that he works with is Syria and Bashar Assad: Eamon Aloyo, 'Just
Assassinations' 5 (2013) International Theory 347.

[24] Gabriella Blum, 'The Individualization of War: From Collectivism to Individualism in the
Regulation of Armed Conflicts' in Austin Sarat, Lawrence Douglas and Martha Merrill
Umphrey (eds.), Law and War (Stanford University Press 2013) http://ssrn.com/abstract=
2231168 accessed 10 May 2015, p. 22.

norms and eschew large-scale conventional warfare, play away from the strengths of powerful states and are difficult to defeat with conventional means. Indeed, guerrilla movements' success against more powerful foes has been striking. Trans-national terrorist organizations present an even more difficult challenge: not only are there no easily identifiable armed forces to engage in combat, there are seldom specific geographic locations around which the threat is centered. In both cases, the foe is likely to melt into the civilian population, creating significant political obstacles for a state using conventional force on a large scale. Perhaps out of frustration, states confronting non-traditional foes have proved more willing to employ non-traditional means, including targeted killings.[25]

Thomas' description of a shift in the perception of assassination of specifically non-state enemies tracks the development of the emergence of targeted killing described in the foregoing chapters. In particular the emergence of targeted killing in the United States was accompanied by testimonies to what Thomas glosses as a 'dramatic structural transformation involving nothing less than the erosion of the institution of sovereignty itself'.[26] Continuing this train of thought Thomas writes:

> The question of what types of actors are able to project force across international borders is tied to the problem of the tractability of force in the international system and, therefore, to international order. Governments can be lobbied, cajoled and coerced, as can in some cases the populations to which they are ultimately accountable. Militant non-state (and especially non-territorial) organizations such as terrorist groups, however, represent the nightmare scenario of violence without accountability.[27]

In keeping with this insight Thomas deplores the fact that, in the United States, the threat of transnational terrorism has been considered less in these terms of international order than in moral terms and as hatred of the United States and its freedoms. To conceive of the problem in terms of international order, he argues, may yield a different perception of the place for international law in this struggle. Rather than conceiving of international law as part of the problem, it can be considered as part of the solution. This is so because, according to Thomas, 'international law does far more to empower states than to shackle them'.[28] He continues: 'International law has long provided states with a powerful means of limiting access to military force and has helped consolidate the state monopoly of violence. It would be shortsighted to marginalize the law as a means of

---

[25] Thomas, 'The New Age of Assassination' p. 29f.
[26] *Ibid.* p. 30.   [27] *Ibid.* p. 36f.   [28] *Ibid.* p. 37.

slowing this monopoly's erosion'.[29] In this way, the war on terror may be placed in 'its proper context: a policy aimed at strengthening, rather than undermining, the rule of international law'.[30] Thomas recognises that this may require some reassessment of 'provisions of international law that may be inadequate to deal with modern challenges'.[31] Such reassessment will have to recognise that 'the threat posed by terrorist networks falls somewhere between traditional notions of war and peace'.[32]

While the marginalisation of international law may also have had its moments in the war on terrorism, I find ample evidence, in the *history* through which targeted killing emerged, of precisely the use of international law that Thomas suggests as the way *forward*. Accordingly, in both the Israeli and the US context we noticed *not the turning away from* international law but the consolidation of the state's monopoly of violence in a cross-border setting and the *reassessment* of provisions of international law that were found to be inadequate to deal with the challenge of transnational terrorism.

From what has been said so far we can see that Thomas argues for retaining the public nature of enmity, and thus a negative perception of assassination, in wars between states. Now he endorses an individualised or private form of enmity and the relaxation of the prohibition of assassination in the case of non-state actors. In fact, Thomas follows the lead of one of the earliest and most influential critics of international assassination – Hugo Grotius – in making this distinction between state and non-state actors. For, as Thomas reminds us, Grotius made explicit exception for 'pirates and brigands' whose actions threatened international order. Thomas concludes: 'A policy that targeted modern pirates and brigands while sparing national leaders would therefore be consistent with a longstanding tradition recognizing that some actors belong outside the law's protection'.[33]

The idea that designated terrorists belong outside the law's protection is also well represented in the history of targeted killing. We can see this in the inclusion of the terrorist enemy in the law of armed conflict as a legitimate target and the simultaneous exclusion from practically all of its protections. This was the position adopted by Military Advocate

---

[29] *Ibid.*   [30] *Ibid.*   [31] *Ibid.*   [32] *Ibid.*

[33] *Ibid.* p. 37. Grotius writes '"tho" it [assassination of 'robbers' and 'pirates'] be not altogether blameless, yet it is not punished amongst Nations, in Detestation of those against whom it is committed' (Hugo Grotius, *The Rights of War and Peace*, vol. 3 (Richard Tuck ed., Indianapolis: Liberty Fund 2005) p. 1300).

General David Yahav when he asserted that the course of treating certain individuals in the context of the first Intifada as criminals had been taken as mere internal state policy and that international law views 'armed terrorists' as 'illegal combatants' who can be 'shot on the spot'. This was also the stance taken by the international law department of the Military Advocate General's office in the context of the second Intifada and the position defended by the Israeli government before the Israel Supreme Court. In the American context, this was the position taken by W. Hays Parks when given the task of providing legal advice on law of war aspects of the military strikes against terrorist-related targets in Libya in 1986 as well as in his 1989 memo on the executive order banning assassination and the lawful killing of terrorists under the law of war. Likewise it was the position taken in the aftermath of the 9/11 attacks, when it was determined that the law of war does not protect members of al-Qaeda, which as a non-state actor cannot be a party to the international agreements governing war. It was even the case that the precedent of 'pirates and brigands' was invoked in the context of recasting the US war on terrorism as a question of *international* as opposed to *national* security.

In both the Israeli and the American contexts, however, we can see that the international legal position of the subject of targeted killing has changed in recent times, a shift that can be described as a shift from exclusion to inclusion. The Israel Supreme Court targeted killing judgment and the US Supreme Court in the *Hamdan v. Rumsfeld* judgment have both contributed to this shift and in both cases the Court rejected the respective government's exclusion of the terrorist enemy from the protection of the law of armed conflict. However, the Courts were only able to do that by reconfiguring this law: the Israel Supreme Court by conceiving of an *international armed conflict* between a state and a non-state actor on occupied territories because crossing the borders of Israel proper (when the defining characteristic of this type of conflict always has been its inter-state, rather than its cross-border nature);[34] the US Supreme Court by conceiving of a transnational non-international armed conflict between a state and its non-state enemy (when the defining characteristics of a non-international armed conflict used to be not only that it takes place between a state and its non-state enemy but also its intrastate character). I will have more to say about the territorial aspects of these changes in the

---

[34] Milanovic, 'Lessons for Human Rights and Humanitarian Law in the War on Terror: Comparing Hamdan and the Israeli Targeted Killing Case' p. 384.

coming section; the question here is what this change means in terms of the international legal position of the subject of targeted killing, a subject that, throughout these changes, remains at once an enemy, criminal and risk.

This shift from exclusion to inclusion has caused a surge in interest, among states, international law scholars and, not least, the ICRC, in the legal categories in which the non-state enemy may be included.[35]

In a recent book Sibylle Scheipers describes how the exclusion from the law of armed conflict of irregular fighters started to change already in the era of decolonisation.[36] Although such exclusion extended beyond the colonies, it had been particularly pervasive there.[37] Faced with anti-colonial violence and granted the expansion envisaged in the 1949 Geneva Conventions common Article 3 and the decline of the 'standard of civilization' as a valid international legal argument, the colonial powers had to come up with new ways of explaining repressive measures such as mass detentions, summary executions, etc.[38] Determined not to apply common Article 3, this included declaring the struggles of decolonization to be questions within the domestic jurisdiction of the colonial power and the adoption of emergency laws to suppress anti-colonial violence. To be

---

[35] Nils Melzer, *Interpretive Guidance on the Notion of Direct Participation in Hostilities under International Humanitarian Law* (Geneva: International Committee of the Red Cross (ICRC) 2009). The vast commentary on the ICRC study includes a forum published in the New York Journal of International Law and Politics: Ryan Goodman and Derek Jinks, 'The ICRC Interpretive Guidance on the Notion of Direct Participation in Hostilities Under International Humanitarian Law: An Introduction to the Forum' 42 (2010) New York Journal of International Law and Politics 637; Kenneth Watkin, 'Opportunity Lost: Organized Armed Groups and the ICRC "Direct Participation in Hostilities" Interpretive Guidance' 42 (2010) New York Journal of International Law and Politics 641; Michael N. Schmitt, 'Deconstructing Direct Participation in Hostilities: The Constitutive Elements' 42 (2010) New York Journal of International Law and Politics 697; Bill Boothy, '"And For Such Time As": The Time Dimension to Direct Participation in Hostilities' 42 (2010) New York Journal of International Law and Politics 741; Parks, 'Part IX of the ICRC Direct Participation in Hostilities Study: No Mandate, No Expertise, and Legally Incorrect'; Nils Melzer, 'Keeping the Balance Between Military Necessity and Humanity: A Response to Four Critiques of the ICRC's Interpretive Guidance on the Notion of Direct Participation in Hostilities' 42 (2010) New York Journal of International Law and Politics 831.

[36] Sibylle Scheipers, *Unlawful Combatants: A Genealogy of the Irregular Fighter* (Oxford University Press 2015).

[37] For an argument about the continuities between the colonial era and today's war on terrorism in this particular regard see Frédéric Mégret, 'From "Savages" to "Unlawful Combatants": A Postcolonial Look at International Law's "Other"' in Anne Orford (ed.), *International Law and Its Others* (Cambridge University Press 2006) 265–317.

[38] Scheipers, *Unlawful Combatants: A Genealogy of the Irregular Fighter* pp. 146–187.

on the safe side, it also included labelling the adversary not as rebels or insurgents but as terrorists.[39]

Scheipers accedes that a stronger consideration of legal issues during the wars of decolonisation in comparison to the height of colonial power may have stopped the worst atrocities but she also describes the regimes created as a 'twisted legality' with extensive and vague authorities offering next to no legal protection.[40] The watershed moments for the 'standard of civilization' of the Second World War, the 1955 Bandung Conference denouncing both Nazism and colonialism as equally linked to a system of oppression, the drafting of the 1977 Additional Protocols to the Geneva Conventions and other events in the wake of decolonization pushed the terms of the debate on irregular fighters further into the sphere of legality.[41]

David Kennedy is right when he points out that modern war reflects modern political life, particularly with regard to the pervasiveness of law.[42] The shift from exclusion to inclusion of the terrorist enemy in the law of armed conflict is a case in point and can further be understood as a continuation of a trajectory of legalisation starting in the era of decolonisation.

In this environment, although clearly not without a certain international legal pedigree, the notion of 'unlawful combatant' seems too self-serving, too much the product of the state's instrumental objectives, and thus out of touch with prevailing conceptions of the imperative to treat 'everyone humanely and legally'.[43] This explains the significant pushback against the exclusion from the law that the concept entails and the embrace of the shifting away from it by rights-minded critics of targeted killing.[44]

Curtis A. Bradley has argued that while the shift from exclusion to inclusion might come across as a step towards the imperatives to treat everyone humanely and legally; it is very likely that the categories in which the non-state enemy is included 'will be stretched in order to

---

[39] *Ibid.* p. 171.   [40] *Ibid.* p. 181.   [41] *Ibid.* p. 147.

[42] David Kennedy, *Of War and Law* (Princeton University Press 2006) p. 13.

[43] *Ibid.* p. 94.

[44] See in particular Werner, 'The Changing Face of Enmity: Carl Schmitt's International Theory and the Evolution of the Legal Concept of War' arguing that the development through which irregular fighters have been redescribed as civilians and the introduction of criteria associated with human rights (more about the latter below) in targeted killing, suggests that it is possible to escape a situation in which states and irregulars treat each other as criminals and parasites, that is, Schmitt's 'logic of *justa causa* (just cause) without recognition of a *Justus hostis* (just enemy)'. p. 352.

accommodate the security needs of the nation'.[45] This is also what Samuel
Moyn points to when he considers the so-called Phoenix programme of
the US Vietnam war as a predecessor to contemporary American targeted
killing practices:[46]

> The chilling fact may be that targeted killing today ... differs from the
> assassinations of the Phoenix programme primarily because no one at the
> time felt the need to claim that the latter's targets were not civilians or
> close enough to the boundary between combatant and non-combatant
> to be legitimate targets. The legalization of war has thus gone along with
> a potential expansion of what an 'active part' in conflict (in the crucial
> phrase of the Geneva Conventions Common article 3) means.[47]

Indeed, in both the Israeli and the US contexts we have seen how the shift
from exclusion to inclusion of the terrorist enemy has been something of a
pyrrhic victory for those aiming to use international law to stop targeted
killing. This can be seen among other places in Judge Aharon Barak's
rejection of the category of unlawful combatants for the benefit of the
notion of *civilians* who constitute *unlawful combatants* turning precisely
on an expansive interpretation of the category of civilians taking a direct
part in hostilities. Judge Rivlin's concurring opinion to the judgment in
which we learn that there is no difference between the two paths in terms
of the result because Barak adapts the notion of civilians taking a direct
part to a new reality reminds us of the 'twisted legality' – the extensive
and vague authorities offering next to no legal protection – that Sibylle
Scheipers saw in the increasingly legalised way in which colonial powers
dealt with anti-colonial violence in the decolonisation era.

Deterritorialisation of Enmity?

The emergence of targeted killing signals a shift in international law from
its traditional concern with public forms of enmity to individual or private

---

[45] Curtis A. Bradley, 'The United States, Israel & Unlawful Combatants' 12 (2009) The Green
    Bag 397.
[46] On the Phoenix programme as a predecessor to contemporary US targeted killings see
    Seymour M. Hersh, 'Moving Targets: Will the Counter-insurgency Plan in Iraq Repeat
    the Mistakes of Vietnam?' The New Yorker (15 December 2003) www.newyorker.com/
    archive/2003/12/15/031215fa_fact accessed 10 May 2015; Tal Tovy, 'The Theoretical Aspect
    of Targeted Killings: The Phoenix Program as a Case Study' 11 (2009) Journal of Military
    and Strategic Studies 1.
[47] Samuel Moyn, 'Drones and Imagination: A Response to Paul Kahn' 24 (2013) European
    Journal of International Law 227 at 231.

forms of enmity. Derek Gregory has argued that the individualisation of enmity 'impels the war to go wherever the individual-as-target goes', in other words, the unmooring of enmity from the demarcated domains of the state system.[48] The dynamic driving this development was touched upon in the foregoing with Thomas' argument about how the rise of 'non-traditional violence' is part of a dramatic transformation involving nothing less than the erosion of the institution of sovereignty itself. The law of armed conflict scholar Louise Arimatsu captures this shift when she writes:

> Our view of the world, based on clearly demarcated spaces is challenged by the reality of violence that spills across borders. While the desire of states to respond with unmitigated authority in a 'global war' functions as a reaffirmation of sovereign power, it paradoxically serves to inflict self-injury to the shell of sovereign power – the territorial boundaries of the nation-state. As rhetoric and reality collide, spaces are created to make and un-make the law, disquieting and liberating in equal measure.[49]

This reaffirmation of sovereign power in a 'global war' (and simultaneous infliction of self-injury to the shell of sovereign power) is, of course, particularly manifest in the geographically expansive American targeted killing scheme.

Thus we saw in the preceding chapter how the emergence of targeted killing formed part of a development through which conceptions of the global national security interests of the United States were taken up in the context of counterterrorism. We also noticed how Abraham Sofaer learned how difficult it is to square an American active defense against terrorism with an international law premised on the territorial compart-mentalisation of the world characteristic of a Westphalian distribution of the right to wage legitimate force. This involved the project of guarding against the protection offered by national borders and the creation of legal categories and interpretations for gaining extraterritorial access to the terrorist enemy. The United States' decision to go to war against the Taliban regime in Afghanistan for allowing the parts of Afghanistan it controls to be used by al-Qaeda as a base of operations caused renewed attention to this question. Further, indirect criteria for determining state

---

[48] Gregory, 'Drone Geographies' p. 14.

[49] Louise Arimatsu, 'Territory, Boundaries and the Law of Armed Conflict' 12 (2010) Yearbook of International Humanitarian Law 157 at 160. A similar argument can be found in Frédéric Mégret, 'War and the Vanishing Battlefield' 9 (2012) Loyola University Chicago International Law Review 131.

responsibility are, alongside pre-emptive (or preventive) self-defence, examples of topics raised by Shultz and Sofaer that are major current debates in the context of the war against terrorism.[50]

While there is an element of continuity in these *jus ad bellum* debates, the idea that the law of armed conflict not only apply to military action against terrorism but that the United States, at least since 9/11, is engaged in a transnational armed conflict with al-Qaeda and its associated forces, represents a new development.

Frédéric Mégret has described the application of the law of armed conflict post-9/11 as a

> bizarre mixture of real battlefields (some of the traditional battles that occurred in Afghanistan and Iraq), unorthodox battlefields (e.g. fight waged by special forces in the territory of foreign countries outside an all-out invasion), and not-battlefield-at-all type violence (drone attacks on suspected terrorists).[51]

This situation has triggered an extensive debate on the application of the law of armed conflict, a debate that, according to Louise Arimatsu, reveals 'an uncomfortable disconnect between the static and territorialized attributes of the law that attempts to govern the ever dynamic, de-territorialized *relational* fact of armed conflict',[52] and this is what we will focus on in this section.

Pursuing the line of thought just introduced, Arimatsu has set out to analyse how the law of armed conflict is framed by an historically determined territorial viewpoint, a viewpoint which is currently being reconsidered in the context of the war on terrorism generally and targeted

---

[50] On the topic of pre-emptive or preventive self-defence see for example, Amos N. Guiora, 'Anticipatory Self-Defence and International Law – A Re-evaluation' 13 (2008) *Journal of Conflict & Security Law* 3; Michael W. Doyle and others, *Striking First: Preemption and Prevention in International Conflict* (Stephen Macedo ed., Princeton University Press 2008); Michael Byers, 'Preemptive Self-defense: Hegemony, Equality and Strategies of Legal Change' 2 (2003) The Journal of Political Philosophy 171; Michael W. Reisman, 'Editorial Comment: Assessing Claims to Revise the Laws of War' 97 (2003) American Journal of International Law 82; Christine Gray, 'The US National Security Strategy and the New "Bush Doctrine" on Preemptive Self-defense' 1 (2002) *Chinese Journal of International Law* 437. On the topic of terrorism and state responsibility see in particular Tal Becker, *Terrorism and the State: Rethinking the Rules of State Responsibility* (Oxford: Hart Publishing 2006); Proulx, *Transnational Terrorism and State Accountability: A New Theory of Prevention*; Marja Lehto, *Indirect Responsibility for Terrorist Acts: Redefinition of the Concept of Terrorism Beyond Violent Acts* (Leiden: Martinus Nijhoff Publishers 2009).

[51] Mégret, 'War and the Vanishing Battlefield' p. 148.

[52] Arimatsu, 'Territory, Boundaries and the Law of Armed Conflict' p. 178.

killing particularly. The territorial viewpoint of the law of armed conflict is most clearly visible in the distinction between classic *international armed conflict* or interstate armed conflict and *non-international armed conflict,* traditionally understood as intrastate armed conflict. This distinction is intimately linked to the emergence and dominance of the territorially-bounded state as both the maker and enforcer of the law. This is a law that 'serves to reaffirm the territorial integrity and sovereignty of the nation-state and with it, its monopoly of violence'. Perceived in this way, the law of armed conflict remains, in Arimatsu's words 'the loyal champion of the foundations laid at Westphalia'.[53]

Now, faced with factual situations that exceed this historically-determined territorial viewpoint of the law of armed conflict, government lawyers, courts and international lawyers more generally have tended to rely on what Arimatsu describes as 'descriptive accuracy'.[54] We can see this at work in the Israel Supreme Court targeted killing judgment and the notion of an *international armed conflict between a state and a non-state enemy,* as well as in the US Supreme Court *Hamdan* judgment, widely interpreted to have asserted the armed conflict between the United States and al-Qaeda and associated forces to be a *transnational non-international armed conflict.* In both cases, the Courts avoided the binary structure of international armed conflict and non-international armed conflict based on the territorially-bounded state.[55] This deterritorialisation or unmooring of enmity from the demarcated domains of the state system takes different forms, and I shall try to describe positions ranging from the most radically deterritorialised view to a conservative territorial view in the context of the contemporary debate over targeted killing.

The most extreme form of deterritorialisation of enmity is that which takes the notion of a global war on terrorism literally in the sense that it pertains to an armed conflict of global proportions between the United States and al-Qaeda and associated forces. Kenneth Anderson has in a number of publications attempted to reconstruct what he refers to as the 'traditional US legal view' on the topic:

> The United States has broadly embraced the view that there in fact is an armed conflict (the one named in US domestic law under the AUMF) with transnational nonstate terrorist actors and thus is a NIAC [Non-International Armed Conflict]. That being so, in the traditional US legal view, the armed conflict goes where the participants go, as it did in World War II and does today. It goes where the targets go and goes where hostilities

[53] *Ibid.* p. 170.   [54] *Ibid.* p. 160.   [55] *Ibid.*

conducted against the targets go. Moreover, once conflict got under way, at least as early as 9/11, it 'isn't over until it's over.' The conflict has extension in both space and time. As a consequence, if targetable enemies move from Afghanistan to Pakistan to Yemen to Somalia over a period of years in which they are sometimes actively engaged in attacks and sometimes quiescent, they remain the enemy no less than before and targetable as such until the armed conflict is over. This position raises difficult and highly controversial issues of so-called direct participation in hostilities by civilians and when they can lawfully be targeted; the general position of the United States has been that terrorists hiding in safe havens are not immune from attack. Moreover, new persons or parties that join with them also become connected to the original NIAC and thus become targetable as well.[56]

Anderson hastens to add that the threshold of armed conflict still has to be met for the existence of such an armed conflict: 'that threshold is not merely instances of fighting with nonstate groups that is fleeting and discrete. Instead it must rise to the customary law threshold of being sustained, intense, systematic, and organized'.[57] However, this determination is also deterritorialised, or, as Anderson puts it, 'the threshold of armed conflict issue exists independent of the geography issue', something which allows individual instances of targeted killing to be lawfully aggregated

---

[56] Kenneth Anderson, 'Targeted Killing and Drone Warfare: How We Came to Debate Whether There is a "Legal Geography of War"' in Peter Berkowitz (ed.), *Future Challenges in National Security and Law: Hoover Institution WCL Research Paper No 2011–16* Available at SSRN: http://ssrn.com/abstract=1824783 accessed 14 May 2015 (2011) p. 4. Anderson's exposition can be compared with what John Brennan, at the time Assistant to the President for Homeland Security and Counterterrorism, stated in a speech at the Program on Law and Security at Harvard Law School on 18 September 2011: 'An area in which there is some disagreement is the geographic scope of the conflict. The United States does not view our authority to use military force against al-Qa'ida as being restricted to 'hot' battlefields like Afghanistan. Because we are engaged in an armed conflict with al-Qa'ida, the United States takes the legal position that – in accordance with international law – we have the authority to take action against al-Qa'ida and its associated forces without doing a separate self-defense analysis each time. And as President Obama has stated on numerous occasions, we reserve the right to take unilateral action if or when other governments are unwilling or unable to take the necessary actions themselves. That does not mean we can use military force whenever we want, wherever we want. International legal principles including respect for a state's sovereignty and the laws of war, impose important constraints on our ability to act unilaterally – and on the way in which we can use force – in foreign territories' (John Brennan, 'Counterterrorism and the Law' (*Homeland Security Watch*, 19 September 2011) www.hlswatch.com/2011/09/18/brennan-counterterrorism-and-the-law/ accessed 10 May 2015).

[57] Anderson, 'Targeted Killing and Drone Warfare: How We Came to Debate Whether There is a "Legal Geography of War"' p. 5.

and be taken together as a single armed conflict across space and time.[58] Anderson is very aware of the issues of territorial integrity that such a deterritorialised armed conflict inevitably comes up against. This is dealt with by way of a return to the protean right to self-defence developed by Shultz, Sofaer and Parks in the 1980s, coupled with indirect means for determining responsibility of the state for allowing its territory to be used by the non-state enemy, or, alternatively, by reference to law of neutrality rights and responsibilities in the context of this transnational non-international armed conflict. In both cases the extraterritorial access to the non-state enemy hinges on whether the territorial state is 'unable or unwilling' to deal with the threat.[59] This was expressed in a previously cited US Department of Justice white paper in the following way:

> Moreover, a lethal operation in a foreign nation would be consistent with international legal principles of sovereignty and neutrality if it were conducted, for example, with the consent of the host nation's government or after a determination that the host nation is unable or unwilling to suppress the threat posed by the individual targeted.[60]

Kenneth Anderson does not even shy away from embracing a notion of *unequal* sovereigns in the international legal order in the context of targeted killing:

> Individual terrorists on missions easily shift around the world, concealed in airports, foreign cities in many lands, so as to strike at vulnerable targets in extraordinarily diverse settings: New York, Mumbai, London, not to mention Pakistan and Afghanistan. Counterterrorism, obviously, must be similarly mobile. But this mobility means different things in different places in its political and legal senses. In dealing with London or Paris, the United States can rely on the cooperation of local security services and the police, as well as broadly shared aims, values, and methods.

---

[58] *Ibid.* p. 6.

[59] On this notion see the article by the former assistant legal adviser for political-military affairs in the US Department of State's Office of the Legal Adviser's Ashley S. Deeks, '"Unwilling or Unable": Toward a Normative Framework for Extraterritorial Self-Defense' 52 (2012) Virginia Journal of International Law 483. For an application of the 'unwilling or unable' test on the killing of Osama bin Laden in Pakistan see Ashley S. Deeks, 'Pakistan's Sovereignty and the Killing of Osama Bin Laden' ASIL Insights www.asil.org/insights/volume/15/issue/11/pakistans-sovereignty-and-killing-osama-bin-laden accessed 10 May 2015.

[60] Department of Justice, 'White Paper: Lawfulness of a Lethal Operation Directed Against a U.S. Citizen who is a Senior Operational Leader of Al-Qa'ida or an Associated Force', published online at: www.law.upenn.edu/live/files/1903-doj-white-paper accessed 10 May 2015 p. 16.

This is not the case in Yemen and numerous other places, occasional official protestations to the contrary. States are not all the same when it comes to terrorism, in other words. No rational US leader is going to take the solemn international law admonition of the 'sovereign equality of states' too seriously in these matters – and the United States has never regarded a refusal to do so as contrary to international law but instead as something built into international law as a qualification on the reach of the 'sovereign equality' of states. There will not be 'Predators over Paris, France,' anymore than there will be 'Predators over Paris, Texas,' but Pakistan, Yemen, Somalia, and points beyond are a different story.[61]

The distinction that Anderson makes between sovereign *equals* and sovereign *unequals* in the context of targeted killing is an illustration of what Gerry Simpson has referred to as the hegemonically-asserted allocation of 'the benefits of sovereignty on the basis of conformity to some standard of behaviour or moral characteristic'.[62] As Gerry Simpson has shown, there is a case to be made for a certain continuity of such claims of legalised hegemony in international law, all the way from the demarcation between Christian/non-Christian or European/non-European to this kind of unequal distribution of equal rights between Great Powers and outlaw states in the present era of formal sovereign equality.[63] Through such legalised hegemony, 'the legal scope for the use of force by Great Powers is widened while the territorial integrity and political independence of the outlaw state shrinks. The result is a highly permissive environment in which the use of force can be more readily employed'.[64]

Noam Lubell and Nathan Derejko also affirm the deterritorialisation of armed conflict although they at the same time recognise the commanding role of the *jus ad bellum* in restraining the apparent *jus in bello* deterritorialisation. For, in Lubell and Derejko's words, 'it is . . . the *ius ad bellum*, rather than the *ius in bello*, which will more often serve as the primary barrier to prevent the precipitous spread of armed conflict to new territories'.[65] That being said, they stress that

---

[61] Anderson, 'Targeted Killing and Drone Warfare: How We Came to Debate Whether There is a "Legal Geography of War"' p. 8f.

[62] Simpson, *Great Powers and Outlaw States: Unequal Sovereigns in the International legal Order* p. 325.

[63] *Ibid.*   [64] *Ibid.* p. 336.

[65] Lubell and Derejko assert that unless acting with consent, with UN Security Council authorisation, or under conditions satisfying the test for action in self-defence, targeted killing would be unlawful, regardless of its compliance with IHL. Noam Lubell and Nathan Derejko, 'A Global Battlefield? Drones and the Geographical Scope of Armed Conflict' 11 (2013) Journal of International Criminal Justice 65 at 87.

the *ius in bello* is not as geographically bound as may have been assumed. It is not designed to follow state borders and, moreover, while the applicability of IHL revolves around a number of concepts, a hot-zone battlefield is not an indispensable requirement for every operation.[66]

The 'number of concepts' around which the applicability of the law of armed conflict revolves in the context of targeted killing is referred to by Lubell and Derejko as a nexus between the target and the armed conflict consisting of three elements: (a) the geographical distance from the primary sphere of hostilities; (b) the level and nature of military operations occurring at the target area; (c) the link between the target and an already occurring armed conflict.

> The latter point is a key question in the context of the 'war on terror', as it is not always clear whether the individuals targeted are in fact members of the same organised armed groups the United States is combatting in Afghanistan. The more tenuous this connection, the more vital it is to see if the first two elements above might nevertheless still lead to the applicability of IHL. This is because in the absence of an ability to encompass the target within the framework of an existing armed conflict, it will become necessary to show that a separate armed conflict exists between the state and the targeted armed group. The difficulty here is that if there is no other fighting elsewhere between members of this armed group and the state, then the only indication for the existence of an armed conflict will be the drone strikes themselves. It is, however, highly questionable as to whether a one-sided drone strike can meet the threshold of intensity for armed conflict. The very concept of armed conflict signifies 'protracted armed violence' *between* two (or more) Parties, and drone strikes from the skies with all the attacking done by one side, and all the casualties on the other, hardly fits the bill ... absent the third element of a link with a pre-existing armed conflict, the second element must encompass more than one-sided drone strikes, and include collective hostilities rising to the level of NIAC.[67]

As is clear from this elaboration on the three elements providing a nexus between the target and an armed conflict, 'as central a role as national borders continue to play in the context of the *ius ad bellum* and any sovereignty related matters, their impact on the applicability of the *ius in bello* is not of the same magnitude'.[68]

By taking the example of the US legal view (as it has been fleshed out by Kenneth Anderson), but also Lubell and Derejko's less radical view (largely because of the commanding role of the *jus ad bellum*), I

---

[66] *Ibid.* p. 86.   [67] *Ibid.* p. 78. Emphasis in the original.   [68] *Ibid.* p. 79.

do not mean to say that a territorial conception of enmity is absent in the debate over targeted killing. Among international law scholars Mary Ellen O'Connell has perhaps been the most outspoken defender of a territorialised conception of armed conflict and the 'zone of combat' in which the law of armed conflict applies in the context of targeted killing.

> Armed conflict occurs when organized armed groups exchange protracted, intense, armed hostilities. The groups must be associated with territory. In addition to the concept of armed conflict, the concept of conflict zone is important. Killing combatants or detaining them without trial until the end of hostilities is consistent with the principles of necessity and proportionality, as well as general human rights, when related to a zone of actual armed hostilities. Outside such a zone, however, authorities must attempt to arrest a suspect and only target to kill those who pose an immediate lethal threat and refuse to surrender.[69]

Applying this reasoning to the American war against terrorism, O'Connell finds that

> In addition to exchange, intensity, and duration, armed conflicts have a spatial dimension. It is not the case that if there is an armed conflict in one state – for example, Afghanistan – that all the world is at war, or even that Afghanis and Americans are at war with each other all over the planet. Armed conflicts inevitably have a limited and identifiable territorial or spatial dimension because human beings who participate in armed conflict require territory in which to carry out intense, protracted, armed exchanges.[70]

O'Connell continues: 'outside of armed conflicts involving United States in Afghanistan, Iraq and Somalia, Al-Qaeda's actions and U.S. responses have been too sporadic and low-intensity to qualify as armed conflict'.[71]

In a 2013 interim report to the UN General Assembly on the use of remotely piloted aircraft in counterterrorism operations, Special Rapporteur Ben Emmerson notes that the ICRC has found a lack of a clear international consensus on the 'territorial' character of the law of armed conflict. Emmerson further looks at the view of the ICRC that 'international humanitarian law does not permit the targeting of persons directly participating in hostilities who are located in non-belligerent states' and the claim of a Dutch Advisory Committee on issues of public international law that 'international humanitarian law "applies only to the territory of

---

[69] Mary Ellen O'Connell, 'Combatants and the Combat Zone' 43 (2009) University of Richmond Law Review 845 at 863f.
[70] *Ibid.*   [71] *Ibid.*

the State where a conflict is taking place"'. On that basis he affirms an 'essentially territorial approach' to the application of the law of armed conflict.[72]

In contrast to O'Connell's and Special Rapporteur Emmerson's positions, what characterises the different approaches that deterritorialise enmity is the following: that which determines enmity is no longer territorial jurisdiction but the *relation* between the enemies. The result is the bizarre battlefield of which Mégret writes. While this would appear to be a development in keeping with the notion of a post-Westphalian international law, it is also true that this position resembles the situation in pre-territorial Europe in which the rules of war were applicable to the respective parties engaged in warfare across the continent based on a *relation* of enmity rather than contingent on notions of territorial jurisdiction.[73] Samuel Moyn has interpreted the same development not as a return to pre-territorial Europe but to the territorially informal orders of colonial governance:

> In colonial governance, war was not a matter of enemies met at the border; it frequently involved shadowy groups of rebels posing a nebulous threat to a territorially informal order. And surely the identification of individual leaders for targeted death, a familiar part of such engagements in European and later American history, is not new.[74]

Enemy or Rights-bearer?

If the legal framework that sustain targeted killing constitutes a refashioning of international law's sanctioning of lethal force in an individualising and deterritorialising direction, this is a development that would appear to be on a collision course with a similarly individualising and deterritorialising movement in international law, namely, human rights – in particular because targeted killing affects what is often said to be the most basic of human rights, the right to life.[75]

Indeed, after having resigned from his mission as UN Special Rapporteur on extrajudicial, summary or arbitrary executions, Philip Alston wrote the following about targeted killing:

---

[72] UNGA, 'Promotion and Protection of Human Rights and Fundamental Freedoms while Countering Terrorism' (18 September 2013) UN Doc A/68/389 paras. 64–65.

[73] Arimatsu, 'Territory, Boundaries and the Law of Armed Conflict' p. 187.

[74] Moyn, 'Drones and Imagination: A Response to Paul Kahn' p. 229.

[75] Inter alia in the Israel Supreme Court targeted killing judgment: *Public Committee Against Torture* v. *The Government of Israel* para. 50.

from the perspective of both domestic and international law, the practice of secret killings conducted outside conventional combat settings, undertaken on an institutionalized and systematic basis, and with extremely limited if any verifiable external accountability, is a deeply disturbing and regressive one. These developments threaten to do irreparable harm to the international legal framework designed to establish and uphold foundational protections for the right to life and human dignity.[76]

While targeted killing creates serious concerns from a human rights perspective there are also ways of explaining, from within human rights law, the coincidence of the emergence of targeted killing and the progressive development of international human rights.

Gregor Noll has shown that the structure of international law conditions human rights in a way that makes it difficult to fulfil the promise of both inalienability and universality. Noll contends that international law cannot sustain inalienability because it would require insulation from politics and human rights obligations, much as other international legal obligation arise, can be altered, abolished even, through the 'will representation of a particular political community'.[77] Further, Noll argues that human rights treaties fail to deliver on universality because they are biased towards 'the trinity of state-population-territory', where 'the force of obligation decreases with the distance to each of these determinants'.[78] This can be observed when their territorial, jurisdictional as well as personal delimitations create 'white spots in the universe of human rights – spots where no meaningful legal responsibility can be determined'.[79] What comes to mind is, of course, the case of Guantanamo Bay and the solemn assertion of the US government that

> by its express terms and clear negotiating history, the International Covenant on Civil and Political Rights ('ICCPR') applies to each State Party only with respect to 'individuals within its territory and subject to its jurisdiction.' The ICCPR thus does not cover operations in Guantanamo, which is not within U.S. territory.[80]

---

[76] Philip Alston, 'The CIA and Targeted Killings Beyond Borders' 2 (2011) Harvard National Security Journal 283 at 289.

[77] Gregor Noll, 'The Exclusionary Construction of Human Rights in International Law and Political Theory' 10 (2003) Institute for International Integration Studies Discussion Paper 1 at 10.

[78] *Ibid.* p. 8.   [79] *Ibid.*

[80] 'Reply of the Government of the United States of America to the Report of the Five UNCHR Special Rapporteurs on Detainees in Guantanamo Bay Cuba' 45 (2006) International Legal Materials 742 at 743.

What also comes to mind is the Israeli government's response to the human rights committee, in its recent fourth periodic report, that while the ICCPR is 'implemented by the Government throughout the State of Israel', with regard to the occupied territories and 'in line with basic principles of treaty interpretation, Israel believes that the Convention, which is territorially bound, does not apply, nor was it intended to apply, to areas beyond a state's national territory'.[81]

Dialogue on pressing human rights issues such as Guantanamo, occupation or targeted killing takes this form of, on the one hand, expressions of the bias towards the trinity of state-population-territory and, on the other, emphatic assertions that 'it is the *law* that human rights are universal and that they accrue to every human being, war or no war'.[82]

The history of targeted killing, but also the way in which Israel and the United States consistently have responded to human rights bodies on the matter, gives us good reason to consider another explanation as to the coincidence of the rise of targeted killing and of international human rights. Thus, the US assertion of the non-applicability of the ICCPR at Guantanamo Bay referred to earlier comes after having asserted that 'the United States is engaged in a continuing armed conflict against Al Qaida, The Taliban and other terrorist organizations' and that 'certain laws of war govern the conduct of that conflict and related detention operations'.[83] Moreover, when the UN Special Rapporteur on extrajudicial, summary or arbitrary executions Asma Jahangir sent a communication to the US government querying whether a drone attack in Yemen on

---

[81] Human Rights Committee, 'Consideration of reports submitted by States Parties under article 40 of the Covenant pursuant to the optional reporting procedure – (Fourth periodic reports of States parties due in 2013) Israel', (14 October 2013) Advance Unedited Version published on the website of the Human Rights Committee: www.ccprcentre.org/country/israel/ accessed 10 May 2015 p. 9. For an accomplished rebuttal (with frequent examples from the war on terrorism generally and targeted killing particularly) of this understanding of the extraterritorial non-applicability of human rights treaties see Marko Milanovic, *Extraterritorial Application of Human Rights Treaties* (Oxford University Press 2011).

[82] Marko Milanovic, 'Norm Conflicts, International Humanitarian Law, and Human Rights Law' in Orna Ben-Naftali (ed.), *International Humanitarian Law and International Human Rights Law* (Oxford University Press 2013) 95–126 at 101. Emphasis in the original.

[83] 'Reply of the Government of the United States of America to the Report of the Five UNCHR Special Rapporteurs on Detainees in Guantanamo Bay Cuba' 45 (2006) International Legal Materials 742. See also Philip Alston, Jason Morgan-Foster and William Abresch, 'The Competence of the UN Human Rights Council and its Special Procedures in Relation to Armed Conflicts: Extrajudicial Executions in the "War on Terror"' 19 (2008) European Journal of International Law 183.

3 November 2002 was consistent with applicable international legal norms, she got the response that

> the Government of the United States respectfully submits that inquiries related to allegations stemming from any military operations conducted during the course of an armed conflict with Al Qaida do not fall within the mandate of the Special Rapporteur. The United States also disagrees with the premise of the letter and the conclusions contained in the report that military operations against enemy combatants could be regarded as 'extrajudicial executions by consent of Governments'. The conduct of a government in legitimate military operations, whether against Al Qaida operatives or any other legitimate military target would be governed by the international law of armed conflict.[84]

Likewise, the Israeli assertion of the non-applicability of the ICCPR on the occupied territories in its fourth periodic report referred to earlier comes after having stated the following about the relationship between human rights and humanitarian law:

> The relationship between different legal spheres, primarily the Law of Armed Conflict and Human Rights law remains a subject of serious academic and practical debate. For its part, Israel recognizes that there is a profound connection between human rights and the Law of Armed Conflict, and that there may well be a convergence between these two bodies-of-law in some respects. However, in the current state of international law and state-practice worldwide, it is Israel's view that these two systems-of-law, which are codified in separate instruments, remain distinct and apply in different circumstances.

To this it should be added that the Israeli government in the third periodic report responded to the concern of the Committee about 'what the State party calls "targeted killings" of those identified by the State party as suspected terrorists in the Occupied territories'[85] in the following way:

---

[84] Commission on Human Rights, 'Letter dated 14 April 2003 from the Chief of Section, Political and Specialized Agencies, of the Permanent Mission of the United States of America to the United Nations Office at Geneva addressed to the secretariat of the Commission on Human Rights' (14 April 2003) UN Doc E/CN.4/2003/G/80 p. 2f. The stance taken by the United States in relation to whether targeted killing falls within the competence of the Human Rights Council in general and the Special Rapporteur in particular is laid out and criticised by the then Special Rapporteur Philip Alston in Alston, Morgan-Foster and Abresch, 'The Competence of the UN Human Rights Council and its Special Procedures in Relation to Armed Conflicts: Extrajudicial Executions in the "War on Terror"'.

[85] Human Rights Committee, 'Consideration of Reports Submitted By States Parties Under Article 40 of the Covenant, Concluding Observations of the Human Rights Committee, Israel' (21 August 2003) UN Doc CCPR/CO/78/ISR para. 15.

'Israel's occasional resort to the targeting of terrorists, as a matter of military necessity, is carried out in compliance with international law of armed conflict'.[86]

Against this background, and with a view to a better understanding of the human rights dimension of the struggle over international law's sanctioning of lethal force in targeted killing, we turn to the relationship between human rights and the law of armed conflict. First the history of the idea that there is a relationship between human rights and the law of armed conflict is considered. Thereafter, the foremost doctrine dealing with this relationship – *lex specialis derogat legi generalis* – is considered. Finally, the tendency to substitute a hybridised for a mutually exclusive relation in the context of targeted killing is analysed.

Brief History of the Relation of Human Rights and Humanitarian Law

That human rights and the law of armed conflict relate to one another at all is an idea of relatively recent origin. In a recently published research handbook on human rights and humanitarian law, Robert Kolb has taken 'the two drum-rolls of 1948 and 1949', the Universal Declaration on Human Rights (UDHR) and the Geneva conventions on the protection of victims of armed conflicts, as his point of departure. Investigating the travaux préparatoires for the two texts he finds that they were

> not cast into the mould of complete mutual ignorance, but it must also be recognized that the cross-fertilizations between them remained extremely marginal. In the late 1940s, IHL and international HRL [Human Rights Law] were set largely on separate tracks. Their meetings were at once short, exceptional and marginal.[87]

What Kolb refers to as a 'quite neat separatism' continued well into the post-war period.[88] Kolb summarises the main reasons for it in five points: First, the reorientation of the law of armed conflict from the old military law to a humanitarian law centring on protected persons (a re-orientation

---

[86] Human Rights Committee, 'Comments by the Government of Israel on the Concluding Observations of the Human Rights Committee' (24 January 2007) UN Doc CCPR/CO/78/ISR/Add. 1 p. 4.

[87] Robert Kolb, 'Human Rights Law and International Humanitarian Law between 1945 and the Aftermath of the Teheran Conference of 1968' in Robert Kolb and Gloria Gaggioli (eds.), *Research Handbook on Human Rights and Humanitarian Law* (Cheltenham and Northampton: Edward Elgar Publishing 2013) 35–52 at 40.

[88] *Ibid.* p. 41.

that would bring its ethos significantly closer to human rights law) was yet to get traction. Second, human rights law was still in its infancy with a non-binding UDHR and the two covenants not adopted until 1966, whereas the law of armed conflict had a very distinguished pedigree in international law and was codified in a series of undoubtedly hard law texts. Third, distinct classes of lawyers championed human rights law and the law of armed conflict with a mutual mistrust for each other. The law of armed conflict was the business of military lawyers often working for states. The body of rules over which they asserted jurisdiction were technical rules for hostile relations *between* polities. In contrast, the cause of human rights law in this time was man in civil society or *in* these polities. Fourth, the institutional settings of the two areas of law were such that the ICRC guarded the law of armed conflict, and the political organs of the UN guarded human rights law. While the ICRC feared that opening the law of armed conflict to the new human rights law would politicise and thus discredit the law of armed conflict in military circles, the ICRC's preparation of rules for war was not welcomed by the UN, because it was seen as suggesting doubts in the organisation's capacity to maintain peace. Fifth, and as already touched upon, the predominant conception at the time was that human rights law applied inside the polity in peacetime, and the law of armed conflict applied in times of war or armed conflict between polities. This means essentially that there were few, if any, meeting points between the two areas of international law.[89]

At this early stage it is already possible to discern some key factors for the subservience of human rights in the law of targeted killing, particularly the conception that human rights are the rights of the citizen dwelling inside the polity and that human rights law only apply in times of normality or peace. Before we get to this, however, we must consider the various reasons for the convergence of the separate tracks of human rights law and humanitarian law starting somewhere in the late 1960s. Kolb summarises them in the following way: the institutional gap where ICRC refused to deal with human rights and the UN refused to deal with the law of armed conflict was breached and the mutual mistrust to some extent overcome. What also occurred was that the asymmetry of hard law, law of armed conflict, soft law, human rights, was redressed by the positivisation of human rights law through the entering into force of the two human rights covenants together with a number of regional human

---

[89] This entire section summarises Kolb's conclusions in *ibid.* p. 41ff.

rights treaties. Additionally, the increasing traction of 'humanitarian law' properly speaking – that part of the law of armed conflict that centres on protected persons – at the expense of the old state-centred military law, also contributed to the convergence. Those focusing on the humanitarian nature of this law argued that both humanitarian law and human rights basically pursue the same objectives, namely to protect the basic rights of the human person from abuse, oppression or violence.[90] While the old state-centred military law favours maintaining a gulf between the 'law of war' and human rights, it is easy to see how a co-operative conjunction would be in the interest of the new 'humanitarian law' effort at strengthening the protection of civilians in armed conflict. This development in the law of armed conflict converged with the advancement of human rights in the 1970s and 1980s, through which human rights discourse emancipated itself from the strictures of the rights of the citizen dwelling inside the polity and started to be thought more and more in terms of belonging to the individual by virtue of being human – in other words, as inalienable and universal.[91]

The 1968 UN Conference on Human Rights in Teheran is often held up as the beginning of the convergence of human rights and the law of armed conflict. Here the notion of 'human rights in armed conflict' received an official imprimatur. The context in which this concept was introduced was in particular the recent commencement of the occupation of the Palestinian territories and Israel was severely criticised for not living up to the standards of both human rights and the law of armed conflict in its occupation of Palestinian lands in the final act of the conference.[92] In 1971, an international symposium under the auspices of the Faculty of Law at Tel Aviv University was held. The two themes at the symposium were 'Human Rights in Peace-time' and 'Human rights in time of war, with particular emphasis on the administered territories'. The proceedings of the symposium were published in the very first volume of

---

[90] Medard R. Rwelamira, 'Human Rights and International Humanitarian Law: The Link or Common Ground Revisited' 3 (1992) Stellenbosch Law Review 329 at 340.

[91] This entire section summarises Kolb's conclusions in Kolb, 'Human Rights Law and International Humanitarian Law between 1945 and the Aftermath of the Teheran Conference of 1968' p. 44ff. On the advancement of international human rights particularly in Western countries from the 1970s see Samuel Moyn, *The Last Utopia: Human Rights in History* (Cambridge Massachusetts: Harvard University Press 2010). See also the contributions in the edited volume: Jan Eckel and Samuel Moyn, *The Breakthrough: Human Rights in the 1970s* (Philadelphia: University of Pennsylvania Press 2014).

[92] UNGA, 'Final Act of the International Conference on Human Rights' (Teheran, 22 April to 13 May 1968) UN Doc A/CONF.32/41.

the *Israel Yearbook on Human Rights*, a publication that ever since has been at the forefront as far as scholarly investigations of the relationship between human rights and humanitarian law is concerned. Included in the section 'human rights in warfare' is an article by the esteemed British humanitarian lawyer G.I.A.D. Draper. I want to pick up on this text by Draper (as well as a follow-up on it that he published a couple of years later) because it is an early text that tries to grapple with the convergence of human rights and the law of armed conflict and does it in a way that carries great explanatory value for how human rights are kept at bay by the legal framework for targeted killing. In a key section of the article Draper writes:

> War, from its nature, presents the supreme denial of human rights and the maximum regime for inhumanity. Yet, throughout its latter history, some prohibitions were introduced to mitigate this inhumanity by man to man, at least insofar as they were consistent with the balance of securing military considerations . . . the modern system of human rights seeks to become the normal ordering of society. Its approach to war is as something exceptional, but not outside of society, something derogatory in the technical sense, but nevertheless a temporary inroad upon itself.[93]

It is significant that Draper finds a legal basis for this 'essential juxta-position of the law of armed conflicts to the regime of human rights' in the positive law of human rights: more particularly, the derogation clauses of the major human rights instruments, particularly Article 15 of the European Convention on Human Rights, which he considers a 'prototype provision'.[94]

The first section of Article 15 reads: 'In time of war or other public emergency threatening the life of the nation any High Contracting party may take measures derogating from it obligations under this convention to the extent strictly required by the exigencies of the situation'. Further on in Section 2 it is stated that Article 2 or the right to life cannot be derogated from 'except in respect of deaths resulting from lawful acts of war'.[95] Now, in this schema, Draper explains, human rights is the

> normal ordering of civil and civilized society. War, international or inter-nal, is the exceptional situation derogating from the full application of

---

[93] G.I.A.D. Draper, 'The Relationship Between the Human Rights Regime and the Law of Armed Conflict' 1 (1971) Israel Yearbook on Human Rights 191.

[94] *Ibid.* p. 197.

[95] Convention for the Protection of Human Rights and Fundamental Freedoms (European Convention on Human Rights, as amended) (ECHR).

human rights. Only that which permits the taking of life in time of war or 'other emergency threatening the life of the nation' will be considered a legitimate inroad upon the prohibition contained in Article 15.[96]

In fact, Draper writes that through Article 15 of the European Convention on Human Rights, 'the whole of the law of war as to killing has been incorporated by reference'.[97] Further on in the same piece Draper reflects on the historical importance of this shift:

> We have therefore got ourselves into the position that the law of war may take its place within the general system of international law not as an alternative to the law of peace, the old and classic positioning, but seen as an exceptional and derogating regime from that of human rights, contained, controlled and fashioned by the latter at every point possible. The law of war is a regime which descends when that of the normal one of human rights lifts in time of armed conflict (international or internal). It is a second-best system, exceptional, but certainly not alien to that of human rights, and must be with us until man can learn to avoid applying the scourge of war to himself and his fellows.[98]

A few years after the conference in Tel Aviv and the publication of the Year-book, Draper would return to the question of the relationship between human rights and the law of armed conflict. This occurred against the background of the Diplomatic Conference on the Reaffirmation and Development of International Humanitarian Law at Geneva 1974–1977 and a series of UN General Assembly Resolutions under the rubric of 'Respect for Human Rights in Armed Conflict' following from the 1968 UN Conference in Teheran. It is clear that these developments had brought human rights and humanitarian law far too close to one another for Draper's tastes. In seeking to 'dispel' the idea of a conjunction between human rights and humanitarian law, Draper investigates the trajectories through which human rights and humanitarian law have developed.[99] In this context he emphasises how the internationalisation of human rights in the twentieth century has not implied the abandonment of the idea that human rights are essentially the rights of the citizen dwelling inside the polity; he thus establishes a continuity in human rights-thinking that stretches as far back as Aristotle, through, inter alia, the 1789 Declaration

---

[96] Draper, 'The Relationship Between the Human Rights Regime and the Law of Armed Conflict' p. 196.

[97] *Ibid.* p. 197.   [98] *Ibid.* p. 198.

[99] G.I.A.D. Draper, 'Humanitarian Law and Human Rights' (1979) Acta Juridica 193.

of the Rights of Man to the 1948 UDHR and the 1966 UN human rights covenants.

> When one studies the lists of human rights and fundamental freedoms that have found a place in the main international instruments for their protection, it is apparent that these rights appear as a form of internationalized constitutional law, by inter-state guarantee. Human rights fall within that part of constitutional law which deals with the relationship between government and the governed, i e the citizenry. This has been the consistent theme since the Virginia Bill of Rights of 1776, the Declaration of the Rights of Man of 1789, the Universal Declaration of 1948, the European Convention of Human Rights of 1953 and the two UN covenants of 1966. The establishment of these rights is not designed to express an antinomy or clash between government and citizen. On the contrary, they express the necessary harmony and civic solidarity within the 'city' formulated by Aristotle. These rights are designed to accommodate both the essential climate of freedom for the development of the human person and man's essential need for life in society. The ambitious design of our century to lift these human rights into the international level, and translate them into international law, by conventions, has not transformed the nature of these rights but has highlighted their importance for the community of states and for the governed in all states. It is these qualities and purposes of the conception of human-rights regimes that fall to be considered when juxtaposing such regimes with the international law of war, now styled the international humanitarian law of armed conflict.[100]

In doing this – in juxtaposing the conception of human rights as essentially the rights of the citizen dwelling inside the polity with the law of armed conflict – Draper finds that 'in dealing with a relation between a government and the governed which has reached the level of armed resistance by the latter', internal conflicts seem, prima facie, to be an area where the law of armed conflict and human rights might conjoin.[101] However, as was also stressed in his 1971 article, human rights operate in times of normality 'and are neither designed for nor adequate to control an armed conflict between government and dissident armed or unarmed, elements of the population', hence the right to derogate from human rights in times of war or emergency.[102] It is different with international armed conflicts because in international armed conflicts the point of contact between human rights and humanitarian law (a relation between a government and the governed) is missing. Instead, the law of international armed

---

[100] *Ibid.* p. 194f.   [101] *Ibid.* p. 203.   [102] *Ibid.* p. 203f.

conflicts purports to govern the hostile relations of states engaged in armed confrontation:

> a war or 'emergency' situation impinges, within specified limits, upon those guaranteed rights and freedoms, in relation to the governed i.e. 'everyone within their jurisdiction', and not in relation to an enemy. The relevance of war to a human-rights regime is that the regime determines what happens to those human rights in that event. The regime in no way purports to regulate the conduct of the war between two states even assuming that both were subject to that human-rights regime.[103]

As is clear from the preceding two sections in this chapter, the individualised and deterritorialised form of enmity brought about in targeted killing fits neither of the two established forms of armed conflict considered by Draper: it is neither an armed conflict between a government and the governed that has reached the level of armed resistance, nor an armed conflict between states. However, as we have seen both in this and in the preceding chapters the idea that human rights apply in times of normalcy and the law of armed conflict in times of 'war' or 'emergency' is understood to apply here too. For targeted killing emerged both in the Israeli and the American context by way of extending the application of the law of armed conflict to encompass a war against terrorism and thus by extending precisely what was described by Draper as the one legitimate inroad upon the right to life in the effort of countering terrorism. To take but three examples from the history of targeted killing: first, the reason that Parks, in his 1989 legal memo on the prohibition against assassination, does not even consider the applicability of human rights law is that he considers assassination in counterterrorism operations within the context of 'assassination in wartime'. And, the extraterritorial element notwithstanding, Parks thinks that in time of war or other emergency threatening the life of the nation, killing in accordance with the law of war is a legitimate inroad upon the right to life.[104] Second, when Daniel

---

[103] *Ibid.* p. 204.

[104] Commenting on the notion of 'respect for human rights in armed conflict', Parks has asserted that this associates the law of war with human rights in an unfortunate way. This is so because 'the former are specific rules relating to legal rights and obligations of a nation engaged in war, some of which involve deprivation of the most fundamental of human right, the right to life, and for the violation of which individuals can be held criminally responsible. They also are frequently a product of military considerations. In contrast, the latter is largely philosophical and political, with little or no individual criminal responsibility for its breaches; in the words of one author, "even their discussion (not to mention their implementation) is dependent on political bodies and their conjectural

Reisner, at the press conference held in the context of the second Intifada, restates a question about the international lawfulness of an instance of targeted killing not as a question of international lawfulness per se, but as the more specific question of lawfulness in application of the law of armed conflict, and then adds that the specific person targeted was a legitimate military target, he does not and need not consider the right to life. This is because, again, the extraterritorial element notwithstanding, a decision was taken to apply the principles applicable to warfare to the situation, rather than the principles applied in time of peace. A third example is the case of Anwar al-Aulaqi. The Department of Justice memo that apparently was written in preparation for the operation to kill al-Aulaqi relies extensively on the legal categories and justifications analysed so far in this chapter – what has been referred to as the individualisation and deterritorialisation of enmity. Nowhere does the memo mention human rights law.[105] The fact that the memo was written at all, but also the diminished form of constitutional protection it grants to a non-state enemy who is also an American citizen, may be explained by the fact that as an American you are obviously closer to the trinity of state-population-territory that Gregor Noll argues determines the state's rights obligations. Yet, when Anwar al-Aulaqi's father claimed a violation of the right to life of both constitutional and human rights law, the Court refused jurisdiction with reference in particular to the claim that if an individual so threatens the United States as to warrant military action against that individual then this is a 'political judgment' that belongs in the domain of political power not subject to judicial intrusion or inquiry.

The Doctrine of Lex Specialis

In the Israel Supreme Court targeted killing judgment we see something which is also present elsewhere in the history of targeted killing, as well as in the contemporary debate over targeted killing in international law, namely, the negotiation of the encounter of the enemy and the

majorities"' (W. Hays Parks, 'Air War and the Law of War' 32 (1990) Air Force Law Review 1 at 69). On the law of war as lex specialis to human rights in armed conflict see Parks, 'Part IX of the ICRC Direct Participation in Hostilities Study: No Mandate, No Expertise, and Legally Incorrect' p. 797.

[105] Department of Justice, 'White Paper: Lawfulness of a Lethal Operation Directed Against a U.S. Citizen who is a Senior Operational Leader of Al-Qa'ida or an Associated Force', published online at: www.law.upenn.edu/live/files/1903-doj-white-paper accessed 10 May 2015.

rights-bearer through the doctrine of *lex specialis derogat legi generalis*. The most important precedent here comes from two advisory opinions of the ICJ: the 1996 Nuclear Weapons Advisory Opinion and the 2004 The Wall Advisory Opinion.[106] In particular, The Nuclear Weapons Advisory Opinion is relevant for our purposes because it specifically concerns the relationship between the right to life and the applicable rules for the taking of life during the conduct of hostilities in armed conflict. This is what the Court has to say on this matter:

> The Court observes that the protection of the International Covenant of Civil and Political Rights does not cease in times of war . . . In principle, the right not arbitrarily to be deprived of one's life applies also in hostilities. The test of what is an arbitrary deprivation of life, however, then falls to be determined by the applicable *lex specialis*, namely the law applicable in armed conflict which is designed to regulate the conduct of hostilities.[107]

As this pronouncement of the Court has been called upon to do very different work in the context of targeted killing it may be worthwhile to call attention to a few different interpretations of it. The first interpretation approximates the position on the relationship between human rights law and the law of armed conflict that has been so influential in the history of targeted killing and that was articulated by Draper in 1971: in armed conflict, the law which is designed to regulate the conduct of hostilities supersedes any human rights criteria for the taking of life. While this interpretation would appear to disregard the Court's insistence that the protection of human rights law does not cease in times of war, it is consistent with the Court allowing the law of armed conflict to determine the conditions in which it is to apply, to the detriment of human rights. In other words, this interpretation suggests that when the conditions for the applicability of the law of armed conflict (as laid down in that law) are met, this law is more 'special' and, for this reason, supersedes human rights law. When *lex specialis* is invoked in this way what is suggested is, precisely as Draper said in his 1971 article, that the exceptional circumstances of armed conflict justify a deviation from the 'normal' law of human rights. Granted that international law can indeed sustain the individualised and deterritorialised enmity described in the foregoing two sections in this chapter, in this interpretation of the Court's pronouncement, the doctrine

---

[106]   ICJ, *Legality of the Threat or Use of Nuclear Weapons* (Advisory Opinion) 1996 available at the website of the Court: www.icj-cij.org/docket/files/95/7495.pdf accessed 10 May 2015; ICJ, *Legal Consequences of the Construction of a Wall in the Occupied Palestinian Territory.*
[107]   *Ibid.* para. 25.

of *lex specialis derogat legi generalis* provides the disregard for human rights in targeted killing with a Latin imprimatur.

The second interpretation is similar to the first: it too allows the law of armed conflict to determine the conditions in which it is to apply and thus places human rights law at the disposal of the law of armed conflict. However, it does so in a way that takes seriously the Court's determination that the protection of human rights does not cease in times of war. In this interpretation, the *lex specialis* doctrine is used not as a tool for setting aside human rights law for the benefit of the law of armed conflict, but as a tool for harmonious interpretation, assisting in the interpretation of the concept of 'arbitrary deprivation of life' in human rights law by way of the more special norms for the taking of life in armed conflict. Here, human rights law and the law of armed conflict apply concurrently or within each other.[108] However, this would appear to entail precisely that the whole of the law of war as regards killing is incorporated in human rights law (Draper) and it is difficult to see any practical difference between this and the previous model, which excludes human rights law from application in the context of targeted killing. Granted that international law can sustain the individualised and deterritorialised enmity brought about in targeted killing, in this interpretation of the Court's pronouncement, targeted killing may be cast as lawful not through derogation but in *application* of human rights (as determined by the law of armed conflict).[109]

The third interpretation takes the Court's insistence on the concurrent application of human rights law and the law of armed conflict to its logical conclusion. However, it does so at the expense of allowing the law of armed conflict to determine the conditions in which it is to apply and may thus be considered insensitive 'to the exception that war continues to be to the normality of peace'.[110] In this interpretation there is no general priority, in armed conflict, between the law of armed conflict and human rights law, but rather this matter has to be determined on a case-by-case

---

[108] On concurrent or application 'within each other' of two norms in application of the doctrine of *lex specialis* see ILC, 'Fragmentation of International Law: Difficulties Arising From the Diversification and Expansion of International Law: Report of the Study Group of the International Law Commission Finalized by Martti Koskenniemi' (13 April 2006) UN Doc A/CN.4/L.682 para. 96.

[109] See for example, Chris Jenks, 'Law From Above: Unmanned Aerial Systems, Use of Force and the Law of Armed Conflict' 85 (2010) North Dakota Law Review 649 at 662.

[110] ILC, 'Fragmentation of International Law: Difficulties Arising From the Diversification and Expansion of International Law: Report of the Study Group of the International Law Commission Finalized by Martti Koskenniemi' (13 April 2006) UN Doc A/CN.4/L.682 para. 104.

basis, taking the relevant circumstances into consideration. While this may create opportunities for applying human rights law and the law of armed conflict concurrently or through harmonious interpretation, in circumstances such as targeted killing we are presented with conflicts that are difficult to overcome. Here, I claim, the doctrine *lex specialis derogat legi generalis* leaves us entirely without guidance; further, whatever normative considerations we might bring to bear in casting either human rights or the law of armed conflict as more 'special' in a particular case of targeted killing, there can be no question of this entailing an actual legal compulsion to accord priority to one or the other.[111]

Substituting a Hybridised for a Mutually Exclusive Relation

There is a noticeable tendency to substitute a hybridised for a mutually exclusive relation of human rights and the law of armed conflict in targeted killing. While appearing to rely primarily on the principle of proportionality of Israeli domestic law, this was arguably what the Israel Supreme Court did in the 2006 targeted killing judgment when disallowing targeted killing if a less harmful means can be employed.[112]

David Kretzmer had suggested this position in a 2005 article published in the *European Journal of International Law*. Kretzmer proceeds by way of identifying the main problems with a mutually exclusive applicability of human rights and the law of armed conflict for the targeting of active members of transnational terrorist groups who are not within the jurisdiction of the state. His conclusion is:

> The law-enforcement model is not suitable when the scale of violence has reached that of a non-international armed conflict and the terrorists operate from the territory of a state that is either unwilling or incapable of cooperating in law enforcement. The armed conflict model was not developed with the case of international terror in mind. Under the rules

---

[111] Cf. Milanovic, 'Norm Conflicts, International Humanitarian Law, and Human Rights Law' p. 100. Relatedly, Martti Koskenniemi has described how 'in a world of plural regimes, political conflict is waged on the description and re-description of aspects of the world so as to make them fall under the jurisdiction of particular institutions' (Martti Koskenniemi, 'The Fate of Public International Law: Between Technique and Politics' 70 (2007) Modern Law Review 1 at 7).

[112] *Public Committee Against Torture* v. *The Government of Israel* para. 40; Milanovic, 'Lessons for Human Rights and Humanitarian Law in the War on Terror: Comparing Hamdan and the Israeli Targeted Killing Case' p. 389ff. Lesh, 'Public Committee Against Torture in Israel v the Government of Israel: The Israeli High Court of Justice Targeted Killing Decision' p. 388f.

of international armed conflicts, terrorists are generally not combatants and may therefore only be attacked for such time as they take a direct part in hostilities, a legal conclusion that does not seem credible when the very conflict is between the victim state and the transnational terrorist group. On the other hand, if an armed conflict with a terrorist group is regarded as a non-international conflict, the state would seem to enjoy almost unlimited power to target persons it claims to be active members of that group, even when they pose no immediate danger and it might be feasible to apprehend them and place them on trial.[113]

On this basis Kretzmer suggests a hybridised or 'mixed model'. Kretzmer argues that when suspected terrorists are not subject to law enforcement jurisdiction and the violence has reached the scale and intensity required for the situation to be regarded as armed conflict, the norms for the conduct of hostilities do not apply exclusively but 'the parameters of absolute necessity' that he finds in the law enforcement model are 'reconsidered'.[114] This is done by drawing a parallel to a state's inherent right to self-defence under Article 51 of the UN Charter, which is subject to the requirements of necessity and proportionality. 'Necessity' here means that

> a state may not target suspected terrorists if there is a reasonable possibility of apprehending them and putting them on trial. Whether apprehension, arrest and trial are reasonable alternatives will depend on whether the victim state has effective control over the territory in which the terrorists are operating, and if it does not, on the degree of willingness or capability of the *de facto* force in control of that territory to arrest and try the terrorists, to extradite them, or, at the very least, to take effective steps to stop their activities.[115]

Kretzmer suggests that proportionality should, in this context, be based on balancing three factors:

> 1. the danger to life posed by the continued activities of the terrorists; 2. the chance of the danger to human life being realized if the activities of the suspected terrorist are not halted immediately; and 3. the danger that civilians will be killed or wounded in the attack on the suspected terrorist.[116]

---

[113] David Kretzmer, 'Targeted Killing of Suspected Terrorists: Extra-judicial Executions or Legitimate Means of Defence?' 16 (2005) European Journal of International Law 171 at 201f.

[114] *Ibid.* p. 203.   [115] *Ibid.*   [116] *Ibid.*

Kretzmer's 'mixed model' is presented as a 'middle road' and as a 'realistic alternative that allows states to defend their residents against terrorist attacks without abandoning commitment to standards of human rights *and* humanitarian law'.[117]

As mentioned, Kretzmer's 'mixed model' should probably be seen as a way of helping human rights regain lost ground in targeted killing. However, and as Kretzmer is well aware, restrictive effects comes at the expense of licensing or sanctioning the cases of targeted killing that fall within the scope of the criteria set – and this model is thus part of the refashioning of international law's sanctioning in the context of targeted killing.

While human rights lawyers may find reasons to resist such hybridisation for the benefit of applying human rights criteria to the exclusion of the law of armed conflict, so, law of armed conflict lawyers have been concerned about the wider implications of the introduction of human rights in the context of what they perceive as the conduct of hostilities. Most notably, Section IX of the ICRC interpretive guidance on the notion of direct participation in hostilities laying down legal constraints on the use of force,[118] has been interpreted as a direct consequence of the hybridisation of human rights and humanitarian law in the context of targeted killing and nothing less than a direct threat, across the conflict spectrum, to the ancient right to kill the enemy.[119]

---

[117] *Ibid.* p. 212. My emphasis.

[118] Melzer, *Interpretive Guidance on the Notion of Direct Participation in Hostilities under International Humanitarian Law* pp. 77–82.

[119] For a painstakingly critical review written by one of the experts participating in the study see Parks, 'Part IX of the ICRC Direct Participation in Hostilities Study: No Mandate, No Expertise, and Legally Incorrect'. Along with at least one-third of the experts participating in the meetings, Parks asked his name to be deleted from the list of participants (*Ibid.* p. 784 footnote 56). See also the rebuttal of the author of the report: Melzer, 'Keeping the Balance Between Military Necessity and Humanity: A Response to Four Critiques of the ICRC's Interpretive Guidance on the Notion of Direct Participation in Hostilities'.

5

The Law of Targeted Killing

In spite of the title, the chronicling style and the historical material used, the idea with this book was always to provide a perspective on the present. This ambition has been further spurred on by the increasing intensity with which targeted killing has been both practised and debated during the time of completing it. But why turn to the past if the concerns are in the present? I found this turn to targeted killing's past helpful in articulating the political implications of targeted killing, political implications that, in the words of Susanne Krasmann, 'are rather tacitly involved in the talk about threats and security, and in the dispute about targeted killing operations' legality'.[1] I found the turn to targeted killing's past helpful also for understanding the legal justifications for targeted killing and the fault lines of the contemporary debate about its legality.

Moreover, in this material the contemporary debates' established positions and forced choices was substituted for a sense of historical motion and political struggle. In this material we could see that targeted killing is irreducible to explanations in terms of the timeless nature of sovereignty, state protection or law but also irreducible to the agency of the protagonists of this history. The complex, contingent and still very much open-ended history of targeted killing can instead be explained with reference to basic questions of the law and politics of protection, the trajectories of state protection in Israel and the United States and the discursive processes of the articulation of problems and threats and a constant turn to law and to lawyers in the provision of answers, definitions and interpretations.

Michel Foucault once claimed, 'what is most dangerous in violence is its rationality. Of course violence itself is terrible. But the deepest root of violence and its permanence come out of the form of the rationality we use'.[2] If this is true, critical engagement, with precisely this kind of

---

[1] Krasmann, 'Targeted Killing and Its Law: On a Mutually Constitutive Relationship' p. 682.
[2] Michel Foucault, 'Truth is in the Future' in Sylvère Lotringer (ed.), *Foucault Live: Collected Interviews, 1961–1984* (New York: Semiotext(e) 1996) 298–301 at 299.

history and historical texts, appears to me to be not only useful but a matter of some urgency for the present. For, *legal* texts, laying down a specifically *legal* rationality, have played an enormously important role in the emergence of targeted killing.

The consistency with which decision makers have turned to law and to lawyers in dealing with the situations and the problems with which they were seized in this history is truly striking. It confirms an aspect of liberal legality captured by David Dyzenhaus when he writes about a 'compulsion of legality' also in cases of threats to the state;[3] in this case, the threat of terrorism and the framing of the extraterritorial killing of designated terrorists in legal terms and a significant amount of legal work creating the necessary legal authorities. Dyzenhaus, himself a strong defender of liberal legalism argues that the compulsion of legality may, in situations of crisis, trigger two very different cycles of legality: one where legal institutions cooperate in creating controls on public authorities which ensure that their decisions comply with 'the principle of legality, understood as a substantive conception of the rule of law'; the other one in which 'the *political* constitution asserts itself under the guise of the *legal* constitution' and the rule of law is reduced to a '"thin veneer of legality" such that it serves to cloak what is in substance arbitrary executive power'.[4]

As suggested by Dyzenhaus, and as the history of targeted killing shows, this 'compulsion of legality' prepares for a struggle not between *politics* and *law* but between *different politics of law*. This was illustrated inter alia in the exchange between Steven R. David and Yael Stein over the legality of Israeli targeted killing in the second Intifada. In this exchange, Stein's 'black-and-white' claim that the Israeli state is in breach with its legal obligations because relying on a legal framework applicable only for the conduct of hostilities was met by David's call for humility in declaring targeted killing inconsistent with international law because taking place in neither war nor peace and because seen in the context of a state legitimately seeking to protect its people from terrorist attacks.[5] Apparently, David is willing to exploit the possibilities opened up by the broad authority, granted by the law of belligerent occupation, to the military commander in choosing between the kind of maintenance of law and order that implies

---

[3] David Dyzenhaus, 'The Compulsion of Legality' in Victor V. Ramraj (ed.), *Emergencies and the Limits of Legality* (Cambridge University Press 2008) 33–59; Dyzenhaus, 'Emergency, Liberalism, and the State'.

[4] Dyzenhaus, 'The Compulsion of Legality' p. 56.

[5] David, 'If Not Combatants, Certainly Not Civilians: Reply to Yael Stein' p. 138.

peace and that which implies war or armed conflict. Stein on the other hand claims that defining the circumstances as one of armed conflict disregards the decades-long occupation, which imposes on Israel, as an occupying power, an extra duty to protect the civilian population living there.

Something similar occurred in the US Congress when Chairman Fascell questioned if the US President could take the country to war wherever an act of terrorism has taken place, and do it all under the rubric of saying this is self-defence and every nation has the right to defend itself; a question that subsequently was reiterated by Congressman Berman with the demand that such an authority be supported by constitutional law. Sofaer responds to this demand by pointing to the commander-in-chief clause, the president's power over foreign affairs and the power to ensure that the laws of the United States are implemented. The exchange was described in that context as a contestation over the sovereign voice in American political life and the role of law in that voice. I am sure that Sofaer would disagree on the description of his position as a thin veneer of legality, cloaking what is in substance arbitrary executive power, but I would stand by the assessment that his legal argument in that context represents a case of the assertion of the *political* constitution over the *legal* constitution.

I have made an effort of trying to understand the conception of law that heeds to the compulsion of legality and yet is able to produce a legal authority to engage in the extraterritorial killing of designated terrorists. Aharon Barak's decision to exercise jurisdiction over targeted killing, his decision on the applicable law and his particular interpretation of that law is clearly a significant event in the history of targeted killing in Israel and beyond. In this judgment, Barak overturned a previous judgment determining targeted killing as non-justiciable, arguing that even what was referred to in that earlier judgment as 'the choice of means of warfare' must be subject to the rule of law. The judgment itself was influenced by Barak's purposive theory of interpretation described as a way to bridge the gap between law and the needs of society. Sofaer, on the other hand, has on numerous occasions expressed his debt to former Legal Adviser Abram Chayes' 'common lawyer' approach to international law.[6] This

---

[6] Abraham D. Sofaer, 'Book Review: International Law and the United States Military Intervention in the Western Hemisphere. By Max Hilaire' 92 (1998) American Journal of International Law 586; Sofaer, 'On the Necessity of Pre-emption'; Sofaer, 'The Reagan and Bush Administrations (1985–1990)'.

is a conception in which the concern over international *legal obligation* is substituted for a concern over the strength of the *legal position* in mobilising international assent.[7]

Michael Marder refers to the *political* hermeneutics of legal interpretation arguing that

> it is deeply erroneous to draw a strict line of demarcation between the active constitution-making capacity and the passive routine of interpretation . . . In doing so, one fails to realize that every interpretation is already an existential decision, which is necessarily active, transformative, and reconstituting. Since the law does not – indeed, cannot – interpret and apply itself, interpretation becomes one of the most crucial loci of the political, where the hermeneutical decisions of concrete subjects 'activate' the impersonal logic and political structures, often transgressing the norm.[8]

Marder arrives at this conclusion through a reading of Carl Schmitt, but the same conclusion was arrived at in the Israeli context through Walter Benjamin's understanding of the indistinct relationship between lawmaking and law-preserving violence, particularly with regards to questions of security.

Legal theorist and former judge of the German Constitutional Court Ernst-Wolfgang Böckenförde has usefully contrasted the exercise of political jurisdiction found in Schmitt's work on constitutional law, with the sovereign decisionism associated with Schmitt's work on sovereignty[9] which is often used to explain the war against terrorism, including targeted killing.[10] Böckenförde begins by asserting 'the common conviction of political philosophers as different as Thomas Hobbes and Immanuel Kant that the state and the concentration of sovereign power established

---

[7] Abram Chayes, 'A Common Lawyer Looks at International Law' 78 (1965) Harvard Law Review 1396 at 1410.

[8] Michael Marder, *Groundless Existence: The Political Ontology of Carl Schmitt* (New York: Continuum 2010) p. 8f.

[9] Ernst-Wolfgang Böckenförde, 'The Concept of the Political: A Key to Understanding Carl Schmitt's Constitutional Theory' 10 (1997) Canadian Journal of Law and Jurisprudence 5 at 18f.

[10] For an early sophisticated account of the war on terrorism along these lines see Frédéric Mégret, "War"? Legal Semantics and the Move to Violence' 13 (2002) European Journal of International Law 361. Another is Paul W. Kahn, 'Imagining Warfare' 24 (2013) European Journal of International Law 199. A recent comprehensive decisionist account of the American war on terrorism and the 9/11 exception is Jason Ralph, *America's War on Terror: The State of the 9/11 Exception from Bush to Obama* (Oxford University Press 2013).

by the state are necessary to protect the individual against the dangers
and threats by their fellow people'.[11] Bringing this conception of political community and the end of sovereign power to bear on Schmitt's
constitutional thinking, Böckenförde writes:

> Constitutional law then appears as the binding normative order and form
> determining the existence, maintenance, and capability for action of a
> political unity . . . It is and must be the specific telos of constitutional law
> to facilitate, preserve, and support the state as a political order and unity.
> An interpretation of constitutional law challenging or even undermining
> such an order would thus be an oxymoron. In this sense constitutional
> law is a genuinely political law: It deals with politics not only directly and
> incidentally, but immediately addresses the existence, form and action of
> the political unity; its object, so to speak, affects the gravitational field of
> the political itself.[12]

Furthermore, Böckenförde writes that Schmitt's concept of the political
informs the general thesis in *Constitutional Theory* that

> a genuine constitutional jurisdiction is a political jurisdiction. Recall that
> constitutional law, with respect to its content, is political law. It is polit-
> ical law not only in the sense that law always has to deal with politics
> by regulating and shaping coexistence within a political unity; rather it
> is political in the sense of defining the conditions, procedures, authoriza-
> tions, and limits of state activities as well as the options and authorizations
> for maintaining the political unity of the state. Accordingly, constitutional
> law, in its very content and telos, refers to the political from which in turn
> it receives its own definition. It is with regard to this political definition
> that constitutional law must be interpreted and applied; moreover, this
> interpretation and application is part of specifically political conduct.[13]

If the telos of constitutional law is to facilitate, preserve and support
the state as a political order and unity and to deal with politics in the
immediate sense of addressing the existence, form and action of political community, this is clearly a very different liberal constitutional state
from the one Schmitt described in his 1922 *Political Theology* as a 'mechanism' that has become 'torpid by repetition'[14], and that for this reason is

---

[11] Böckenförde, 'The Concept of the Political: A Key to Understanding Carl Schmitt's Constitutional Theory' p. 12 footnote 19.
[12] *Ibid.* p. 8.   [13] *Ibid.* p. 12.
[14] Schmitt, *Political Theology: Four Chapters on the Concept of Sovereignty* p. 15.

understood to require miraculous sovereign intervention when placed under threat.[15]

The emergence of this distinct form of political jurisdiction or, in other words, the introduction of apocryphal sovereignty in Schmitt's work reflects the legal and political developments specific to Weimar Germany. However, as Ernst-Wolfgang Böckenförde, David Dyzenhaus and Ellen Kennedy have in different ways suggested: we are in this particular regard still living the predicament of Weimar. This is why we can hear, in the history and debate on targeted killing, an uncanny echo of Benjamin's solemn note from the year 1920 in the context of the Kapp-Lüttwitz putsch: '"only the State has the right to use force" (and every use of its force stands in need of a particular law)'.[16]

The history of targeted killing testifies to the wielding of a dynamic conception of law, responsive to the call for state protection, in international as much as in domestic law. Indeed, Martti Koskenniemi, in *The Gentle Civilizer of Nations: The Rise and Fall of International Law 1870–1960*, refers to the 'Weimar heritage' in international law when analysing how the threat of the irrelevance of the discipline was avoided by the adoption of a deformalised conception of international law unwary of its autonomy in relation to the political.[17] This international law is a *rule of law writ large* complete with the tensions of a *Weimar law writ large* following

---

[15] In Chapter 3 of *Political Theology*, after having declared that 'all significant concepts of the modern theory of the state are secularized theological concepts', Schmitt asserts: 'the exception in jurisprudence is analogous to the miracle in theology' (*ibid.* p. 36). The theological and jurisprudential contexts in which this analogy is valid are a deistic theology and the liberal constitutional state. The enlightenment saw to it that God's direct intervention in the normal course of nature's activity was banned and in the same manner sovereignty was ousted from the constitutional state (John P. McCormick, *Carl Schmitt's Critique of Liberalism: Against Politics as Technology* (Cambridge University Press 1999) p. 150). In *Political Theology*, Schmitt explicitly associates himself with the 'fundamentally systematic and methodological analogies' with which 'conservative authors of the counter-revolution who were theists could . . . attempt to support the personal sovereignty of the monarch ideologically, with the aid of analogies from a theistic theology' (Schmitt, *Political Theology: Four Chapters on the Concept of Sovereignty* p. 37). For a reading that stresses not the decisionist but the concrete order underpinnings of *Political Theology* see Leila Brännström, 'Schmitt's definition of Sovereignty as Authorized Leadership' in Matilda Arvidsson, Leila Brännström and Panu Minkkinen (eds.), *The Contemporary Relevance of Carl Schmitt: Law, Politics, Theology* (Abingdon: Routledge 2015) 19–33.

[16] Walter Benjamin, 'The Right to Use Force' in Marcus P. Bullock and Michael W. Jennings (eds.), Rodney Livingstone (tr), *Walter Benjamin: Selected Writings 1913–1926* (Cambridge Massachusetts: Harvard University Press 1996) p. 231.

[17] Koskenniemi, *The Gentle Civilizer of Nations: The Rise and Fall of International Law 1870–1960* Chapter 6, especially 465–480.

from the abandoning of the 'safety valve' of an exterior political sphere. If it makes sense to follow Koskenniemi in referring to the '*fall* of international law' in an era, and in relation to a practice, that by all accounts attest to the proliferation, indeed, the pervasiveness of international law; then targeted killing is part of that 'fall'.

If Weimar, the compulsion of legality and this distinct form of exercise of political jurisdiction can be used as reference points in accounting for the emergence of targeted killing from the perspective of *international law in history*, then the immediately foregoing chapter – analysing targeted killing from the perspective of *the history of international law* – shows that the nature of the law produced resists any neat localisation in time and space.

Notions of a 'twisted legality' (because of extensive and vague authorities) wielded on a bizarre battlefield (ranging from the conventional to the entirely unconventional) were used to describe the double bind between authority and force emerging from the law of targeted killing. The disjunction between that law and an international law that still clings to territorial jurisdiction for its distribution of the exercise of legitimate violence is illustrated by how victims of drone strikes in Waziristan successfully challenge the lawfulness of the American targeted killing campaign in a Pakistani High Court with little effect on the American legal position and the practice of targeted killing in the area.[18]

This chapter also showed that targeted killing did not emerge without historical precedent, whether it be in a history of legalised hegemony in international law stretching all the way from the distinction between Christian/non-Christian, subsequently European/non-European, to the *unequal* distribution of *equal* rights in the contemporary era of formal sovereign equality; the application of the law of armed conflict to belligerents based on their relation of enmity rather than on territorial jurisdiction characteristic of pre-territorial Europe; or the territorially informal orders of colonial governance. A more recent precedent was found in the 2004 Israeli disengagement plan in which Israel asserted its fundamental right of self-defence, both preventive and reactive, including where necessary the use of force, in respect of threats emanating from the Gaza Strip.

Granted that sovereign equality prevents us from asserting hegemony as a fundamental aspect of international law; that Westphalian territoriality

---

[18] 'US Drone Strikes Illegal, Govt Should Stop Them – Pakistani Court' *RT* (10 May 2013) http://rt.com/news/pakistan-us-drone-illegal-093/ accessed 10 May 2015.

is too strong a narrative to make unimaginable a return to the legal order preceding it; and that colonial governance is too vested in backward ideas about civilisation. Perhaps then the question that the contemporary debate about targeted killing needs to answer is if Gaza can be allowed to form the paradigm for the future of the international law of force.

BIBLIOGRAPHY

Abramowitz, David, 'The President, the Congress, and Use of Force: Legal and Political Considerations in Authorizing Use of Force Against International Terrorism' 43 (2002) *Harvard International Law Journal* 71.

Adalah: The Legal Center for Arab Minority Rights in Israel, 'Discriminatory Laws in Israel' www.adalah.org/en/law/index accessed 20 May 2015.

Agamben, Giorgio, *State of Exception* (Attel K tr, University of Chicago Press 2005).

al-Awlaki, Nasser, 'The Drone That Killed My Grandson' *The New York Times* (17 July 2013) www.nytimes.com/2013/07/18/opinion/the-drone-that-killed-my-grandson.html accessed 10 May 2015.

Allott, Philip, *The Health of Nations: Society and Law Beyond the State* (Cambridge University Press 2002).

Aloyo, Eamon, 'Just Assassinations' 5 (2013) *International Theory* 347.

Alston, Philip, 'The CIA and Targeted Killings Beyond Borders' 2 (2011) *Harvard National Security Journal* 283.

Alston, Philip, Morgan-Foster, Jason and Abresch, William, 'The Competence of the UN Human Rights Council and Its Special Procedures in Relation to Armed Conflicts: Extrajudicial Executions in the "War on Terror"' 19 (2008) *European Journal of International Law* 183.

Anderson, Benedict, *Imagined Communities: Reflections on the Origin and Spread of Nationalism* (Revised edn, London: Verso 2006).

Anderson, Kenneth, 'Targeted Killing in U.S. Counterterrorism Strategy and Law' in Wittes B (ed.), *Legislating the War on Terror: An Agenda for Reform* (Washington DC: Brookings Institution Press 2009).

'Targeted Killing and Drone Warfare: How We Came to Debate Whether There Is a "Legal Geography of War"' in Berkowitz P (ed.), *Future Challenges in National Security and Law* (Hoover Institution 2011). WCL Research Paper No 2011–16 http://ssrn.com/abstract=1824783 accessed 14 May 2015.

Anghie, Antony, *Imperialism, Sovereignty and the Making of International Law* (Cambridge University Press 2004).

Arendt, Hannah, *The Human Condition* (University of Chicago Press 1958).

'Antisemitism' in Kohn J and Feldman RH (eds.), *The Jewish Writings: Hannah Arendt* (New York: Schocken Books 2007) 46–121.

'The Great Tradition I. Law and Power' 74 (2007) *Social Research: An International Quarterly* 713.

'The Jewish State: Fifty Years After, Where Have Herzl's Politics Led? [originally published 1945–46 in Commentary 1]' in Kohn J and Feldman RH (eds.), *The Jewish Writings: Hannah Arendt* (New York: Schocken Books 2007) 375–401.

'To Save the Jewish Homeland [originally published 1948 in Commentary 5]' in Kohn J and Feldman RH (eds.), *The Jewish Writings: Hannah Arendt* (New York: Schocken Books 2007) 388–401.

'Zionism Reconsidered [originally published October 1944 in the *Menorah Journal*]' in Kohn J and Feldman RH (eds.), *The Jewish Writings: Hannah Arendt* (New York: Schocken Books 2007) 343–374.

Arendt, Hannah, Kohn, Jerome and Feldman, Ron H., *The Jewish Writings: Hannah Arendt* (New York: Schocken Books 2007).

Arimatsu, Louise, 'Territory, Boundaries and the Law of Armed Conflict' 12 (2010) *Yearbook of International Humanitarian Law* 157.

Auerbach, Anthony, 'Remarks on Walter Benjamin's Critique of Violence' (aauerbach.info) http://aauerbach.info/research/urban/benjamin_violence.html accessed 10 May 2015.

Azoulay, Ariella and Ophir, Adi, *The One-state Condition: Occupation and Democracy in Israel/Palestine* (Haran T tr, Stanford University Press 2013).

Balibar, Étienne, *We, The People of Europe? Reflections on Transnational Citizenship* (Swenson J tr, Princeton University Press 2004).

Barak, Aharon, 'The Role of the Supreme Court in a Democracy' 3 (1998) *Israel Studies* 6.

Purposive Interpretation in Law (Bashi S tr, Princeton University Press 2005).

Bartelson, Jens, 'Double Binds: Sovereignty and the Just War Tradition' in Kalmo H and Skinner Q (eds.), *Sovereignty in Fragments: The Past, Present and Future of a Contested Concept* (Cambridge University Press 2010) 81–95.

Barzilai, Amnon, 'New Israeli Drone Would Destroy Missile Launch Pads' *Haaretz* (17 December 2001) http://www.haaretz.com/print-edition/news/new-israeli-drone-would-destroy-missile-launch-pads-1.77561 accessed 15 May 2015.

Baxter, Richard R., 'The Duty of Obedience to the Belligerent Occupant' 27 (1950) *British Yearbook of International Law* 235.

Beard, Jennifer, 'The International Law in Force' in Johns F, Joyce R and Pahuja S (eds.), *Events: The Force of International Law* (New York: Routledge Cavendish 2010) 18–28.

Becker, Tal, *Terrorism and the State: Rethinking the Rules of State Responsibility* (Oxford: Hart Publishing 2006).

Bell, Colleen, 'War and the Allegory of Medical Intervention: Why Metaphors Matter' 6 (2012) *International Political Sociology* 325.

Ben-Naftali, Orna, 'A Judgment in the Shadow of International Criminal Law' 5 (2007) *Journal of International Criminal Justice* 322.

Ben-Naftali, Orna and Michaeli, Keren R., 'Justice-Ability: A Critique of the Alleged Non-Justiciability of Israel's Policy of Targeted Killings' 1 (2003) *Journal of International Criminal Justice* 368.

'Public Committee Against Torture et al v. the Government of Israel et al' 101 (2007) *American Journal of International Law* 459.

Ben-Yehuda, Nachman, 'Gathering Dark Secrets, Hidden and Dirty Information: Some Methodological Notes on Studying Political Assassinations' 13 (1990) *Qualitative Sociology* 345.

Political Assassinations by Jews: A Rhetorical Device for Justice (New York: SUNY Press 1993).

Bendersky, Joseph W., 'The "Fourth" (Second) Interrogation of Carl Schmitt at Nuremberg' 139 (2007) *Telos* 35.

Bendor, Ariel L., 'Justiciability of the Israeli Fight Against Terrorism' 39 (2007) *The George Washington International Law Review* 149.

Benjamin, Walter, 'Theses on the Philosophy of History' in Arendt H (ed.), Zohn H (tr), *Illuminations: Essays and Reflections* (New York: Schocken Books 1968) 253–264.

'Critique of Violence' in Demetz P (ed.), Jephcott E (tr), *Reflections: Essays, Aphorisms, Autobiographical Writings* (New York: Schocken Books 1978) 277–300.

The Correspondence of Walter Benjamin 1910–1940 (Scholem G and Adorno TW eds., Jacobson MR and Jacobson EM trs, University of Chicago Press 1994).

'The Right to Use Force' in Bullock MP and Jennings MW (eds.), Livingstone R (tr), *Walter Benjamin: Selected Writings 1913–1926* (Cambridge Massachusetts: Harvard University Press 1996).

Benvenisti, Eyal, *The International Law of Occupation* (2nd edn, Oxford University Press 2012).

Bhuta, Nehal, 'The Antinomies of Transformative Occupation' 16 (2005) *European Journal of International Law* 721.

'States of Exception: Regulating Targeted Killing in a "Global Civil War"' in Alston P and Macdonald E (eds.), *Human Rights, Intervention, and the Use of Force* (Oxford University Press 2010) 243–274.

Blakesley, Christopher L., 'Jurisdiction as Legal Protection Against Terrorism' 19 (1987) *Connecticut Law Review* 895.

Blau, Uri, 'License to Kill' *Haaretz* (27 November 2008) http://www.haaretz.com/license-to-kill-1.258378 accessed 13 May 2015.

Blum, Gabriella, 'The Individualization of War: From Collectivism to Individualism in the Regulation of Armed Conflicts' in Sarat A, Douglas L and Umphrey MM (eds.), *Law and War* (Stanford University Press 2013) http://ssrn.com/abstract=2231168.

Blumenberg, Hans, *The Legitimacy of the Modern Age* (Wallace RM tr, Cambridge, Massachusetts: MIT Press 1985).

Blumenfeld, Laura, 'In Israel a Divisive Struggle Over Targeted Killing' *The Washington Post* (27 August 2006) http://www.washingtonpost.com/wp-dyn/content/article/2006/08/26/AR2006082600917_pf.html accessed 15 May 2015.

Bobbitt, Philip, *Terror and Consent: The Wars for the Twenty-First Century* (New York: Anchor Books 2009).

Boothy, Bill, ' "And For Such Time As": The Time Dimension to Direct Participation in Hostilities' 42 (2010) *New York Journal of International Law and Politics* 741.

Boyle, Francis A., 'Preserving the Rule of Law in the War Against International Terrorism' 8 (1986) *Whittier Law Review* 735.

Boyle, Michael J., 'The Costs and Consequences of Drone Warfare' 89 (2013) *International Affairs* 1.

Bradley, Curtis A., 'The United States, Israel & Unlawful Combatants' 12 (2009) *The Green Bag* 397.

Breen, Keith, 'Law Beyond Command' in Goldoni M and McCorkindale C (eds.), *Hannah Arendt and the Law* (Oxford: Hart Publishing 2012) 15–34.

Brennan, John, 'Counterterrorism and the Law' (*Homeland Security Watch*, 19 September 2011) http://www.hlswatch.com/2011/09/18/brennan-counterterrorism-and-the-law/ accessed 10 May 2015.

'The Efficacy and Ethics of U.S. Counterterrorism Strategy' (*White House*, 30 April 2012) http://www.wilsoncenter.org/event/the-efficacy-and-ethics-us-counterterrorism-strategy accessed 14 May 2015.

Briggs, Herbert W., 'Recognition of States: Some Reflections on Doctrine and Practice' 43 (1949) *American Journal of International Law* 113.

Brown, Philip Marshall, 'The Recognition of Israel' 42 (1948) *American Journal of International Law* 620.

Brown, Wendy, *Walled States, Waning Sovereignty* (New York: Zone Books 2010).

Brännström, Leila, 'Schmitt's definition of Sovereignty as Authorized Leadership' in Arvidsson M, Brännström L and Minkkinen P (eds.), *The Contemporary Relevance of Carl Schmitt: Law, Politics, Theology* (Abingdon: Routledge 2015) 19–33.

B'Tselem – The Israeli Information Center for Human Rights in the Occupied Territories, 'Documents Published by Ha'aretz Raise Grave Suspicions that the Army Performs Illegal Assassinations' (2010) www.btselem.org/press_releases/20100408 accessed 13 May 2015.

Butler, Judith, 'Critique, Coercion and Sacred Life in Benjamin's "Critique of Violence" ' in D Vries H and Sullivan LE (eds.), *Political Theologies: Public Religions in a Post-Secular World* (New York: Fordham University Press 2006) 201–219.

Parting Ways: Jewishness and the Critique of Zionism (New York: Columbia University Press 2012).

Byers, Michael, 'Preemptive Self-defense: Hegemony, Equality and Strategies of Legal Change' 2 (2003) *The Journal of Political Philosophy* 171.

Böckenförde, Ernst-Wolfgang, 'The Concept of the Political: A Key to Understanding Carl Schmitt's Constitutional Theory' 10 (1997) *Canadian Journal of Law and Jurisprudence* 5.

Canestaro, Nathan, 'American Law and Policy on Assassinations of Foreign Leaders: The Practicality of Maintaining the Status Quo' 26 (2003) *British Columbia International and Comparative Law Review* 1.

Carty, Anthony, 'Israel's Legal Right to Exist and the Principle of the Self-determination of the Palestinian People?' 76 (2013) *The Modern Law Review* 158.

Cassese, Antonio, 'On Some Merits of the Israeli Judgment on Targeted Killings' 5 (2007) *Journal of International Criminal Justice* 339.

Chamayou, Grégoire, *A Theory of the Drone* (Lloyd J tr, New York: The New Press 2015).

Chayes, Abram, 'A Common Lawyer Looks at International Law' 78 (1965) *Harvard Law Review* 1396.

Chemerinsky, Erwin, 'Against Sovereign Immunity' 53 (2000) *Stanford Law Review* 1201.

Clarke, Richard A., *Against All Enemies: Inside America's War on Terror* (New York: Free Press 2004).

Cloud, David S., 'CIA Drones Have Broader List of Targets' *Los Angeles Times* (5 May 2010) http://articles.latimes.com/2010/may/05/world/la-fg-drone-targets-20100506 accessed 10 May 2015.

Cohen, Amichai, 'Legal Operational Advice in the Israeli Defense Forces: The International Law Department and the Changing Nature of International Humanitarian Law' 26 (2011) *Connecticut Journal of International Law* 367.

Cohen, Amichai and Cohen, Stuart A., *Israel's National Security Law: Political Dynamics and Historical Development* (Abingdon: Routledge 2012).

Cohen, Ed, *A Body Worth Defending: Immunity, Biopolitics and the Apotheosis of the Modern Body* (Durham and London: Duke University Press 2009).

Cohen, Stuart A., '"Masqueraders" in the IDF: The Military Unit and the Public Debate, 1991–1992' 2 (1993) *Low-Intensity Conflict and Law Enforcement* 282.

Commission on Human Rights, 'Letter dated 14 April 2003 from the Chief of Section, Political and Specialized Agencies, of the Permanent Mission of the United States of America to the United Nations Office at Geneva addressed to the secretariat of the Commission on Human Rights' (14 April 2003) UN Doc E/CN.4/2003/G/80.

Craig, Alain, *International Legitimacy and the Politics of Security: The Strategic Deployment of Lawyers in the Israeli Military* (Plymouth: Lexington Books 2013).

Craven, Matthew, 'Introduction: International Law and Its Histories' in Craven M, Fitzmaurice M and Vogiatzi M (eds.), *Time, History and International Law* (Leiden: Martinus Nijhoff Publishers 2007) 1–25.

Crawford, James, *The Creation of States in International Law* (2nd edn, Oxford University Press 2006).

Crenshaw, Martha, 'The Debate over "New" vs. "Old" Terrorism' 4 (2009) *Values and Violence* 117.

Critchley, Simon, *The Faith of the Faithless: Experiments in Political Theology* (London and New York: Verso 2012).

David, Steven R., 'If Not Combatants, Certainly Not Civilians: Reply to Yael Stein' 17 (2003) *Ethics & International Affairs* 138.

'Israel's Policy of Targeted Killing' 17 (2003) *Ethics & International Affairs* 111.

Deeks, Ashley S., 'Pakistan's Sovereignty and the Killing of Osama Bin Laden' *ASIL Insights* http://www.asil.org/insights/volume/15/issue/11/pakistans-sovereignty-and-killing-osama-bin-laden accessed 10 May 2015.

'"Unwilling or Unable": Toward a Normative Framework for Extraterritorial Self-Defense' 52 (2012) *Virginia Journal of International Law* 483.

'Detention, Treatment, and Trial of Certain Non-Citizens in the War Against Terrorism – Military Order of November 13, 2001, Federal Register: 16 November 2001 (volume 66, Number 2) Presidential Documents Page 57831–57836' in Greenberg KJ and Dratel JL (eds.), *The Torture Papers: The Road to Abu Ghraib* (Cambridge University Press 2001).

Department of Justice, 'White Paper: Lawfulness of a Lethal Operation Directed Against a U.S. Citizen who is a Senior Operational Leader of Al-Qa'ida or an Associated Force', published online at: www.law.upenn.edu/live/files/1903-doj-white-paper accessed 10 May 2015.

Department of Defense, 'Report of the Department of Defense Commission on Beirut International Airport Terrorist Act', 23 October 1983. Published online by the Federation of American Scientists: http://www.fas.org/irp/threat/beirut-1983.pdf accessed 10 May 2015.

Derrida, Jacques, 'Force of Law: The Mystical Foundation of Authority' in Cornell D and others (eds.), *Deconstruction and the Possibility of Justice* (Abingdon: Routledge 1992) 3–67.

'Force of Law: The Mystical Foundation of Authority' in Anidjar G (ed.), *Acts of Religion: Jacques Derrida* (Abingdon: Routledge 2002) 230–300.

Dieckhoff, Alain, *The Invention of a Nation: Zionist Thought and the Making of Modern Israel* (Derrick J tr, London: Hurst & Company 2003).

Dinstein, Yoram, *The International Law of Belligerent Occupation* (Cambridge University Press 2009).

Doolittle, J. H. and others, 'Report on the Covert Activities of the Central Intelligence Agency', published online by Cryptome: http://cryptome.org/cia-doolittle.pdf accessed 10 May 2015.

Doyle, Michael W. and others, *Striking First: Preemption and Prevention in International Conflict* (Macedo S ed., Princeton University Press 2008).

Draper, G.I.A.D., 'The Relationship Between the Human Rights Regime and the Law of Armed Conflict' 1 (1971) *Israel Yearbook on Human Rights* 191.

'Humanitarian Law and Human Rights' (1979) *Acta Juridica* 193.

Dyzenhaus, David, 'The Compulsion of Legality' in Ramraj V V (ed.), *Emergencies and the Limits of Legality* (Cambridge University Press 2008) 33–59.

'Emergency, Liberalism, and the State' 9 (2011) *Perspectives on Politics* 69.

Editorial, 'Punished and be Damned' *The Economist* (27 August 1998) http://www.economist.com/node/162475 accessed 10 May 2015.

Eichensehr, Kristen, 'On Target: The Israeli Supreme Court and the Expansion of Targeted Killings' 116 (2006) *Yale Law Journal* 1873.

Elden, Stuart, *Terror and Territory: The Spatial Extent of Sovereignty* (Minneapolis: University of Minnesota Press 2009).

    'Reading Schmitt Geopolitically: Nomos Territory and Großraum' in Legg S (ed.), *Spatiality, Sovereignty and Carl Schmitt: Geographies of the Nomos* (Abingdon: Routledge 2011) 91–105.

Elia, Zureik, Anita, Vitulla and Abu Harthiyeh, Mohammad, *Targeting to Kill: Israel's Undercover Units* (Palestine Human Rights Information Center), published online at: http://www.thejerusalemfund.org/ht/a/GetDocumentAction/i/2942 accessed 10 May 2015.

Elsea, Jennifer K., *Memorandum: Legal Issues Related to the Lethal Targeting of U.S. Citizens Suspected of Terrorist Activities* (CRS Report for Congress 2012), published online by the Federation of American Scientists: http://www.fas.org/sgp/crs/natsec/target.pdf accessed 10 May 2015.

Esposito, Roberto, *Bíos: Biopolitics and Philosophy* (Campbell T tr, Minneapolis: University of Minnesota Press 2008).

    Communitas: The Origin and Destiny of Community (Campbell T tr, Stanford University Press 2010).

    Immunitas: The Protection and Negation of Life (Hanafi Z tr, Cambridge: Polity Press 2011).

Feldman, Ron H., 'Introduction: The Jew as Pariah: The Case of Hannah Arendt (1906–1975)' in Kohn J and Feldman RH (eds.), *The Jewish Writings: Hannah Arendt* (New York: Schocken Books 2007) xli–lxxvi.

Feldman, Yotam and Blau, Uri, 'Consent and Advise' *Haaretz* (29 January 2009) http://www.haaretz.com/consent-and-advise-1.269127 accessed 10 May 2015.

Ferraro, Tristan, Occupation and Other Forms of Administration of Foreign Territory: Expert Meeting (Geneva: International Committee of the Red Cross (ICRC) 2012).

Finn, Peter and Miller, Greg, 'Anwar al-Awlaki's Family Speaks out Against his Son's Death in Airstrike' *The Washington Post* (17 October 2001) https://www.washingtonpost.com/world/national-security/anwar-al-awlakis-family-speaks-out-against-his-sons-deaths/2011/10/17/gIQA8kFssL_story.html accessed 10 May 2015.

Fiss, Owen, 'Law Is Everywhere' 117 (2007) *The Yale Law Journal* 256.

Fitzpatrick, Peter, 'Latin Roots: The Force of International Law as Event' in Johns F, Joyce R and Pahuja S (eds.), *Events: The Force of International Law* (New York: Routledge Cavendish 2010) 43–54.

Foucault, Michel, *The History of Sexuality: An Introduction* (Hurley R tr, New York: Pantheon 1978).

'Truth is in the Future' in Lotringer S (ed.), *Foucault Live: Collected Interviews, 1961–1984* (New York: Semiotext(e) 1996) 298–301.

'Society Must be Defended', *Lectures at the Collège de France 1975–76* (Macey D tr, New York: Picador 2003).

Security, Territory, Population: Lectures at the Collège de France, 1977–78 (Burchell G tr, New York: Palgrave Macmillan 2007).

Frazer, Elizabeth and Hutchings, Kimberly, 'On Politics and Violence: Arendt Contra Fanon' 7 (2008) *Contemporary Political Theory* 90.

Fulghum, David A., 'More UAVs Shift to Afghan Duty' 155 (2001) *Aviation Week and Space Technology* 44.

Gazit, Shlomo, 'Policy in the Administered Territories' 1 (1971) *Israel Yearbook on Human Rights* 278.

Geertsema, Johan, 'Exceptions, Bare Life and Colonialism' in Ramraj VV (ed.), *Emergencies and the Limits of Legality* (Cambridge University Press 2008) 337–359.

Gellman, Barton, 'Broad Effort Launched After '98 Attacks' *The Washington Post* (19 December 2001) http://www.washingtonpost.com/wp-dyn/content/article/2010/03/11/AR2010031102582.html accessed 10 May 2015.

'A Strategy's Cautious Evolution' *The Washington Post* (20 January 2002) http://www.washingtonpost.com/wp-dyn/content/article/2006/06/09/AR2006060900885.html accessed 10 May 2015.

Gellman, Barton and Priest, Dana, 'CIA Had Fix on Hussein: Intelligence Revealed "Target of Opportunity"' *The Washington Post* (March 20, 2003) AD1 www.washingtonpost.com/wp-dyn/articles/A58177-2003Mar20.html accessed 10 May 2015.

Ghanim, Honaida, 'The Urgency of a New Beginning in Palestine: An Imagined Scenario by Mahmoud Darwish and Hannah Arendt' 38 (2011) *College Literature* 75.

Glennon, Michael J., 'Mr. Sofaer's War Powers "Partnership"' 80 (1986) *American Journal of International Law* 584.

Goodman, Ryan and Jinks, Derek, 'The ICRC Interpretive Guidance on the Notion of Direct Participation in Hostilities Under International Humanitarian Law: An Introduction to the Forum' 42 (2010) *New York Journal of International Law and Politics* 637.

Gorali, Moshe, 'Easier to Kill, Harder to Judge' *Haaretz* (31 January 2002) http://www.haaretz.com/print-edition/features/easier-to-kill-harder-to-judge-1.54240 accessed 10 May 2015.

Gordon, Neve, *Israel's Occupation* (Berkeley: University of California Press 2008).

Gordon, Peter E. and McCormick, John P., 'Introduction: Weimar Thought: Continuity and Crisis' in Gordon PE and McCormick JP (eds.), *Weimar Thought: A Contested Legacy* (Princeton University Press 2013).

Gordon, Robert W., 'Foreword: The Arrival of Critical Historicism' 49 (1997) *Stanford Law Review* 1023.

Gray, Christine, 'The US National Security Strategy and the New "Bush Doctrine" on Preemptive Self-defense' 1 (2002) *Chinese Journal of International Law* 437.

Greenberg, Joel, 'Israelis Debate Army's Rights Record in Uprising' *The New York Times* (24 May 1993) http://www.nytimes.com/1993/05/24/world/israelis-debate-army-s-rights-record-in-uprising.html accessed 10 May 2015.

Greenwald, Glenn, 'US Drone Strikes Target Rescuers in Pakistan – and the West Stays Silent' *The Guardian* (12 August 2012) www.theguardian.com/commentisfree/2012/aug/20/us-drones-strikes-target-rescuers-pakistan accessed 10 May 2015.

Gregory, Derek, 'Drone Geographies' 183 (2014) *Radical Philosophy* 7.

Grimmet, Richard F., Authorization For Use of Military Force in Response to the 9/11 Attacks (P.L. 107–40): Legislative History (CRS Report for Congress 2001, published online by the Federation of American Scientists: http://www.fas.org/sgp/crs/natsec/RS22357.pdf accessed 10 May 2015.

Grotius, Hugo, *The Rights of War and Peace*, vol. 3 (Tuck R ed., *Indianapolis: Liberty Fund* 2005).

Guiora, Amos N., 'Targeted Killing as Active Self-Defense' 36 (2004) *Case Western Reserve Journal of International Law* 319.
    'Anticipatory Self-Defence and International Law – A Re-evaluation' 13 (2008) *Journal of Conflict & Security Law* 3.

Gunneflo, Markus, 'The Targeted Killing Judgment of the Israeli Supreme Court and the Critique of Legal Violence' 23 (2012) *Law and Critique* 67.
    The Life and Times of Targeted Killing (Lund: Faculty of Law 2014).
    'Political Community in Carl Schmitt's International Legal Thinking' in Arvidsson M, Brännström L and Minkkinen P (eds.), *The Contemporary Relevance of Carl Schmitt: Law, Politics, Theology* (Abingdon: Routledge 2015).

Hajjar, Lisa, *Courting Conflict: The Israeli Military Court System in the West Bank and Gaza* (University of California Press 2005).

Handelzalts, Michael, 'Advice and Dissent' *Haaretz* (21 December 2001) http://www.haaretz.com/culture/books/advice-and-dissent-1.77879 accessed 10 May 2015.

Hansen, Beatrice, *Critique of Violence: Between Poststructuralism and Critical Theory* (Abingdon: Routledge 2000).

Heller, Kevin Jon, 'Symposium on the Functional Approach to the Law of Occupation' (*Opinio Juris*, 23 April 2012) http://opiniojuris.org/2012/04/23/symposium-on-the-functional-approach-to-the-law-of-occupation/ accessed 10 May 2015.

'"One Hell of a Killing Machine": Signature Strikes and International Law' 11 (2013) *Journal of International Criminal Justice* 89.

Hersh, Seymour M., 'Moving Targets: Will the Counter-insurgency Plan in Iraq Repeat the Mistakes of Vietnam?' *The New Yorker* (15 December 2003) www.newyorker.com/archive/2003/12/15/031215fa_fact accessed 10 May 2015.

Hobbes, Thomas, *Leviathan* (Oxford University Press 1996).

Holder, Eric, 'Attorney General Eric Holder Speaks at Northwestern University School of Law' (2012) http://www.justice.gov/opa/speech/attorney-general-eric-holder-speaks-northwestern-university-school-law accessed 10 May 2015.

Holmqvist, Caroline, *Policing Wars: On Military Intervention in the Twenty-First Century* (New York: Palgrave Macmillan 2014).

Hooker, William, *Carl Schmitt's International Thought: Order and Orientation* (Cambridge University Press 2009).

Hudson, Leila, Owens, Colin S. and Callen, David J., 'Drone Warfare in Yemen: Fostering Emirates Through Counterterrorism?' 14 (2012) *Middle East Policy* 142.

Human Rights Committee, 'Consideration of Reports Submitted By States Parties Under Article 40 of the Covenant, Concluding Observations of the Human Rights Committee, Israel' (21 August 2003) UN Doc CCPR/CO/78/ISR.

'Comments by the Government of Israel on the Concluding Observations of the Human Rights Committee' (24 January 2007) UN Doc CCPR/CO/78/ISR/Add. 1.

'Consideration of Reports Submitted by States Parties under Article 40 of the Covenant Pursuant to the Optional Reporting Procedure – (Fourth periodic reports of States parties due in 2013) Israel', (14 October 2013) Advance Unedited Version published on the website of the Human Rights Committee: www.ccprcentre.org/country/israel/ accessed 10 May 2015.

ILC, 'Fragmentation of International Law: Difficulties Arising From the Diversification and Expansion of International Law: Report of the Study Group of the International Law Commission Finalized by Martti Koskenniemi' (13 April 2006) UN Doc A/CN.4/L.682.

'Israel Acknowledges Killing Palestinian Deputy in 1988 Raid' *The Guardian* (1 November 2012) http://www.guardian.co.uk/world/2012/nov/01/israel-acknowledges-killing-palestinian-deputy accessed 10 May 2015.

'Israel Bars 3 Reporters over "Undercover" Articles' *The New York Times* (25 October 1988) http://www.nytimes.com/1988/10/26/world/israel-bars-3-reporters-over-undercover-articles.html accessed 10 May 2015.

Israel Ministry of Foreign Affairs, 'Israel Supreme Court Decision on Targeting Terrorist Operatives' (2006) www.mfa.gov.il/MFA/Government/Law/Legal+Issues+and+Rulings/Israel+Supreme+Court+decision+on+targeting+terrorist+operatives+20-Dec-2006.htm accessed 10 May 2015.

Israel Prime Minister's Office, 'The Cabinet Resolution Regarding the Disengagement Plan' (6 June 2004), published online by the Israel Ministry of Foreign Affairs: http://www.mfa.gov.il/mfa/foreignpolicy/peace/mfadocuments/pages/revised%20disengagement%20plan%206-june-2004.aspx accessed 10 May 2015.

Jabotinsky, Ze'ev, 'The Iron Wall (We and the Arabs)' (1923) First published in Russian in Rassvyet in 1923, published in English in Jewish Herald (South Africa) in 1937, published online by Marxistsde: www.marxists.de/middleast/ironwall/ironwall.htm accessed 10 May 2015.

Jenkins, Brian Michael, 'Combatting Terrorism Becomes a War, P-6988' (1984) The Rand Corporation, published online: http://www.rand.org/content/dam/rand/pubs/papers/2005/P6988.pdf accessed 10 May 2015.

Jenks, Chris, 'Law From Above: Unmanned Aerial Systems, Use of Force and the Law of Armed Conflict' 85 (2010) *North Dakota Law Review* 649.

Johns, Fleur, *Non-legality in International Law: Unruly Law* (Cambridge University Press 2013).

Johnsen, Gregory D., '60 Words and a War Without End: The Untold Story of the Most Dangerous Sentence in U.S. History' (*BuzzFeed BuzzReads*, 16 January 2014) http://www.buzzfeed.com/gregoryjohnsen/60-words-and-a-war-without-end-the-untold-story-of-the-most accessed 14 May 2015.

Johnson, James Turner, 'Just War Tradition and Low-Intensity Conflict' in Coll AR, Ord JS and Rose SA (eds.), *Legal and Moral Constraints on Low-Intensity Conflict*, vol 67 (Newport, Rhode Island: U.S. Naval War College 1995) 147–169.

Joint Chiefs of Staff, 'Foreign Internal Defense', Joint Publication 3–22 (12 July 2010) available at: www.dtic.mil/doctrine/new_pubs/jp3_22.pdf accessed 14 May 2015.

Jones, Craig, 'Where Drones Matter: Notes on Israeli Sikul Memukad' (*War, Law & Space – Thoughts on Violence in the Historical Present*, 8 May 2013) https://warlawspace.wordpress.com/2013/05/08/where-drones-matter-notes-on-israeli-sikul-memukad/ accessed 15 May 2015.

'Frames of Law: Targeting Advice and Operational Law in the Israeli Military' 33 (2015) *Environment and Planning D: Society and Space* doi:10.1177/0263775815598103.

Kahn, Paul W., *Political Theology: Four New Chapters on the Concept of Sovereignty* (New York Columbia University Press 2011).

'Imagining Warfare' 24 (2013) *European Journal of International Law* 199.

Keller, Helen and Forowicz, Magdalena, 'A Tightrope Walk Between Legality and Legitimacy: An Analysis of the Israeli Supreme Court's Judgment on Targeted Killing' 21 (2008) *Leiden Journal of International Law* 185.

Kennedy, David, *Of War and Law* (Princeton University Press 2006).

Kennedy, Ellen, *Constitutional Failure: Carl Schmitt in Weimar* (Durham: Duke University Press 2004).

Foreword to *Constitutional Theory*, by Carl Schmitt, (Seitzer J ed., Seitzer J tr, Durham: Duke University Press 2008) xv–xvi.

Khen, Even and Moodrick, Hilly, 'Can We Now Tell What "Direct Participation in Hostilities' is?" 40 (2007) *Israel Law Review* 213.

Klaidman, Daniel, *Kill or Capture* (New York: Houghton Mifflin Harcourt 2012).

Klein, Aaron J., *Striking Back: The 1972 Munich Olympics Massacre and Israel's Deadly Response* (New York: Random House 2005).

Koh, Harold Hongju, 'The Obama Administration and International Law' (*Department of State*, 25 March 2010) www.state.gov/s/l/releases/remarks/139119 .htm accessed 15 May 2015.

'Foreword: America's Conscience on International Law' in Scharf MP and Williams PR (eds.), *Shaping Foreign Policy in Times of Crisis: The Role of International Law and the State Department Legal Adviser* (Cambridge University Press 2010) xi–xvii.

Kolb, Robert, 'Human Rights Law and International Humanitarian Law between 1945 and the Aftermath of the Teheran Conference of 1968' in Kolb R and Gaggioli G (eds.), *Research Handbook on Human Rights and Humanitarian Law* (Cheltenham and Northampton: Edward Elgar Publishing 2013) 35–52.

Korn, Alina, 'Israeli Press and the War against Terrorism: The Construction of the "liquidation policy"' 41 (2004) *Crime, Law & Social Change* 209.

Koskenniemi, Martti, *The Gentle Civilizer of Nations: The Rise and Fall of International Law 1870–1960* (Cambridge University Press 2001).

'International Law as Political Theology: How to Read Nomos der Erde?' 11 (2004) *Constellations* 492.

From Apology to Utopia: The Structure of International Legal Argument (2nd edn, Cambridge University Press 2005).

'The Fate of Public International Law: Between Technique and Politics' 70 (2007) *Modern Law Review* 1.

Krasmann, Susanne, 'Targeted Killing and Its Law: On a Mutually Constitutive Relationship' 25 (2012) *Leiden Journal of International Law* 665.

Kreitner, Roy, 'Justification Between Positivism and Decisionism' 7 (2006) *Theoretical Inquiries in Law* 229.

Kremnitzer, Mordechai, 'Targeted Killing Policy: Insufficiently Limited' 44 (2007) *Justice – The International Association of Jewish Lawyers and Jurists* 38.

Kretzmer, David, *The Occupation of Justice: The Supreme Court of Israel and the Occupied Territories* (New York: SUNY Press 2002).

'Targeted Killing of Suspected Terrorists: Extra-judicial Executions or Legitimate Means of Defence?' 16 (2005) *European Journal of International Law* 171.

'Israel' in Sloss D (ed.), *The Role of Domestic Courts in Treaty Enforcement: A Comparative Study* (Cambridge University Press 2009) 273–325.

Kunz, Josef L., 'Critical Remarks on Lauterpacht's "Recognition in International Law"' 44 (1950) *American Journal of International Law* 713.

Kurtulus, Ersun N., 'The New Counterterrorism: Contemporary Counterterrorism Trends in the United States and Israel' 35 (2012) *Studies in Conflict and Terrorism* 37.

Lavi, Shai, 'The Use of Force Beyond the Liberal Imagination: Terror and Empire in Palestine, 1947' 7 (2006) *Theoretical Inquiries in Law* 199.

Lehto, Marja, *Indirect Responsibility for Terrorist Acts: Redefinition of the Concept of Terrorism Beyond Violent Acts* (Leiden: Martinus Nijhoff Publishers 2009).

Leiser, Burton M., 'Enemies of Mankind' in Netanyahu B (ed.), *Terrorism: How the West can Win* (New York: Farrar, Straus and Giroux 1986) 155–156.

Lemke, Thomas, *Biopolitics: An Advanced Introduction* (Trump EF tr, New York University Press 2011).

Lesh, Michelle, 'Public Committee Against Torture in Israel v the Government of Israel: The Israeli High Court of Justice Targeted Killing Decision' 8 (2007) *Melbourne Journal of International Law* 373.

Limone, Noah, 'Chronicling Walter Benjamin's Final Hours' *Haaretz* (9 July 2012) http://www.haaretz.com/chronicling-walter-benjamin-s-final-hours-1.449897 accessed 10 May 2015.

Lindahl, Hans, 'Give and Take: Arendt and the Nomos of Political Community' 32 (2006) *Philosophy and Social Criticism* 881.

Linderfalk, Ulf, 'The Post-9/11 Discourse Revisited: The Self-image of the International Legal Scientific Discipline' 2 (2010) *Goettingen Journal of International Law* 893.

Lippens, Ronnie, 'Viral Contagion and Anti-terrorism: Notes on Medical Emergency, Legality and Diplomacy' 17 (2004) *International Journal for the Semiotics of Law* 125.

Liska, Vivian and Eisenberg, Tamara, 'A Travel Guide to Palestine: Walter Benjamin in Israel' 2 (2009) *Naharaim-Zeitschrift für deutsch-jüdische Literatur und Kulturgeschichte* 301.

Livingstone, Neil C., *The Cult of Counterterrorism: The Weird World of Spooks, Counterterrorists, Adventurers and Professionals* (Lexington: Lexington Books 1990).

Lubell, Noam and Derejko, Nathan, 'A Global Battlefield? Drones and the Geographical Scope of Armed Conflict' 11 (2013) *Journal of International Criminal Justice* 65.

Malanczuk, Peter, 'Israel: Status, Territory and Occupied Territories', in Bernhardt R (ed.), *Encyclopedia of Public International Law II* (Elsevier 1995) 1468–1497.

Marder, Michael, *Groundless Existence: The Political Ontology of Carl Schmitt* (New York: Continuum 2010).

Martel, James R., *Textual Conspiracies: Walter Benjamin, Idolatry, and Political Theory* (Ann Arbor: University of Michigan Press 2011).

Mazetti, Mark and Schmitt, Eric, 'Two-year Manhunt Led to Killing of Awlaki in Yemen' *The New York Times* (30 September 2011) http://www.nytimes.com/2011/10/01/world/middleeast/anwar-al-awlaki-is-killed-in-yemen.html accessed 10 May 2015.

McCormick, John P., *Carl Schmitt's Critique of Liberalism: Against Politics as Technology* (Cambridge University Press 1999).

McFarlane, Robert C., 'Background Material on Terrorism' The White House, Washington (15 August 1984), published online by Washington Decoded: www.washingtondecoded.com/files/nsdd.pdf accessed 10 May 2015.

Mégret, Frédéric, '"War"? Legal Semantics and the Move to Violence' 13 (2002) *European Journal of International Law* 361.

'From "Savages" to "Unlawful Combatants": A Postcolonial Look at International Law's "Other"' in Orford A (ed.), *International Law and Its Others* (Cambridge University Press 2006) 265–317.

'War and the Vanishing Battlefield' 9 (2012) *Loyola University Chicago International Law Review* 131.

Melzer, Nils, 'Targeted Killing or Less Harmful Means? Israel's High Court Judgment on Targeted Killing and the Restrictive Function of Military Necessity' 9 (2006) *Yearbook of International Humanitarian Law* 87.

Interpretive Guidance on the Notion of Direct Participation in Hostilities under International Humanitarian Law (Geneva: International Committee of the Red Cross (ICRC) 2009).

'Keeping the Balance Between Military Necessity and Humanity: A Response to Four Critiques of the ICRC's Interpretive Guidance on the Notion of Direct Participation in Hostilities' 42 (2010) *New York Journal of International Law and Politics* 831.

Middle East Watch, *A License to Kill – Israeli Operations against "Wanted" and Masked Palestinians* (Ron J and others eds., New York, Washington, Los Angeles and London: Human Rights Watch 1993).

Milanovic, Marko, 'Lessons for Human Rights and Humanitarian Law in the War on Terror: Comparing Hamdan and the Israeli Targeted Killing Case' 89 (2007) *International Review of the Red Cross* 373.

Extraterritorial Application of Human Rights Treaties (Oxford University Press 2011).

'Norm Conflicts, International Humanitarian Law, and Human Rights Law' in Ben-Naftali O (ed.), *International Humanitarian Law and International Human Rights Law* (Oxford University Press 2013) 95–126.

Mongoven, Ann, 'The War on Disease and the War on Terror – A Dangerous Metaphorical Nexus?' 15 (2006) *Cambridge Quarterly of Healthcare Ethics* 403.

Morris, Benny and Black, Ian, *Israel's Secret Wars: A History of Israel's Intelligence Services* (New York: Grove Press 1991).

Moyn, Samuel, *The Last Utopia: Human Rights in History* (Cambridge Massachusetts: Harvard University Press 2010).

'Drones and Imagination: A Response to Paul Kahn' 24 (2013) *European Journal of International Law* 227.

Moyn, Samuel and Eckel, Jan, *The Breakthrough: Human Rights in the 1970s* (Philadelphia: University of Pennsylvania Press 2014).

Müller, Jan, 'Carl Schmitt: An Occasional Nationalist?' 23 (1997) *History of European Ideas* 19.

Nachman, Ben-Yehuda, *Political Assassinations by Jews: A Rhetorical Device for Justice* (New York: SUNY Press 1993).

National Commission on Terrorist Attacks upon the United States, The 9/11 Commission Report: Final Report of the National Commission on Terrorist Attacks upon the United States (1st edn, New York: W.W. Norton & Company 2004).

National Security Council, 'Combatting Terrorism', National Security Decision Directive 138 (NSDD 138) Signed by President Ronald Reagan on April 3, 1984. Published online by the Federation of American Scientists: http://www.fas.org/irp/offdocs/nsdd/nsdd-138.pdf accessed 15 May 2015.

'U.S. Policy on Counterterrorism', Presidential Decision Directive 39, signed by President Bill Clinton on 21 June 1995. Published online by the Federation of American Scientists: http://www.fas.org/irp/offdocs/pdd/pdd-39.pdf accessed 10 May 2015.

'Combatting Terrorism', National Security Presidential Directive 9 signed by President George W. Bush on 21 October 2001. Published online by the Federation of American Scientists: http://www.fas.org/irp/offdocs/nspd/nspd-9.htm accessed 10 May 2015.

National Security Planning Group, 'Summary of National Security Planning Group Meeting on Combatting Terrorism', 2 March 1984. Retrieved from The Reagan Files: http://www.thereaganfiles.com/nspg-meetings.html On file with author.

Newey, Glen, *Routledge Philosophy Guidebook to Hobbes and Leviathan* (Abingdon: Routledge 2008).

Niva, Steve, 'Disappearing Violence: JSOC and the Pentagon's New Cartography of Networked Warfare' 44 (2013) *Security Dialogue* 185.

Noll, Gregor, 'The Exclusionary Construction of Human Rights in International Law and Political Theory' 10 (2003) *Institute for International Integration Studies Discussion Paper* 1.

'Force, Dislocation, Partisanship: An Essay on International Law in the State of the Exceptional' in Petman J and Klabbers J (eds.), *Nordic Cosmopolitanism: Essays in International Law for Martti Koskenniemi* (Leiden: Martinus Nijhoff Publishers 2003) 207–219.

Nolte, Georg, 'Targeted Killing' in Wolfrum R (ed.), *The Max Planck Encyclopedia of Public International Law – online edition* (Oxford University Press 2008) www.mpepil.com accessed 20 May 2015.

Norris, Andrew, 'Carl Schmitt on Friends, Enemies and the Political' 112 (1998) *Telos* 68.

O'Connell, Mary Ellen, 'Combatants and the Combat Zone' 43 (2009) *University of Richmond Law Review* 845.

O'Keefe, Roger, 'Israel/Palestine Sixty Years On' in Giegerich T and Proelß A (eds.), *Krisenherde im Fokus des Völkerrechts – Trouble Spots in the Focus of International Law* (Berlin: Duncker & Humblot 2010) 13–55.

Obama, Barack, 'Remarks by the President on a New Strategy for Afghanistan and Pakistan' (*White House*, 2009) www.whitehouse.gov/the_press_office/Remarks-by-the-President-on-a-New-Strategy-for-Afghanistan-and-Pakistan/ accessed 10 May 2015.

Orford, Anne, *International Authority and the Responsibility to Protect* (Cambridge University Press 2011).

'In Praise of Description' 25 (2012) *Leiden Journal of International Law* 609.

'On International Legal Method' 1 (2013) *London Review of International Law* 166.

Pan, David, 'Against Biopolitics: Walter Benjamin, Carl Schmitt, and Giorgio Agamben on Political Sovereignty and Symbolic Order' 82 (2009) *The German Quarterly* 42.

Parks, W. Hays, 'Rolling Thunder and the Law of War' 33 (1982) *Air University Review* 11.

'Crossing the Line' 4 (1986) *US Naval Institute Proceedings* 22.

'Teaching the Law of War' (1987) *The Army Lawyer* 4.

'Memorandum of Law: Executive Order 12333 and Assassination' (1989) *The Army Lawyer* 4.

'Air War and the Law of War' 32 (1990) *Air Force Law Review* 1.

'The Laws of War, Methods and Means of Combat, Assassination and the Law of War' in Nash M (ed.), *Cumulative Digest of United States in International Law 1981–1988*, vol. 3 (Office of the Legal Adviser, Department of State 1993) 3411–3421.

'Book Review (Review of the Books Terrorism in War – The Law of War Crimes by Dobbs Ferry and Non-Combatant Immunity as a Norm of International Humanitarian Law by Judith G. Gardam)' 28 (1994) *George Washington Journal of International Law and Economics* 207.

'Deadly Force is Authorized' 127 (2001) *US Naval Institute Proceedings* 32.

'Lessons From the 1986 Libya Airstrike' 36 (2002) *New England Law Review* 755.

'Teaching the Law of War: A Reprise' 3 (2007) *IDF Law Review* 9.

'Combatants' 85 (2009) *International Law Studies Series – US Naval War College* 247.

'Jus in Bello in the Struggle Against Terror' in Moore JN and Turner RF (eds.), *Legal Issues in the Struggle Against Terror* (Durham, North Carolina: Carolina Academic Press 2010) 359–401.

'Part IX of the ICRC Direct Participation in Hostilities Study: No Mandate, No Expertise, and Legally Incorrect' 42 (2010) *New York Journal of International Law and Policy* 769.

'Washington Post Opinions: Reaction to Post Coverage of bin Laden's death' *The Washington Post* (6 May 2011) www.washingtonpost.com/opinions/ reaction-to-post-coverage-of-bin-ladens-death/2011/05/02/AFMTojCG_ story.html accessed 10 May 2015.

'Perspective and the Importance of History' 14 (2012) *Yearbook of International Humanitarian Law* 361.

'Update on the DOD Law of War Manual' American Bar Association 22nd Annual Review of the Field of National Security Law, Ritz Carlton Hotel, Washington DC, 30 November 2012, published online by the Lawfare blog: https://lawfare.s3-us-west-2.amazonaws.com/staging/s3fs-public/ uploads/2012/12/Parks.Manual.pdf accessed 15 May 2015.

Perliger, Arie and Weinberg, Leonard, 'Jewish Self-Defence and Terrorist Groups Prior to the Establishment of the State of Israel: Roots and Traditions' 4 (2003) *Totalitarian Movements and Political Religions* 91.

Pfeffer, Anshel, 'Israel Should Stop Suppressing Debate about its Drone Policy' *Haaretz* (19 February 2013) www.haaretz.com/opinion/israel-should-stop-suppressing-debate-about-its-drone-policy.premium-1.504482 accessed 10 May 2015.

Pictet, Jean S., The Geneva Conventions of 12 August 1949: Commentary, Geneva Convention Relative to the Protection of Civilian Persons in Time of War (Pictet JS ed., Griffin R and Dumbleton C trs, Geneva: International Committee of the Red Cross (ICRC) 1958).

Piterberg, Gabriel, *The Returns of Zionism: Myths, Politics and Scholarship in Israel* (London: Verso 2008).

Plaw, Avery, *Targeting Terrorists: A License to Kill?* (Burlington and Hampshire: Ashgate Publishing Company 2008).

Porras, Ileana M., 'On Terrorism: Reflections on Violence and the Outlaw' 1 (1994) *Utah Law Review* 119.

Porter, Patrick, *The Global Village Myth: Distance, War and the Limits of Power* (Washington DC: Georgetown University Press 2015).

'President Signs Authorization for Use of Military Force bill' (White House, 18 September 2001) http://georgewbush-whitehouse.archives.gov/news/ releases/2001/09/20010918-10.html accessed 10 May 2015.

Preston, Stephen W., 'CIA and the Rule of Law' (*Lawfare*, 10 April 2012) www.lawfareblog.com/2012/04/remarks-of-cia-general-counsel-stephen-preston-at-harvard-law-school/ accessed 10 May 2015.

Proulx, Vincent-Joël, *Transnational Terrorism and State Accountability: A New Theory of Prevention* (Oxford: Hart Publishing 2012).

Rajkovic, Nikolas M., Aalberts, Tanja and Gammeltoft-Hansen, Thomas, *The Power of Legality: Practices of International Law and their Politics* (Cambridge University Press forthcoming 2016).

Ralph, Jason, 'War as an Institution of International Hierarchy: Carl Schmitt's Theory of the Partisan and Contemporary US Practice' 39 (2010) *Millennium: Journal of International Studies* 279.

America's War on Terror: The State of the 9/11 Exception from Bush to Obama (Oxford University Press 2013).

Ranstorp, Magnus, 'Statement of Magnus Ranstorp to the National Commission on Terrorist Attacks Upon the United States March 31, 2003' (National Commission on Terrorist Attacks Upon the United States) http://govinfo.library .unt.edu/911/hearings/hearing1/witness_ranstorp.htm accessed 14 May 2015.

Rasch, William, 'Introduction: Carl Schmitt and the New World Order' 104 (2005) *South Atlantic Quarterly* 177.

Raz, Avi, *The Bride and the Dowry: Israel, Jordan, and the Palestinians in the Aftermath of the June 1967 War* (New Haven: Yale University Press 2012).

Reagan, Ronald, 'Address to the Nation on Events in Lebanon and Grenada' (*White House*, 27 October 1983) www.reagan.utexas.edu/archives/speeches/1983/ 102783b.htm accessed 10 May 2015.

'Remarks to Citizens in Chicago Heights, Illinois' (*White House*, 28 June 1985) https://www.reagan.utexas.edu/archives/speeches/1985/62885b .htm accessed 10 May 2015.

'Speech to the Nation on Air Strikes Against Libya' (*White House*, 14 April 1986) http://millercenter.org/president/reagan/speeches/speech-5864 accessed 10 May 2015.

Reeve, Simon, *One Day in September: The Full Story of the 1972 Munich Olympics Massacre and the Israeli Revenge Operation "Wrath of God"* (New York: Skyhorse Publishing Inc. 2000).

Reisman, Michael W., 'Editorial Comment: Assessing Claims to Revise the Laws of War' 97 (2003) *American Journal of International Law* 82.

Reisner, Daniel, 'Press Briefing by Colonel Daniel Reisner – Head of the International Law Branch of the IDF Legal Division 15 November 2000' (Israel Ministry of Foreign Affairs, 15 November 2000) http://mfa.gov.il/MFA/ PressRoom/2000/Pages/Press%20Briefing%20by%20Colonel%20Daniel%20 Reisner-%20Head%20of.aspx accessed 10 May 2015.

'Remarks by Daniel Reisner (Panel on Constraints on the Waging of War: Jus In Bello and the Challenge of Modern Conflicts)' 97 (2003) *Proceedings of the Annual Meeting (American Society of International Law)* 200.

'Reply of the Government of the United States of America to the Report of the Five
     UNCHR Special Rapporteurs on Detainees in Guantanamo Bay Cuba' 45
     (2006) *International Legal Materials* 742.
Richter, Paul, 'Congress Ponders Whether the U.S. Should Ease Ban on Assassi-
     nations' *Los Angeles Times* (18 September 1998) http://articles.latimes.com/
     1998/sep/18/news/mn-24038 accessed 10 May 2015.
     'White House Justifies Option of Lethal Force' *Los Angeles Times* (29 October
     1998) http://articles.latimes.com/1998/oct/29/news/mn-37327 accessed 10
     May 2015.
Rose, Jacqueline, *The Question of Zion* (Princeton University Press 2005).
Ross, Brian and Ferran, Lee, 'How Anwar Al-Awlaki Inspired Terror From Across
     the Globe' *ABC News* (30 September 2011) http://abcnews.go.com/Blotter/
     anwar-al-awlaki-inspired-terror/story?id=14643383 accessed 10 May 2015.
Rwelamira, Medard R., 'Human Rights and International Humanitarian Law: The
     Link or Common Ground Revisited' 3 (1992) *Stellenbosch Law Review* 329.
Salter, Michael G., 'Neo-fascist Legal Theory on Trial: an Interpretation of Carl
     Schmitt's Defence at Nuremberg from the Perspective of Franz Neumann's
     Critical Theory of Law' 5 (1999) *Res Publica* 161.
     Law as Politics, Ideology and Strategic Myth (Abingdon: Routledge 2012).
Sandia National Laboratories, 'Osama Bin Laden: A Case Study' (1999), pub-
     lished online by George Washington University, www2.gwu.edu/~nsarchiv/
     NSAEBB/NSAEBB253/sandia.pdf accessed 10 May 2015.
Scahill, Jeremy, *Dirty Wars: The World is a Battlefield* (New York: Nation Books
     2013).
Schachter, Oscar, 'The United States and the World Court' 80 (1986) *Proceedings
     of the Annual Meeting (American Society of International Law)* 204.
Scharf, Michael P. and Williams, Paul R., *Shaping Foreign Policy in Times of Cri-
     sis: The Role of International Law and the State Department Legal Adviser*
     (Cambridge University Press 2010).
Scheipers, Sibylle, *Unlawful Combatants: A Genealogy of the Irregular Fighter*
     (Oxford University Press 2015).
Schmitt, Carl, *Political Theology: Four Chapters on the Concept of Sovereignty*
     (Schwab G tr, London and Cambridge, Massachusetts: MIT Press 1985).
     The Crisis of Parliamentary Democracy (Kennedy E tr, London and Cambridge,
     Massachusetts: MIT Press 2000).
     State, Movement, People: The Triadic Structure of the Political Unity (Dragichi S
     tr, Corvalls: Plutarch Press 2001).
     Legality and Legitimacy (Seitzer J tr, Durham: Duke University Press 2004).
     On the Three Types of Juristic Thought (Bendersky JW tr, London and Westport,
     Connecticut: Praeger Publishers 2004).
     The Nomos of the Earth in the International Law of the Jus Publicum Europaeum
     (Ulmen GL tr, New York: Telos Press Publishing 2006).

The Concept of the Political – Expanded Edition (Schwab G tr, University of Chicago Press 2007).

Theory of the Partisan: Intermediate Commentary on the Concept of the Political (Ulmen GL tr, New York: Telos Press Publishing 2007).

Constitutional Theory (Seltzer J tr, Durham: Duke University Press 2008).

'The Großraum Order of International Law with a Ban on Intervention for Spatially Foreign Powers: A Contribution to the Concept of Reich in International law (1939–1941)' in Timothy Nunan (ed. & tr), *Writings on War* (Cambridge and Malden: Polity 2011).

'Großraum Versus Universalism: The International Legal Struggle over the Monroe Doctrine', in Legg S (ed.), Hannah M (tr), *Spatiality, Sovereignty and Carl Schmitt: Geographies of the Nomos* (Abingdon: Routledge 2011) 46–54.

Dictatorship: From the Origin of the Modern Concept of Sovereignty to Proletarian Class Struggle (Hoelzl M and Ward G trs, Cambridge and Malden: Polity 2014).

Schmitt, Michael N., 'State-Sponsored Assassination in International and Domestic Law' 17 (1992) *Yale Journal of International Law* 609.

'Review of Nils Melzer's Targeted Killing in International Law' 103 (2009) *American Journal of International Law* 813.

'Deconstructing Direct Participation in Hostilities: The Constitutive Elements ' 42 (2010) *New York Journal of International Law and Politics* 697.

Schondorf, Roy S., 'The Targeted Killing Judgment' 5 (2007) *Journal of International Criminal Justice* 301.

Schwab, George, 'The Decision: Is the American Sovereign at Bay?' 16 (1978) *Revue Européenne des Sciences Sociales* 67.

Scobbie, Iain, 'An Intimate Disengagement: Israel's Withdrawal from Gaza, the Law of Occupation and of Self-determination' 11 (2007) *Yearbook of Islamic and Middle Eastern Law* 107.

Shamgar, Meir, 'The Observance of International Law in the Administered Territories' 1 (1971) *Israel Yearbook on Human Rights* 262.

'Legal Concepts and Problems of the Israeli Military Government: The Initial Stage' in Shamgar M (ed.), *Military Government in the Territories Administered by Israel 1967–1980: The Legal Aspects* (Hebrew University Jerusalem – Faculty of Law, The Harry Sacher Institute for Legislative Research and Comparative Law 1982) 13–59.

Shamir, Ronen, '"Landmark Cases" and the Reproduction of Legitimacy: The Case of Israel's High Court of Justice' 24 (1990) *Law and Society Review* 781.

'Occupation as Disorientation: The Impossibility of Borders' in Ophir A, Givoni M and Hanafi S (eds.), *The Power Of Inclusive Exclusion: Anatomy of Israeli Rule In The Occupied Palestinian Territories* (New York: Zone Books 2009) 587–596.

Shane, Scott, 'U.S. Approves Targeted Killing of American Cleric' *The New York Times* (6 April 2010) http://www.nytimes.com/2010/04/07/world/middle east/07yemen.html accessed 10 May 2015.

Shehadeh, Raja, 'Occupier's Law and the Uprising' 17 (1988) *Journal of Palestine Studies* 24.

'Apologia for Occupation: Israel, the "Intifada" and the Rule of Law' 23 (1994) *Journal of Palestine Studies* 104.

Shlaim, Avi, *The Iron Wall: Israel and the Arab World* (New York: W. W. Norton & Company 2001).

Shultz, George P., 'New Realities and New Ways of Thinking' 63 (1984) *Foreign Affairs* 705.

'Power and Diplomacy in the 1980s [Address before the Trilateral Commission on 3 April 1984]' 84 (1984) *Department of State Bulletin* 12.

'Terrorism and the Modern World [Address before the Park Avenue Synagogue New York City on 25 October 1984]' 84 (1984) *Department of State Bulletin* 12.

'Terrorism: The Challenge to the Democracies [Address before the Jonathan Institute's second Conference on International Terrorism on 24 June 1984]' 84 (1984) *Department of State Bulletin* 31.

'Terrorism: The Problem and the Challenge [Statement before the House Foreign Affairs Committee on 13 June 1984]' 84 (1984) *Department of State Bulletin* 29.

'Low-Intensity Warfare: The Challenge of Ambiguity [Address Before the Low-Intensity Warfare Conference, National Defense University, Washington, D.C., 15 January 1986]' 86 (1986) *Department of State Bulletin* 204.

Turmoil and Triumph: My Years as Secretary of State (New York: Charles Scribner's Sons Macmillan Publishing Company 1993).

'A More Accountable World?' 13 (2002) *Mediterranean Quarterly* 1.

Simpson, Gerry, *Great Powers and Outlaw States: Unequal Sovereigns in the International Legal Order* (Cambridge University Press 2004).

Skouteris, Thomas, 'Engaging History in International Law' in Beneyto JM (ed.), *New Approaches to International Law* (The Hague: T.M.C. Asser Press 2012).

Slaughter, Anne-Marie, 'Mercy Killings' 136 (2003) *Foreign Policy* 72.

Sloane, Robert D., 'The Cost of Conflation: Preserving the Dualism of Jus ad Bellum and Jus in Bello in the Contemporary Law of War' 34 (2009) *The Yale Journal of International Law* 47.

Slomp, Gabriella, *Carl Schmitt and the Politics of Hostility, Violence and Terror* (New York: Palgrave Macmillan 2009).

Sofaer, Abraham D., *War, Foreign Affairs and Constitutional Power: The Origins* (Cambridge, Massachusetts: Ballinger Publishing Company 1976).

'Terrorism and the Law' 64 (1986) *Foreign Affairs* 901.

'The United States and the World Court' 80 (1986) *Proceedings of the Annual Meeting (American Society of International Law)* 204.

'International Law and the Use of Force' 82 (1988) *Proceedings of the Annual Meeting (American Society of International Law)* 420.

'Luncheon Address (10 May 1988)' (1988) ALI Meeting Speeches 23.

'Terrorism, the Law and the National Defense' 126 (1989) *Military Law Review* 89.

'Book Review: International Law and the United States Military Intervention in the Western Hemisphere. By Max Hilaire' 92 (1998) *American Journal of International Law* 586.

'Playing Games with Terrorists' 36 (2002) *New England Law Review* 903.

'Terrorism as War' 96 (2002) *Proceedings of the Annual Meeting (American Society of International Law)* 254.

'On the Necessity of Pre-emption' 14 (2003) *European Journal of International Law* 209.

'Responses to Terrorism: Targeted killing is a Necessary Option' *SFGatecom* (26 March 2004) www.sfgate.com/opinion/openforum/article/Responses-to-Terrorism-Targeted-killing-is-a-2775845.php accessed 15 May 2015.

The Best Defense? Legitimacy & Preventive Force (Stanford, California: Hoover Institution Press 2010).

'The Reagan and Bush Administrations (1985–1990)' in Scharf MP and Williams PR (eds.), *Shaping Foreign Policy in Times of Crisis: The Role of International Law and the State Department Legal Adviser* (Cambridge University Press 2010) 65–86.

Sofaer, Abraham D. and Williams, Paul R., 'Doing Justice during Wartime' 111 (2002) *Policy Review* 3.

Sontag, Susan, *Illness as Metaphor* (New York: Farrar, Straus and Giroux 1978).

Stahl, Adam, 'The Evolution of Israeli Targeted Operations: Consequences of the Thabet Thabet Operation' 33 (2010) *Studies in Conflict and Terrorism* 111.

Stares, Paul B. and Yacoubian, Mona, 'Unconventional Approaches to an Unconventional Threat: A Counter-Epidemic Strategy' in Campbell KM and Darsie W (eds.), *Mapping the Jihadist Threat – The War on Terrorism Since 9/11* (Washington DC: Aspen Strategy Group 2006) 85–95 www.aclu.org/files/fbimappingfoia/20111110/ACLURM000944.pdf accessed 10 May 2015.

Stein, Yael, 'By Any Name Illegal and Immoral' 17 (2003) *Ethics & International Affairs* 127.

Stephens, Bret, 'Target Assad' *The Wall Street Journal* (27 August 2013) http://online.wsj.com/news/articles/SB10001424127887323407104579036740023927518 accessed 10 May 2015.

Stickle, Douglas R., 'Malignants in the Body Politic – Redefining War Through Metaphor' (School of Advanced Airpower Studies for Completion of Graduation Requirements 2002).

Stirk, Peter M., 'Carl Schmitt, the Law of Occupation, and the Iraq War' 11 (2004) *Constellations* 527.

 The Politics of Military Occupation (Edinburgh University Press 2009).

Strauss, Leo, 'Notes on Carl Schmitt, The Concept of the Political' in Schwab G (ed.), *The Concept of the Political Expanded Edition* (University of Chicago Press 2008) 99–122.

Sultany, Nimer, 'The Legacy of Justice Aharon Barak: A Critical Review' *Harvard International Law Journal Online* www.harvardilj.org/wp-content/uploads/2011/05/HILJ-Online_48_Sultany.pdf accessed 15 May 2015.

Tal, David, 'Israel's Concept of Preemptive War' 57 (2006) *Syracuse Law Review* 601.

Tams, Christian J., 'The Use of Force Against Terrorists' 20 (2009) *European Journal of International Law* 359.

Thomas, Ward, 'Norms and Security: The Case of International Assassination' 25 (2000) *International Security* 105.

 The Ethics of Destruction: Norms and Force in International Relations (Ithaca and London: Cornell University Press 2001).

 'The New Age of Assassination' 25 (2005) *SAIS Review* 27.

Tilly, Charles, *Coercion, Capital, and European States, AD 990–1990* (Cambridge: Basil Blackwell 1990).

Toaldo, Mattia, *The Origins of the US War on Terror: Lebanon, Libya and American Intervention in the Middle East* (Abingdon: Routledge 2012).

Tovy, Tal, 'The Theoretical Aspect of Targeted Killings: The Phoenix Program as a Case Study' 11 (2009) *Journal of Military and Strategic Studies* 1.

Ulmen, G. L., *Translator's Introduction* to *Theory of the Partisan – Intermediate Commentary on the Concept of the Political*, by Carl Schmitt (New York: Telos Press Publishing 2007).

Ulrich, Jonathan, 'The Gloves Were Never On: Defining the President's Authority to Order Targeted Killing in the War Against Terrorism' 45 (2005) *Virginia Journal of International Law* 1029.

UNGA, 'Final Act of the International Conference on Human Rights' (Teheran, 22 April to 13 May 1968) UN Doc A/CONF.32/41.

 'Declaration of the Assembly of Heads of State and Government of the Organization of African Unity on the Aerial and Naval Military Attack Against the Socialist People's Libyan Arab Jamahiriya by the present United States Administration in April 1986' (20 November 1986) UN Doc A/RES/41/38.

 'Promotion and Protection of Human Rights and Fundamental Freedoms while Countering Terrorism' (18 September 2013) UN Doc A/68/389.

UNSC, Verbatim Record (27 July 1948) UN Doc S/PV.339.

 'Letter dated 19 April 1988 from the permanent representative of Tunisia to the United Nations addressed the President of the Security Council' (1988) UN Doc S/19798.

'International Political Relations' (1998) *United Nations Yearbook* 1219.

'Letter from the Permanent Representative of the United States of America to the United Nations addressed to the President of the Security Council' (20 August 1998) UN Doc S/1998/780.

Res 611 (April 25, 1988) UN Doc S/RES/611.

Res 1368 (12 September 2001) UN Doc S/RES/1368.

Res 1373 (28 September 2001) UN Doc S/RES/1373.

US Congress, Senate, Select Committee to Study Governmental Operations with Respect to Intelligence Activities, 94 Cong., 2nd sess., 'Interim Report: Alleged Assassination Plots Involving Foreign Leaders', 1975 available online at www.aarclibrary.org/publib/contents/church/contents_church_reports_ir .htm accessed 10 May 2015.

'War Powers, Libya and State-sponsored Terrorism', Hearings before the Subcommittee on Arms Control, International Security, and Science of the Committee on Foreign Affairs, House of Representatives, Ninety-ninth Congress, second session, 29 April, 1 and 15 May 1986.

'US Drone Strikes Illegal, Govt Should Stop Them – Pakistani Court' RT (10 May 2013) http://rt.com/news/pakistan-us-drone-illegal-093/ accessed 10 May 2015.

US Mission to the UN Press Release No. 106(85), 4 October 1985, extract reprinted in 80 (1986) *American Journal of International Law* 165.

Vagts, Detlev F., 'Hegemonic International Law' 95 (2001) *American Journal of International Law* 843.

Valverde, Mariana and Mopas, Michael, 'Insecurity and the Dream of Targeted Governance' in Larner WW and Walters W (eds.), *Global Governmentality* (Abingdon: Routledge 2004) 233–250.

Vinx, Lars, 'Carl Schmitt' in *Stanford Encyclopedia of Philosophy* (2010) http://plato .stanford.edu/entries/schmitt/ accessed 20 May 2015.

Vitullo, Anita, 'Yitzhak Rabin and Israel's Death Squads' 22 (1992) *Middle East Report* 40.

Vlasic, Mark Vincent, 'Cloak and Dagger Diplomacy: The U.S. and Assassination' 95 (2000) *Georgetown Journal of International Affairs* 95.

'Assassination & Targeted Killing: A Historical and Post-bin Laden Legal Analysis' 43 (2012) *Georgetown Journal of International Law* 259.

Warren, Craig A., '"It Reads Like a Novel": The 9/11 Commission Report and the American Reading Public' 41 (2007) *Journal of American Studies* 533.

Watkin, Kenneth, 'Opportunity Lost: Organized Armed Groups and the ICRC "Direct Participation in Hostilities" Interpretive Guidance' 42 (2010) *New York Journal of International Law and Politics* 641.

Weber, Samuel, 'Rogue Democracy' 38 (2008) *Diacritics* 104.

'Bare Life and Life in General' 46 (2012) *Grey Room* 7.

Weinberger, Caspar, 'The Uses of Military Power' (PBS, 1984) www.pbs.org/wgbh/pages/frontline/shows/military/force/weinberger.html accessed 15 May 2015.

Weizman, Eyal, *Hollow Land: Israel's Architecture of Occupation* (London: Verso 2007).

Werner, Wouter, 'The Changing Face of Enmity: Carl Schmitt's International Theory and the Evolution of the Legal Concept of War' 2 (2010) *International Theory* 351.

'What War Powers Does the President Have?' *Slate* (13 September 2001) www.slate.com/articles/news_and_politics/explainer/2001/09/what_war_powers_does_the_president_have.html accessed 10 May 2015.

Whittle, Richard, *Predator: The Secret Origins of the Drone Revolution* (New York: Henry Holt and Company 2014).

Wills, David C., *The First War on Terrorism: Counter-terrorism Policy During the Reagan Administration* (Maryland: Rowman& Littlefield Publishers, Inc. 2003).

Witte, Bernd, *Walter Benjamin: An Intellectual Biography* (Rolleston J tr, Detroit, Michigan: Wayne State University Press 1997).

Wittes, Benjamin, 'Lawfare Podcast Episode #57: General Stanley McChrystal and Kristina Talbert-Slagle on Lessons on Counterinsurgency from the Human Body' (*Lawfare* 9 January 2014) https://www.lawfareblog.com/lawfare-podcast-episode-57-general-stanley-mcchrystal-and-kristina-talbert-slagle-lessons#.Us_VcPZZVC4 accessed 10 May 2015.

Wojcik, Mark E., 'Introductory Note to Public Committee against Torture in Israel v. Government of Israel' 46 (2007) *International Legal Materials* 373.

Woods, Chris and Lamb, Christina, 'CIA Tactics in Pakistan Include Targeting Rescuers and Funerals' *The Bureau of Investigative Journalism* (4 February 2012) www.thebureauinvestigates.com/2012/02/04/obama-terror-drones-cia-tactics-in-pakistan-include-targeting-rescuers-and-funerals/ accessed 10 May 2015.

Wrange, Pål, *Impartial or Uninvolved? The Anatomy of 20th Century Doctrine on the Law of Neutrality* (Visby: eddy.se 2007).

Yagoda, Ben, 'The Genius of The 9/11 Commission Report: How a Government Committee Made a Piece of Literature' *Slate Magazine* www.slate.com/articles/arts/books/2004/11/the_911_commission_report.html accessed 10 May 2015.

Yahav, David and others, *Israel, the "Intifada" and the Rule of Law* (Tel Aviv: Israel Ministry of Defense Publications 1993).

Yashuvi, Na'ama, *Activity of the Undercover Units in the Occupied Territories* (Bonn J tr, Jerusalem: B'Tselem– The Israeli Information Center for Human Rights in the Occupied Territories) available at: www.btselem.org/Download/199205_Undercover_Units_Eng.doc accessed 10 May 2015.

Yoo, John C., 'The President's Constitutional Authority to Conduct Military Operations Against Terrorists and Nations Supporting Them, U.S. Department of Justice, Office of the Legal Counsel (September 25, 2001)' in Greenberg KJ and Dratel JL (eds.), *The Torture Papers: The Road to Abu Ghraib* (Cambridge University Press 2005) 3–24.

Yoo, John C. and Delabunty, Robert J., 'Memorandum for William J. Haynes II General Counsel, Department of Defense – Re: Application of Treaties and Laws to al Qaeda and Taliban Detainees (January 9, 2002)' in Greenberg KJ and Dratel JL (eds.), *The Torture Papers: The Road to Abu Ghraib* (Cambridge University Press 2005) 38–79.

Zeisberg, Mariah, *War Powers: The Politics of Constitutional Authority* (Princeton University Press 2013).

Zulaika, Joseba, *Terrorism: The Self-fulfilling Prophecy* (The University of Chicago Press 2009).

TABLE OF CASES

ICJ, *Case Concerning Military and Paramilitary Activities in and Against Nicaragua*
(Jurisdiction and Admissibility) 1984 available at the website of the Court:
www.icj-cij.org/docket/files/70/6485.pdf accessed 10 May 2015   139

———, *Case Concerning Military and Paramilitary Activities in and Against Nicaragua*
(Merits) 1986 available at the website of the Court: www.icj-cij.org/docket/files/
70/6503.pdf accessed 10 May 2015   142

———, *Legality of the Threat or Use of Nuclear Weapons* (Advisory Opinion) 1996
available at the website of the Court: www.icj-cij.org/docket/files/95/7495.pdf
accessed 10 May 2015   227–229

———, *Legal Consequences of the Construction of a Wall in the Occupied Palestinian
Territory* (Advisory Opinion) 2004 available at the website of the Court: www.icj-
cij.org/docket/files/131/1671.pdf accessed 10 May 2015   18–19, 227

Israel Military Court sitting in Ramallah, *Military Prosecutor* v. *Omar Mahmud Kassem
and Others* (13 April 1969) (1971) 42 International Law Reporter 470   69–70,
138

Israel Supreme Court, *Ziv* v. *Gubernik and Others* (2 December 1948) (1949) 16
Annual Digest of Public International Law Cases 7   40–41

———, *Ahmed Shauki el Kharbutli* v. *Minister of Defence* (3 January 1949) (1949) 16
Annual Digest of Public International Law Cases 7   41

Israel Supreme Court sitting as the High Court of Justice, *Barakeh* v. *Prime Minister*
(2002) HCJ 5872/01. Translated from Hebrew in Orna Ben-Naftali and Keren
R. Michaeli, 'Justice-Ability: A Critique of the Alleged Non-Justiciability
of Israel's Policy of Targeted Killings' 1(2003) *Journal of International Criminal
Justice* 368   15–18

———, *Ajuri* v. *IDF Commander* (2002) HCJ 7015/02. http://elyon1.court.gov.il/
Files_ENG/02/150/070/A15/02070150.A15.pdf accessed 10 May 2015.   75

———, *The Public Committee Against Torture et al.* v. *The Government of Israel
et al.* (2006) HCJ 769/02. Available in English at the website of the Court:
http://elyon1.court.gov.il/files_ENG/02/690/007/a34/02007690.a34.pdf accessed
10 May 2015   15–24, 30–32, 39, 215, 229

US District Court for the District of Columbia, *al-Aulaqi* v. *Obama*, 727 F.Supp.2d. 1, 8 (D.D.C.2010) Available online at: https://www.aclu.org/legal-document/al-aulaqi-v-obama-decision accessed 10 May 2015   83–89

US Supreme Court, *Hamdan* v. *Rumsfeld*, 126 S. Ct. 2749 (2006) available at the website of the Court: http://www.supremecourt.gov/opinions/05pdf/05-184.pdf accessed 10 May 2015   174–175, 203, 209

INDEX

Abayat, Hussein, 71, 74, 77, 79
Abramowitz, David, 169, 171
Achille Lauro cruise ship, 137, 154
active defense, 115–124, 127–145, 154–166, 207
Afghanistan. *See also* al-Qaeda
attempts to kill bin Laden in, 157–160
planning of 9/11 attacks in, 185
Soviet invasion of, 178, 179
Taliban targets in, 166, 175–176
targeted killings in, 5, 185
use of Predator drones in, 164
Against All Enemies: Inside America's War on Terror (Clarke), 178–179
aggression, act of, 139
Ahmed Shauki el Kharbutli v. Minister of Defence, 41
Ajuri case, 75
al-Aulaqi, Anwar, 83–84, 85–86, 87, 171, 185, 226
al-Aulaqi, Nasser, 88
al-Aulaqi v. Obama, 83–87, 88
Alien Tort Statute, 85–86
al-Qaeda
armed conflict against, 217–218
attempts to capture bin Laden and, 157–160
base of operations, 207
disease metaphor and, 186, 189–190
law of war and, 203
as a new kind of terrorism, 178, 181, 182–184
Alston, Philip, 215–216
American Constitution (1789), 97

American Society of International Law (ASIL), 74–75, 139–140, 171, 173
Amnesty International, 79
Anderson, Kenneth, 5, 209–212
Anghie, Antony, 123
Anti-Terrorism Act of 1986, 136
Arendt, Hannah, 35–37
Arimatsu, Louise, 207, 208
armed conflict
conventional, 87, 98, 150, 151
international, 19, 21, 30–31, 149, 173–174, 209
non-international, 149, 150, 173–174, 191, 209–210
precision targeting in, 172
targets in, 213
territorialised conception of, 214
transnational non-international, 174
Army Field Manual, 146
ASIL. *See* American Society of International Law
Assad, Bashar, 199–200
assassinations. *See also* targeted killing
banning of, 89
killing of Osama bin Laden and, 155–156
legality and legitimacy of, 195–197
of non-state enemies, 199–201
in peacetime, 148–149
political, 1, 45–46, 48, 149, 193. *See also* assassinations
of state leaders, 198–199
statutory ban on, 143–145
in wartime, 149–152
international armed conflict, 149–150

interstate armed conflict, 149–150
peacetime counterterrorism,
150–152
auctoritas principis, 146
AUMF. *See* Authorization for Use of
Military Force
Authorization for Use of Military Force
(AUMF), 167–171, 209–212

Balibar, Étienne, 93
Barak, Aharon, 16–17, 29
on customary international law, 28,
39
findings in 2002 *Ajuri* case, 75
on international armed conflict,
19–23
targeted killing judgment of, 18, 234
on unlawful combatants, 206
dynamic interpretation, 23, 31–32,
75–76, 234
purposive interpretation, 23, 31–32,
75–76, 234
Barakeh, Mohammed, 15
Bartelson, Jens, 7
Bates, John, 85, 86
Baxter, Richard, 55
Begin-Sadat Center for Strategic
Studies, 62
Beinisch, Dorit, 16–17
belligerent occupation, 3–4, 19. *See also*
occupied territories
approaches to, 64–65
constitutional structure of, 59, 73–74
Hague Regulations and, 63
international law of, 87, 233–234
legal regime of, 55–59, 63
of Palestine, 29
Ben-Gurion, David, 44
Benjamin, Walter, 2, 9–10, 24–32
and belligerent occupation, 59
Critique of Violence, 25–27, 33, 90
and establishment of state of Israel,
44
and Israeli-Palestinian relations, 40
and Kapp-Lüttwitz putch, 237
Ben-Naftali, Orna, 16
Benvenisti, Eyal, 63
Ben-Yehuda, Nachman, 45–48

Berger, Sandy, 163
Berman, Howard, 135, 234
Biden, Joseph R., 161
bin-Laden, Osama, 155–156, 157–160,
183, 184
biopolitics, 7–8
Black September, 50
Blakesley, Christopher L., 137
Blum, Gabriella, 200
Blumenberg, Hans, 120
Böckenförde, Ernst-Wolfgang,
235–236, 237
Boyle, Francis, 118–119
Bradley, Curtis A., 205
Brennan, John, 189–191
Brit Shalom, 33
Brown, Wendy, 108
B'Tselem, 66–67
Bush, George H.W., 124, 156, 180
Bush, George W., 164, 167, 169–170,
176
Butler, Judith, 28, 39

Cabinet Committee to Combat
Terrorism, 109
Canestaro, Nathan, 114
Carter, Jimmy, 112
Carty, Anthony, 43
Casey, William, 117, 121
Cassese, Antonio, 19, 138
Central Intelligence Agency (CIA), 111,
144, 165, 175–176
Chayes, Abram, 234
Church Committee, 112–113
civilians
casualties, 5, 20, 152–153
as unlawful combatants, 21–23,
30–32
taking direct part in hostilities,
22–23, 31, 79, 205–206, 210,
230–231
Clarke, Richard
*Against All Enemies: Inside America's
War on Terror*, 178–179
in campaign against al-Qaeda and
bin Laden, 159–160
on use of Predator drones, 164, 176
Clausewitz, Carl von, 149

Clinton, Bill, 157, 160, 164, 182
Cohen, Amichai, 44, 71
Cohen, Stuart A., 44, 62
collateral damage, 152–153, 178
colonialism, 34, 100, 101, 205
Committee on International Relations,
169
Concept of the Political, The (Schmitt),
91, 93, 102–103
constitutional law, 95
Constitutional Theory (Schmitt),
90–91, 93, 94, 95–96, 97, 236
Contras, 142
conventional armed conflict, 151
in First World War, 98
uniforms in, 87, 150
counterinsurgency, 149, 151, 173–174
attack of civilians in, 150
deterritorialisation of enmity in, 209
enemy-centric, 191
as foreign internal defence, 191
lawful killing in, 209–210
population-centric, 191
unprivileged belligerents in, 150
counterterrorism, 5, 49–50, 75,
180–181, 184
American, 184, 186
assassination in, 49, 225
CIA's role in, 165
Clinton's policy on, 157
corporal destruction as mode of,
184
drones in, 164, 214–215
extraterritorial, 89, 193
fear of indecision in, 124–127
foreign internal defence in, 191
hot pursuit in, 49
and individualisation of enmity,
194–206
legally sanctioned, 39
military's role in, 180
Parks' writings on, 146
peacetime operations of, 149,
150–152, 173–174
Predator drones in, 83, 157,
163–166, 175–177
Presidential Decision Directive
39 and, 157

Reagan-era policy on, 110
right to self-defence in, 140
Sofaer on, 127–128, 137
targeted killing in, 185, 193
in Tunisia, 48–49
War Powers Act and, 136
War Powers Resolution and, 134
Craven, Matthew, 3–4
Crisis of Parliamentary Democracy, The
(Schmitt), 126–127
Critique of Violence (Benjamin), 25–27,
33, 90
cruise missiles, 160, 161, 175, 176, 199
*Cumulative Digest of United States in
International law*, 153
customary international law, 28. *See
also* international law

Darwish, Mahmoud, 38
David, Steven R., 78
Dayan, Moshe, 54
*Decision, The: Is the American Sovereign
At Bay?* (Schwab), 132
Declaration of the Rights of Man
(1789), 223–224
Delabunty, Robert J., 174
Derejko, Nathan, 212–213
Derrida, Jacques, 27, 32
Dieckhoff, Alain, 34–35
Dinstein, Yoram, 64
Diplomatic Conference on the
Reaffirmation and
Development of International
Humanitarian Law, 223
domestic law. *See also* international law
armed conflict and, 209–210
duality of, 87
Israeli
historical origin of law and, 40–41
proportionality of, 23, 229
state of emergency and, 44–45
national security and, 142
self-defence and, 140
state protection in, 237
terrorism and, 123
Draper, G.I.A.D., 222–225, 227, 228
drones, 83, 157, 163–166, 175–177
Dyzenhaus, David, 233, 237

Eban, Abba, 42, 53
Egypt, 50, 58
Elden, Stuart, 102
el-Wazir, Khalil, 48–49, 50, 51, 139
Emmerson, Ben, 214–215
enmity
    deterritorialisation of, 206–215
    friend-enemy distinction, 36, 90,
        92–93, 102, 122, 149
    individualisation of, 194–206
Esposito, Roberto, 6, 7–8, 92
Etzel, 45, 46
European Convention on Human
        Rights, 224
    article 15 of, 222–223
    article 2 of, 222
*Ex captivitate salus – Erfahrungen der
    Zeit 1945/47* (Schmitt), 98
Executive Order 12333, 111, 146, 153,
        157, 165
extradition, 137

Fascell, Dante B., 132–133, 135, 234
fatwa, 178
Fawzi, Mahmoud Bey, 40
fedayee, 70
Federal Bureau of Investigation (FBI),
        181–182
first Intifada, 60–70, 202
Ford, Gerald, 112
foreign internal defence, 191
Foucault, Michel, 7–8, 232–233
Fourth Geneva Convention, 58–59, 64
friend-enemy distinction, 93

Gaza, 7
Gaza Strip. *See also* occupied territories
    disengagement from, 79–80
    entrapment of enmity and, 52–53
    IDF anti-terrorist units in, 63
    Israel's effective control of, 55
    occupation of, 50
    rules of engagement in, 72
    security measures in, 54
    settlements in, 60
Geneva Convention, 58–59
    article 3 of, 106, 204–205
    article 4 of, 150

Geneva Diplomatic Conference
    on the Reaffirmation of
    International Humanitarian
    Law Applicable in Armed
    Conflict, 138
Gentili, Alberico, 195
Gentle Civilizer of Nations, The
    (Koskenniemi), 237
geopolitical space, 103
Ghanim, Honaida, 38, 44, 52, 70
Glennon, Michael J., 134, 135
globalism, 120, 184
Gordon, Neve, 53–54
Gordon, Robert W., 2
Gregory, Derek, 207
Großraum, 103
Grotius, Hugo, 149, 202
Guantanamo Bay, 184, 216–217
guerrilla movement, 151, 201
Guiora, Amos N., 77
Gulf of Sidra, 132
Gulf War of 1991, 180

Haganah, 34, 45, 46
Hague Convention, 56, 149
Hague Regulations, 56, 63
Hamas, 61
Hamdan v. *Rumsfeld*, 174–175, 203,
        209
Hamilton, Lee H., 178
Hamlet, 125–126
Harel, Isser, 46
Hasan, Nidal Malik, 84
Hellfire missile, 164, 175–176
Hezbollah, 109
Hobbes, Thomas, 5–7, 8, 89, 92,
        187–188, 235
Holy Roman Empire, 100
human rights, 215–231
    and humanitarian law, 219–226
    lex specialis derogat legi generalis
        doctrine and, 226–229
    substituting a hybridised for a
        mutually exclusive relation,
        229–231
Human Rights Watch, 79
humanitarian law, 219–226
Hussein, Saddam, 197, 199

ICCPR. *See* International Covenant of
    Civil and Political Rights
ICJ. *See* International Court of Justice
ICRC. *See* International Committee of
    the Red Cross
IDF. *See* Israel Defence Forces
illegal combatants, 68
Illness as Metaphor (Sontag), 187–188
injustus hostis, 195, 198
international armed conflict, 19, 21,
    30–31, 149, 173–174, 209
International Committee of the Red
    Cross (ICRC), 64–65, 204,
    214–215, 220
International Court of Justice (ICJ),
    18–20, 42, 139–140
International Covenant on Civil and
    Political Rights (ICCPR),
    216–218, 227
international law. *See also* domestic law
    customary, 28
    duality of, 87
    European, 98–101, 103
    in history, 3–4
    history of, 3–4
    injustus hostis, 195
    justus hostis, 194–195
    post-Westphalian, 97–108, 139, 195
    targeted killing and, 1–5
    transnational terrorism and,
    201–202
    Weimar heritage in, 237–238
    Westphalian, 97–108, 139, 195
International Law of Belligerent
    occupation, 58
international terrorism, 88
intifada
    armed terrorists as illegal
    combatants in, 68–69
    first, 60–70, 202
    IDF's legal defence in, 61–62
    rules of engagement in, 68–69
    second, 70–81
intrastate armed conflict. *See*
    non-international armed
    conflict
Iranian Revolution, 179
Iraq, 180–181

Irgun, 45
Islamic Jihad, 109
Israel, 70–81
    common entrapment of enmity and,
    52–55
    domestic law
      historical origin of law and, 40–41
      proportionality of, 23, 229
      state of emergency and, 44–45
    first Intifada and, 60–70
    Jewish-Arab relations in, 38–43, 188
    non-applicability of ICCPR on
      occupied territories of, 218–219
    occupation of Palestinian territories,
    50
      disengagement from Gaza, 79–80
      Jordanian option in, 53
      legal regime of, 55–59
      maintenance of law and order in,
      64–65
      Palestinian option in, 53
      strike capabilities in, 79–81
      surveillance in, 79–81
    second Intifada and, 70–81
    state of emergency in, 44–45
    state protection in, 32–51
      common entrapment of enmity
      and, 38–43
      history of wars of existence and
      assassinations, 43–51
      political Zionism as, 34–37
    targeted killing in, 193
      as active self-defense, 77–79
      second Intifada, 70–81
    territory, 38–39
Israel Defence Forces (IDF), 16, 54,
    56–57, 61–62, 71
Israel Security Agency, 48
Israel Supreme Court, 15, 17–19,
    28–30, 40–41, 80, 193, 203, 229
Israel Yearbook on Human Rights, 222
Israeli Basic Law, 29
Israel's Occupation (Gordon), 53–54
ius ad bellum, 212–213
ius in bello, 212–213

Jabotinsky, Ze'ev, 36
JAG. *See* Judge Advocate General

Jahangir, Asma, 217
Jefferson, Thomas, 196
Jenkins, Brian Michael, 109, 157
Johns, Fleur, 3
Johnson, James T., 146–147
Jones, Seth, 83
Jordan, 50, 58
Judge Advocate General (JAG), 130–131, 134, 140
Jünger, Ernst, 97
jus ad bellum, 98, 138, 139, 148, 173, 208, 212–213
jus in bello, 98, 148, 173
Just War theory, 146–147
justus hostis, 194–195, 198

Kahn, Paul, 136
Kant, Immanuel, 235
Kean, Thomas H., 178
Kellogg-Briand Pact, 102–103
Kennedy, David, 205
Kennedy, Ellen, 93, 97, 108, 237
Kennedy v. *Mendoza-Martinez*, 113
Kill or Capture (Klaidman), 189
Klaidman, Daniel, 189
Knesset, 15
Koh, Harold, 171–172, 175
Koskenniemi, Martti, 237
Kreitner, Roy, 73
Kretzmer, David, 17, 229–231
Kritik der Gewalt (Benjamin), 25–27

La Belle Disco bombing, 154
Lavi, Shai, 25
law
    constitutional, 95
    domestic, 23, 40–41, 44–45, 87, 123, 140, 142, 209–210, 229, 237
    international. *See* international law
    positive, 26
    of war, 152–154
Law of Armed Conflict and Human Rights, 218–219
law-enforcement model, of targeted killing, 229–230
lawmaking violence, 30
law-preserving violence, 27–28, 30
Laws and Customs of War on Land, 56

Lebanon, 80, 116–117
Lehi, 45, 46
Leiser, Burton M., 50
Leviathan (Hobbes), 5–7, 89, 187
lex specialis derogat legi generalis doctrine, 219, 226–229
Libya, airstrikes on, 132
    as acts of aggression, 138
    assassination of state enemies in, 197
    authorisation of, 135
    counterterrorism and, 180
    law of war and, 145, 152, 203
    state-sponsored terrorism and, 180–181
Lincoln, Abraham, 113
Lubell, Noam, 212–213

Machiavelli, 187–188
Madison, James, 196
Marder, Michael, 235
Marine Battalion Landing Team, attack on (1983), 116–118, 121, 185
McChrystal, Stanley, 191
McFarlane, Robert C., 110
Meese, Edwin, 110, 112
Mégret, Frédéric, 208
Meir, Golda, 50–51
Memorandum of Law: Executive 12333 and Assassination (Parks), 145, 146
Michaeli, Keren, 16
Middle East Research and Information Project (MERIP), 62
Middle East Watch, 63, 66, 67, 68–69
Military Commissions Act (2006), 175
Military Prosecutor v. *Omar Mahmud Kassem and Others*, 69–70
military violence, 27
mista'arvim, 62
Monroe, James, 103
Monroe doctrine, 103–105
More, Thomas, 196
Mossad, 46, 48
Moyn, Samuel, 206, 215

Nakba, 42
naksah, 52

National Commission on Terrorist Attacks Upon the United States, 177–186
National Security Council, 165
National Security Decision Directive 138, 82, 109–112, 114
National Security Planning Group, 112, 121, 142
National Security Presidential Directive 9, 165–166
Nazism, 90–91, 97, 188, 205
necessity, 230
Netanyahu, Benjamin, 49
New World, 99
Nicaragua case, 139, 142
9/11 Report, 177–186
Noll, Gregor, 137, 216
Nomos of the Earth (Schmitt), 87, 99, 106
Nuclear Weapons advisory opinion, 227

Obama, Barack, 176, 185, 189
occupied territories, 17. *See also* belligerent occupation
    authorities of military commanders in, 56–57, 64
    international armed conflict in, 21, 203
    international law and, 71
    Israel Supreme Court's jurisdiction over, 17
    legal system in, 56–57
    maintenance of law and order in, 64–65
    non-applicability of ICCPR on, 218–219
    security measures in, 48, 54
    self-determination in, 60
    targeted killing in, 71
O'Connell, Mary Ellen, 214
On the Three Types of Juristic Thought (Schmitt), 8–10
Oppenheim, L., 149
Orford, Anne, 6
Oslo Agreement, 70

Pakistan, 5–7, 158

Palestine
    belligerent occupation of, 29
    first Intifada, 60
    Jewish-Arab relations in, 38
    occupation of, 50
    surveillance in, 79–81
    Zionism and, 33
Palestinian Liberation Organization (PLO), 61
Palmach, 46, 62
Pan Am 103 bombing (1983), 180
Parks, W. Hays
    on assassination of state enemies, 172, 197
    on combatant's privilege, 148
    Crossing the Line, 152
    on exclusive authority to wage war, 147
    on guerrilla infrastructure, 151
    on killing of Osama bin Laden, 155–156
    and lawful killing of terrorists, 145–154
    legal roles within American military, 145–146
    Memorandum of Law: Executive 12333 and Assassination, 145–146
    on peacetime assassination, 148–149
    on prohibition against assassination, 161–162, 203, 225
    on wartime assassination, 149–152
partisan, 105–107
peacetime assassination, 148–149
peacetime counterterrorism operations, 149, 150–152, 173–174
personality strikes, 176
PFLP. *See* Popular Front for the Liberation of Palestine
Phoenix programme, 206
piracy, 137
Plaw, Avery, 50
PLO. *See* Palestinian Liberation Organization
Poindexter, John, 112
political assassinations, 1, 46. *See also* assassinations

extra-legal, 193
by Jewish groups in Palestine-Israel, 45–48
in wartime, 149
Political Assassinations by Jews (Ben-Yehuda), 45–48
political execution, 46
political question doctrine, 85
Political Theology (Schmitt), 92, 94, 236
Politico-Military plan, 160
Popular Front for the Liberation of Palestine (PFLP), 69
Porter, Patrick, 117, 120
Power and Diplomacy in the 1980s (Schultz), 118–119
Predator (unmanned aerial vehicle), 83, 157, 163–166, 175–177
Presidential Decision Directive 39, 157
President's Constitutional Authority to Conduct Military Operations Against Terrorists and Nations Supporting them, 170
Preston, Stephen, 171
Princeps legibus solutus est, 96
principle of proportionality, 20
proportionality, 230
Public Committee Against Torture v. *the Government of Israel*, 15–24
    Court decision in 2002, 15
    international armed conflicts, 21
    international law and, 18–20
    jurisdiction in, 17–18
    reversal of 2002 decision in 2006, 16–17
    unlawful combatants and, 21–23

Qadhafi, Muammar, 152, 180

Rabin, Yitzhak, 61, 70
Ralph, Jason, 107, 174
Ranstorp, Magnus, 185–186
Raz, Avi, 52–53
Reagan, Ronald, 109, 116–117
Rechtsstaat, 91, 94–95, 135
Reisner, Daniel, 71–76
Richter, Paul, 161
right authority, 146–147, 148, 175
Rivlin, Eliezer, 16–17, 23, 206

Roosevelt, Theodor, 104
Rose, Jacqueline, 34, 35
Rumsfeld, Donald, 164, 166

Salter, Michael, 125–126
Schachter, Oscar, 140
Scheipers, Sibylle, 204–205, 206
Schlesinger, Arthur, Jr., 128–129
Schmitt, Carl, 2, 235
    Concept of the Political, The, 91, 93, 102–103
    Constitutional Theory, 90–91, 93, 94, 95–96, 97, 236
    Crisis of Parliamentary Democracy, The, 126–127
    Ex captivitate salus – Erfahrungen der Zeit 1945/47, 98
    on friend-enemy distinction, 122
    on Hobbes, 8–10
    on international legal order, 118
    and law of politics and protection, 89–108
    Nomos of the Earth, 87, 99, 106
    Political Theology, 92, 94, 236
    on sovereign protection, 91–94
    State, Movement, People, 90–91
    Theory of the Partisan, 105–107
    US District Court and, 87–89
    on Westphalian to post-Westphalian international law, 195
Scholem, Gershom, 33
Schwab, George, 132
Schwebel, Stephen M., 128
second Intifida, 70–81
Second World War, 150
Security Council, 40, 48–49, 159, 172, 198–199
self-defence
    active, 50, 82, 115, 123, 167, 175, 193
        targeted killing as, 77–79
    airstrikes as acts of, 152–153, 180
    forms of, 141
    international law of, 140, 141
    law of war and, 152
    precision targeting in, 172
    pre-emptive, 207
    restricting right to, 103, 139
    right of state to, 139–142

self-defence (*cont.*)
  right to, 6, 139, 141, 159, 171,
    230–231, 234
  Six-Day War as Israel's preemptive,
    52
  sovereignty and, 103
  terrorist attacks and, 173
Senate Foreign Relations Committee,
  161
Senate Select Committee on
  Intelligence Agencies, 112–113
Shabak, 48
Shamgar, Meir, 17, 56–58
Shamir, Ronen, 17
Shehadeh, Raja, 60
Shin Bet, 48
Shomer, 34
Shultz, George P.
  active defense policy of, 109,
    154–166
  on active self-defense, 50, 82, 115,
    123, 167, 175, 193
  on globalism in counterterrorism,
    184
  of the need for a 'world's policeman',
    122
  Park Avenue Synagogue speech,
    123–124
  Power and Diplomacy in the 1980s
    speech, 118–119
  on terrorism
    indecision in fighting, 124–125
    international, 120–121
    legal authority to engage, 126
    threat of, 187
  Terrorism and the Modern World
    speech, 119–120
  Turmoil and Triumph, 110
signature strikes, 176
Sikul Memukad, 78, 163
Simpson, Gerry, 212
Six-Day War, 50, 52
Slaughter, Ann-Marie, 198–199
Slomp, Gabriella, 105
Sofaer, Abraham D., 234
  on active defense, 127–145, 207
  on Anti-Terrorism Act of 1986, 136
  on assassination of state enemies,
    197

on designating terrorist enemies,
  131–136
on extradition, 137
on extraterritorial access to terrorist
  enemies, 136–143
on International Court of Justice's
  authority, 139–140
as Legal Adviser, 127–130
on right of self-defence, 141
on state responsibility, 142–143
on statutory ban on assassination,
  143–145
*Terrorism, The Law, and the National
  Defense* speech, 130–131
*War, Foreign Affairs and
  Constitutional Power*, 128–129
on War Powers Resolution, 131–135
Somalia, 7
Sontag, Susan, 187–188
sovereignty
  apocryphal acts of, 94–97
  combatant's privilege and, 148
  contingent, 102
  double bind 7, 55, 122, 147–148, 238
  extralegal, 94–97
  Hobbes on, 5–7
  protection of, 92, 94–97
sphere of influence, 103
Spinoza, Baruch, 96
State, Movement, People (Schmitt),
  90–91
Stein, Yael, 78–79, 234
Stephens, Bret, 199–200
Stirk, Peter, 59
Strauss, Leo, 91
Sudan, 158
surveillance, 79–81
Syria, 40, 80

Tal Zataar camp, 188
Taliban, 166, 175–176, 207
Tams, Christian J., 138
targeted killing, 193–231
  after 9/11, 166–192
  as active self-defense, 77–79
  of Americans, 82–192
  al-Aulaqi v. *Obama*, 83–87
  concept of, 161–163
  disease metaphor in, 186–192

history of, 2–5
human rights and, 215–231
international law and, 1–5, 193–231
in Israel, 1–2, 15–81
  second Intifida, 70–81
law of, 167–175, 232–239
law-enforcement model of, 229–230
legal, 193
lex specialis derogat legi generalis
  doctrine and, 226–229
mixed model of, 229
practice of, 2–5
sovereignty and, 5–7
in United States, 1–2
Tenet, George, 165, 166
territorial integrity principle, 140–141
terrorism. *See also* counterterrorism
  active defense against, 122–124
  as emerging global national security
    threat, 116
  passive to active defense against,
    115–127
  in post-cold war period, 184
  state responsibility in, 142–143
  state-sponsored, 131, 180–181
*Terrorism, The Law, and the National
  Defense* (Sofaer), 130–131
Terrorism and the Law (symposium),
  137
Terrorism and the Modern World
  (Shultz), 119–120
terrorists
  extraterritorial access to, 136–143
  lawful killing of, 145–154
  measures to neutralise, 109–114
  targeted killing of, 75
  trans-national, 201
Theory of the Partisan (Schmitt),
  105–107
Third Reich, 90
Thirty Years' War, 89
Thomas, Ward, 195–197, 200–202, 207
Toaldo, Mattia, 117–118
Tomahawk missiles, 180
Trans World Airlines (TWA)
  847 hijacking, 109, 127–128,
    137
transnational non-international armed
  conflicts, 174

treachery, 196
Truman, Harry, 122
Tunisia, 48–49, 139
Turmoil and Triumph (Schultz), 110

UDHR. *See* Universal Declaration of
  Human Rights
uniforms, in conventional war, 87,
  150
United Nations Charter (1945)
  article 2(4), 102, 103
  article 51, 103, 139, 180, 230–231
United Nations Conference on Human
  Rights (1968), 221, 223
United Nations Convention Against
  the Taking of Hostages, 138
United Nations Convention on the Law
  of the Sea (1982), 137
United Nations General Assembly, 42
United Nations Human Rights
  Committee, 44–45
United States
  counterterrorism and, 49–50
    fear of indecision in, 124–127
  globalism, 120, 167, 184–186
  homeland as the planet, 184
  international terrorism and, 49–50
  terrorism as global national security
    threat to, 116–121
  war against unspecified terrorists
    foes, 109–154
United States District Court for the
  District of Columbia, 87–89
United States Supreme Court, 203
Universal Declaration on Human
  Rights (UDHR), 219–220,
  223–224
unlawful combatants, 21–23, 30–32
  targeted killing of, 75
unmanned aerial vehicles, 80, 83, 157,
  163–166, 175–177

Vattel, Emmerich de, 196
violence
  fate-imposed, 26
  lawmaking, 30
  law-preserving, 27–28, 30
  for legal ends, 26
  military, 27

for natural ends, 26
Vitullo, Anita, 62
Vlasic, Mark Vincent, 162

Walters, Vernon A., 49
wanted persons, 62, 66–67
war
 conventional, 149–150
 counterinsurgency, 149, 150, 151,
  173–174, 191, 209–210
 international armed conflict, 19, 21,
  30–31, 149–150, 173–174, 209
 interstate armed conflict, 149–150
 law of, 152–154
 legalized killing in, 149
 non-international armed conflict,
  149, 150, 173–174, 191,
  209–210
 as political activity, 149
 uniforms in, 150
*War, Foreign Affairs and Constitutional
 Power* (Sofaer), 128–129
War Powers Act, 136
War Powers Resolution (1973), 126,
 131–135, 144, 169–170
Weber, Samuel, 103
Weimar constitution, 96
Weimar Germany, 9–10, 25, 90,
 237–238
Weinberger, Caspar, 125, 156

Weinberger doctrine, 125
Weizman, Eyal, 79, 81
Weizmann, Chaim, 35
Werner, Wouter, 10, 194
West Bank. *See also* belligerent
 occupation; occupied territories
 entrapment of enmity and, 52–53
 IDF anti-terrorist units in, 63
 Israel's effective control of, 55
 occupation of, 50
 rules of engagement in, 72
 security measures in, 54
 settlements in, 60
Westphalia, 89, 100, 108
Wills, David C., 115, 155
Wilson, Woodrow, 98, 104
World Trade Center bombing (1993),
 181

Yahav, David, 63, 65–66, 68, 202
Yamamoto, Isoroku, 3
Yemen, 7
yishuv, 35
Yoo, John, 170, 174
Yunis, Fawaz, 143–145

Zeisberg, Mariah, 129
Zionism, 34–37
Ziv v. *Gubernik and Others*, 40–41

Printed in the United States
By Bookmasters